THE
PRETENDER

THE PRETENDER

MY LIFE UNDERCOVER FOR THE FBI

Marc Ruskin

Thomas Dunne Books
St. Martin's Press ✹ New York

THOMAS DUNNE BOOKS.
An imprint of St. Martin's Press.

THE PRETENDER. Copyright © 2017 by Marc Ruskin. All rights reserved. Printed in the United States of America. For information, address St. Martin's Press, 175 Fifth Avenue, New York, N.Y. 10010.

www.thomasdunnebooks.com
www.stmartins.com

The Library of Congress Cataloging-in-Publication Data is available upon request.

ISBN 978-1-250-06863-7 (hardcover)
ISBN 978-1-4668-7710-8 (e-book)

Our books may be purchased in bulk for promotional, educational, or business use. Please contact your local bookseller or the Macmillan Corporate and Premium Sales Department at 1-800-221-7945, extension 5442, or by e-mail at MacmillanSpecialMarkets@macmillan.com.

First Edition: June 2017

10 9 8 7 6 5 4 3 2 1

To the memory of my father,
Asa Paul Ruskin.

Physician, inventor, professor, always calm, wise,
quick to smile, his humor unparalleled.

Author's Note

For self-evident reasons, I have changed the names of all whose security could be adversely affected by revealing their involvement with the FBI. However, I have used the true names of all individuals who are already associated with the Bureau, either through court records, social media, or other publicly accessible sources. Similarly, the names of certain under-cover operations have been changed.

The opinions expressed in *The Pretender* are mine alone. It will come as no surprise that they are not the opinions of the FBI.

Contents

If quick, I survive.
If not quick, I am lost.
This is "death."
—SUN TZU (孫子), 544–496 BC

We sleep safe in our beds because rough men
stand ready in the night to visit violence
on those who would do us harm.
—GEORGE ORWELL

Marc Ruskin, aka Alex Perez,
aka Sal Morelli, aka Edwardo Dean,
circa 1994

THE
PRETENDER

Introduction

A t any given time, the FBI has about one hundred full-time under-cover agents (or UCs, as we referred to ourselves) in the field. In the 1990s and 2000s, I was proud, *very proud,* to be one of them. Thanks to the three languages I speak as a native (English, Spanish, and French), prior experience as a prosecutor, all-purpose physiognomy, and the luck of the draw, I had the most diverse case list, the most notorious cases, the broadest experience within the FBI bureaucracy, including overseas, and the most pertinent outside experience.

Before I signed with the Bureau in 1985, I was a staffer for New York senator Pat Moynihan and an assistant DA in Brooklyn; today, I practice law. I know that of all the tools available to the FBI or any other government agency—no matter the nature of the target (counterfeiter, banker, racketeer, car thief, terrorist), the reams of Big Data at the various agencies' disposal, the number of drones (armed or unarmed) in their warehouses (stateside or overseas)—the living, breathing undercover operative remains the gold standard for *actionable* information. It's true on *24* and *Homeland,* and it also happens to be true in the real world—and it will be even truer in the future, as criminals and terrorists become ever less likely to trust any kind of recordable or traceable medium. Their expectation of privacy is already approaching zero (and ours isn't much higher). The National Security Agency (NSA) could announce that it is unilaterally shutting down its entire electronic surveillance operation, or the debate over the constitutional legality of such snooping could be settled in favor of privacy (a political impossibility, at the time of this writing), and the bad guys would *still* scoff. They know which way the wind's blowing—and they also know how to employ the newest commercially available encryption technology.

As the effectiveness of the traditional methods of electronic investigation decreases, the importance of UC work necessarily increases. Even if the NSA does collect every single communication generated in every corner of the globe, where's the value without evaluation and corroboration? I'm not going to pass judgment on the various drone campaigns, but I know that intelligence developed and *directed* by people on the ground in the target area is vital for their effectiveness. The absence of that direction is exactly why innocent people are killed.

One reason legal cases against terrorists are so hard to prosecute is the difficulty of planting undercover agents in those environments. As the FBI's ill-fated Detroit Sleeper Cell case confirmed following 9/11, reliance on information provided by informants is not and never will be enough. Eager, perhaps too eager to provide a frightened public with successes in the war on terror, the Bureau had relied on a source who may have provided the inspiration and means for the subjects' plans. Plans to commit violent acts of jihad that may have remained dormant, if they had ever existed, but for the timely (for the Bu) intervention of the source. Informants may not be trustworthy; their information has to be confirmed. In the end, the judge in that notorious case overturned the jury's conviction because the prosecution failed to turn over to the defense key evidence, including facts casting doubt on the informant's reliability.

The bottom line: In the era of electronic surveillance, undercover work is not passé. It is not obsolete. In fact, it's just the opposite. It enforces accountability. It prevents mistakes. I want readers (and policy makers) to understand why undercover agents are often the most valuable of all the boots on the ground.

During my long career, I worked many long-term, short-term, and cameo cases: financial fraud, insurance fraud, health-care fraud, public corruption, corporate espionage, La Cosa Nostra, narcotics, the Foreign Corrupt Practices Act, international stolen car rings, counterfeit documents, terrorism, espionage, the Brooklyn rabbis kidnapping and torture case of recent fame, and many more. About a dozen of these operations were major Group I (long-term) initiatives lasting a year or longer, with large budgets and resources, including teams of special agents and analysts, and requiring approval from Washington. Another dozen or so were Group IIs, also large-scale and expensive but not requiring approval from the very top. I'd have a hard time counting all the cameo jobs, some of which were only one-night stands. Often I had three or four cases going at the same time, switching identities as required, making certain I walked out the door with the correct ID, bling—and frame of mind. Years ago, a clerk in the ELSUR (Electronic Surveillance) unit (which maintains every taped—now digitally recorded—conversation, no matter how brief, and creates official logs for "chain of custody" purposes) told me that he had *thousands* of entries under my name.

For four years, I also managed the UC bureaucracy from our covert headquarters in Northern Virginia. Three years were spent working the legal attaché desks in Buenos Aires, Paris, and Madrid. I speak Spanish and French fluently, and have a working knowledge of Mandarin (one reason I was asked to take on so many one-off cameo UC roles). I've seen a lot—not everything, but a lot. I want this book to give readers what none of the others in UC work have even tried to do: *perspective* on the scope and scale of undercover work domestically and around the world; the bureaucratic inefficiencies spawned by the denizens of remote offices and conference rooms that can undermine the best work in the field (after all, we're dealing with three distinct cultures: management, analyst, and field agent); the increasing importance of UC work in this brave new electronic world. My narrative focuses on just ten or so of the dozens of cases I worked, while referencing others, as necessary. And I'll allude to cases that did not involve me directly.

I want readers to understand the kind of men and women who make good UC agents; the training received; the dangers and stresses faced. I have laid out in detail how UC cases are brainstormed, then painstakingly designed and presented for approval, assembled over many months *before* the first encounter with a target; how a bogus identity is carefully "backstopped" to withstand scrutiny; the ins and outs of working targets; how investigations succeed, and how they fail. I hope this book will prove to be the definitive narrative of undercover operations.

Can I reveal everything I know? Almost. Most of the investigative material for these cases is in the public record (as court documents, usually). A few of the "False Flag" cases are still classified. (This book has been vetted by the Bureau, as required by the contract of my employment.) Obviously, I won't betray active or possibly active sources or operations, but that's not really a problem, because my cases are closed. I have changed some names and telltale details. I do not reveal any techniques or trade secrets that really are secret. In fact, there aren't many of them: the perpetrators know and use the same tricks as the investigators. In the burgeoning field of digital and online crime, almost all of the tools are available. The crooks and some of the terrorists are almost as sophisticated as the agencies.

I indulge in no long rants against Bureau management. Nor is there uncritical praise of the institution. I have no axes to grind. I'm critical when necessary, but I'm not going to shake the FBI establishment to its foundations with revelations of incompetence and recommendations for change. That's not my agenda. On the contrary, I want to illustrate those attributes that make the FBI the world's premier law enforcement agency, while simultaneously shedding light on those characteristics that hinder a monolithic bureaucracy's capacity for change.

In the foreground throughout is my story, that of a lone undercover agent who served four FBI directors serving at the pleasure of five presidents, first as an eager rookie carrying a pistol and badge, then prime-of-career veteran, then seasoned éminence grise. I was part and parcel of both the "Old Bu" with its G-men and the New-Era FBI, the one born on September 11, 2001: same agency, expanded mission; always a work in progress. I wish it the best, because we need its best.

1

Quantico NAC 85-7

It was midafternoon on a Sunday when I took the exit ramp off I-95 South and steered toward Marine Corps Base Quantico. After passing through the military guard post, I drove along what seemed like a long and winding, desolate two-lane road—or was it just my anxious state of mind? I finally came to a small sign: "FBI Academy." A right turn, another half mile, and then another guard post, this one manned by uniformed FBI police. My name was on their list, my driver's license satisfied them, and I proceeded farther down the road. On my right was a series of firing ranges. Then, to my left, the somewhat menacing—and strikingly out of place amid the rolling Virginia woodlands—multibuilding compound that is the FBI Academy. I had arrived for New Agent Training.

My worst fears—of having unwittingly removed myself from the familiar multicultural world of New York City, only to enter a zone of rigid conformity—were soon confirmed. Seated at a table inside the lobby, along with other WASPy-looking individuals registering and greeting new arrivals, was a tall blond woman with a middle-American athletic cheerleader attractiveness and a Southern twang. She introduced herself as Susan Walton from the *New York* office (could it be?!) and explained that she would be one of my class's two field counselors (as in "from the field": real agents). Yes, I had landed on Mars and would soon be surrounded by androids bent on transforming me into a disciplined, rule-following cog in their well-oiled machine of an organization. And in order to indulge my FBI fantasy, I had resigned from a good job as an assistant

DA in Brooklyn—the kind of position that can lead just about anywhere in the legal profession, as more than one Supreme Court justice has proved. My first impressions, of the people, of the culture—fueled by inaccurate preconceptions—would prove erroneous, but it would take a while.

They don't waste time at Quantico. That very evening all of us wannabes were sitting in our classroom, dressed in professional attire, staring at Mike, who would be our primary class counselor (as opposed to field counselor; Mike was based at Quantico). A short, lean, hawk-nosed Texan in his midforties, he clearly liked his job and wore his FBI lapel pin with pride. After we were sworn in, Mike got our instruction off to a rollicking start with a lecture on the many ways that we could flunk out of training, and with assurances that some of us would do just that. We were then invited to stand, introduce ourselves, and give a recitation as to why we had joined the FBI. One of the women explained that becoming an FBI agent had been her life's dream. So dedicated was she to achieving this goal, she had undergone eye surgery in order to correct for nearsightedness. I'll never forget her—but I didn't know her long. The following day, she was gone. Disappeared. No explanation provided, then or later.

Amazing at the time, but it turned out to be the way the system worked. Suddenly, someone was gone, never to return. No good-byes, no handshakes, no tears. We'd return to the floor in our dorm to change clothes for firearms training, perhaps, or gym—and there would be the naked mattress, the empty closet, the vacant air. The effect was chilling, as it was no doubt calculated to be. Failure to make the grade in any area would result in just such a vanishing, but disaster could also strike from the violation of unwritten and unknown rules as well. Here's the cold arithmetic: Annually, six hundred of the twelve thousand *qualified* FBI applicants jump through all the hoops and make it to Quantico as a New Agent (exponentially more don't meet the minimum qualifications). Of the six hundred, another 10 to 20 percent fail to reach the graduation ceremony—four *long* months later—and receive those coveted Credentials.

That first night in Quantico, Mike made the significance of the Bureau's mission, and our role in furthering it, maximally clear. This was 1985, eight years before the first WTC bombing, ten years before the Okla-homa City bombing, sixteen years before 9/11. Yet the threats from in-ternational terrorism were already on the radar. The seventies had seen the rise of the Red Brigades, the Baader-Meinhoff Gang, the Palestine Liberation Organization, the Popular Front for the Liberation of Pales-tine, as well as numerous domestic organizations, such as the Weather Underground and the Black Panthers. Combined with myriad other threats—organized crime, outlaw biker gangs, cocaine cartels, huge financial swindlers—the responsibility was enormous. The FBI was the last line of defense. We were the last line of defense. The public, that is, *everybody else,* was depending on us: ten thousand FBI agents to protect three hundred million men, women, and children. Mike was deadly seri-ous, and I, for one, appreciated it.

Mike's point was driven home a few months later. A few weeks be-fore graduation, each New Agent class takes a field trip to FBI Headquar-ters for a guided tour and a meeting with the Director. We were seated in the back rows of the special amphitheater used for the firearms demon-stration. Tourists decked out in Bermuda shorts and T-shirts, overweight and underweight mom and dads with their gaggles of children, occupied the rest of the seats. The dapper agent who served as emcee fired off some rounds from his submachine gun, and the *ooo*s and *ahhh*s arose collec-tively from the audience. Then he made an announcement: "Today we have special visitors. In the back rows, a class of new FBI agents about to graduate." Immediately, spontaneously, these tourists in their T-shirts turned as one, located our professionally attired group, stood, and clapped. And clapped. Enthusiastically. For several minutes. Those waves of emo-tion washed over all of us in the back rows, and any cynicism we might have harbored was washed away with it. These fellow citizens *believed in us and our mission.* Their pride and their reception left an indelible impression.

Our class was officially designated "NAC 85-7" (that is, the seventh new agent class in 1985) and lodged in Jefferson Dorm, our home away from home for four months—assuming we made it that far. I was in room 1313 (lucky number?), and had the good fortune of having Jesse Ramirez as my roommate—Ramirez . . . Ruskin: the rooms were assigned alpha-betically. Jesse was also a former assistant DA—Kansas City, in his case.

He was a short and muscular Pancho Villa look-alike, and we were instant friends.

Then the first major exciting event of our training: receiving functioning firearms. For a few weeks, we had been allowed only "red handles." These were revolvers with the firing pin removed, featuring red grips, which readily identified them as inoperable and therefore "safe." Working with the red handles, we learned all there is to know about handling and using a revolver, other than actually shooting a bullet. When the big day finally came, Mike escorted us down a long hallway deep inside one of the academy buildings until we reached the heavy doors of the gun vault, with an exit across the street from the firearms ranges. One by one, we were handed our future duty weapons: Smith & Wesson Model 13 revolvers, "blued" (which means black), with 3-inch barrels, capable of firing a .357 Magnum round. In the future, on the way to the range, we would sign the gun out from the vault, then return it before going anywhere else. No firearms other than red handles are allowed inside the academy buildings.

The FBI takes firearms training very seriously, and with good reason. Guns are serious business, exceedingly dangerous when in the hands of the poorly trained or ill intentioned. I guess we Americans understand that, if nothing else. Sykes Houston, an agent in Dallas (and direct descendant of Sam Houston), told me years later that the average FBI agent is a markedly better shot than most Texas Rangers. The FBI "Revolver Qualification Course" involved the firing of 50 high-power "+P+" .38-caliber hollow-point rounds within strict time limits, starting with 18 shots at the 50-yard line, 6 prone, 6 kneeling, and 6 standing. That's *50 yards,* 150 feet, with a 3-inch barrel, which is essentially a snub-nosed gun. Years later, my friend Will Godoy quipped during weapons qualification in Puerto Rico that he didn't care how good he was at 50 yards. It wouldn't *matter.* "At that distance," he said, "I'll have enough of a running start, they'll never hit me."

The FBI doesn't feel that way (nor did my friend, really). The FBI believes that if you're good at 50 yards, you'll be even better at the shorter distances you're more likely to encounter in real life, and I agree. Combat training and shooting at Quantico involved (and still involves) the use of cars, pop-up targets, and makeshift cabins. Kick in the door of the cabin, identify any targets, and react accordingly. There might be three (cardboard) motorcycle gang members pointing guns directly at you. There might be an attractive (cardboard) woman with a revolver in her outstretched hand. Or there might be the same woman grasping an ice-cream cone. The training was good—excellent—but not, of course, infallible. Special Agent Robin Ahearn, whose class at Quantico had been two weeks ahead of mine, was assigned to perimeter security during her first fugitive arrest in Phoenix. This was less than six months after graduation. Near the entrance of the motel complex where the felon was hiding out, hearing shots, the rookie agent ran toward the sound. Two equally inexperienced agents, startled by the approaching armed woman emerging from the dark, informed that the fugitive was known to be holed up with his girlfriend, opened fire. Struck numerous times, Robin Ahearn died where she fell. Such a tragedy would shake any organization to its foundations.

And it was due to the firearms training that I came within a hair's breadth of flunking out and, I guess, slinking back to NYC, tail between my legs, unemployed. Training is divided into three areas: Academic, Defensive Tactics, and Firearms. There are tests in each, and any failing score results in dismissal. I was set to be our class valedictorian for Academics, and was doing well if not the best in both others. On a Friday afternoon, halfway through our four-month course, we fired the required two qualification courses. On the first one, I shot the first 18 rounds from the 50-yard line well under the 1-minute-50-seconds allowed. *Too far* under the time limit, because in my haste to beat the buzzer I hadn't taken the time to properly aim. I missed the qualifying score by one round. Shaken, on the second course I missed by two rounds. Three or four of us had failed to qualify. On Monday, we would have one more opportunity. Those who failed to fire two qualifying courses would be on their way home by sunset. Reapplying for my old job in the DA's office in Brooklyn would require some creativity, but Quantico's near-total cloak of mystery would actually be an advantage in this case . . . *of course, I had to resign . . . I was unwilling to compromise my principles . . .* blah blah blah. *Maybe* it would have worked. But I had no intention of finding out.

That weekend found me on the firing range, red handle in hand, dry-firing through the qualification course, as my man Jesse Ramirez stood behind me, stopwatch in hand. (Jesse had passed without a problem.) For each of the 50 rounds, I would need to integrate into my brain exactly how many seconds I had in order to take aim, to breathe, and to squeeze (not *pull!*) the trigger. Over and over again, we went through the course as I fired the phantom bullets. And on Monday, I sailed through the "qual" with scores in the mid-eighties, a B+, as it were. All of us made it over the hurdle—a cause for celebration by the entire class, believe me. By this point, a tangible esprit de corps had developed. That was the whole idea. The seeds of the camaraderie that binds all FBI agents were already well sown.

And it was camaraderie between a very culturally diverse group numbering just twenty-four. (Budget constraints dictated the low number. Classes generally numbered forty-plus.) For most of us, who were in our late twenties to early thirties, this was a second career. One woman had been an assistant curator at an art museum. One fellow, who was from the backwoods of Arkansas, *named his gun* as soon as it was issued (apparently his revolver was female). There were four attorneys (one having specialized in criminal defense); a few accountants; a high school vice principal; a flight attendant; a half dozen former police officers, sheriff's deputies, and state troopers; and about the same number of military personnel. Four Jews: an MIT-educated mechanical engineer, a Navy pilot, and two attorneys, one of whom was yours truly. (The other one was Ben Berry. He and I were the fastest runners, alternating for first place in the timed two-mile test.) Initially, seven females, five Hispanics, and only three blacks. That last number dropped to two just two weeks into our training, when the woman, some kind of civil rights lawyer, vanished overnight. She had been overweight from the beginning and was then unable to pass the initial physical fitness trials. Mike offered her the opportunity to be "recycled" and start with another class a few months later. She declined. Her heart had never been really set on becoming an FBI agent—she had not concealed her ambivalence from her fellow classmates. (She might have been more enthusiastic had she seen the as yet to be made film, *Mississippi Burning,* with Gene Hackman and Willem Dafoe, based on MIBURN, the mid-sixties FBI investigation into the murder of three civil-rights workers.)

Two of us from NAC 85-7 had dreams of becoming undercover agents. At the beginning of their careers, SAs (special agents) don't choose specialties, certainly not undercover. But it was already on my mind—and also on Danilo Perez's mind. A veteran of the Colombian navy, and fellow native Spanish speaker, who later took U.S. citizenship, Danilo was assigned to a nearby dorm room. Tall and skinny, with scruffy black hair, a mustache, and a heavy accent, he did not fit anyone's stereotype of an FBI agent. Of course, neither did I. (Years later, Danilo and I would meet up at undercover schools, both as instructors, both with many years of experience working behind enemy lines.) This was the *Miami Vice* era. It was a huge hit on television. Danilo would lie on his bed, with Phil Collins's "In the Air Tonight" playing over and over again on his Walkman cassette player. We both saw ourselves as Sonny Crockett and Rico Tubbs, driving that high-end sports car on Miami's Biscayne Boulevard, in our Gucci suits, en route to a meeting that would enable us to take down a Colombian cartel boss. In order to further that goal, I showed some initiative and submitted a memo requesting an assignment to Miami as my first office. Being a native Spanish speaker, with an Argentine mother, and years of experience in Latin America, I thought I would be ideally suited for conducting investigations in Miami's Latino community. And so I suggested. I didn't realize that my memo actually had another destination stamped all over it, only in invisible ink.

There is a tradition endured by all graduating agents a couple of weeks prior to the big day. We sat in our regular classroom chairs, Mike at the front desk, a pile of envelopes before him. After he read the name on the envelope, the agent was to come to the front of the classroom, pick up the envelope, and turn to the class. He was then to name three places: where he was from, where he *hoped* to be assigned, and where he *expected* to be assigned. Then open the envelope, take out the orders, and read aloud a fourth place, the actual Office of Assignment. Followed by lots of laughing and clapping and cheers. When it came my turn, I held the envelope and said, "New York . . . Miami . . . San Juan." I opened the envelope and smiled. San Juan.

Spanish speakers in the classes just ahead of ours had all received orders to San Juan, *not* Miami. I had seen it coming. It would be an adventure nonetheless.

Mom and Dad and my little brother and sister drove down to Quantico for graduation. It's safe to say that the FBI wasn't what Francine and Asa Ruskin had imagined for their oldest son's legal career, much less for his liberal arts degree from Vassar. They were liberal, secular Jews. My father couldn't forget COINTELPRO, but those notorious domestic spying and dirty tricks activities dated to the late fifties and sixties, and died with J. Edgar Hoover in 1972. Nor could Dad get around the association between Hoover's FBI and McCarthyism and blacklisting. In fact, the McCarthy committee investigators intimidating Americans on national TV were *not* FBI agents. They were staffers for the House Un-American Activities Committee, but the collective memory, aided by the media, had melded the two groups. However, it was FBI special agents who risked their lives south of the Mason-Dixon Line, investigating the racists who were tormenting civil-rights activists. (*Mississippi Burning* is one of the few movies that got it right.)

I discussed all this with my parents. Nevertheless, sitting in the third row at the graduation ceremony in Quantico, they were still not thrilled at my change of employment. They *were* gratified to learn that my fellow graduates could boast all kinds of advanced academic degrees and other achievements. During the reception afterward, Dad gravitated toward Ben Berry's father, both commiserating. Two young and promising Jewish lawyer sons—where had they gone wrong?

In my own mind, the transition to the FBI wasn't all that radical. In Brooklyn, I was the hard-nosed aggressive prosecutor, passionate about helping the victims of violent crime, almost all of them residents of the same ghettos and living in the same dire straits as the accused. I loved the work but realized after a few years that I didn't want to spend my entire career and life in Brooklyn. Nor did I want to follow my fellow prosecutors into the big law firms across the East River, only to end up lamenting the loss of our exciting careers as ADAs. I wanted to move in the opposite direction: more, not fewer, encounters with the juiciest field the law has to offer—the law of the wild. You can't prosecute the criminals unless you catch them first. And I had seen many potentially good cases fail due to errors by investigators. I intended to put together cases that would be slam-dunks for prosecutors. And I did. Let the record—including this book—show that I never failed to infiltrate my targets and be accepted, and thanks to my legal background, to construct my cases with never a glimmer of entrapment. And then there's this: I had been a good lawyer, maybe an excellent one, but I really wanted to be one of the *best* at something. Literally. The best. Maybe this was it.

A month later, my flight touched down at Luis Muñoz Marín airport, in Isla Verde, San Juan, Puerto Rico.

2

San Juan

There were no screeching tires and guns in hands, but the big waves *were* pounding the World War II–era landing craft crossing the Caribbean from Puerto Rico to the island of Vieques, eight miles east of Puerto Rico. A couple of Navy corpsmen manned the boat while my partner, Lowell Walker, and I hung on hard. Lowell—a Fulbright scholar in European literature and a former teacher at a prestigious boys' prep school—wore Bermuda shorts and a tropical shirt and cradled a shotgun. I sported cargo pants, a baggy T-shirt, a .357 Model 686 large-frame stainless-steel revolver on my waist, and an additional snub-nosed 5-shot .38 on my ankle.

It was a beautiful night, with a cloud of stars overhead, perfect for reverie, crashing waves aside. Less than five weeks before, I had graduated from Quantico. Now here I was, heavily armed and on my way to arrest a dangerous felon on the run from the law. We still had a few miles of ocean to negotiate. Lowell Walker reached out, poked me, grinned, and shouted above the racket, "You're a long way from Brooklyn now, Marc!"

I'll say. We know that *Miami Vice*, then into its second great season, had been a major influence in my request for an initial assignment to that action-filled paradise. Instead, because of an acute shortage of Spanish speakers—*real*, colloquial street Spanish—the Bureau airmailed me direct to the San Juan Division. *Another* action-filled paradise: Puerto Rico was particularly dangerous because of the *Macheteros* and its splinter group, the *Organización de Voluntarios para la Revolución Puertorriqueña*

(OVRP), terrorist organizations that idolized Fidel Castro and his regime, and employed explosives and assassinations in their campaign for Puerto Rican independence and a Cuban-like socialist state. Their sister organization stateside was the more well-known New York–based FALN (*Fuerzas Armadas de Liberación Nacional*). In the view of the *Macheteros*, FBI agents were "combatants" and thus fair game. Moreover, San Juan had a higher homicide rate than any city in the United States, and Ponce, on the south side of the island, was close behind. The island was far more dangerous territory than any stateside posting. In fact, this was officially a "hazardous duty" assignment and theoretically forbidden to FOAs (First Office Agents; that is, rookies), but that year a temporary exception had been carved out for those of us with prior law enforcement experience (even if it was white collar, I guess). I arrived in San Juan on a Monday evening and showed up at the office in the Federal Building in Hato Rey the following morning, at what seemed to me to be the crack of dawn (a mistake not to be repeated, as we will see), sweating in a wool suit and with absolutely no idea what to expect. Things got better almost immediately, when the suit came off. One of my first objectives would be to buy several guayaberas (Caribbean business-casual shirts).

John Navarette was my Supervisory Special Agent, my "SSA," boss of the Reactive Squad to which I was assigned. John called me into his office and got right to the point: "Listen, Marc, to do this job well you need to be able to lie well. If you're tracking a fugitive and you tell people he robbed a bank, chances are no one has heard of him. If you tell them he molested a ten-year-old girl, you'll get his address. Just remember who you're lying to. Try and be honest with yourself and when you can, with the ones you love. If you have any questions and need advice, feel free to come in. Otherwise I'll see you every couple of months at your file review." This was my kind of supervisor, and definitely not the overly regimented environment I had contemplated as a disquieting possibility. And, as I would soon learn, where burdensome regulations were in place, they weren't necessarily set in concrete. There were means to get around them.

On the Reactive Squad, about a dozen of us worked violent street crimes, and we always had more than enough to do. My desk was in the very large "bullpen," where each squad had a cluster of desks near the entrance to their respective supervisor's office. Obscuring a clear view of the ceiling was a permanent haze of cigarette and cigar smoke. Navarette assigned me a handful of cases, ranging from fugitive investigations to theft of government property (such as an agent's gun from a parked car), gave me the keys to my BuCar (as the newest agent, I rated the oldest vehicle, naturally, a clunker reminiscent of the '65 Ford Falcon I owned in college), and assigned me a Training Agent named Mark Llewellyn. Any concerns I may have had about the stringency with which Mark would keep tabs on me were rapidly dispelled. He was an old-timer by San Juan standards (that is, five or six years on the job), affable but aloof and with the look of a retired prize fighter. I quickly gleaned that I was free to contact him at any time and for any reason— so long as that reason was a dire emergency and my life was in peril. With Navarette and Llewellyn, I was batting 2-for-2 when it came to immediate supervisors. Not always the case with rookies, believe me.

Years earlier, J. Edgar Hoover, had promulgated the 10% Rule: Agents were to spend no more that 10 percent of any given day in the office. The remaining 90 percent was to be spent in the field, investigating cases. That would be a job unlike anything I could have dreamed of, but did the FBI actually work like that? So far, yes. It was a great relief. Other than a daily morning appearance in the office, I was on my own with my BuCar, my BuWeapon, and my BuCases. However, that "daily morning appearance" was not pro forma, and the subtleties of that little bureaucratic dance were one of the first important lessons my fellow agents on the Reactive Squad made certain I learned, because my performance could affect them directly. Here's how it played out. On a table or podium outside each supervisor's office door in the bullpen was a clipboard with a sheet of paper, the all-important "1 Register," its significance emphasized by its numeric designation. Each agent, upon arriving in the office, would sign on the highest open line, and indicate time arrived. Now, the official BuDay was 8:15 a.m.–5:00 p.m. And in order to qualify for overtime—an extra 25 percent on the paycheck, which, when you're paid peanuts is *not* peanuts—ten additional hours per week were required. So the first agent in the office would sign in at somewhere in the neighborhood of 6:05 a.m. Regardless of the time his wristwatch may have erroneously reflected. The next agent would time his arrival at 6:08 a.m., say. Everyone would have arrived by 6:25 a.m., despite what any of their wristwatches might have reflected. The missing ten minutes could be made up at the end of the day. At 8:15—usually right on the nose—the supervisor would walk out of his office and draw a diagonal line across the register under the last name, with his initials, in order to prevent late arrivals from cheating Uncle Sam. This practice was enforced by the supervisor's boss, the Assistant Special Agent in Charge, aka the dreaded "ASAC," who was traditionally the hatchet man for Special Agent in Charge. The ASAC would patrol the office searching for minor infractions. Our man Navarette would first look across the squad area. If any faces were missing, he would draw the line on the sheet in such a manner as to allow the missing agent to squeeze in a signature, just above it. This agent might then sign in at 7:10 or 7:20 a.m., in order to avoid the appearance of abusing the favor.

Let me be real clear here: All of the agents averaged way more than forty hours a week—more than the overtime-triggering fifty hours—and all would and did work around the clock, without hesitation or complaint, in time of crisis—in San Juan, a frequent state of affairs—but few were bound by petty rules. As to what I was learning of BuCulture, I liked it. My preconceptions concerning the buttoned-down image of the FBI had already been in enthusiastic free fall, beginning with Navarette's and Llewellyn's carte blanche dispensations, and continuing with my early dealings with real street agents. I was in my element.

An important note about weaponry. In those days, FBI agents didn't yet carry pistols with extra magazines, which were more likely to jam than revolvers, and more complicated to maintain. They were not "agent-proof," in management parlance. However, the revolvers took much more time to reload. In San Juan, therefore, everybody carried a backup to the .357. Even agents working white-collar crime carried two guns—a point noted in the squad's plea to FBIHQ for enhanced security measures for agents on the *Isla del Encanto*. (The weapons didn't change, however headquarters agreed to finance alarm systems in all the residences, with quick response by armed private security guards. This was a major relief for agents out conducting investigations, who were concerned for their families' well-being.)

In Puerto Rico, I had a lot more faith in my new guns than in the elaborate defensive tactics I'd just learned at Quantico. In fact, I had no intention of getting into a mano a mano physical confrontation with anyone, be it in San Juan or elsewhere. I made a point, from the very beginning, never to carry a canister of pepper spray or an expanding baton. Some agents, usually young ones, carry as many accoutrements as will fit on their persons. But as a former aggressive prosecutor, I knew that other aggressive prosecutors, anticipating the tactics of aggressive defense attorneys, would challenge the carrier of pepper spray for not having used "less drastic methods" before escalating to the use of deadly force. I'd be able to say, "The gun was the only weapon available. Sorry." A firearms instructor at Quantico had taught us, "Any confrontation between an agent and someone else is an armed confrontation. There is always, *always,* at least one gun present."

These issues are still pertinent today. The risks to a law enforcement officer of being shot with his or her own weapon are inherent to the job, leading most recently to the devastating events in Ferguson, Missouri, and their aftermath. I want only to point out how "avoidance of deadly force" is not always so easy . . . or safe.

Now let's flash-forward to that Friday evening—less than a week after my arrival in San Juan—when I was crashing across the ocean to Vieques on a Navy troop landing craft, the kind one sees in World War II movies transporting soldiers to the Normandy beaches. I had been in-division (to get technical about it) for less than a week. Four others from the Reactive Squad were on board for this adventure: my overall supervisor, John Navarette; my daily (but hands-off) supervisor, Mark Llewellyn; my partner, Lowell Walker; and Mark's partner, Van Camacho. Van's official BuName (the one that goes on the paycheck) really was "Van," and that was the only name the tough, macho, muscular Puerto Rican answered to. It wasn't until years later that I learned his name at birth: Vanesa. He grew up fast, with such a name. It reminded me of a certain song by Johnny Cash: "A Boy Named Sue."

The fugitive we were after on Vieques? He occupied a prominent place on the New Jersey Top-Twelve Most Wanted list, was sought in connection with various homicides and violent assaults, and was indeed worthy of his high standing among his peers in the Pagans, a notorious outlaw biker gang, second only to the Hell's Angels for brutality and a Neanderthal lifestyle. His name: Alan Shapiro, more suitable to a personal injury lawyer than a chain-wielding chopper jockey. We would be able to identify him by the swastika tattoos. Our landing craft made it safely on the beach at Vieques, where we were met by a friend of Navarette's, a retired cop. At this friend's cabin, we planned the arrest and imbibed a couple of Heinekens apiece. (It's a particularly popular brew in Puerto Rico, second only to the locally produced Medalla.) With the adrenaline racing, it may as well have been ginger ale, at least in my case, but still, this was definitely not something they taught at Quantico.

An hour later, just after 10:00 p.m., we charged through the door to Shapiro's ramshackle house with guns drawn, not knowing if he would be alone with his common-law wife, or with a dozen other Pagans, or sitting in his leather recliner enjoying . . . a Heineken. He jumped off a cot, shouting angrily, rushing forward. One solid punch from Mark took the fight out of him. As Van assisted in the cuffing, the rest of us cleared the house, disregarding the high-pitched verbal abuse from the only other occupant, his (unarmed) girlfriend. An hour later we dropped him off at the local Comisario, with a dirt floor and single bulb dangling from the ceiling, and then headed to the town square for a late dinner and more Heinekens.

The next morning we picked up Shapiro at the Comisario, banged across the ocean, and returned the trusty landing craft at Rosey Roads (Roosevelt Roads Naval Station). Driving back to San Juan, I sat in back with our prisoner. At one point he said to me, "You know, you and I have something in common."

"Really, what's that?" I had nothing in common with this lunatic biker charter member of the Pagan outlaw motorcycle gang.

"We're both members of The Tribe."

"The Tribe?"

"We're both Jewish."

That's nice, I thought, but I don't have swastikas tattooed all over my body. I asked my fellow tribesman about his tattoos. He explained that they were simply an essential part of the Pagans' dress code. Nothing personal. I pursued the small talk. He explained that he and another

Pagan had kidnapped a drug dealer who had "disrespected" them with a short count. In order to teach him respect and proper Pagan etiquette, they'd cut him a few times. Sixty or seventy times. We all turned to stare at him, even Mark Llewellyn, who was driving and had seen and heard just about everything in his many years as a police officer and special agent. Noting our reaction, our Pagan captive was quick to mitigate. "They were only thumbnail deep." (Eleven years later, I ran into Shapiro in federal court in White Plains. He was still having trouble with the law. The decade had taken a heavy toll on this guy, but the ID was easy. I'll never forget those proud swastikas.)

Then, a couple of weeks later, in mid-August, came the WELLROB arrests. The crime that had most immediately instigated this bust had been committed almost two years earlier, on September 12, 1983, in West Hartford, Connecticut, when a Wells Fargo armored car had been assaulted and robbed of seven million dollars, with one guard and one police officer killed in the shootout. Most of the money, supposedly intended to fund the envisioned Puerto Rican revolution, had ended up in Cuba instead. The long trail forward had led to this day, when thirty *Macheteros* were to be arrested simultaneously. This paramilitary cadre was categorized by the U.S. government as domestic terrorists. The entire leadership and core operational players were to be swept up in the one net. All would be well trained and heavily armed. The FBI's Hostage Rescue Team (the Bureau's Special Forces), the U.S. Marshals' Special Arrests Unit, and a dozen FBI SWAT teams had flown in for the operation.

I had been in San Juan less than a month, had already participated in a high-risk-fugitive arrest, and now the *Macheteros*. The grass wasn't growing under the feet of the lawmen on the *"Isla del Encanto,"* that's for sure. This was the place to be.

On a sweltering August morning, the arrest teams had set up well before dawn. Befitting my status as an FOA, I was assigned to securing the entrance to the Federal Building parking lot, where the prisoners would be brought initially before heading to court. The terrorists had all sworn never to be taken alive, but better judgment prevailed and all but one surrendered without resistance. Although my assignment in the busy parking lot seemed to pose limited physical risk, another source of exposure soon arose. A steel-mesh fence was the only barrier to a neighboring public parking lot. As word of the arrests spread, the adjacent lot soon filled with journalists. Arrestees came and went, yet only one FBI agent made for an ongoing perfect photo op featuring his obligatory blue FBI cap snugly in place and FBI raid jacket damp with perspiration. An attractive young woman reporter from the *independentista* newspaper *Clarín* must have used several rolls of film capturing my likeness (and later my BuCar's license plate). As the *Macheteros* were known to conduct active intelligence-gathering and surveillance of their enemy combatants (us), this did little for my peace of mind. Visions of my photo on a *Machetero* bulletin board floated through my imagination.

The one exception to the pattern of peaceful surrender that morning was the *Macheteros'* Cuban-trained leader, Filiberto Ojeda Ríos, who opened fire with a machine gun outside his rural home. A bullet fragment hit my colleague Abe Alba in the eye. Returning fire, one member of the Hostage Rescue Team nailed Ríos in the hand, causing him to drop the weapon. He was arrested, otherwise unharmed. (This would turn out to be a case of justice delayed: twenty years later the same arrest scenario would be replayed, but this time Ríos would be shot dead.) In fact, I was to work against this organization full-time over the next few years, and the more one knows an enemy, the less fearsome he appears. But as the *Machetero* Rules of Engagement became clear to me, I became somewhat infuriated. The way they worked was as follows: They viewed themselves as brave revolutionaries fighting for a free and independent Puerto Rico, with the support of their Cuban fellow idealists. Shooting and killing U.S. military personnel and other symbols of tyranny (FBI agents) was, in their view, fully justifiable—and convenient when it came to uniformed army and navy personnel stationed in Puerto Rico, who were unarmed. (Shooting at Puerto Rico police and FBI agents did pose more risks—we could shoot back—but they did consider us fair game, too.) On the flip side, if we, their imperialist oppressors, busted through the door one morning, these "revolutionary combatants" could shout "Don't shoot . . . I've got my hands up . . . Call my lawyer." And we wouldn't shoot and they'd get their lawyers.

With the *Machetero* operation concluded and most of the bad guys arrested, I was finally in a position to acclimate to the quotidian duties of my Reactive Squad. We made arrests on a weekly basis, which is a lot for the Bureau, and I soon came to know the entire island, the lost corners never seen by tourists nor by most Puerto Ricans. A lawman sees the underbelly of whatever world he protects, and we saw all kinds of crimes. I should point out—and it's an important point throughout this book—that the federal crimes investigated by federal authorities (the FBI, in my case) are generally more complex and involve bigger—usually smarter—players than those investigated by the local police. The scope of these criminals and their crimes is greater, having as they necessarily do an effect on "interstate commerce"—the broadly interpreted Constitutional language by which federal jurisdiction is granted. Simply put, *any* activity that involves more than one state (or territory, such as Puerto Rico or the Virgin Islands) is used to justify federal investigation of *all* the related activity that a subject is involved in, whether or not it is "interstate." If Bad Guy #1 mails an extortion letter using the U.S. mail, it's a slam-dunk, we have jurisdiction. If he makes a phone call from New York City to Bad Guy #2 in the same city, using lines that are relayed through Newark, New Jersey—bingo: federal jurisdiction. Most of the criminal activity the FBI investigates involves what it is famous for: La Cosa Nostra, Al-Qaeda, TWA 800, Lockerbie, Enron, Bernie Madoff. However, smaller fish would also fall within the net, and therein would come the work of the Reactive Squad in Puerto Rico. Extortion, kidnapping, bank robbery, theft of government property, and more populated our caseload. When Fugitive A traveled from New York to San Juan to avoid arrest—it was Interstate Flight to Avoid Prosecution, an official federal crime. This was the *federal* charge that had given the Bureau jurisdiction to arrest Pagan Alan Shapiro, to face justice on the underlying New Jersey *state* charges.

These flight cases quickly became my favorite work. Never having been much of a team player, I seized these opportunities to work independently. Reminiscent of one of my favorite stories as a boy, *The Most Dangerous Game,* working a fugitive was truly a hunt, a match of wits. As I got closer to the prey, a second sense would awaken in me, an incorporeal awareness that the confrontation was approaching. For example, a communication would arrive from the Chicago office—a telephone call or a teletype—revealing that an informant in Chicago had spoken to a friend in the remote Puerto Rican town of Jayuya. The friend had seen Luís Guzman (a name I have created for this illustration), who was wanted as a material witness in a gruesome homicide, at the home of a local Jayuya gang boss. A few hours later, driving my old BuCar along two-lane gravel roads winding through the mountainous landscape, I would pull into town. No cell phones then, and radio contact was spotty in the mountainous inland regions. First stop—not the local saloon—the local Comisario. Thanks to my native Spanish, I would quickly establish rapport with the detective in charge. Without fail, I would soon be riding with two local plainclothes detectives who were thrilled to be working an FBI investigation. This was their turf and we would work it together until Guzman was in cuffs.

For particularly important cases, Navarette would assign a few of us to assist the case agent, and off we'd go, at a moment's notice. One afternoon, we came upon a one-room wooden hut, alone in an open field, built on stilts to avoid flooding, with a rickety ladder leading to the door. Inside was supposed to be a fugitive from New York. We parked our two vehicles by the treeline. Then my squad-mates Fernando and Ricardo approached the ladder, covered by two veterans. I was fifteen yards back, off to the side, gun pointed at the door, providing cover. Suddenly, an unmistakable sound: someone has just racked a shotgun. I turned my head. It was Oz Tinsley, a fellow rookie and former Sacramento police officer. Along with another agent, he was covering the rear. Oz was grinning as he shouldered the Bureau-issued pump-action and pointed it at the cabin's rear window. *Jesus Christ.* This had the makings of a true cluster-fuck. *I* knew who had loaded the chamber, but our leaders, directly in front of the entrance, didn't. Neither did the fugitive. Loud shouting followed, barked commands to come out, *¡manos arriba! hands up!* a half-dozen revolvers and rifles pointed at the ramshackle structure. Out came the skinny, terrified fugitive from his family home, waving his empty hands and pleading not to be shot. When the older agents found out that it was Oz who had racked the round, their anger, fueled by their recent fear, was something to behold. Oz was about my height but with an additional seventy-five pounds, most of it muscle. He had a real presence, but his expression was a sorry one indeed, with both Fernando and Ricardo shouting at him like a couple of furious drill sergeants in a movie. Even our handcuffed fugitive quaked in fear, uncertain as to whom the vehemence was being directed. Having no desire to incur the wrath of fellow agents—and newbies will make mistakes, it's inevitable—I resolved to follow my instincts and keep a low profile, working alone or with fellow rookies.

For the more important cases, Navarette would be out there, in the middle of the action. Highly unusual for an FBI supervisor, all of whom are burdened with a mass of paperwork and administrative tasks. And he knew how to take quick, decisive action. He had first demonstrated this with the Vieques outlaw biker fugitive (though a secondary motivation may have been to observe and evaluate me, the rookie agent, in action). He did it again two months later. A tip had come in from one of the squad's many paid informants. A hold-up at a suburban bank was planned for the next morning, when the robbers, all experienced, violent felons, would assault an armored car that was scheduled to arrive, thus assuring the presence of large amount of cash. The information was reliable: the tipster *had been offered a place on the hold-up team.*

Within hours, the FBI op was set and ready to go the following morning. The armored car would arrive at the bank, on schedule at 11:00 a.m., operated, as usual, by two uniformed guards. With one twist: the guard driving the vehicle would be Navarette, and the other guard would be SA Roger Gomez, a former Illinois State Police undercover agent. On the rooftop of the one-story bank, our local SWAT team would be waiting for the robbers to arrive. The rest of the agents on the squad would be parked in their BuCars within view of the bank, ready to swoop in. I should point out that in the New-Era twenty-first-century FBI, it would be virtually impossible for a supervisor to obtain authorization for such a covert scenario—two undercovers set up as virtual walking targets—with so little time for advance preparation. This is a subject for much future discussion.

The bank was situated on a corner. The trap called for the SWAT team to climb up the wall on the side street under cover of darkness. At 6:00 a.m. I was parked a half block away, with a direct view of the entrance as well as the street to the side of the bank. Sipping my coffee, all the possible scenarios played out in my imagination, most of them involving some kind of a shootout—it seemed virtually inevitable. Along with my .357, I had a pump-action 12-gauge within reach. The SWAT team did not arrive and did not slither under cover of darkness. Soon enough, it was no longer dark. *Well, the streets are still empty, they can still slither up discreetly.* By 8:30, there was still no SWAT team, and by now there were plenty of people around. At nine the bank opened. At 9:15, I watched as the SWAT truck finally pulled up on the side street. The team leader, a gray-haired, affable chain-smoker, got out, stretched, and leisurely dragged on the cigarette dangling from his lip as his team in full SWAT gear—uniforms, helmets, tactical hip holsters, machine guns, radio—climbed down from the back of the truck carrying a ladder. *Okay, I'm a rookie, but this can't be right.* A crowd of curious onlookers watched the team climb the ladder and assemble on the roof, but they seemed unfazed by what I would have thought was a highly unusual scenario unfolding before them. The minutes ticked by. As the team leader periodically strode across the roof, checking on his dispositions while still smoking, all was business as usual down below. *This just cannot be right. Why won't the robbers see them up there?* I was befuddled.

The armored car, driven by Navarette, arrived on time at 11:00. But the robbers didn't. To the disappointment of the by-now considerable crowd of bystanders, there was no hold-up. Navarette was livid. Within an hour, we were all on our way back to the office. Postscript: The incredulous tipster from the streets called Navarette that afternoon. The hold-up team *had* been on the scene at the bank, on time, and ready to rob, but their boss had asked someone in the big crowd what was going on. *Espera un ratito,* stick around, the local had replied, the FBI is all over the place—pointing at the roof—there's going to be one hell of a show!

Unbelievable. The lesson learned would prove to be invaluable throughout my undercover career: take nothing for granted with respect to performance by fellow agents. Even in the FBI, incompetence can make an occasional appearance. In this case, the SWAT team just packed up and left. There were no repercussions.

The entire San Juan Division of the FBI consisted of fewer than seventy agents—covering a territory with a population of more than four million—and a third of those agents were assigned to Squad 4—the

Terrorism Squad, the balance being distributed among six other under-manned and overworked squads. The bulk of Squad 4's caseload was occupied by the *Macheteros* and splinter groups. The WELLROB arrests previously described resulted in no more than a short pause in the groups' operational pursuits. Absurdly—or so it seemed to us—most of the arrestees were free on bond. They were being prosecuted as defendants back in the Federal District Court in Hartford, Connecticut, and in order that their status as accused parties to a major federal case not unduly burden their lifestyle, they continued to reside in San Juan. To attend their court appearances, they would receive from the U.S. Marshals vouchers for *free* flights back to the mainland. Although the prosecutions resulted in convictions and lengthy jail sentences, there followed a bitter footnote. The San Juan agents of my generation, who had worked long hours and often taken huge risks, were stunned when most of those serving time received executive clemency from President Bill Clinton during "Pardongate," January 20, 2001, hours before he left office. Many of those pardons were based on recommendations from then Deputy Attorney General Eric Holder.

Typically, a Squad 4 agent would be assigned one or more known (or suspected) terrorists to investigate. Veteran agents would be assigned veteran terrorists, such as Ojeda Ríos. Rookies would be assigned rookie and low-level *Macheteros*. The substance of the cases varied significantly, as the *Machetero* foot soldiers were a mix of academic university intellectuals and hardcore common criminals. A senior agent would coordinate all the intelligence that was being developed on large sheets of paper, stitching it together to create a unified database. There were no computers and no electronic spreadsheets.

Additionally, the large-scale cases—a machine-gun attack on a Navy bus resulting in several fatalities (1979), the assassination of an off-duty Navy sailor (also '79), the blowing-up of eleven National Guard fighter jets (1981), the firing of a shoulder-launched missile at the FBI office in the Federal Building (1983, six weeks after the Wells Fargo robbery in Connecticut), the attempted murder of an Army major as he drove his motor scooter to work at Fort Buchanan in the heart of San Juan (1986—being close by, I was one of the first agents on the scene), and the ambush-murders of various officers of the local Puerto Rican constabulary (shooting a poorly trained cop in the back, at night, being an exception to the *Machetero* policy of only killing unarmed victims)—would be assigned to teams with a veteran case agent in charge.

International terrorism had its place in Puerto Rico as well. In the pre–Twin Towers world of 1985, Middle Eastern operatives had yet to earn a place of prominence in the assessments of the FBI. Domestic organizations posed the immediate threat. Hezbollah did have a presence in Puerto Rico, consisting primarily of "sleepers," agents put in place over a long term, operating as ordinary merchants, awaiting the call to duty, many providing operational support—false documentation, transport, and lodging—to active operational terrorists transiting through San Juan en route to the mainland. Squad 4, generally with the assistance of the Special Operations Group (the covert surveillance team), monitored and reported on the Hezbollah presence. But FBIHQ demanded that the focus be on the *independentistas*.

A few months after the WELLROB arrests, the Squad 4 supervisor called the case agent, Art Balizan, into his office. "Art, the SAC is very impressed with the job you did. It was exceptional. And he wants you to know just how much this means to the FBI, and to the San Juan Division. Here are the keys to his BuCar. It's yours." Art proudly drove that large late-model luxury sedan with tinted windows. For about two weeks. Then, Art learned, as we all did, that an informant had reported that the *Macheteros* had planned a revenge killing, specifically the assassination of . . . *the SAC*! Art's torrent of loud invective, a skillful blend of Spanish and English, emanated from his supervisor's office as Art slammed the car keys onto the desk.

A couple of months later, there was new informant info. The assassination target was now an FBI agent whose residence the *Macheteros* had ascertained. They were working out the plan, but the source could not find out who the targeted agent was, or where he or she lived. It could be any one of us. The already high level of paranoia in the office now became intolerable. *Just because you're paranoid doesn't mean they're not out to get you.* The old refrain took on added meaning. Raul Fernandez, a friendly, broad-faced Texan on the Terrorism Squad, told me that his commute home to the suburbs of Rio Piedras was taking an additional forty-five minutes as a result of the "dry-cleaning" (spy talk for counter-surveillance) he employed as a precaution: surprise U-turns (just like the one on the bridge in *The Godfather*), backing-up on exit ramps, driving through red traffic lights—all calculated to identify vehicles attempting to follow you unnoticed. I didn't have the heart to point out that all the dry-cleaning in the world wouldn't be of much use if they already had Raul's address. The feared assassins would already be parked across the street when he got home.

In my building lived five FBI agents. It was a new condo, across the street from the beach in Ocean Park. In back was the notorious *casario* (housing project) of Lorenz Torres. One of the building's security guards told us that, on several mornings, he had noticed a car parked near the entrance to our building, with two men inside. Just sitting there. His counterpart on the evening shift had made the same observation. These two guards were unaware of the informant's information concerning the planned hit, so we had no reason to believe they were indulging in imagined threats or fanciful observations. Their intel had a chilling cred-ibility. The condo parking lot, in the rear, housed my trusty navy-blue, personally owned Bronco II. As I had no spot for my BuCar, I typically parked it in back, in a cul-de-sac ending in a locked mesh-gate rear door to the lot. Driving home on the first Thursday evening after the alert was issued, I approached the building. The quiet, narrow street was al-ready dark. As I made the left turn into the dimly lit cul-de-sac, I observed to my right a parked car. With two men sitting in the front seat. No lights, inside or out. I parked the BuCar on the left side of the street, at the end of the cul-de-sac, a few feet from the gate. I looked at the gate, then up at my rearview mirror. I waited, but after two or three minutes, I decided it was time to put this to an end. I got out of the car, walked around the front then turned toward the entrance of the cul-de-sac. As I walked toward their car, I drew my massive .357 Smith & Wesson. I held it pointed at the ground, my arm slightly angled away from my hip, so they would be sure to see it—it's a psychologically heart-stopping *Dirty Harry* weapon. My eyes fixed on the two silhouettes and the car win-dows. No movement at all inside the car. As the distance closed to a few yards, the engine coughed to life. Without lights, and without haste, the car backed away. As I stood, in the middle of the street, following with my eyes, the car turned, stopped, shifted into drive, and calmly drove away. After that night, there were no more observations of suspect behavior made by the security guards at the condo across the street from Ocean Park.

It was a threshold moment for me, though I didn't recognize it as such at the time. Walking *toward* a hostile confrontation. Solo, determined, calm. Concerns about my physical well-being, self-doubts regarding my capacity for being a lawman, reservations as to the wisdom of having abandoned my "normal world" career—all had evaporated. The foundation had been set for the next three decades.

After eighteen months in Puerto Rico, I shifted from the Reactive Squad into the covert Special Operations Group (SOG), five agents primarily working surveillance on the two main terrorist groups on the island. From time to time, we'd also work a narcotics dealer or an organized crime figure, of whom there were plenty on the island. Thus, less than two years after arriving at Quantico for basic training, my career as a street agent had come to an end. For the next twenty-five years, I would work in the shadows, never using my true name, always hiding my true purposes. In the beginning with SOG, I considered it relatively safe work, because unlike the undercover work in my future, we generally had no intentional direct interaction with the targets. But in my time in the Bu, there were three SOG fatalities that I know of, one killed by a subject in Newark, one by "friendly fire" (also in Newark), and one in a car crash. And there were a few spectacular firefights.

In San Juan, our little surveillance group of five, led by Ed Bejerano, leased, under a fictitious company name, a warehouse in an industrial district. It had storage space for our cars and equipment and an office area for doing paperwork, of which there wasn't too much. No longer were we permitted in the office in Hato Rey. We were cut off from Bureau life and culture, and were essentially on our own, virtually free of management oversight (what a shame). We would on occasion meet with a case agent in an isolated area, to pass on information or discuss strategy; otherwise we just had each other. First order of business for me was cultivating a non–law enforcement look—in my case, a surfer expat's heedless nonchalance. I let my hair grow, developed a deep tan, and routinely wore shorts, sneakers, and a baggy T-shirt—to conceal my .357 Smith, of course. The Puerto Rico driver's license, credit cards, and wallet filler (health insurance/frequent flyer/Blockbuster/etc. cards) all told the watching world that my name was Jean-Marc Haddock. My first alias.

"Dave to Marc, Dave to Marc."

"Go ahead."

"We've got a white SUV pulling out of Roach's *marquesina* (carport). Appears to be his vehicle." In those days, the nicknames did not have to be politically correct. "Headed west toward General La Paz."

"Got him, thanks."

At night, in remote areas when discreet surveillance of a target's car by our cars was much more difficult, when the potential for being burned was significant, the ground forces would sometimes pull back as a team, leaving the job entirely to the Cessna—a tricky business for the co-pilot/observer, keeping track of the correct auto, then relaying its position to us on the ground at critical moments. An involuntary blink of the eye up in the sky, and down below we might spend an hour or two following the wrong car.

These were the "secret spy planes" that became the subject of a flurry of political and media attention in 2015. In response to real privacy concerns raised by the Patriot Act and Edward Snowden's infamous revelations about the National Security Agency's domestic and international spying, legislators predictably overreacted. The purple prose concerning mysterious FBI airlines registered to shell corporations owned by people who did not exist—fantasy images of the Bureau's very own Men In Black operating ultra-sophisticated aircraft, bristling with antennas and super-long-distance video lenses, was harrowing indeed. In fact, the use of these planes—whose most sophisticated technology might have been a GPS—for surveillance was sanctioned by the Supreme Court long ago (*California v. Ciraolo* being the seminal case, decided in 1986). Yet this did not interfere with the hysteria, nor impede the legislators from seeking to prohibit the use of the old-fashioned surveillance planes.

My surveillance work in Puerto Rico was not technically undercover work, but the experience turned out to be valuable training for my official UC career. In that trial run as a "ghost," I needed about six months to get the hang of being invisible. One develops a sixth sense, an intuition, an awareness that someone may be lurking in the shadows, which can be life-saving, before, during, and after a covert encounter. I was also beginning to understand the telltale markers for behavior that just doesn't fit. For example, one night, standing in the checkout line at my neighborhood supermarket, something almost "implicit" about the body language of the guy right in front of me triggered closer inspection and consideration. Lo and behold, he was the dangerous narcotics dealer we'd had under surveillance for months. There we were, our shopping carts full of foodstuffs.

The other vital skill I acquired on Special Ops: patience. Sitting quietly, two or three hours, in a darkened car parked in a quiet alley in a high-crime *caserio,* waiting for a gang chieftain to adjourn a meeting with his lieutenants—initially this was not easy for a big-city boy. However, it became etched into my character and proved invaluable over the following two-plus decades. Late one night I needed a different kind of patience when two off-duty San Juan cops mistook me and my partner for hoods intent on robbery. Looking back, I wonder how all four of us paused for that vital split-second before firing our drawn .357s. According to the book, maybe we shouldn't have. There's an example of *split-second patience*. Both kinds come in handy. That night, it undoubtedly saved lives.

During my surveillance work, my new home-away-from-home was a silver Mazda 626 which inexplicably still had that distinctive new-car odor. Prior to the start of each shift, I would bring down my gear from my tenth-floor beachside condo, crowding into the elevator with a folding luggage rack: large nylon camera case with Nikon and a variety of lenses; nylon gear bag with high-power binoculars, handi-talkie, miscellaneous high-tech surveillance equipment, insulated food case with sufficient nourishment and beverages, no Heinekens, nylon shotgun case (rectangular, so as to not look like a gun case) with a Remington 12-gauge and extra shells. The shotgun, a pump-action short-barreled law enforcement model, I would usually place within easy reach in the rear right passenger foot well, covered by a beach towel. Then, I would drive off to meet the rest of the team at a prearranged spot, often a parking lot at a BK or Mickey D's not too far from a target's home or workplace.

In the cop films, conducting a moving surveillance is a piece of cake. Subject pulls out of driveway or garage, cop pulls out of parking space and falls into place right behind the subject's car. Both cars then proceed for however long through crowded urban streets and deserted country roads, the cop always one car-length behind. Whenever one of the cops needs to communicate by radio, he holds the mic up to his mouth, rather than keeping it below dashboard level and out of sight. In the movies, the bad guys don't use rearview mirrors. Eventually the subject pulls into the driveway of Mr. Big's mansion, and the cop car pulls over, twenty-five yards back from the gate. Douse the engine. The bad guy having no idea that he was tailed.

Following terrorists, cocaine dealers, or organized crime characters is a bit different. Using the Hollywood surveillance technique, the lawmen would be "burned" in five minutes. Under the most benign scenario, the target then might decide to not proceed to his true destination, drive around for a bit, do a little shopping, return to where he started. Or the target might lead the burned surveillers into a deserted warehouse area for an unpleasant confrontation with a malevolent reception party.

Here's a typical scenario: At the BK parking lot in San Juan, we SOG operatives lean against a couple of cars, sip at a soda, and chat. We're working a major target, the number two in the *Machetero* chain of command who had been trained in Cuba.

Me, on our encrypted radio, to the guys in the Cessna: "I did a drive-by on the way over, Toad's car is in the *marquesina,* as usual, nose in. Didn't see any movement." They all had similarly flattering nicknames. Toad was driving his late-model Toyota SUV.

Red Cap (Ed Bejerano; we all had nicknames): "Okay, I'll take the first eye, on the cross street with a view of his house." With his droopy mustache, easy smile, and mischievous, slow eyes, Ed could have been typecast as a Mexican *bandolero.* He was so laid-back, he hardly appeared to be breathing. And sometimes with such folks you might mistakenly wonder if what's happening between the ears is equally slow. Not the case with Ed. You knew the brain was razor-sharp, working at lightning pace.

The rest of us would take up positions covering the different directions Toad could travel in. Once his car pulled out, the "eye" would not move. Instead:

Marc (no suitable nickname managed to stick): "He's headed toward you eastbound on Godoy y Cruz."

"Got him." I pull out, half a block in front of Toad, with one eye on my rearview mirror. All the cars are moving now, fast. "He just made a right turn onto Ortega toward the on-ramp for the Panamericana Southbound."

Carmen (the only woman on the team): "I'm getting onto the Panamericana now . . . I'll pick him up . . . got him."
Oso: "Let me know when you're getting warm, I'm about number ten [cars] behind, on your left."
Five minutes later, Carmen: "Okay, Oso, I'll take the next exit." She signals the turn, exits, as Oso takes the eye. She pulls over at the bottom of the ramp, acts like she's searching in her purse, waits to see what other cars might be getting off, satisfied that she's clean, takes the next ramp back on and rejoins the pack. And so it goes.

One night Toad led us to an apartment building in a quiet section of Santurce, arriving there after ten. He had been driving for over an hour, apparently aimlessly, therefore clearly dry-cleaning. As this dry-cleaning maneuver—conducted fairly well, I have to admit—was a significant change from his routine, we were particularly careful that night. Any sign of something out of the ordinary and he would have scrubbed his meet. At the nonluxury building, with open parking lot and darkened lobby, Carmen set up with an eye.

"He's inside."

Quickly I parked around the corner and slowly walked toward the entrance. Had I seen him, I would have walked past, without entering. Instead, the lobby was empty. Above the single elevator, the numeral 5 was illuminated. We noted many license plate numbers. Some we recognized as belonging to other *Macheteros*. Others would be cross-checked by Squad 4 office agents. The next day we learned from one of those agents that a suspected safe house was situated on that fifth floor of the Santurce building. A good night's work and a good survival lesson: It became routine for me never to take an elevator directly to the floor of my destination. I would always push two or three buttons (if alone), and I would *always* have it come to a stop on another floor. Should there be someone surveilling me, they would not know at which I had gotten off.

Because the *Macheteros* tended to be more active after dark, we usually worked after dark, setting up on whomever we were following that week, or that month, at around two or three in the afternoon, and usually putting him to bed around ten or eleven, maybe twelve, depending on his routine. Many had "day jobs," so if they weren't moving by then and the lights had been out for an hour or two, they weren't going anywhere. (They didn't have the patience to play games, sit in the dark for an extended period, on the off chance that there might be a surveillance team outside.) On those occasions that they did enter their cars late in the evening, we would be in for a long, often productive shift.

After a typical shift, Armando Rodriguez (Oso) and I would drive down to Condado, get a bite to eat, then move on to one of the two or three clubs that catered to a mix of expats and young Puerto Ricans. Eventually, we'd head back to our beachside condos. When I got up midmorning the next day, I'd go for a run, maybe put in a little beach time, then load up the BuCar and head off to work. Altogether, not a bad life for a single guy.

And then, suddenly (or so it seemed), it was August 1988, three years since my graduation from Quantico, and I had orders for reassignment to the New York office. My Transfer Luncheon (the Bu has a capitalized name for everything, and I mean Everything; I'm sparing readers most of them) was held at Mona's, a beachfront Mexican restaurant, one of our favorites. All SOGers, ground and aerial, were on hand, but only a couple of the office supervisors; the SOG agents who weren't leaving the island had to remain covert and could not be seen with a full Bureau complement. The gang presented me with a plaque commemorating my assignment to the *Isla del Encanto*—and then, as per tradition, roasted the hell out of me. I wasn't going to take this lying down. Fueled by screwdrivers, I retaliated with my own observations and jibes, some prepared beforehand. There were lots of laughs that afternoon, and few of the jokes would pass muster with today's politically correct thought police. Driving away in our respective BuCars, all of us were soused, and I, for one, was also thoughtful. Puerto Rico had been a big deal for me—truly a major transitional stage in my life. I had loved the transition from the courtroom in Brooklyn to the FBI Academy in Quantico to the mean streets of Puerto Rico. Not for a moment did I doubt that I'd made the right call by changing careers.

But what about where I was going? Would the New York gig be as enlightening and rewarding as my first Bureau assignment? I was pretty confident that the answer would be yes. I've already admitted that I had joined the FBI because I thought it might provide the opportunity for me to be the best at something important. Three-plus years later, I knew that I had made the right move.

3

Learning to Live a Lie

Learning to lie is one thing, and it takes practice, but learning to *live a lie*—that's something else entirely, a much greater challenge, and that's what undercover work is. The seed for my interest in working behind enemy lines had been planted many years before, watching old movies about the OSS agents in Nazi-occupied Europe. Then, while working for Pat Moynihan in Washington, I met a retired undercover agent from the Bureau of Narcotics and Dangerous Drugs (predecessor to the DEA). This man had as much character as anyone I met in the capital, particularly on the Hill, where character often seemed to be an actual impediment to career advancement. In Puerto Rico, I found gratification in the surveillance work against the local terrorist groups, but I also realized that I didn't want to be *just* a watcher, a voyeur, a ghost. Not for the next twenty-five years. The goal was to become a *player*, maybe the best one, to see how far I could push the envelope, and in the FBI, I figured out, one elite job leads the way in that regard.

But first things first. My initial assignment stateside was not going to be undercover. I knew that. Inside the walls of the fortress, the Bureau works like any other organization: whom you know counts, along with who's on vacation and who's retiring next month. In New York, the usual first job for young agents, even those with extensive street experience, as I now had, is with the "applicant squad." These agents run background investigations on applicants to the Bureau, mainly, but also on political appointees and the like. The running joke about this tedious work: "Gear up, guys, we're going out on an applicant arrest tonight."

But fortunately, I had in hand an introduction to James Kallstrom, czar of the fifteen or so SOG squads in the Big Apple. (Eight years later, in 1996, as Assistant Director in Charge of the NYO, Jim would head the Bureau's investigation of the crash of TWA Flight 800 off the southern coast of Long Island—and rule that it was not terror related, but a failure of the aircraft. After eighteen months, the final report concluded that there was no evidence of a terrorist act. Civilian investigators eventually determined that the cause had been an electrical short circuit triggering an explosion of flammable vapors in a fuel tank.) Jim took me on board and assigned me to a newly formed squad, SO-13. A mixed blessing, as I was soon to learn.

Our supervisor on SO-13 was Thom Nicoletti, "Crazy Thom," one of the two genuinely out-of-control agents I came to know in my quarter century with the Bu. Despite bringing an NYU coed to a covert "off-site" for a tryst (she was of age—Thom was in his midforties), despite punching Special Agent in Charge Carson Dunbar (a big boss) in the face, Thom somehow managed to survive and thrive. He was a former Marine, former Secret Service Agent, who looked like, and patterned himself after—in my story, almost predictably—Sonny Crockett from *Miami Vice*. Down to the $10,000 Rolex and the Gucci suits. After New York he ended up in Hawaii, a plum assignment . . . but stepped on some toes and was exiled to the Guam Resident Agency. Until the governor of Guam personally declared Thom "PNG" (persona non grata), and had him deported. After Thom's retirement, he was observed on various telecasts toting an AK-47 while standing guard behind former Afghan president Hamid Karzai. I came to like this man but would tread with care in his presence. For two years, I was happy enough working under him on a wide array of cases—surveillance in the investigation of the murder of DEA agent Everett Hatcher, a few organized crime cases, several foreign counterintelligence ops—but also feeling that surely this wasn't *quite* my destiny. I chafed at the bit. I was growing tired of being a ghost, a shadow, an invisible agent. I had learned all there was to learn about the surveillance and countersurveillance business. The time was approaching for me to make a move. But to what squad? Openings for inexperienced wannabe undercover agents were rare indeed. And how to get there without incurring Crazy Thom's wrath and retribution, because he was well known for interpreting any request for transfer to another squad as a betrayal worthy of retribution. Agents naïve enough to approach him for a frank discussion about filling a vacancy in the Bank Robbery Squad, or, heaven forbid, another Special Operations Squad, would elicit a smile and "I'll do what I can." Then they'd find themselves working the worst possible shifts until the transfer came through—and not to the squad they had asked for, but to their worst-nightmare squad, such as working applicants.

My big break came in 1990. At the SO-13 off-site, sitting in our large kitchen snack room before a shift, I was leafing through the NYO internal announcements (yes . . . this was before email). A posting caught my eye: a job working UC on a new large-scale operation targeting commodities exchanges on Wall Street. Wow. I called one of the case agents, Ed Cugell, who scheduled an interview for the *next* day at his office in downtown Manhattan. As Thom was out of town, I did not have to use a pretext for a trip downtown. (The standard excuse was "need to stop by Health Services," but you can't use it too often, obviously.)

It was clear at the interview that this was a major operation. Sitting in the conference room with Ed Cugell were two SSAs (Supervisory Special Agents), Ed's co-case agent, and several others supporting the nascent investigation. C-1 SSA Mary Jane Bocra explained that her squad and C-21 SSA Craig Dotlo's squad would have joint responsibility for the op, which would require six UCs. After an hour's worth of questions about my background, Craig laid down the primary ground rule. This was a *deep*-cover op, working and living my UC role day in, day out, contact with family and friends infrequent. The case could be expected to run *at least* one or two years, but could go on for who knows how long. So the commitment was open-ended, but once in I would stay in. Was I still interested?

It would be a gross understatement to say that I was eager to be selected. A couple of years earlier, I had sat one weekend in my parents' apartment reading the *New York Times* coverage of the arrest of nearly fifty commodities brokers in Chicago following an FBI sting against that famous exchange. I had thought, *now that would be one fascinating job.* And here was the possibility, the glimmer of a possibility, for that fanciful dream to be realized.

The next day, at the off-site, I was caught off guard in our kitchen by Thom, who was suddenly back in town.

"Hey Marc, were you in the office yesterday interviewing for a transfer to another squad?"

Busted.

"Well, er, I was, I did go to the office, actually, I was, I did, well it wasn't exactly . . ." Then—and if I had seen this scene in a film, I would not have believed it—the phone rang. After a very short exchange, Thom hung up and turned toward me, his mounting anger replaced by an expression of confusion, of pure befuddlement.

"You've been transferred to C-1. Effective immediately."

That was the commodities UC job. I actually got it, with zero UC experience? How had this happened? I was ecstatic! And to my surprise, Thom was anything but a sore loser. He knew what fights to pick. He even organized a Transfer Pizza Party. I received another plaque for my collection and was out of there. Later, I learned that Mary Jane Bocra had gone straight from my interview to the office of the big boss, Jim Esposito, the Assistant Director in Charge of the New York office—and my boss in San Juan five years earlier.

"You want Marc, he's yours."

The New York sting was designed to follow up on the big success at the commodities exchange in Chicago that I had read about in the *Times*. That one had started three years earlier, in the mid-eighties, with FBI agents posing as traders and infiltrating the trading floor. The first subpoenas were issued in early 1989, with the indictments coming down eight months later. The main scam of the indicted brokers and traders was using advance knowledge of customers' orders to aid their own trades. This illegal "front-running" necessarily entailed other crimes, including racketeering, mail fraud, commodities fraud, skimming profits, filing false tax returns, lying to federal agents, conspiring to defraud the IRS, and probably more, but the front-running was the primary crime.

Despite the wide publicity that accompanied the Chicago case, the FBI and other agencies had every reason to believe that the same practices were still rampant on the two commodities exchanges on Wall Street. Of course, the bosses must also have understood that the Chicago publicity would now make a successful infiltration of the closed world in New York a much more difficult task. By their natures, these exchanges rely on trust among the traders, many of whom have known each other from their school days. It's a club, and not an easy one to join, but the Bureau decided to give it a try on the biggest financial stage of all—Wall Street. This would be another "Group I" investigation, that is, highest priority, with major resources in time and money allocated. (At any given time, the Bureau is engaged nationwide in about fifty Group I ops.) Code name: COMMCORR, an elision of "commodities" and "corruption." I liked the ring of it.

I was now one of what ultimately would be six UC agents who would try to obtain membership on the COMEX exchange after being inserted onto the floor working as clerks, the support employees who make up the bulk of the personnel buzzing around the vast halls. The hope was to obtain membership as traders within a year. All of us were rookies in this clandestine netherworld of undercover. I don't know this for a fact, but the all-rookie lineup could have been a first for the FBI. Highly unusual, that's for sure, and for obvious reasons: it was the blind leading the blind. Today, with a formalized UC training and certification program in place, new guys (and gals) are usually mixed with veterans. I have participated in hundreds of UC meets while accompanied by a rookie in the role of sidekick or maybe girlfriend, getting acclimated to the dark side. In the early days, there simply weren't enough UCs to go around.

Our first task was establishing new identities that would withstand the close scrutiny they'd be subjected to after starting our first jobs as humble clerks, followed by *intense* scrutiny when we applied for our broker's licenses and actual seats on the exchange. A new identity is rooted in a new name, of course. For major operations, UC agents select their own names, for the good reason that we need to be *completely* comfortable with that name. In my career, I used about a dozen aliases. This one, following the French theme set in San Juan with Jean-Marc Haddock, was

H. Marc Renard. My new last name means "fox" in French—an inside joke for my benefit only: the fox set loose among the hares. When asked by brokers on the floor of the exchange about the initial "H," I would respond, "—for Henri, which no one here can pronounce, not correctly." A small touch, but the sort of comment that built on my image as a guy of European origin, and simply not the kind of detail one would expect from a lawman.

From the garage of available UC vehicles, I scrounged a dark-blue, late-model Mercedes 500SEL seized from some narcotics dealer, in all likelihood. (Later, to go along with the enviable wheels, I rented an enviable upscale techno-furnished apartment on 10th Street and University Place.) I flew to San Juan to set up prior employments and residences down there. The whole process of setting up the new identity is called "backstopping" a legend, and in those days we UC agents did the work almost on our own, and without guidance. It was all OJT, on-the-job training, and it requires great diligence and attention to detail, and a fair amount of specialized and arcane know-how. Which I didn't have at first. This is one reason that in the early nineties the Bureau set up a specialized, dedicated backstopping unit codenamed Janus (destined to play a major role in my story soon enough). But backstopping H. Marc Renard was my problem—a full-time job for a full six months. I assumed my fellow UC rookies on Wall Street were doing the same thing with the same laborious, even obsessive attention to detail, but we were all operating more or less independently—not as a team.

Let's get specific. What would I need to have? There was no manual, no checklist of items necessary to establish one's footprint in the world of real people. Some were obvious, like a real driver's license and Social Security card. Those were also easy enough, because the Bureau already had established the necessary contacts in those state and federal agencies. However, once our contacts put our paperwork into their systems, it would be processed by clerks who did *not* know it was fictitious, and thus the documents could not be expedited, or given any priority.

Other requirements were not so easy, and many were fraught with unexpected obstacles. Credit cards? Everyone has them, but take a look at an application, and the task is daunting when the answers are all lies. Rent an apartment? Again, lots of questions to answer and lies required, and the landlord might check some of those bogus answers, especially concerning finances. So a bank checking account would be mandatory. Why not include a savings account as well? Armed with my new driver's license, my Social Security card, and a new Renard P.O. box (thanks to a kindly Upper East Side postmaster), I walked into a Chase branch in Lower Manhattan. Sitting across from the bank officer, I confidently filled out the forms, listing as my physical (not mailing) address a large apartment complex on 86th and Second. The paperwork completed, he carried it off, along with my identification documents. After a disconcertingly long absence, he reappeared.

"Your Social Security number was issued a month ago, Mr. Renard." It was a statement, but, from his expression, it was clearly also a question. When the agent who provided the contact at Social Security gave me the card, he failed to mention, and I hadn't thought about the not-insignificant vulnerability imposed by the fact that the card would be real, but it would *not* be backdated. Nor would I have thought that a bank officer performing such a routine task would have the capacity to unearth such a detail so easily.

"Oh, I had a very messy divorce," I replied totally off the cuff, with what I thought was reasonable aplomb. It was the best I could come up with on short notice. "My ex abused my credit cards for all sorts of things to get back at me, destroying my credit, to the point where my lawyer had to obtain a new Social Security number for me."

He looked at me—to my somewhat agitated mind, it seemed close to an outright glare—for a few seconds and left again. Then he returned with temporary checks and a bankbook. His final look and final words conveyed his suspicion, "Okay, but . . ." I clearly needed more history in my life as Henri. Having lived in San Juan for three years, it seemed an obvious choice. But those three years had to be expanded to account for *eleven* years, covering my entire life as an adult. (I had already subtracted five years from my true age, which was thirty-five. Clerks on the exchanges were on the youngish side. The fictitious age of thirty was already pushing the envelope.) So this became the new big lie: I, Henri Marc Renard, had moved to San Juan from Buenos Aires when I was nineteen. My French dad and Argentine-bred mom had moved there from Paris when I was in grade school. Good luck to anyone try-

ing to corroborate my overseas upbringing. The backstopping had to
be done on the ground. Should the fictitious identity come under close
scrutiny—and it probably would, in this instance—the trail had to appear as real as possible. Anyone associated with my new history would,
if interviewed (probably by phone from New York), need to speak of me
with a credible degree of familiarity. So I had to return to San Juan, an
unexpected fringe benefit. At Banco Popular, my old friend Deputy Chief
Security Officer Carlos Guzman and his boss readily agreed to open a fictitious account for me. More importantly, they agreed to *backdate* this
account (sometimes I learn fast) in their computer system. I later learned
that it took their software engineer two full days to override their operating system. Taking the challenge seriously, the Banco Popular team
even created a worn bankbook, with deposits and withdrawals dating
back a decade. Beautiful craftsmanship.

An Isla Verde–area real-estate agent friend agreed to serve as my former "landlord" in an apartment he owned, and a small business owner
agreed to have been my boss in that career. Sounds simple, but it took a
couple of weeks on the island to get that and more set up. It was worth
it. Now I could rent the apartment in the trendy Greenwich Village area.
Mary Jane Bocra and Craig Dotlo, my supervisors, had been pushing for
all the UCs to rent apartments in Battery Park City, then a newly created
(literally—on landfill) upscale yuppie neighborhood near the financial
district. Not wanting to be under a management microscope, I opted instead for the ultramodern expensive loft in the hipper Greenwich Village. I successfully argued that such digs would better suit H. Marc's
image. And for some vaguely felt reason, I thought it was unwise for me
to have *too* much in common with my fellow UC "clerks"—an unfortunately correct premonition, as things turned out. Lease and San Juan–
based legitimacy in hand, I could get the electricity turned on. And the
phone line. And, finally, the credit cards.

What about college? While not indispensable for a commodities trader,
a college degree would help, because my persona was more along the
lines of "international and refined," rather than crude and vulgar in a Joe
Pesci, Danny DeVito, *Wolf of Wall Street* kind of way. (The full spectrum
can be found on the exchange floors.) A backstopped BA was in order,
but the University of Puerto Rico, which seemed logical, would be a

problem. I had no familiarity with the school and would have been unable to survive a conversation with someone who did.

Plan B was a long shot, but I contacted the father of my closest college friend, president of a prestigious northeastern university. The president knew only that in my capacity as an FBI agent, I was working an important undercover case and that a fictitious degree would be an important element in my cover story. Without more specifics than the subject matter—white-collar crime—and the general area of interest—Wall Street—he agreed to the scheme after a short meeting at his bucolic on-campus home. I was amazed but very happy, because I didn't have much of a Plan C. Only the president and the registrar would know. The registrar had a need to know: she created an actual fabricated file—physical documentation—for H. Marc Renard and placed it in the appropriate cabinet.

One day, the backstopping process nearing completion, Mary Jane called me at my new place in the Village with the news that she had set up a meeting for us COMMCORR undercover agents with one of the UCs from the Chicago case. For security reasons—the Chicago case had been prominent news, and many of those UCs' true identities were in wide circulation as a result of the public trials arising out of the indictments—we would meet this sleuth in a hotel room in Newark, rented with a covert credit card. This would be my—our—first opportunity to learn about the nuts and bolts of the task that lay ahead, as well as a chance to get a feel for my fellow UCs and size them up—at least three of them, the number present. The remaining two were yet to be selected. Mary Jane and Craig were on hand, of course. One of the other UCs was a relief to see: Ben Berry, my classmate from Quantico, five long years ago, the fellow Jewish attorney in NAC 85-7, and my challenger for first place in the two-mile run, whose father had commiserated with mine at the graduation ceremony. This was great. I didn't know that Ben was one of us. I didn't know what he had been up to for the past five years. Answer, in two words: Kansas City. The native New Yorker had discovered that there was civilization west of the New Jersey border. And they have challenging crimes out there, too. Ben had just flown back from that First Office, and he was annoyed that the Bu was not reimbursing him for the extra seat he had required to accommodate his beloved cello. Then

there was hawk-nosed, long-haired Jim Clemente, he of the calm demeanor, which would soon be dissipated on the manic floor of the
exchange. Representing our sister agency in the op—the U.S. Postal
Inspection Service—was Jeff Davis, a blond, chisel-featured inspector,
who had previously earned his living as a model. Jeff would later prove
to be made of the same granite used in the chiseling, always maintaining
his calm when all about him were losing theirs.

The Chicago UC guy did little to encourage us. In addition to the
heightened suspicions—extreme caution really—to be expected after
the wave of arrests in Chicago, he painted a grim picture of the obstacles
that awaited us. And of the workload. We would be working two jobs:
daytime at the exchange, evenings FBI agents. Seated in our covert apartments with the typewriters, all alone, documenting our covert activities
and progress. Meeting with our contact agents. Planning strategy. Those
nights that were a little different—jovial eating and drinking and bonding with target brokers—would only result in extra paperwork the following evening. The paperwork chore required an average of two hours
every night. But I didn't begrudge the tedium. It was important.

That was the bad news. The good news was that the Chicago case had
proved and highlighted the importance of the undercover technique and
its value as the gold standard for investigation and then prosecution in
this kind of case, as well as so many others. This point is very important
for both my story and twenty-first-century law enforcement at most
levels. Specifically, how does any prosecutor make cases involving terrorism, organized crime, white-collar crime, without UC work and testimony? With great difficulty. Many journalists and other interested
parties are upset that the prosecutions that flowed from the '08 financial
crisis, and every other financial crisis, featured huge fines but almost no
perp walks. A key reason is that *the prosecutions were hamstrung by the
lack of UC testimony*. Without this professional eyewitness element, making a tight case—in white-collar investigations especially—is exponentially more difficult. With the UC on the witness stand, the jurors hear
the criminal activity described by the most reliable of all witnesses, and
with audiotape or video on which they can see and hear the scheming,
the winks and nods, the money actually changing hands. Without the
UC, the jurors usually have only ream after ream of paper, from which

they're expected to draw the right inferences. Wiretaps may provide incriminating conversation and exchanges, but just as often, probably more often, they're ambiguous. *What did that mean?* The jurors' doubt makes it much harder to send guilty people to prison. Meanwhile, the skilled undercover agent is *guiding* the meetings and conversations to yield clear, incriminating results. So would it play out in my UC roles, again and again, in the years and decades to come.

In the hotel room in Newark, Mary Jane and Craig laid out the scenario they and the two case agents had developed for our new COMM-CORR sting on Wall Street. The entire undertaking relied on the assistance of the CEO of Planet Oil, LTD, a leading international energy company with a presence on the COMEX exchange, specifically in the crude oil pit. (I have changed the name of the company, of course.) As I would come to learn, Craig, always an indefatigably resourceful agent, had developed Planet Oil's CEO as a "Friend of the Bureau" through an introduction from Planet Oil's Chief Security Officer, a retired FBI agent. The company's presence at this time consisted of a booth, two traders, and two clerks. The basic idea was to expand this presence with the hiring of six new clerks, with the expectation that these new clerks would, with time, develop into traders and make everyone a lot more money. The CEO, going against the advice of his floor traders, wanted to bring in "new blood" (i.e., us, the FBI UC team). The basic assumption: the criminal behaviors that had been discovered in Chicago—primarily front-running in its many permutations—were also rampant in New York. How could they *not* be? The money was too easy.

After nearly a half year of preparation, it was show-time. In the early winter months of 1990, I, Henri Marc Renard, arrived at 4 World Trade Center for work on my first day, went through security, entered the enormous cavern that housed both of New York's huge commodities exchanges, and found my way to the Planet Oil booth. My only previous observation of the floor having been on the film screen, watching Dan Ackroyd and Eddie Murphy in the very funny *Trading Places*. Trading had not yet commenced. The two genuine clerks, tall and fat Greg and short and fat and bearded Eddie (a Hobbit, I suspected) were not *openly* hostile to the new clerk, who they had to suspect might bypass them on the road to the Holy Grail, Traderdom. Eddie introduced me to the other new clerks, that is, my fellow UC operatives. Jeff was courteous; Jim and Ben were more standoffish than the role required, in my view. All now had new surnames, of course, though pursuant to conventional wisdom, the true first names had been retained, the idea being that we humans are less likely to trip up if using our real given names. (A related trick among border-patrol personnel is to casually ask folks where they were born. If you hesitate answering that question, you weren't born there.) I was skeptical about automatically retaining the first name. I had no problem with H. *Marc* Renard, but with future ops I'd always select a name that was operationally appropriate (Hispanic, Italian American, etc.), rather than one that would be easy to respond to.

Filling out the immediately pertinent dramatis personae of the COMM-CORR sting—and present that morning, of course—were Planet Oil's two licensed traders: Pete, short, gray-haired, surprisingly soft-spoken (which is rare for his occupation) when not trading, about forty-two going on sixty-two; and his partner Tommy, midthirties, with a broad porcine face, black hair brushed back, toting an extra fifty or sixty pounds, lending him a more fixed position on the floor. Tommy did not suffer the impediment of being soft-spoken. Loud and vulgar, he was reflective of a great many in his profession: a born blowhard.

The trading bell rang. The place instantly erupted. I found myself in a human anthill: deafening shouting, thousands of bodies pressed together, standing, swaying, and pushing. Bedlam. This was the era of Desert Storm, the first Iraqi war, and no other commodity compared in volatility to crude. Fortunes were made and lost in minutes. The volume and pace was dizzying. Eventually, I came to comprehend the activity, in much the same way that hearing a crowd shouting in an unknown language begins as unintelligible noise, which gradually acquires meaning as one's language skills develop. But in the beginning, the pits consisted of masses of men shouting at the top of their lungs and frantically waving their arms back and forth. Ringing the pits were masses of clerks, moving from booth to booth, hurriedly talking to traders to relay orders, or talking on the banks of phones attached to the flimsy booth walls. Eddie, the clerk, would get off the phone, run (literally run, seconds meant money) to the pit, where Tommy, the trader, was stationed like a statue, and whisper (read: with hands cupped, shout into Tommy's ear) the order: "Buy 500 Oct at 10." Translation: Buy 500 futures contracts for delivery of crude oil in October at 10 cents of the dollar value they were trading at. If they were trading at $90.05 per barrel, he was to offer $90.10, and buy as close to that price as possible. As each contract consists of 1,000 barrels, minor fluctuations rapidly translate into big money.

As soon as the rest of the pit realizes Tommy is buying a large number of contracts, the reaction is akin to what might be expected when raw meat is thrown into a pit of hungry lions. Impossibly, the volume *rises,* the frantic waving becomes *more frantic,* and Tommy is scribbling even *more* frantically onto a notepad of buy/sell order forms. As soon as a page's lines are all filled, he tears off the sheet, throws it to a hovering Eddie, who in turn runs over to me, as I stand at the booth, yelling into one phone and holding another to my free ear (jumping ahead now, I wasn't doing this on the first day). I am already working on the prior page from Tommy's order pad when Eddie thrusts the new scribble at me and runs off. My job was to confirm each of the trades with a clerk for the trader on the other side of each transaction, identified by the oversized rectangular badge pinned to his shirt. If there were fifteen trades on the page, each of the fifteen clerks had to be called, or tracked down at their booth, as rapidly as possible. Any discrepancy as to price, number of contracts, or identity of the trader on the other end of the transaction could have an impact of several thousand dollars.

While it was not my money, and I could not have cared less about the trades, I had to do as good a job as possible—both to advance my career at Planet Oil and my career as an FBI undercover.

The opportunities for skullduggery in this system are probably pretty apparent. (Today those opportunities are more limited; the use of hand-held computers has eliminated much of the paper-based fraud.) It all came down to front-running—traders using prior knowledge of customers' orders to aid their own trades. This was accomplished by large-volume traders, such as Tommy, who passed their insider information to small-volume independent brokers (referred to as "Locals"), who would then make a huge profit using the illegal tip, and later split the gain with Tommy. One objective of COMMCORR was for me to climb the ladder and become a local and participate in these crooked trades.

Ironically, it was an error made in executing my clerk duties that led to the first real break in the case. One midmorning about three months after I had started work for Planet Oil, I could not find the clerk to confirm the details of a large trade between Tommy and a broker standing next to trader QQQQ, as identified by the badge pinned on his chest (that was his actual ID, one that constituted knee-slapping humor on the floor—a pun: Four-Q . . . fuck you). I moved on to the next trade, then the next, then the next, and then, ten minutes later, found the broker's young, overloaded clerk at her booth, juggling several phones. She denied the trade. It wasn't on her trader's card. Uh oh . . . This was the first time this had happened to me. When I relayed the news to Tommy, he went postal. As the others looked on, grateful they were not standing in my shoes, his shouts drowned out even the background din of the pit.

"You fucking moron! Asshole! Dumb shit . . . !"

I stared at him, mute. Every ounce of control, all my reserves of strength, self-discipline, were dedicated to not punching his Porky Pig face and breaking his nose. But did I want to be fired from Planet Oil, pulled off of my first UC op, sent back to SO-13, or more likely, a permanent slot on the Applicant Squad? I just stood there until he lost interest and returned to his place in the pit. The missing trade issue would be handled after-hours. This would be just one of many episodes on Wall Street that convinced me that the brokers on the trading floor—Tommy, Four Q's neighbor, and the rest—were, quite frankly, some of the most despicable people I'd ever met, or would ever meet. Generally speaking, the drug dealers and car thieves and other street professionals I'd later deal with (and, in some cases, get to know well) had more sympathy for their fellow men and women than those ravenously greedy Jordan Belfort (*The Wolf of Wall Street*) and Gordon Gekko wannabes on the floor of the commodities exchanges.

After trading closed, I took my time at our booth, completing the forms that, as junior clerk, it was my daily responsibility to complete. Tommy and Pete had waved three or four of their friends over, traders for large brokerage houses or multinational oil companies. The loss from the missed and denied trade was over $25,000. As the traders studied their notecards and made changes, Tommy completed a new sheet from the order pad, handed it to me for processing, and tossed the old sheet into the garbage. The new sheet (which I later photocopied) was minus the trade with Four Q's neighbor in the pit. The old sheet—well, I scooped that one out of the garbage after they were all gone. Here, finally, was real, tangible evidence of fraud. Two documents covering the *same* set of transactions, one true, one altered. And a UC as eyewitness. Mary Jane and Craig had something besides hopes and aspirations to report back to FBIHQ and Justice. COMCORR was beginning to provide returns.

In those first months, none of us UCs were wearing recording devices, primarily because there was nothing to record. We were not yet in a position to engage in any kind of criminal activity. We were not yet brokers, and certainly had not developed the relationships necessary to become partners in fraudulent transactions. On a more practical level, there remained the problem of passing through the metal detector at the COMEX entrance, and of concealing a device in a chicken-farm environment where privacy is a quaint memory, a luxury for the evening hours. The constant high decibels of the pit and environs would require mics to be as close to mouth/ear level as possible, if anything discernible as communication was to be recorded. A real problem. In Chicago, they had managed without adequate recordings, relying on the detailed notes of the UCs, meticulously corroborated by the documents reflecting the fraudulent activity. While the evidence had proved sufficient for successful prosecutions, Craig sought to make the cases bulletproof, unassailable by defense attorneys, and, not surprisingly, he came up with a kind of Rube Goldberg solution.

The standard law enforcement recording devices of the day, solid and reliable, were the Swiss-made Nagra and mini-Nagra—the former, the size of a trade paperback; the latter, a bit larger than a deck of cards. The plan was to hollow out the sole of a high-top sneaker, creating a space to fit the mini-Nagra. Then a series of wires would run up the inner-pants leg and then the shirt, with the mic at collar level.

My fellow (Jewish) tribesman, Ben Berry, and Jim Clemente were selected to carry the first devices. Unlicensed traders-in-training were permitted limited time in the pits, under supervision of an experienced broker. Ben and Jim, the first UC clerks hired by Planet Oil, had recently been granted this privilege. Wearing the devices was somewhat of a gamble, as the likelihood of actually capturing clearly audible, incriminating conversations in the din of the trading pit was remote, while the risk of discovery was not negligible. Jim enjoyed believing that wearing a wire around the trading pit would be dangerous, but I felt that was histrionics. It wouldn't be dangerous, in the sense of exposing us to physical injury. We might get caught, but we weren't going to get killed. Only a few years after COMMCORR did I realize the tremendous advantage I had by starting my UC career with a white-collar investigation. I could learn to live the lie, to walk the walk, and talk the talk of an alternate persona *without* having to worry about being murdered should I slip up. At a time when all UC training was OJT, COMMCORR was my Undercover Academy.

After three or four months on the job, the last two UC agents, Ralph Nessman and Fatime Hajdari joined the four of us already in place. Ralph, a natural jokester, and calm, steady Fatime were welcome additions to the team. Relieved of the more arduous duties, which are always assigned to the latest newcomers by the traders, I was free to do a little exploring on the cavernous COMEX and NYMEX floor of the World Trade Center. Both exchanges shared the space, and nothing else. Already, I was losing patience with what appeared to me to be the snail's-pace progress of the investigation. More specifically, I felt that working at Planet Oil with so many UCs was cramping my style. I started to look for another path to achieving the op's goals, one that would not involve the cast and crew of Planet Oil.

The break came one morning when I bumped into—literally—Joseph Bernstein, one of my closest friends in the Brooklyn DA's office. He was no longer an ADA but had switched gears and was working as an attorney at NYMEX. The surprise in this encounter was mutual; I kept my cool, we smiled and shook hands. I hastily—and quietly—told Joseph that I could not explain my presence there at that moment, but would call him in the evening. Which was a way of communicating precisely what I *was doing there,* without breaking any rules. Joseph had organized my farewell dinner from the DA's office in Brooklyn, knew full well what my new career was, and was nobody's fool. On the contrary, he was one of the sharpest minds in our old office, and combined with his sardonic, ever-present wit, an exceptional companion. Here was a winning hand dealt by destiny, a close friend working on one of the exchanges, no doubt well connected, and perhaps willing to help.

That evening, back in my Village apartment, I called Craig first. While he wasn't thrilled that an unknown actor was now aware of an FBI agent's presence on the trading floor, he gave me the green light to tell Joseph what he had no doubt already figured out. I would, of course, leave out any mention of Planet Oil or the presence of other UCs. This was followed by a long call to Joseph, then a discreet dinner the next week. Joseph explained that he had lost interest in criminal law and had been working for NYMEX for three years, looking to develop an expertise in financial markets. He knew a few traders—*honest* traders, I wouldn't want to imply that all were dishonest—and he was close friends with the owner of one of the clearinghouses, the private banks which processed all the financial transactions occurring on the exchanges. And he was indeed willing to help. Uncovering corruption in the exchanges was fully consistent with his values, and he had the courage to step out on a limb to further that end.

Now the wheels between the ears of H. Marc Renard began to spin. Would I be able to convince Mary Jane and Craig to let me divert from the "Approved at All Levels" scenario (that is, the detailed scenario as authorized all the way up to the corner offices at FBIHQ in Washington) and set off on my own in the NYMEX pits? In order to set the stage, I asked Joseph to introduce me to Steve Weinstein, the owner of the clearinghouse. In preparation, Joseph and I had concocted a story about having met ten years earlier while he was vacationing in Puerto Rico, and that we'd been close friends ever since. He explained to Weinstein that I had accumulated a fair bit of equity and was now looking to lease a seat on the NYMEX and establish myself as a Local, an independent, self-employed broker, trading in one of the pits on my own account.

Steve was only too happy to meet a potential new client, certainly one whose bona fides were provided by Joseph. He in turn introduced me to Enzo Alioto, a Local, unaffiliated with the big brokerage houses, trading on his own account in the gold pit. Enzo was friendly and willing to act as a mentor, at Steve's behest. Of course, neither of them knew I was an undercover agent for the FBI. In this new set-up I was developing, only Joseph knew the truth. He saw no harm in the deception—Weinstein and Alioto would be playing a role in fighting the corrupt element on the floor of the exchange, albeit unwittingly.

From that juncture on, at every opportunity, I would wander away from the COMEX, cross the floor to the gold pit, and hang out with Enzo, my trading mentor. It was all a far cry from clerking for Tommy and the crude pit. Mary Jane and Craig had obtained approval for my new gambit. I would soon resign from Planet Oil. I was on a roll. The encounter with Joseph had opened new doors; I now had, in effect, a new assignment. And even more luck soon seemed to be enhancing my likelihood of success. On the NYMEX floor, I had noticed a senior clerk in the Goldman Sachs booth who looked familiar. He was a lithe, athletic man with a shaved head and mustache. His glances at me reflected potential mutual recognition. One day, I finally stopped him.

"Hey, did you use to study Tae Kwon Do with Master Sun?"

"That's where I know you from! Wow, good to see you, man."

"You had a second-degree black belt and a black belt in Aikido, right?"

We had not seen each other in thirteen years, and didn't remember each other's last names, conveniently . . . no, fortunately . . . no, *thank the lord*. I reintroduced myself as Marc Renard. He was Lester Goodwin and had been working for NYMEX brokers for over a decade. I now had another "old friend" to vouch for me on the floor.

But then disaster struck at Planet Oil. Jim Clemente, trader-in-training and wearing the wire, was one day in the pit, crunched between the traders on either side, and on the steps above and below. E821, the trader to Jim's left, waving and signaling with his right hand inadvertently brushed against Jim's chest.

"What's that?" He stares hard at Jim, in disbelief. "Feels like a wire. A wire."

"Er . . . ah . . ." Jim turns around, bolts up the steps through the other traders and out of the pit. The rest of us could see him as he came over the lip of the pit, face blanched. He did not come down to the booth, but turned and trotted away from the trading area. Inside the pit there was a new buzz of conversation, centered around E821, but not the shouts and waving that accompany trading. When Jim returned from the men's room, where he'd gone to remove the mic and wires, he was met by stares, some hostile, some merely curious. Pete and Tommy, Planet Oil's two traders, exchanged urgent whispers with the other traders in the pit. Would a confident smile and rejoinder by Jim—something like "It's a buzzer for signals from the booth" or "an external monitor for my pacemaker"—have worked? In any event, his rapid exit from the pit did little to assuage the suspicions already heightened by Chicago. For the rest of that day, Jim bluffed it out. The traders in the pit did not confront him, being otherwise occupied with the fluctuating market for crude.

At the emergency meeting that night, Craig and Mary Jane decided that we would proceed as though nothing had occurred, and would all be at our jobs the next morning, minus any recording devices. At this point in COMMCORR, the six UC agents were meeting every other Wednesday evening with the entire team supporting the op, a wide range of personnel—contact agents, case agents, financial analysts, ancillary agents, and, on occasion the Assistant U.S. Attorneys assigned to handle the eventual prosecution. These meetings had a way of becoming painfully long and boring, usually due to griping by a couple of my fellow UCs. This one was even longer—but less boring than usual. There was a lot of justified speculation and concern regarding the fallout from the episode between our Jim and broker E821. Moreover, Jim had to be convinced that he needed to return to the floor. His absence now would in all likelihood be interpreted as confirmation of the traders' suspicions and would surely doom the case. COMMCORR down the drain. Mary Jane argued effectively that these were Wall Street brokers and traders, not La Cosa Nostra. They wouldn't put out a contract on Jim. Finally, although not fully convinced, Jim agreed to show up in the morning. The worst that might happen on Wall Street—well, it did happen, but that was later on, and . . . and it didn't concern Jim.

The following morning, trading at Planet Oil and in the crude pit resumed as normal. The traders were courteous with Jim, though distant. No more small talk. They would trade with him, as an employee of Planet Oil, and that was it. They would never know for sure, but they would not be taking any chances. In the days to come, it was clear that the new status quo would remain the status quo. Craig briefed the CEO at Planet

Oil. If the incident was raised by his traders or business associates, he would not be caught off guard. As the big boss, he would brush it off as the fruit of the paranoia inspired by Chicago. No one would argue.

Not long after the near debacle with Jim, I had a new idea and called Craig, asking for a meeting with him and Mary Jane—alone, without the other UCs. This wasn't kosher, but he was curious and amenable, probably because he and everyone else now had to consider COMMCORR as in some jeopardy. My proposal, a long shot just a couple of weeks earlier, was now a lifeboat for a ship that was slowly sinking. I suggested that once I had established myself as a licensed local trader in the NYMEX, with a leased or purchased seat, I could in turn sponsor some of my fellow Planet Oil UCs. Jim was irrevocably tainted, and Ben as well, by association. Their reputations would follow them on the floor. But the others still had a chance. Shortly after the private meeting, Craig and Mary Jane signed onto my scheme, got their approvals, and within a week I resigned from Planet Oil. Good riddance as far as I was concerned. I could come and go as I pleased and develop relationships as I saw fit. I spent as much time as appeared appropriate in the gold pit, without taxing Enzo Alioto's goodwill. From Steve Weinstein, I ascertained all the requirements, financial and otherwise, for leasing a seat and qualifying for a NYMEX broker's license. Co-case agent Ed Cugell obtained the funds for deposit to my Banco Popular account, subsequently transferred to the Chase account. Along with some other assets, that sum—half a million dollars—would buttress my financial bona fides and establish my capability to lease a seat. But first I would need to complete the lengthy and thorough NYMEX application. Any spare time I could find was dedicated to preparing for the next hurdle, the written and practical licensing exams. It was not uncommon for clerks with ten years on the floor to fail this test. I had been there six months.

For me, at least, COMMCORR was going pretty well, and maybe my progress would save a good portion of the rest of the operation. That was the hope—that was *my* hope—and in a few weeks I would have passed the exams and leased my seat on the exchange. I'd be in business, trading in gold contracts for my own account, preferably making money for the operation rather than *losing* it. Once the necessary relationships were in place, I would finally start recording incriminating conversations to prove our insider-trading cases. Altogether, we—the FBI and I—had about a year and half invested in this COMMCORR operation. It was a lesson learned for me: there's a lot of delayed gratification in most long-term UC ops.

And, yes, I was dreaming of glory. Out of the six of us who'd started undercover at COMEX, I was probably the only one still with a chance to convert investigation into prosecution. All the others, still clerks at Planet, were tainted by Jim's episode. It would be a major story, even bigger than the bust three years earlier in Chicago. New York is New York. New York is *Wall Street*. My name wouldn't be in the stories, much less the headlines, but those stories would prominently feature an unnamed UC agent who had saved the case, and everyone in the Bureau would know. My first Group I UC operation would be a career-maker, a dream come true. I was feeling pretty good.

Then the phone rang. It was a Friday morning. I was sitting in my apartment in the Village, studying a text about advanced trading, as it happened. (As a prospective independent floor broker on the verge of leasing his seat, I could come and go as I pleased.) Earlier in the week, I had passed the exams for the broker's license, but I was still studying in order to enhance my proficiency as a professional commodities broker. The specific subject of study that morning was the tricky butterfly trade, wherein a trader buys a number of contracts for a particular month while simultaneously selling a number of contracts for a different month, hedging his exposure and playing off the varying maturity dates. A year earlier, it would all have been gibberish. By now, it made some sense. I put the book aside and answered the ring. On the line was the secretary for Sara Hendriks, the NYMEX General Counsel.

"Mr. Renard, can you hold the phone for Ms. Hendriks?"

I had never met Sara Hendriks, but I did know who she was. She came on the line and immediately asked if I could drop by her office later in the day. Sure, I said, no problem. I assumed she had some question concerning the extensive paperwork backing up my application for my seat, and I had full confidence in my backstopping. At this point, a problem in this area didn't even cross my mind.

That afternoon, I walked into Hendriks's office. After the usual courtesies, she got right to the point.

"Mr. Renard, referring to your application, we're having some problems."

That was a *gulp* moment, no doubt about it.

"Really? Well, we can work them out. Is it references? Bank accounts?"

"It's not quite like that. We have reason to believe your entire application, including your name, is a fabrication."

What?!! Forget the gulp. This was serious. I wasn't expecting anything like this blanket indictment, and I had to figure out my next move, quickly. My brain was suddenly in high gear, aided by a jolt of adrenaline, and I made the instantaneous decision to dig in my heels. What was my choice? I wasn't going to concede without a fight, so I became the very picture of confusion but civility, a man of means courteously and patiently tolerating incompetence by the staff.

"What are you talking about? I'm not Henri Marc Renard? I guess this would surprise my parents. There's been some huge mistake. I don't even know what to say. This is ridiculous."

I don't remember the exact words I used, but those are close. I thought I did a pretty good job of carrying off the charade. Now it was Sara Hendriks's turn to be flustered. I think she had expected me to fold my cards and admit then and there that I was running some kind of scam, and she'd then call security and two burly guys would haul me away and grill me for hours. Or simply toss me out of the building. Instead, here I was, puzzled and maybe a little offended. She asked if I could come back in half an hour. Sure, I said, absolutely, I'll come back and we'll straighten this out and we can get going with my application.

"I don't know how to *prove* I am who I am, but we'll work through this. It's obviously a huge mistake. I'm Marc Renard. Who else would I be? *Why?*"

She had some doubts now. But this was clearly a crisis in the making. I had to call Craig, but we didn't have cell phones in those days, so I had to find a pay phone. I went down the escalator into that huge labyrinthine shopping mall that used to be under the World Trade Center. But I was also a little paranoid now, so I had to dry-clean myself. Thanks to my assignment in Puerto Rico, I'd had a lot of training in this procedure, the equivalent of the ploys used while driving a car, as previously described.

If you're on foot, stop suddenly, look at your watch, pretend to remember something, make a quick U-turn while keeping an eye out for equivalent behavior. Or turn down a corridor, pause for reflection, go through your pants pockets like you've forgotten something, then turn around and check for anyone else hesitating and turning around. All basic stuff, but it works.

No one was following me. I found a pay phone, called Craig, and told him what had happened and what I wanted to do: return to Sara Hendriks's office and continue the bluff. Craig, a total professional and veteran of the UC wars, did not hesitate. He immediately agreed that I had to go back and carry on. Meanwhile, he'd call the civilians on my backstopping list and put them on red alert so they wouldn't hesitate vouching for me, if they got a call. The list was short: two people at my fictitious alma mater, three people in Puerto Rico. Any snoopers at the exchange would have no access to the clerks in the various government offices that had set up my fake IDs (impossible), and everyone else on my paperwork, including the New York real-estate and bank people, knew me as Marc Renard.

I returned to Hendriks's office, where James Johnson was now also present. I'd never met him. I knew only who he was: Executive Vice President of NYMEX. Johnson now took control of the interview and repeated his colleague's allegation about my fabricated identity and added a new one: the exchange had reason to believe I was a former assistant DA in Brooklyn, now an agent for the FBI.

Now I knew that a third party had probably recognized me, which was bad enough, and that they *might* well know that I used to be Marc Ruskin. But what could I do but get back on my high horse? I said, "This is the strangest thing I've ever heard of. What in the world could be going on? Let's see what you need to fill in any gaps in the paperwork."

I was really pumping, not thinking at all, just talking as fast and convincingly as I could as Marc Renard. One ploy I didn't try was mentioning my friend Joseph to vouch for me. I wasn't going to put his job in jeopardy.

"Or maybe someone has confused me with someone else. Could you maybe bring in whoever it is? We could straighten this out now. Let's try to do it today. When he sees me close up, he'll realize he's made a mistake. A big mistake."

Perhaps picking up a little confidence, as they seemed to be buying into my act, I now allowed a little annoyance to creep into my voice. Now Johnson was a little flustered. I think he, like Hendriks in the first meeting, had expected me to throw up my hands and concede defeat. He apologized for any inconvenience, but the person was unavailable. Could I return on Monday, when the individual would be on hand, and we could straighten everything out and I could proceed with my application?

So there *was* a third party. Bad news, but I allowed them to smooth my ruffled feathers and said I understood that they had to check this out, even though it was an absurd mistake. I said I'd be back in their office first thing Monday morning. I'd invested so much time and money to get my trader's license, we had to get this straight. Considering the circumstances, the meeting came to a close on as positive a note as possible. Both the general counsel and the executive vice president were apologizing profusely. Again, in the underground mall, I did my dry-cleaning, then called Craig. I still thought I might be able to bluff it out. The issue was simple: Did they know my real name? If they didn't, if someone just knew me vaguely and thought they recognized me, I might be able to play it through. If they did have my name, COMMCORR was finished, because any kind of investigation would quickly confirm that H. Marc Renard and Marc Ruskin were the same person. But we had to play it out, see what happened.

Again, Craig agreed. We might as well keep up the bluff. This wasn't his squad's only case, but it was by far the biggest and most important one, requiring the two supervisors, the two full-time case agents, and a few other part-timers, and the six UC agents. Craig wasn't going to toss a few million dollars and eighteen months of hard, careful work down the toilet unless he absolutely had to. The five UC agents still working at COMEX weren't getting anything done and had no prospects, but they were still there, still working as clerks. As long as I was making progress at NYMEX, Craig didn't want to pull them. If he did, someone might make the connection between them and me. And, who knows, if they stayed in place, my dream scenario would come true and I could open doors for some of them down the road.

What was the worst that could happen on Monday? Johnson would call the gendarmes, who would show that wily fox Marc Renard the door. Or would they grill the FBI's uncovered undercover agent? Craig and I couldn't see that happening. They'd want me out of there in the worst way. But if they did start—or try to start—an interrogation on the spot, I would play an outraged H. Marc Renard, call my attorney, and have him rush over. Mary Jane would have one on stand-by, a private attorney and "Friend of the Bureau," who would lend a hand without asking questions. Craig and I hung up. I wasn't in panic mode. I really wasn't. Neither was he. We could ride this out. Then, a few hours later, Craig called my apartment. I knew immediately the he had some terrible news. His voice was different. He'd gotten a phone call from the registrar, where I'd set up the fake transcript as Marc Renard. A woman from NYMEX had called and asked if a Marc Renard had attended the school— *and* if a Marc *Ruskin* had also attended.

So they had both names.

Then, almost immediately, Craig had received a second call from the head of Human Resources in the Brooklyn DA's office. A woman from NYMEX—my accuser, no doubt, pressed to corroborate her claims—had called to ask whether a former assistant DA by the name of Marc Ruskin had joined the FBI. Pressed, the caller identified herself by name. She had to, because she was calling in an official capacity. The HR chief provided the correct answer—that policy forbade him from even confirming that someone had been a prosecutor in the office—but the quick thinking didn't really matter. NYMEX had both of my names. I'd been officially fingered.

I begged Craig to let me go in Monday morning and play this out to the bitter end, but he said no. *They* said no. The situation had reached the corner offices in Washington—the Bureau and the Department of Justice and the Postal Inspection Service—and their decision was final. Pull H. Marc Renard from the COMMCORR investigation. I was bitterly disappointed. Eighteen months invested, and zero to show for it. Okay, some great training in living a lie, some great lessons learned, but no indictments, no perp walks, no headlines, no glory. What a long weekend. No need to study butterfly trades. Instead, I met with Craig and Mary Jane to plan my exit strategy. And in the evening drank a wee bit more than my usual dose of Jameson's.

On Monday morning, in a phone booth near my real apartment, I picked up the handset, dropped a quarter in the slot (last operational expense for COMCORR), and called Johnson, the NYMEX executive VP, and explained that I had to go to Puerto Rico on short notice because of a serious illness in the family. Not only would I miss the meeting with him and Ms. Hendriks, much to my disappointment, but with deep regret I was withdrawing my application for a seat on the exchange. What a charade. I kept a straight face on my end of the line, and Johnson played along on his end. He said he understood. He was sorry that it had turned out this way. We wished each other well.

He and everyone else at NYMEX must have been relieved—but it wasn't over for them, because within a few months the U.S. Attorney's office initiated an investigation into possible obstruction of justice, which would be a federal crime. Everyone involved was subpoenaed to testify before a federal grand jury. Nothing came of it, but maybe it put the fear of God into them. (But I doubt it.) When the story broke, a columnist for *The Wall Street Journal* took the FBI's side and called it a "disgrace" that the government's undercover agent had been outed by a lawyer in the regulatory arm of NYMEX, which was duty-bound to monitor and control the traders, *not protect them.*

Who had betrayed me? A former colleague: Dominique Hentoff, who had started in the Brooklyn DA's office the year after me. Now she was working in the regulatory office at NYMEX. She had seen me on the floor with my Renard nametag, and rather than approaching me and asking why I had a new name, she'd taken the information to her bosses. If she had asked me, I might have been able to bring her into the operation. She must also have remembered that I had left the DA's office to join the FBI. When I found out her name, I conjured a vague recollection of perhaps having caught an almost unconscious glimpse of her on the floor of the exchange, but who knows. Nor did it matter. When the op unraveled, I never saw or heard from her.

The real collateral damage was to Joseph Bernstein, my old friend from the DA's office; Steve Weinstein, the clearinghouse owner to whom

Joseph had introduced me; and Lester Goodwin, from Master Sun's Tae Kwon Do class. All three had vouched for me, the latter two unwittingly, and they became pariahs in the exchanges. Joseph resigned. Steve's clearinghouse lost customers and went through severe financial hard times. Lester may ultimately have been able to salvage his career; I never found out.

The most valuable lesson for future UC ops was to never, *never* bring individuals with whom one has personal relationships into any kind of operational law enforcement activities. Regardless of the temptation. There are always going to be unforeseeable consequences, and attaining a successful conclusion is not worth compromising friends and acquaintances. No case is sufficiently important to justify such risks. Throughout the following years, as we'll see, I might involve other special agents or police officers, informants, and cooperating witnesses in a case. These people knew the risks. You won't read about my bringing in a civilian, because I never did.

When setting up the sting, Craig Dotlo and I had understood that as a former lawyer in New York, I might be recognized. My participation was a calculated risk, and it had backfired with a bang heard throughout the Bu, I'm sure. I feared my UC career may have come to a premature demise. Wrong. Very wrong, as future developments would reveal. Still, a lesson learned. Half a dozen years later, when we set up a phony law office in Westchester for a health-care fraud Group I, I kept my name but changed the spelling to Mark, and we backstopped a completely new ID. Mark Ruskin and Marc Ruskin had different pasts, different dates of birth, different Social Security numbers, but if someone recognized me, I'd have the right name and should be able to explain my new circumstances within the legal profession. After Craig and I came up with that scheme, I couldn't help wondering what would have happened if my former colleague in Brooklyn had recognized me on the NYMEX floor, but with the right name. I think she would have approached me and said, "Hey Marc, nice to see you, I thought you'd joined the FBI." This would have given me a fighting chance to run a line. *Yeah, that didn't work out, I quit their lousy academy after two weeks . . . Quantico, what a dump . . . and those assholes expect you to follow their orders like some kind of automaton . . .* Hey, it might have worked. But as it turned out, nothing could save COMMCORR. Craig gave me a couple of weeks to decompress, and I flew down to Key Biscayne to see my girlfriend. Back in New York, I set about closing down "The H. Marc Renard Show." Craig pulled the remaining UC agents clerking at COMEX—but not immediately, and not all at the same time. All of us had to be reassigned to other offices, since the NY office was in the Federal Building, only a few blocks from the World Trade Center and the pits where we'd been working for a year. One very *looong* year.

4

The Stakes Go Up

Once the smoke had cleared on Wall Street, my "attaboy" consolation was a transfer to the satellite office in New Rochelle, just north of the city. Maybe that sounds like a demotion to the far side of the crime world, but it was actually a coveted assignment. First, the New Rochelle beat included—for me, specifically, as a recognized undercover agent—the entire greater NYC metro area, the best terrain there is for the kind of entrepreneurial, innovative crime that provokes Bureau investigation. Second, these smaller FBI offices are, by definition, more limber, and quicker to react. There are fewer supervisors and usually no upper management positions at all. Out of sight, out of mind. With a good SSRA (Senior Supervisory Resident Agent)—and New Rochelle had one at the time—that neighborhood office is an excellent venue for creative stings and investigations, about as good as it gets, and offers the best of both worlds: big-city crime but with minimal BuHassles.

I was assigned to C-21, a Public Corruption and Fraud squad headed by Craig Dotlo, one of my supervisors on COMMCORR. Craig was a big believer in UC cases, and for the next eight years I worked one investigation after another for him, in addition to some moonlighting elsewhere in the metropolitan area and occasionally beyond. As I had learned in COMMCORR, Craig was a really sharp, insightful guy; it was the "beginning of a beautiful friendship," to quote an observation made to a fellow gendarme in a certain movie.

The "public corruption" category that was our squad's specialty affords almost unlimited possibilities for investigation and prosecution, and my first assignment targeted a crime I hadn't thought much about, if at all. This was 1990, and FBI case agents and investigators in other agencies were reporting a troublesome development. The La Cosa Nostra wiseguys collared for whatever crime turned out to be, more often than not, equipped with well-executed but fraudulent driver's licenses, vehicle registrations, and Social Security cards. Fugitives of various sorts were also carrying these documents. So were terrorists, as I was soon to learn. (But this was not only pre-9/11, it was before the 1993 World Trade Center bombing, the prequel to the Al-Qaeda attack. It's hard to comprehend now, but terrorism on American soil simply wasn't high on the radar, and this was just twenty-plus years ago.) Armed with fraudulent documents, extremely dangerous characters could disappear in the vast reaches of the country. I'm sure they did, and no law enforcer would ever be able to track them down.

We know that Ramzi Yousef, the convicted primary conspirator of the 1993 bombing, had claimed asylum in the States using a stolen Iraqi passport. Not so easy today. In fact, the United States probably has the world's best system for screening passports with the help of Interpol's database. Meanwhile, the attacks in Paris in November 2015 revealed the dangers of the European Union's "open borders" policies, and changes are coming; some have already come. Everyone now understands that *tight* standards for documentation are *crucial* in the fight against terrorism.

In the NYC metro area in 1990, the big problem was fraudulent documents—not stolen or fake, *fraudulent*. The difference is critical but often misunderstood. Fraudulent documents are the real thing, issued by government agencies, with the information on the IDs therefore available to law enforcement on the appropriate databases. The *name* on the documents doesn't correspond to the arrestee's actual name, or to anyone else, living or dead, but there's no way any cop or investigator could know this. By contrast, a merely *forged* driver's license might look like the real thing, but when the cop runs it through the databases, nothing will come up, because the license doesn't exist in the records. Same thing with a forged Social Security card, which might be good for show, but try using it as identification for a new bank account and the bankers will find out that it's a fake and call the police. (Yes, as I had learned in COMMCORR, the banks do have access to the databases, at least to the extent of verifying an SSAN, a Social Security Administration Number, as they are officially called).

These fraudulent documents were big business for the bad guys. The "runners" on the street charged at least $1,000, maybe $1,500, for a driver's license. Car registrations and Social Security cards were maybe $500. As we would learn, the collaborating clerks inside the issuing agencies were getting $25, maybe $50 for each fraudulent document created. That's not much, but some clerks cleared a dozen frauds on some days, which was real money for someone working behind a counter: cash, tax-free, at least a car payment and, in a good week, a mortgage payment as well. In their own minds, the participating clerks could dismiss this scam as a "harmless act" or "victimless crime," but the repercussions down the line were neither harmless nor victimless. For example, such documents would later enable a band of terrorists to elude detection long enough to fly jetliners into the World Trade Center and the Pentagon.

I note that fraudulent U.S. passports, specifically, were much more difficult to obtain with the same mechanism because it was harder for the "runners" to set up accomplices in the offices of the State Department. On the other hand, it was *not* difficult for runners to bribe local hires in certain Third World consulates, and that's what usually happened. Fraudulent green cards were also difficult to buy on the street because it was tough for the runners to penetrate the Immigration and Naturalization Services (INS). I did have one green-card case, a subject with corrupt and, as it turned out, widespread INS contacts. The runner in this case, a target named Jabes Ortega, was a very sharp Dominican with a criminal history as a "coyote," smuggling aliens across the border from Mexico. (Technically, a "target" becomes a "subject" once some evidence has been developed, but the terms are often used synonymously, as I did above: both terms for the same guy in the same paragraph.) The resourceful Ortega was even bribing the security guards at 26 Federal Plaza, *the Federal Building*. They waved me and my Walther PPK undercover pistol right on through. I was in there with Ortega a half-dozen times. On every occasion, I murmured to myself: *Memo to FBI agents: Please don't speak to Marc if you see him at 26 Fed.* Ortega charged ten to fifteen *thousand* for one green card, and he had no lack of clientele. Six months after a sale, his INS accomplices would delete the illegal files from the computers, thus destroying any evidence of their wrongdoing, while also creating some unpleasant surprises down the line for the aliens who had purchased them.

In the beginning, Craig and his case agents had some idea about some of the players in the fraudulent ID business, but they didn't know how the system worked. Nor did they know how to penetrate the closed circles of targets and emerge with the necessary *prosecutable detail*. That was the big catch—it always is—but we got the answers with a Group I op that ran for almost three years and resulted in fifty arrests, with widespread media coverage.

Before we could get going, however, we needed the formal proposal, always the first step with any Group I undercover operation. This document is as long as a novel, outlining the crime problem, known targets, personnel requirements, budget, and modus operandi, all in excruciating detail. Once this proposal is written, generally by the case agent, and has been appropriately reviewed and approved at the local level by the Chief Division Counsel and mid-level management, it goes to the regional level—in our case, Headquarters City, the New York office at Federal Plaza in downtown NYC. If it passes muster there, it is shipped to headquarters in Washington, known as JEH to those who work there. (Clue: The building is named after the Bu's slightly controversial founder.) At JEH, it is subjected to the final evaluation by a committee comprised of high-level managers from both the Bureau and the Justice Department.

As onerous as this procedural mechanism sounds, it still doesn't convey the difficulties that major proposals face or the number of acronyms that have to be explained and questions satisfied. Sometimes they aren't satisfied, and if the proposal makes it all the way to JEH only to be skewered at this last stop, that can mean six months of fieldwork down the drain. More likely, JEH will require changes and attach conditions and stipulations. Additionally, the powers at JEH require a Renewal Proposal to be submitted and approved every six months.

Regardless what you might have heard or read, there are no rogue Black UC Ops in today's twenty-first-century FBI. Nor were there any when I was starting on the mean streets in the last decade of the twentieth century. It didn't happen. It *couldn't* happen. The mechanism to hide such an op has never existed. *Within* the Bureau, there aren't that many secrets.

Craig was prepared to devote significant resources to this op. There would be two full-time case agents—a big commitment right there, because the C-21 squad had fewer than a dozen agents altogether. There would be a part-time financial analyst to handle the bookkeeping and a full-time UC guy—me, tasked with infiltrating the world of the "runners" whose fraudulent documents made them much money and caused law enforcement a great deal of trouble.

Dave Clark was selected as one of the case agents. An "Old Bureau" special agent from New England, Dave had been hired during the Hoover era. One of his favorite stories—one of *my* favorite stories—was the day he arrested a Weather Underground fugitive in the late seventies. He and his partner brought this very frightened young lady back to the office in New Rochelle, printed and photographed her, completed their paperwork, then packed up and prepared to take her to court for arraignment.

"When does it begin?" she then asked.

"When does what begin?" asked Dave.

"Please don't play this game with me. You know what I mean. The third degree."

Dave still breaks into laughter when he tells the story, and I do, too. Not until her captors drove her to court and she was standing with an attorney before the magistrate did this poor suspect stop shaking. (Her apprehension isn't so funny, but I don't have *too* much sympathy; she was a fugitive, after all.)

As a polar opposite to Dave, his co-case agent on the op was young and feisty Vicki Barnes Davis, from Huntsville, Alabama. One tough lady: as a corollary duty, she was a firearms instructor. Dave's friendly wisecracks with Vicki, which today would qualify for EEO (Equal Employment Opportunity) prosecution, elicited Southern-fried retorts served with cutting wit. Vicki could take it and dish it back with interest. She and Dave became good friends, and the chemistry binding the entire team was just right.

Our office was on an upper floor of the local Ramada Inn in New Rochelle. Though not covert, few people knew it was there. I'd leave my desk at the Ramada around ten in the morning, hit the streets, usually returning by five or six in the afternoon. The Ramada was ideal: if any subject ever saw me enter—*hey, I had a deal going down on the fifth floor.* Of all the cases I've worked on, the handle for this investigation is my favorite: RUN-DMV, a parody of RUN-DMC, the popular hip-hop trio originally based in Hollis, Queens. I assume almost everyone knows that "DMV" is the Department of Motor Vehicles, but the broader joke might have been lost on someone living a bespoke life on, say, Park Avenue and therefore behind the hip-hop times. Their loss.

The dark-blue Mercedes 500SEL pulled to the curb by the storefront of Holyland Travel, on Morris Avenue in a run-down section of the Bronx. The driver, known as Bim, a burly black man with shaved head and a beard, looked like an ex-prizefighter. He got out of the car, looked deliberately up and down the avenue, then positioned himself on the sidewalk. His passenger stepped out of the sedan, gold chains reflecting the sunlight, and stretched as he closed the door. He was about half the size of the driver and clearly in charge. He looked through his Cartier-framed sunglasses at his Rolex, then appeared to give some orders to his driver, who nodded, crossed his arms, and leaned against the Mercedes. The man with the Rolex walked through the Holyland doorway, where he was approached by an attractive—very attractive—Palestinian woman, perhaps in her late twenties, with almond-shaped eyes and a stunning figure. Fortunately, no burka covered her features.

"Can I help you?"

"I'd like to see Mahmoud."

She glanced back over her shoulder. The man standing by the door in the back nodded. No further questions asked, she pointed the new arrival toward the small office in the rear. The man by the door led the way and gestured for the new arrival to take a seat.

"I am Mahmoud. What can I do to help you?" No small talk. His English was fluent, though heavily accented.

"Well, I have a little problem. I was told that you might be able to help me. To solve my problem."

"What kind of problem?"

"I have a car, a very nice car, that I need to get registered, that needs plates. But I don't have a title. I don't have any paper for the car."

"Who sent you?"

"Jamal. From Newark."

Mahmoud stared hard. For a while. The guy who had arrived in the Mercedes stared back.

"I should be able to handle it. What's your name?"

"Alex."

Alex Perez, and this time, unlike with H. Marc Renard, my new alias for the streets was no in-joke about a fox or anything else. I just liked the sound and the *feel* of the two words. I wouldn't have to think twice before I introduced myself as Alex Perez. This was good, because the stakes were now higher: my new friends in the wider world of metro NYC would be packing guns. My overall UC backstory for RUN-DMV and other investigations was simple: As Alex Perez, I had left Miami under obscure and unexplained circumstances. Maybe I'd been forced to leave. My primary car was a late-model Chrysler Imperial, legally registered to Alex, of course, with Metro-Dade plates, a small but invaluable prop, assuring instant credibility on the streets I'd be working far north of Miami. (The Mercedes from COMMCORR, which I still kept in reserve for special subjects, was a mite too upscale for the day-to-day Alex but it was perfect for Mahmoud, who would have already learned that I'd arrived in the Mercedes with a driver who also served as bodyguard.) I now had a long ponytail halfway down my back, usually a few days growth of beard, and I featured two or three gold chains and bracelets seized by the Bureau in other cases. A little gel in the hair was the finishing touch. That's the look the job required: vulgar, and if not big-money, aspiring to big-money while still a proud denizen of the streets. I was (and still am) about five-foot-nine, slight of build, wiry, muscular, with an angular face and deep-set blue eyes that can project humor or cold cockiness, whatever is appropriate to the moment. All in all, I have an Eastern European/Semitic look crossed with French and can pass as Hispanic, blue eyes notwithstanding, when accompanied by my colloquial Spanish.

Mahmoud Noubani was Palestinian, and a true believer in the cause, as I came to learn. And as I had learned from intel provided by John

Sultan, a new CW, he had no reluctance in applying violence as a business tool. His expertise was providing people with false IDs—his potential client pool from the Middle East, even pre-first WTC bombing, was food for chilling speculation. Going in "cold" as I did with Mahmoud is the most difficult type of initial UC meet, the most prone to failure. The vast majority of meets are bolstered by an introduction from an informant who already has the subject's trust. With a strong introduction, such as "Alex is my cousin's ex, we've been friends, and we've been doing business for over ten years," all of that trust is transferred to the UC. With Mahmoud, we'd didn't have this introduction. He had come across our radar indirectly, when Vicki had found a complaint report submitted to the New York Attorney General's office by a young contractor from Queens, named John Sultan, a scrawny twenty-year-old from Bangladesh. This contactor had accompanied a Greek business acquaintance to Holyland to act as an interpreter, and he had been present when his companion paid for a fraudulent driver's license and Social Security card from Mahmoud. John had made some disparaging comments at the time about the cost of the documents, and he later returned to Holyland seeking a partial refund for his acquaintance. Instead, one of the young Arabs who worked at Holyland slammed John's head into the counter, and Mahmoud himself aimed his pistol at John's head. John considered himself lucky to have walked out alive. He then made the formal complaint to the AG's office, which came to nothing until it worked its way to us, thanks to Vicki's diligence.

After reading the report, Vicki and I interviewed him at his home in Astoria, Queens. Vicki had done her due diligence on John's construction company: it was a going concern. He owned a lot of heavy equipment. He was a Muslim—and his cute blond wife was not. Hard as it was for me and Vicki to believe initially, John was genuinely outraged by what he had witnessed with Mahmoud and Holyland—not just the gun at his head, also the fraudulent documents being channeled onto the streets. What a straight shooter. The details he provided served as RUN-DMV's legal basis—probable cause—for targeting Holyland.

Over the next few days, I would think further about John Sultan: an immigrant, multilingual, speaking Urdu, English, and a fair bit of Arabic; a secular Muslim who would look at home in any mosque in the Middle

East. Clearly very bright, unusually entrepreneurial, and with a profound sense of integrity. Perfect. After talking to Craig Dotlo, I went back to Astoria.

"Hey, John, how would you like to do some work for the FBI? It won't pay much, but I guarantee it will be interesting."

Once the paperwork was processed, John was officially a CW: a "cooperating witness." (Or "confidential witness," the term preferred by prosecutors and the press.) In addition to the innumerable RUN-DMV meets that we worked on over the next several years, we also worked some IT (international terrorism) cases, both gathering intelligence and working undercover, as we will see later. Along with special agents working the International Terrorism Squads, John did UC work targeting Hezbollah and other jihadist organizations, which were active domestically in the mid-nineties, and still are. John was trusted by the targets to the point that at a jihadi conference attended by a rogue's gallery of IT subjects, John worked security. Today, John has changed his name and is an executive in the computer business. He is one of my best friends. According to the book, this is a violation of an FBI truism: Never become friends with a confidential informant or cooperating witness. Hammered home at the FBI Academy and reiterated in in-service training. But first things first with John: Mahmoud and Holyland.

Mahmoud didn't know about the complaint John had filed, but he would certainly have remembered the request for a partial refund—and drawing his gun. So John couldn't provide a direct introduction. I had to go in cold. It was John's suggestion that I use the "Jamal in Newark" introduction. "Newark has a huge Arab population," he explained. "Mohamed and Jamal are the most common names. Mohamed's too obvious. Jamal's best. Mahmoud's got to know a bunch of Jamals."

He did, or at least he accepted the indirect introduction. After making the decision to accept me as a client, he was all business. Details concerning the car, timeline, and price ($500 seemed reasonable) went smoothly. Crooks haggle and an undercover operative *always* haggles, always acts like he is willing to walk away from a transaction if he's not getting a good price. Some haggling is mandatory, but I kept it to a minimum at this first cold call. *Is that the best you can do?* Such a token pro forma effort to negotiate would be expected, but our nascent relationship was too fragile for me to push beyond it. Back in the Mercedes, I turned off the mini-Nagra recorder concealed in my fanny pack and said to Bim, "I was just waiting for him to tell me to get the fuck out of his office." Instead, RUN-DMV now had the first subject to agree with FBI UC Alex Perez to participate in criminal activity.

The cold call at Holyland had worked, thanks to the intel provided by John. Thanks also to the preparation that went into creating the first impression. Years later, as we'll see, I would make a number of cold calls, often in False Flag operations—cases in which I was posing as an intelligence officer, a spy, from another country—and all such cases depend on the success of the initial contact. When you go in cold, if you are not completely convincing, if the person you're dealing with isn't fully persuaded, well, like they say, you don't get a second chance to make a first impression. The recipe for success is lots of preparation followed by some combination of appearance and *attitude*. I turned out to be good at this and had a great cold-call batting average, but it's hardly ideal; fortunately, the RUN-DMV investigation didn't have to rely on them.

Vicki and Dave had unearthed an unlikely confidential informant (CI) from central casting named Timmy, who would be key to the long path that followed. Skinny and rodent-like, Timmy was a runner for the used-car dealers. In fact, it was one of those dealers who introduced him to Vicki and Dave. Every morning, Timmy would make the rounds of his dealers and pick up the paperwork for cars sold the previous day (around a dozen on average) and drop everything off at Yonkers DMV. At the DMV, Timmy would either hang out until the registrations and plates were ready, or he'd return later. His wife, Debbie, worked as a clerk behind one of the DMV windows. Very handy for our investigation. From this happily married couple we learned that many, if not most, of the runners were primarily processing "no-ID" paperwork, that is, registrations with fictitious names submitted with no identification. Of course, identification is technically required, so these applications were processed by certain of Debbie's colleagues who would overlook the missing corroboration—for a price. Debbie didn't know exactly which of her fellow clerks were on the take, and her husband didn't know exactly how the runners got it done, just that at the end of the day, they had the "no-ID" registrations and license plates in hand.

Timmy had been recommended as a reliable and generally honest fellow who could perhaps shed some light on the details of the process. With a little financial encouragement, he agreed to take on a partner, Alex Perez, whom he would present to the DMV world as an old friend from Miami who needed some cash after a hasty departure northward. Timmy was Italian American and had never quite become one of the boys, as most of the runners were Hispanic or Middle Eastern. Alex might be just what he needed—and Timmy was just what Alex needed. He's the guy who indirectly provided me with opportunity to learn the nuts-and-bolts of how the fraudulent registrations were being obtained.

For the first few days of our partnership, I accompanied Timmy on his rounds at the dealerships and DMV. Once I had the routine down, and my face had become familiar to those Timmy dealt with, I started on my own. However, with the runners at the DMV, asking questions was out of the question. This is usually the case, of course. People operating outside the law are highly suspicious of direct questions. As a good crook, therefore, I was obliged to appear totally disinterested in the activities of all new acquaintances. Discreet indirection was called for. Learn from patient observation what kinds of small talk the subjects engage in, then start to participate in the conversations, always on the lookout for opportunities to offer a humorous anecdote. All I could do in Yonkers was hang out, wait for Timmy's work to get done, and pay careful attention to the unguarded conversation around me.

One day, runner Manuel said to runner Julio Dominguez, in Spanish, "I've got a no-ID, but I need someone to do it and I need it today."

"Well . . . all right, but you'll have to wait. I've got two, and my girl can't go on the line again right away, the supervisor's on the floor."

Julio's girl was waiting on the line with all the paperwork, minus proof of ID. Approaching the front, she waited for the right cashier to be free, careful not to attract attention. Passing the title and forms to the cashier, she murmured in a low voice, "This is for Julio." Standing in the background, Julio caught the teller's eye and nodded. Or attached to the paperwork there might be an ID: Julio's driver's license.

Months later Julio Dominguez said to me, "Debbie used to do no-IDs. She was doing them like crazy to pay for her honeymoon, then she stopped." This news flabbergasted me. Debbie was Timmy's wife.

"Debbie did no-IDs? Now she's so stuck-up. Did Timmy know?"

"What do you think? Of course. She was getting them from him and everybody else."

When I mentioned this revelation to Craig, he just shrugged. Vicki shook her head and smiled. I mentioned it in my 302 report, but there was no point in taking it any further. A renewed lesson about how far to trust any informant: *Just as far as you need to.* That's it. With CIs and CWs, cooperating witnesses, one ought still exercise a healthy skepticism. Though with CWs, knowing they will be testifying one day, they are less likely to massage the truth.

Our increasing understanding of what was going down with the fraudulent documents still didn't tell us how we could get in on the scam and prosecute these felons whose craft was causing so many problems for law enforcement at all levels. Assuming I could get the nuances down pat and develop the trust required to get a registration processed illegally without ID—I thought I could—I would still need to provide the crooked DMV clerk with the car title and insurance card, along with the completed DMV forms. Providing titles meant buying real cars. Or so we thought. Following up on this loose end, Craig teamed us up with Jack Wright, the DMV Inspector General in Albany, a retired BuAgent. Jack provided the solution. He had his people at DMV print up titles for nonexistent cars which were being sold by the nonexistent people whose name appeared on the title. So we would use fraudulent titles produced by the good guys to obtain other fraudulent titles produced by the bad guys. These, along with blank insurance cards, and DMV registration forms, would be my tools to make cases. I would complete the forms and insurance cards with invented names and addresses and— of course—for which no form of ID would be presented. We would thus have irrefutable, hard evidence demonstrating that the corrupt DMV employees had issued registrations in names that were demonstrably false. And had accepted bribes directly from FBI agents or cooperating witnesses.

We approached the RUN-DMV objectives from every angle we could come up with. First was Holyland, then Timmy, then came Oscar Cascillo, who became an important cooperating witness, in the same category as John Sultan. The difference between a CW and an informant is significant, as it directly affects how much evidence we will need to develop for a prosecution. A CW agrees to testify if necessary. Hence the name, cooperating *witness*. With an informant, the agreement from the outset is that he/she (as referred to in reports, to hide the gender) will *never* testify and his/her identity will *never* be released (unless a deal to testify is reached at a later time). As the informant will not be testifying, other evidence has to be found to replace what he/she *would have testified to*, if he/she was a CW.

I write the following claim without hesitation: The FBI is the only federal law enforcement agency that keeps its word to informants, and this is one of the most important legacies of J. Edgar. This ironclad agreement is known on the streets, and it is responsible in no small measure for the Bureau's reputation on the streets. This agreement holds for narcotics investigations, terrorism, everything, and it is this credibility with informants that has allowed the FBI to consistently develop outstanding sources, and it accounts for much of the Bureau's success overall. There are, no doubt, state and local agencies scattered about with equivalent credibility on the street. But they are, by definition, operating on a different level.

Some CWs and CIs are selected and recruited based on their specialized knowledge and connections in a specified area, as was the case with Timmy. With others, such as Oscar, the investigative value is their ability to scour the countryside (or, more likely, the cityscape) and pinpoint criminals in the targeted activity, then gain their confidence. (Much like a good undercover agent, in fact.) John Sultan worked in a similar capacity. He didn't live on the streets, he certainly didn't have his acre of criminal turf that he knew like the back of his hand, but John had a great knack for building rapport: criminals, terrorists, they *wanted* to trust John Sultan.

Oscar Cascillo's street connections were already extensive when he started working with us, but he was also a bloodhound. My case agent Dave Clark had merely to point Oscar in the right direction. But Oscar's motivation for working for Dave and the FBI was cash—two hundred here, four hundred there—so we had to watch out for the bullshit. His information had to be interpreted with appropriate circumspection. Or like I just wrote, trust these guys just as far as you need, and no more. Or to put it bluntly, in Oscar's case: maybe half of his information from the streets was worth anything. In stark contrast with John Sultan: the cash wasn't that important to John, and there was never any bullshit from him.

One early summer afternoon—the year is now 1992—I was riding with Oscar in his big old boat of a Chevy convertible, a car that could be, and often was, parked in Washington Heights or the South Bronx, without fear of its disappearing (its value on the hot-car market wouldn't have covered the cost of a good *parillada* (delicious Hispanic BBQ)). With his Hawaiian print shirt, Panama hat, and gold-capped front teeth, the paunchy middle-aged Venezuelan Oscar looked right at home in the big convertible. We were driving to Newark to a gas station/car repair/used-car lot owned by a Bengalese immigrant Oscar had unearthed. The man's name was Nair, and he could, according to Oscar, obtain driver's licenses, Social Security cards, and other fraudulent documents. This could be a good score for RUN-DMV.

Oscar had been out there once, but even though he didn't know the street address or the name of the place or Nair's full name (Nair itself ranks with Smith and Rodriguez for uniqueness), he promised me he could find our target in one of Newark's many run-down South Bronx look-alike neighborhoods. Driving over in Oscar's car was probably not the smartest thing to be doing, either, but Nair had already seen the Chevy. It wouldn't cause any agita when it reappeared at his shop. I was carrying my mini-Nagra and my Walther PPK. I didn't have a transmitter because I was alone (Oscar didn't count), with no surveillance backup. There was no one nearby to listen to any transmission. In those days, we UCs were almost always on our own. Only rarely did I have surveillance covertly covering me from a van down the street (for example). Today, there would be a mandatory surveillance team, lots of preapprovals, other red tape. Nair's establishment would probably be formally surveyed prior to any meets, his criminal history and INS status checked, and so forth. It's safer for the UC now, I guess, but also much more cumbersome and, in some cases, limiting. This is an issue I'll develop as the book unfolds. Moreover, all that background work required today is resource intensive and costly, and the Bureau's resources are not limitless. With the result being, I suspect, fewer UC meets and fewer subjects investigated through covert ops.

And backup surveillance is only *safer*, not *safe*. It is not foolproof. What is? This case in point: Shortly after I had established my relation with Mahmoud at Holyland, Vicki and Dave wanted to take some pictures and get a feel for the place. They arrived before my scheduled meet with Mahmoud and parked the minivan with tinted windows down the street, but with line of sight to the storefront. (If the subjects of such surveillance are considered to be "surveillance conscious," a third agent would have driven the van to the site, parked, stepped out, and walked away, leaving it "empty," as far as anyone could tell.) At Holyland, Dave and Vicki just parked and crawled in back with their equipment. No one on Morris Avenue noticed, or cared. Mahmoud himself was now more at ease with me. Over the course of two or three meets over a period of a couple of months, I had made it clear that I had frequent contact with people in need of false IDs. Mahmoud had no problem understanding why they would be a popular commodity in the circles I frequented, and he went on, at surprising length, as to what he could provide—primarily, real driver's licenses, car registrations, and Social Security cards. He sincerely regretted that he had no sources for green cards. (I guess so, since Ortega charged $15,000 for this service, as mentioned.) Mahmoud and I discussed prices, and now I haggled a little more, because it was necessary.

To be successful, the UC has to think like and act like a real criminal, to project all the indicia of really being what he claims to be. If you agree to whatever price the subject wants, you are too eager to close the deal, you're not looking to make money, you're just looking to complete the buy. To anyone who is the least bit street-smart, alarms will go off, if only in the deepest recesses of the brain. On the other hand, if you make it clear that you're willing to walk away from the deal, that you're not interested in the subject personally, that all you care about is making money, that you can always buy the documents or drugs or guns or whatever from a hundred other guys, *then* you are sending out signals that you are for real.

Mahmoud understood that if his fraudulent docs were going to be worth my while, I needed enough of a margin to add my cut. We struck a deal in principle. After the meet, at a prearranged location (a McDonald's parking lot), I joined Vicki and Dave in the back of the van. My adrenaline was still flowing. I was in that post-UC-meet state of mild euphoria mixed with heightened ego.

"Can you believe what he was saying? Was that an amazing conversation or what?"

A bemused smile from Dave: "All we could hear was static. But as long as you've got it all on your tape, we're fine."

We were fine only because I hadn't needed their help! We might not have been fine if I had needed it. I was developing a new appreciation as to the value of surveillance in UC operations. *If* the surveillance team can hear and make out what's going on, *maybe* they can respond in time, but thirty seconds can be and probably is an eternity if the meet falls apart. For example, some years before, in Philadelphia, undercover agent Chuck Reed, forty-five years old and a father of three, was sitting in the back of drug-dealer Jonathan Cramer's Mercedes-Benz discussing a future buy while the confidential informant sat in the front passenger seat. As no money and no drugs would be changing hands, it was the kind of meet that one would consider very low risk. Neither the UC nor the dealer would be worried about a rip; the dealer would not be contemplating a possible bust. Nothing to be concerned about. It was late morning on a sunny but brisk March day in 1996. They were parked in the lot of the Comfort Inn, in Philadelphia's Old City.

Reed had his portfolio, the kind with a zipper running along the top between the handles. Inside was his Nagra. Placed to his left on the transmission bump, it was situated so as to clearly record all three occupants of the car. Cramer, inexplicably hinky, reached back in a sudden motion, pushed aside the handles of the portfolio, peered inside, and exclaimed: *A wire!* Reed instantaneously drew his gun. *FBI . . . DON'T MOVE.* Cramer also reacted instantaneously: the gun under his right thigh was suddenly in his hand and firing. The one surveillance car *a few hundred yards away* heard a volley of gunfire as Reed and Cramer fired away within the close confines of the Benz. The surveillance team watched as a door opened and someone rolled out—the informant, escaping the rain of bullets. Both Chuck Reed and his subject were mortally wounded.

The bottom line: No matter how close the surveillance backup is positioned, the best I could hope for is for the cavalry to arrive in time to pick up the pieces. As an undercover agent, I was totally responsible for my own well-being. If I wanted to enhance my chances of survival, I needed to do it myself.

I wasn't thinking about all this in the *front* of my brain as Oscar and I rolled toward Newark, but it had to be in the back, didn't it? I knew that 90 percent of the time, being a special agent working the streets is not dangerous. But when it's dangerous, it's very dangerous. The reason there are not more fatalities is that the men and women who become agents are not your average people. Pluck someone off the street and make them an active agent on the streets (not a desk jockey) and see how long they last. It probably goes without saying that this is especially true for UCs. Very few UCs are killed—only Chuck Reed during my career along with one UC fatality each from the NY State Police, DEA, and Newark PD (this officer was waiting to testify *inside the courthouse*)— and this is only because of the nature of the people doing the job. Not your typical people. Not your typical agents. While this may seem obvious, it certainly wasn't obvious to me. Not then. I had sincerely felt that what I was doing every day was as safe as any other job in the Bureau. It took several years for me to realize that almost no one was getting killed only because it was Jack Garcia, or Lee Howell, or Mark Pecora, or, yes, Marc Ruskin, doing the work.

It distresses me to report that Chuck Reed worked undercover only *occasionally*. That terrible afternoon in Philadelphia was just such an occasion. That's an obvious problem. To have an agent who primarily works as a field agent occasionally take the reins as a UC is akin to the cardiologist who *occasionally* performs open-heart surgery. In medicine, this doesn't (it is to be hoped) happen often, and the equivalent shouldn't happen in UC work. But there are not, as a practical matter, enough full-time UCs to handle all the potential cases. It was perhaps a reflection of my exaggerated self-image, but I would never turn down a case, particularly one involving potentially violent subjects. My reasoning: If I didn't handle it, someone else would. If I did the job, there was less likelihood that things would break bad. And if another, perhaps less experienced UC was injured because I had turned down the role, I would be responsible (or so ran my logic).

. . .

On the way to Nair's place, I told Oscar exactly how to explain my background to this new subject. I told him several times, and I had him repeat it back to me, in English and in Spanish, to make sure he had it straight. I said quite clearly, *"Bueno,* Oscar, *escúchame bien.* Alex is an old friend from Miami, a *Cubano,* he's had to leave Florida and needs new ID. Don't tell this guy [Nair] why I had to leave, don't tell him anything he doesn't need to know. It'll just hink him up. He's not going to ask and he's not going to care."

"No te preocupes, Alex. I got it, *entiendo, hermano!"* Like all confidential witnesses and informants I worked with, Oscar knew me only by my street name. If he doesn't even know another one (my real name), he can't possibly slip up and use the wrong one. John was an exception. First: I had initially approached him as Marc, in order to interview him regarding his complaint to the state AG's office. (These were the early days of my UC career. I quickly learned to never participate in noncovert, true-name activities.) Second: He was several cuts above other CWs.

After getting off the highway, we drove along the dreary streets, the tenements interspersed with weedy lots enclosed by rusty fences, ramshackle businesses, and dirty grocery stores. Oscar pulled the Chevy into a large corner lot. There were a couple of gas pumps, a lot of cars, and a fairly large, old garage building with a few bays and a wooden door leading toward an office area. The bays had cars in them, with a few mechanics moving around. We were first approached by a pack of large, well-groomed, and seriously menacing German shepherds, then by a short, stout middle-aged man with long, stringy gray hair. Oscar had provided me with a general description. This was Nair. When he gave a command to the pack, they trotted away obediently. He led us through a large room and into a back office, and waved for me and Oscar to sit opposite his cluttered desk. The door stayed open and the dogs trotted in and out and around, with Nair apparently oblivious to their presence or to any disconcerting effect they might have on his guests. I didn't mind them. "Beautiful dogs," I remarked. Nair smiled. Then Oscar made the introductions.

"This is Alex, I told you about him. He's a major cocaine dealer from Colombia." I looked at Oscar. If the Bu's UC procedural manual had permitted it, I would have shot him dead right there in Nair's little office. He had made a thoughtless, *terrible* mistake. What if Nair had replied "Colombia!" *Excellente*. What part, my friend? My wife and I lived there for ten years before coming to the U.S." Maybe I wouldn't be alive to write these pages.

But he didn't. What Nair did was start the conversation in Spanish, then revert to English once he was apparently satisfied that I was a native speaker. He fished around in his desk and pulled out an envelope containing a number of worn Social Security cards. He asked me to choose one with a name that I liked, and said that he would obtain a New Jersey driver's license to match. He could also, maybe, get me a passport, but it would be expensive. A couple of hundred for the SSAN card alone, another $1,000 for the DL. We haggled. I argued for a discount, saying I could bring him more clients. He countered that he was just making a small profit; there were others he had to pay. Then we struck a deal. Back in the car on the New Jersey Turnpike, I confronted Oscar, "What the fuck where you doing? I told you Miami, *Cubano*. I told you NOT to say anything about any criminal activity, just to hint that I had some problems. You said it back to me. I told you what I wanted you to say!"

Nonplussed by my anger, with broad smile, cigarette dangling: "I thought it would make a better impression. You know, make him think you're a big shot drug dealer."

As a source, Oscar lived up to all the stereotypes, and then some: ready to say anything to anybody if he thought there was some benefit in it. Benefit *to him*.

In the RUN-DMV era, official surveillance was rare, as I've mentioned, but ultimately I *did* have backup on the scene, though it took some creative effort on my part. The whole question of my personal safety and the limitations of surveillance based a block away had focused my attention. My search for a respectable way to make this job and this life less likely to end abruptly was already in the back of my mind when I attended a three-day seminar for NY-based SAs on the Bureau's UC ops. The covert location was a Midtown hotel in Manhattan. Some of the speakers were UCs I had come to know well in the past couple of years, so this would be an opportunity to schmooze and relax for a few days, a break from the street.

Among the attendees I noticed an odd couple, their body language seeming to indicate that they were friends, not more. Perhaps squad-mates with an interest in learning about the subject. The guy looked like the antithesis of UC, what I would have described as the FBI type *least* suited for covert activity. Actually, a caricature of a special agent. Large and slightly overweight, he sported a signature police officer mustache and wore dark-blue "tactical" SWAT-like clothing, inappropriate for the office, *really* inappropriate for a covert conference. On his Sam Brown (police belt, of course) he carried: a large automatic pistol, a double mag-pouch with *two* additional high-capacity ammunition clips, a hand-cuff pouch, a collapsible baton in a pouch, and a handi-talkie in leather clip-on holster. What a character. I concluded that he probably worked foreign counterintelligence, where he'd be unlikely to make more than one arrest every couple of decades. I'll note that I carried a pistol at the conference, nothing else. I had stopped carrying handcuffs six months out of the academy.

Meanwhile, this agent's companion projected a different image. Blond shoulder-length hair, a close-fitting, sleeveless, short white dress, high heels, and long legs, she would have appeared more at home at F.I.T. (Fashion Institute of Technology) about twenty blocks to the south than at this FBI function. During a break in the action I learned her name: Alicia Hilton. She had three years of agent time and was very, very inter-ested in undercover work. I told her that I would be happy to bring her along on some of my meets. She could be Alex Perez's old lady. Did she want to run the idea by her supervisor? She did indeed. If she got the okay, she'd call and we'd set something up.

I also had to check with my immediate boss, Craig, as well as my case agents, Dave and Vicki. They approved my thinking and my plan. The initial reasoning behind bringing along a female UC to some meets was *not* security. I had developed a number of friends among the runners at Yonkers, but in my efforts to develop their trust, developing Alex as a credible and likable scoundrel, I had neglected to present a personal side.

While this alone would not have raised suspicion (just the opposite, such reticence would be perfectly in character for the cautious outlaw), it opened the door for what was becoming an increasing number of offers from my new friends on the street to introduce me to pretty young women. Julio Dominguez's girlfriend had a recently separated best friend, looking to meet someone. Was I interested? Carlos had a cousin, single, and very attractive. Would I like to meet her? Outright refusals would have been rude and harmful to the painstakingly developed relationships, but my continued postponement of all such proffered introductions to available young women would soon become problematic.

Outside of Hollywood, UCs don't allow themselves to become romantically (or otherwise) entangled with subjects of the opposite gender, nor with their friends and families. It's also true that Ben Berry—my classmate at Quantico and one of the UC agents in the ill-fated COMMCORR investigation—had met his future wife while undercover in COMMCORR. But she was not remotely connected to the case. They met playing cello in a string quartet. And that situation had *still* been complicated. And it was equally important not to allow a situation to develop that could lead to speculation, accusations, or awkward circumstances. Several years later, I worked a La Cosa Nostra case in Long Island and Queens along with another, younger UC. After a late-night meet, the wife of one of the subjects asked the UC for a ride home. On the way, she asked him to pull over at a quiet spot. She had said she wasn't feeling well, but as it turned out she was feeling well enough to try to go down on the guy, a maneuver that he (purportedly) was able to dissuade her from executing.

But Alicia was one of us. Her presence would resolve my (Alex's) "personal life" issues and simultaneously enhance my own status as the boyfriend of this beautiful fox. Alicia got her permissions, and within a month after I met her at the conference, she accompanied me on a routine trip to Yonkers DMV. We had decided beforehand what her basic uniform should be: halter-top, tight jeans, teased hair with sequins, flashy nail polish (anything but red). She would chew gum, smile, and say very little beyond hi and bye. Her street name was Alice. For Alice's gun, a 9mm Sig Sauer, we purchased a midsize purse made of supple high-grade leather. The front seam was sealed not by thread but Velcro, permitting instant access to her weapon. (The producer was Guardian Leather, the now-defunct manufacturer of the best UC gear ever.)

As it turned out, Julio, Duardo, Merick, and some of the other guys were on hand at the DMV. True to my appropriately macho character, I acted as though my old lady didn't exist. And so did my fellow runners, out of respect. But the next day, when I returned to the DMV on my own, there were many compliments, nods, sly smiles, winks. Alicia's opening performance as Alice had been a major hit. She became a welcome adornment to almost all of Alex's appearances around town. Her presence was never challenged. In fact, it was always welcome—in sharp contrast to the effect the presence of an unexplained *man* by my side would have had. While I worked my subject, my girlfriend was, to all appearances, minding her own business, vaguely looking around but in fact carefully observing parked but occupied cars, loiterers, guys approaching from behind or across the street. She chewed her gum and maybe started to get bored, to all appearances. But if she said, "I'm getting bored, Alex," that meant someone just entering the scene required close attention. Such was the code we had developed as my confidence in her grew, and vice-versa. In the course of the hundreds of UC meets we worked, she had to employ those code words maybe a dozen times. A dozen *critical* times.

"Bored" was important, but the most important code word is the one to invoke if you decide you're about to get shot and don't want even a split-second hesitation by your partner or surveillance. It also needs to be a word that's hard to mistake over a static-prone radio transmitter. *Hey, did Marc just say* Monday *or* Hyundai? That's no good. *Hey, did that sound like a gunshot?* That's no good. So I always set up a word that, while perhaps out of place, would be unmistakable even with a garbled transmission. One time some years later, when I didn't trust my team, the word was *"Help!"* With Alicia, who was standing right next to me, maybe sitting in the backseat, the word was "Honey." That sounds too common! No, it wasn't. I, Marc Ruskin, would normally never use that word. I just wouldn't say it by accident, so if I *did* say it during a meet, if I called Alice "Honey," she would immediately open fire, shoot, and kill the subject. If during a meet she was seated in the backseat (always the backseat, never the front, pursuant to Alex's Rules of Survival) of my red Jeep Cherokee (now my main ride, replacing the Chrysler, for the most part, which had replaced the Mercedes, for the most part), Alicia might not have been in a position to see the subject's hands, but my "Honey" would inform her of the deadly peril. It perhaps goes without saying that we would never be moving in a subject's car, also pursuant to Alex's Rules of Survival. I just wouldn't do it. *Alex, let's take my car.* When this happened, I would have to come up with something. *We'll follow you, I won't have time to come back and pick up my ride.* No one ever pushed. If they had, their insistence would have justified concerns on *my* part as to what *they* were up to. I would never have gotten in that other vehicle.

I didn't take Alice out to Mahmoud and Holyland for her first two or three months. I knew Mahmoud could turn violent in a flash—recall John Sultan's face slammed onto the desk—and I wanted Alicia and me to really have our act down before meeting him together. When we did, no problem. My old lady smiled, kept quiet, and stood a bit back. Her presence did not raise the least concern with Mahmoud. I was impressed. Alicia appeared fearless.

"I was terrified," she said in the car.

Which doubly impressed me. With Alicia, I'd never need to worry about the surveillance team that wasn't there, or the surveillance team that was a couple of blocks away, trying to decipher an emergency code word over a staticky radio line. I had my surveillance team right by my side. Alicia would just start shooting. Fortunately, she never had to. I never had to say "Honey" (or any of the other red-alert codes I used with other backup agents and surveillance over the years).

One tactical problem remained. I needed to figure out a better system for recording significant conversations. The new set-up had to meet two criteria. First, it had to be virtually undetectable. Still fresh in my mind was the COMMCORR debacle, when Jim Clemente's wire was discovered during accidental jostling. If that happened with my new friends on the street, it would be curtains for both Alex Perez and Marc Ruskin, and for Alicia. Second, it had to reliably produce usable tapes, not shreds of conversation barely, if at all, decipherable through the background noise. On the first count, the Nagra was too large to conceal on skinny Alex. The mini-Nagra was the right size, but where to carry it? Where on my person would the virtually all-male subject population be least likely to find it? Okay, we have that answer, so the next issue was the mechanics. Rita Fitzpatrick, an agent on the organized-crime squad in New Rochelle, came up with the design: an elastic waistband, with two eight-inch by eight-inch pieces of white cloth in front. Sandwiched between them was a cotton pouch, sized for the Mini, attached with Velcro. It was situated right over my crotch, with a twelve-inch wire passing through a hole in my right pants pocket where it connected with a remote on-off switch held in place with a safety pin. The mics, likewise, were held in place with safety pins and attached to the carrier's waistband, a few inches below my belly button. With baggy pants, combined with a small fanny pack containing my Walther PPK, this contraption fit my criterion: virtually undetectable by any but the most careful, invasive pat down. Hats off to Rita, who was even nice enough to stitch together the carrier. She was true FBI family: her father had been an agent—and both his daughters followed in his footsteps.

Some years later, the DeSantis holster company came out with a "concealment" fanny-pack holster that became the (law enforcement) industry standard for covert carry—for three or four years, maybe five, by which time word had spread through the underworld and they were widely recognized on the street as holsters. Their value evaporated. Wearing one had become as discreet as pinning on a badge.

That on-off switch was ticklish. Craig Dotlo had to arm-wrestle with the prosecutors to obtain written authorization for me to have one. The rule in place, and still in place, was that a recording device is turned on before contact with subjects and left on until the contact is over. The rule does make sense, in that it provides the defense counsel no opportunity to ask the UC agent on the witness stand the following question: "So, Agent Jones, you only had the recording device on when my client made seemingly incriminating remarks, and turned it off when he made his repeated refusals to participate in your criminal schemes, is that not correct?"

I contended that the mini's tape had a recording time of two hours, while I was often meeting with multiple subjects over a five- or six-hour period. I couldn't burn valuable tape time recording endless conversations about girls, cars, ball games, different girls, and the rest of it. Nor could I change the tape. The U.S. Attorney's office gave me the green light. They wanted the incriminating conversations recorded and understood that my trial experience as a Brooklyn prosecutor would enable me to withstand the most withering cross-examination. (Really.)

That was one recording device. I also had a second one in my rugged-nylon, black Guardian portfolio, with the level three ballistic (bullet-proof) panel and concealed weapon seam. One end of the portfolio had a real seam; the other end fastened by Velcro, ordinary to sight and touch and providing an easily accessible holster. In one of the two compartments accessed by zippers running along the top, I often carried one of my Nagras. (I had a drawer full of recording devices and transmitter accessories, and next to my desk was the small suitcase-size machine for transferring the recordings to cassette.) The standard mics for Nagras had long wires, for running the mic down from a shirt collar to the recording device, but among my prized tools were three-quarter-inch mics that would screw directly onto the top of the Nagra. No wires. Before a meet, I would place fresh batteries into the Nagra and a new reel of tape. Also into my portfolio would go a few large yellow manila envelopes, rubber bands, and masking tape, maybe some other "believable" stuff. En route to the meet, five or ten minutes away, probably after a little dry-cleaning, I would pull into a parking lot, turn on the Nagra, then place a little masking tape over the switch to make sure it stayed on. Then into the manila envelope went the Nagra, sealed with a belt of masking tape and rubber bands. Before leaving the office, I had made imperceptible pinpricks in the envelope with a sewing needle—experience had shown me that otherwise, the recordings came out muffled. Arriving at the meet, inside my portfolio was a manila envelope containing a small, hard box, which might contain cash, drugs, whatever. If anyone saw it, the likelihood of a "what's that?" was remote. If it happened, my answer was easy. *What's it to you?*

Two recording devices. Of course, one of the runners nearly found the one lodged in my crotch. Standing in the noisy lobby at the DMV, shooting the breeze with Julio, Manuel, and a couple of others, I sensed a motion behind me, perhaps reacting to a smile or glimmer in the eyes of one of the guys. Alicia was not by my side on this occasion (she still had a few regular cases to work for her own squad). Leaning forward, I clapped both hands over my privates just as Neno, one of the regulars, goosed me from behind. His hand squeezed flesh rather than steel.

"MARICON," I shouted, laughing, "You can't get any at home, you want a guy with a ponytail."

Everyone was very amused. Good-natured Alex had once again showed himself to be one of the guys. After what could have been a melancholy end to a nice day.

On another occasion, across the street from the DMV in a small park where the runners and their friends and girls would hang out when the weather was nice, Neno and I were alone in the park, talking about a no-ID title registration. A slender Dominican with long frizzy hair and a scraggly mustache, he was amicable, and somewhat mischievous. But his humor had a crafty side to it, which made me realize that there was more depth and survival instinct to him than was suggested by his happy-go-lucky demeanor. There was no one nearby. Looking directly at my face, without glancing downward, Neno moved his right arm forward and clamped his hand around my fanny pack. What he found was the hard steel barrel of my Walther. His eyes widened. I stared back, moved my right index finger to my lips and smiled. He smiled. Any lingering doubts about Alex's hard-case character were extinguished. My good reputation was sealed. While many of the subjects I was dealing with owned (and sold) guns, carrying on a daily basis was a sign of a heightened machismo. Getting caught with a handgun tucked in one's waistband meant guaranteed jail time. Some didn't care; others used discretion, wearing their guns when they thought it might possibly come in handy.

To be accepted as a real criminal, you have to behave like a real criminal. The appearance of being engaged in some ongoing, low-level petty crime can only help the UC cause—some kind of tangible demonstration that conformity with the law is not a personal hang-up. My personal contribution to the playbook were the Swatches I used with the runners in Yonkers. One day I brought a couple of dozen complete with the display case—acquired legitimately, at full retail price.

"Hey, I got something you may be interested in, in my car."

After a quick (and obvious) scan right and left, I opened the trunk, gestured to the display case with the lid wide open, the $50 price tags clearly visible.

"Twenty each. Anybody want a few?"

The runners quickly scooped up those Swatches. Everybody loves a bargain. That Alex, he's a thief at heart. We can trust him.

Another reason they could trust me is that I had been careful to follow my rule about indirection. I didn't talk about myself except with vague comments, and I didn't ask questions, particularly about matters that were none of my business. In *Donnie Brasco,* Joe Pistone wrote that he spent a half year hanging out at a mob bar before he insinuated himself into any discussions of criminal activity. Pistone's book was one of my principal textbooks. He had had patience, and now I had patience—ingrained after three years as a surveillance agent in Puerto Rico—and so did the Bureau. But there was a limit, of course, and three months after my first appearance at the DMV in Yonkers, the moment of truth had arrived. Well, *a* moment of truth, but an important one. The timing of this moment had been much debated. I was concerned about making a move too early, without being fully accepted by this close-knit cabal of mid-level crooks. My supervisor and case agents were eager to show the bosses results. I said okay. Here goes. I showed up one morning—by myself (Alicia not having yet obtained the green light to join me on the street). The runner named Carlos was leaning against the wall, an eye on the line snaking up to the tellers. Craig, Vicki, and Dave were back in the office waiting.

"*Hermano,* can you help me out, I've got a no-ID I need to get done."

Carlos smiled, looked at me. "Give me the piece. And fifty dollars for the teller. Also, I've got to give my girl twenty-five dollars for going through the line."

Late that afternoon, I proudly returned to the Ramada with a NYS registration and a set of license plates obtained for a nonexistent owner with a bribe paid to the teller. RUN-DMV had its first two subjects—Carlos and the clerk—dead to rights, and we were set for more. Once the threshold had been crossed, the number of Alex's no-IDs mounted quickly. In order to broaden the number of subjects and to prevent developing a reputation as "one-way Alex," I started to bring my own girls to Yonkers, to handle my "pieces." Initially, I'd bring a dressed-down

Jen or Bridget (two agents from my squad). Julio and the others thought it was great to have white girls do the transactions, because they were less likely to catch the eye of the supervisors than Spanish girls. Julio and others would give me their work to process. I just had to be sure that the tellers understood that it was okay to process these no-IDs for Alex's girls. Once Alice became my regular girlfriend, she would do all the pieces, and soon the tellers who were on the take were comfortable processing the no-IDs that she brought to their windows.

There was, of course, as always, a legal issue raised by the AUSA (Assistant U.S. Attorney).

Perhaps a word or three is in order on the subject of these prosecutors. My perception of most AUSAs, particularly in the Southern and Eastern Districts of New York, was that they were (today, most still are) Ivy Leaguers doing their two or three years of make-myself-feel-good public service prior to joining a white-shoe law firm for the rest of their very well-compensated professional lives. Safely ensconced behind their temporary desks, they could comfortably be "tough" and "hard-nosed." Which, given their lack of street smarts and real-life experience, often resulted in harsh and uneven treatment of subjects and unrealistic demands on investigators. Typically, at a meeting with the case agent and the assigned AUSA, the prosecutor would ask me: "Marc, at your next meet with Jose, ask him where he gets the Glocks" (or cocaine, or counterfeit bills, or whatever). I would reply that real criminals don't ask that kind of question. As long as the guns work or the coke is of sufficient purity, as long as the price is right, why should they care where it comes from? As I just noted above, you can't ask questions like that. Only a *cop* is going to be asking a question like that, seeking information that is none of his or her business. Before I knew better, I would argue with the AUSAs, and the meetings would end on a sour note. Then the solution occurred to me. I would agree to whatever request they made. If it was something appropriate, I would follow through at the meet. If not, I wouldn't. If I was later asked why not, I replied, "Yeah, I tried to work that in, but the opportunity never came up."

With RUN-DMV, the AUSAs expressed concern about UC Alex's role in processing the no-IDs for the other runners. While it significantly broadened the pool of subjects, runners, and DMV clerks, there was a liability issue. Someone driving a car with a no-ID registration, obtained with the assistance of an FBI undercover agent, getting into a serious accident, then vanishing . . . such a scenario posed obvious legal issues. The AUSAs finally agreed to let me process the pieces, with the proviso that I would note all the details so that Vicki and Dave could pass them on to Jack Wright at DMV Headquarters in Albany. I would manage this by speaking the information for the mini-Nagra when out of earshot ("Let's see . . . Jane Doe, plate number ABC123; John Smith, plate number . . ."). As soon as the case went down, these no-ID registrations that had been allowed to walk, allowed to reach their crooked purchasers, would be voided.

Six months into RUN-DMV, the CI Timmy/Yonkers DMV thread of the op became somewhat like fishing in a well-stocked stream. In the course of time, I also developed subjects and cases at the Bronx and Harlem DMV offices, but Yonkers was by far the biggest crime scene for fraudulent automobile paperwork. While I continued to fish there, as the number of subjects and criminal counts continued to grow, I started to focus attention on the other angles, fish in the other streams. Holyland, for example. I stopped by Mahmoud's place of illegal business from time to time. There was little progress on our original transaction for the fraudulent auto registration. Even Mahmoud, in his genuine efforts to illegally register my undocumented (i.e., stolen) car, could not get around the absence of a title. No matter. Among criminal businessmen, just as with those who are legitimate, there is often confident agreement followed by an inability to follow through. The incomplete deal provided an excuse for my visits and made Mahmoud all the more eager to come across on new, illegal transactions.

Waiting by the three or four desks that made up Mahmoud's business, I chatted with the attractive woman who had greeted me on the initial cold call. She turned out to be his younger sister, Fatima. Astonishingly gracious and refined, she was totally out of place on Morris Avenue. With her, it was hard for me to remain in character as Alex. Even a crude knowledge of world affairs and cultural distinctions might have seemed a bit much for this shady Miami *Marielito* named Alex Perez. Fatima was married, clearly by arrangement, and clearly unhappily, to Mahmoud's old gnome of a business partner, Hakim. While Hakim was only rarely at Holyland, he was not totally oblivious and was present enough to develop a dislike for me. Not a distrust, just an antipathy toward a man whose presence his young wife seemed to enjoy.

There were a few subjects developed in the course of RUN-DMV whom I really did not want to be arrested. Fatima was at the top of the list. But for her brother and her wretched husband, she would not have been involved in anything like this—it was the family business. My concern for her mounted one afternoon well into the sting. Before telling that story, I need to lay this groundwork. What passed for high tech in those days was the beeper transmitter. Prior to cell phones, people carried beepers. The really old beepers, utilized mostly by doctors, really did just beep, nothing else. The doctor would then call the answering service. The next generation—the first ones I used—would display a number, usually a phone number, but drug dealers would often establish a set of coded number ("44," for example, might mean "the cocaine is ready for pick-up"). The FBI provided me (and other UCs) with a device that *appeared* to be such a beeper but was really a transmitter to send any conversation straight to a nearby surveillance team. This was a big improvement over a shiny metal transmitter with antenna taped to the chest or carried in a pocket. I rarely used those crude transmitters, if only because I seldom had backup nearby to listen to my communication. And I was never comfortable even when I did. Who would be? If discovered, the consequences would be grim indeed. The really good beeper/transmitters actually *could* receive beeped numeric messages, and were thus completely safe to carry. I didn't have one of the really good ones. Mine had little dashes painted on the screen. (Sounds pathetic, I know. And this was the ultra-high-tech Federal Bureau of Investigation!) Upon close inspection, this thing would be revealed as not a beeper at all, only a transmitter, and therefore no safer than the shiny metal transmitter with the antenna.

On the afternoon at Holyland in question, I had as part of my toolkit, and for the first time, one of the devices that looked like a beeper but was actually a transmitter. On this occasion, my case agents, Dave and Vicki, were down the street in the van to take pictures and perhaps hear from me. In addition to the phony beeper, I also had a real beeper on my belt. Two of them? Not unusual for denizens of Alex's world. Different numbers for different connections. Always safer to blur the lines. Waiting to meet with Mahmoud, I chatted with Fatima about this and that until she said, out of the blue and by way of advice, "Alex, there's something you have to be careful about. The police, the undercover cops, they now have beepers that are really radios, you know, microphones so the other cops can hear what's going on and record it. I wouldn't want anything bad to happen to you."

Wow. The word about my new toy was already out. Even Fatima knew about these things. This was sobering. Any chance she had a hunch what I was?! Could her word of advice have been more than that—a warning? In retrospect, I decided she was simply expressing a genuine concern for a charismatic rogue.

On another visit, I leafed through an Arabic newspaper at the front counter, while Mahmoud was in his office on the phone. Looking at the photos, I came across a political cartoon depicting caricatures of a Bedouin and a Jew shaking hands. In his left hand, concealed behind his back, the Jew held a long-bladed knife. I had an inspiration. Finally admitted into Mahmoud's office, I held up the cartoon and said, "It's really terrible the way those Zionists murdered a holy man, while violating the border of another country." I was referring to the recent targeted assassination of a major Hezbollah leader conducted by the Israel Defense Forces in Lebanon. My knowledge and interpretation were a bit of a gamble, but I thought this gambit was worth it. Mahmoud's face lit up. He went into a discourse on the vile character of Jews in general and the viciousness of Israeli Zionists in particular, with which Alex Perez heartily concurred. I wondered what my dad, looking down from up on high, must have been thinking as he heard this exchange.

I had some new best friends—and a new arrangement: I would bring my clients to Holyland, and Mahmoud would fit them out with the full package. NYS driver's license, auto registration and plates if needed, a Social Security card, utility and phone bills. The bills would be forged, but when such bills are used as proof of residence, in conjunction with an *apparently* valid ID, they were (and still are) accepted at face value. For the auto registrations, I would provide the titles we had obtained from DMV's Inspector General in Albany, showing ownership by people or auto dealers who didn't exist. Thanks to these bogus titles, we had an endless supply of phantom cars awaiting no-ID registrations. To play the role of unscrupulous buyer, we wanted reliable and composed people who would be sure to make the right impression—men, no women, because in Mahmoud's world, women would never make the right impression. A pool of such individuals happened to be right at hand: FBI undercover agents and confidential witnesses. If I had brought in *real* clients, mobsters and illegal aliens, and they then disappeared with the false ID . . . the Bureau would have been facilitating criminal activity and incurring a huge exposure to civil liability, as the AUSAs never failed to remind us in our meetings with them. We were not going to let the fraudulent documents walk away if it could possibly be avoided. Imagine a fatal car accident caused by the FBI undercover agent's client driving with fraudulent license and registration. The supervisor's dismissal of the agent in *American Hustle* comes to mind: ". . . Yeah, Richie, you can go home now."

The first client I took to Mahmoud's establishment was Sam Romero, an experienced UC in the past, now a tech agent. A few days prior to the meet, I went to see Mahmoud and said, "This guy is important, he's the boss of one of the biggest cartels in Miami. His organization moves huge amounts of cocaine. Do me a favor, please treat him with kid gloves. He's a real big shot, and if he's pleased, he'll send us a lot of his people to get their documents."

That's the role I described to Sam, a Miami native, over the phone. *He* got it immediately (as opposed to Oscar Cascillo, who could have cost me my life months earlier by spontaneously introducing me to Nair as a Colombian drug lord, when I didn't know a thing about Colombia). The day of the meet with Mahmoud, Sam Romero and I rendezvoused at my office in New Rochelle. Midforties, a bit stout, wearing a dark suit with diamond ring and Rolex. Perfect. He could credibly have ordered a hit on any of his fellow cartel bosses. Sam was a professional, we didn't waste each other's time. I provided the nuts-and-bolts of the meet during the thirty-minute drive to Holyland. In Mahmoud's office, Sam was appropriately arrogant and aloof, and Mahmoud treated him with great deference, with the courtesy and remonstrations due to a man of prominence and power. A home run. On the way back to New Rochelle, Sam and I talked about mutual friends, incompetent managers, and anything that came to mind, the typical chat of friendly colleagues. It would not have occurred to either of us to talk about the case, to dissect the meet, and so forth. Tarantino got it right in *Pulp Fiction,* with the two hit men on their way to the job discussing the attributes of Big Macs and BK Whoppers as served in Europe—and the foot massages, of course. Who can forget them?

Describing a recent raid, the supervisor of the squad investigating the Jamaican drug gangs gave me the idea for an exacting new character from the dark side to introduce to Mahmoud. (Apparently the large sums of money pouring in from the sale of cocaine had not trumped this gang's communal lifestyle. The details revealed in the search of the Brooklyn apartment were graphic. In lieu of the toilet, the many residents—men, women, children—had substituted the bathtub. Firearms and half-smoked ganja cigars littered the rooms.) My Jamaican drug lord would be like Sam, a true professional. Mike Campbell.

"Mahmoud," I said in the preliminary conversation at Holyland, "next week I'm bringing a new client. This one is a real lunatic. The head of one of the Jamaican posses in Brooklyn. He's got plenty of cash, but he's very high-strung. Anything can set him off."

Driving over with Mike, I provided an overview of what the scenario should look like. Like Sam Romero, he had his role ready in twenty minutes. Emerging from the Chrysler Imperial in front of Holyland, tall and thin, with the long dreadlocks and scraggly beard and glaring eyes, he exuded menace. His agitation was such that he loudly refused to enter Mahmoud's office. I went inside and persuaded Mahmoud to come outside. He wasn't sure how to react to the wild man out front, and he could not have been eager to have this hothead inside Holyland. But he was no stranger to rough characters and he appreciated the now certain knowledge that I, Alex Perez, likewise moved in dangerous circles. He was willing to proceed with the deal. The Rasta paced up and down the sidewalk spitting out instructions; Mahmoud and I at his side. Passersby walked right on by, not even glancing at the volatile scene. The next time I saw Mahmoud, he confessed that he was relieved when the Rasta and I finally drove away. And of course he appreciated the profit (at least $2,000—*each time* I brought somebody in).

Not wanting to shortchange South Florida as a hotbed of criminal intent and activity, I brought in the "top lieutenant" of my earlier client, "cartel boss" Sam Romero, played by a handsome young Hispanic agent, Diego Rodriguez. Though relatively new to UC work, Diego gave the role a brash arrogance that worked perfectly. A natural, apparently, he nevertheless did not stay with undercover work. As of this writing, Diego is Chief Global Security Officer for Univision, having retired as the Assistant Director of the NYO, one of the half-dozen most powerful agents in the Bureau.

Next up was Steve Kim, a stocky native of Seoul who spoke flawless Korean should the need arise. As we drove over, he listened impassively to my standard exposition of the game plan. Mahmoud was busy when we entered Holyland, and we waited by the counter. Making small talk, Kim said something about his family in South Korea. When I realized he was talking about his *real* family, not some fictitious story for others to overhear, I made a curt remark, in character for Alex, and Steve stopped talking. When we entered Mahmoud's office, I was surprised to see two young Arab men—midtwenties, perhaps—standing behind the boss's desk. They just stood, arms folded, unsmiling: poster boys for the PFLP. With the door closed, myself directly across from Mahmoud and Kim to my right, it was a bit close in the room. Both Kim and I were wearing recording devices, my mini-Nagra in the customary underwear pouch, Kim's full-size Nagra in an elastic carrier around his belly. Between the two of us we had only one weapon, my standard Walther PPK.

Mahmoud was amiable enough and engaged in the culturally mandatory preliminary small talk—queries about family health, observations concerning the state of the economy, the folly of mainstream politicians—before turning to Kim.

"So, what can I do for you?"

"Uh . . . uh . . . uh"—Kim turned and looked at me, imploring; the proverbial "deer in the headlights."

"Uh . . . uh . . . What was your name again?"

All eyes on Kim. Then, all eyes on me. Mahmoud and the two Palestinian poster boys glaring. Mahmoud finally broke the long silence. I wasn't counting, but it *seemed* like a minute or even more before he finally shouted at me, "*What the fuck?* You're bringing people here you don't even know!"

Mahmoud's shock was equaled by my own stunned amazement. Without a doubt, this was the most dangerous situation in my brief UC career—my considerably longer FBI career. I had not anticipated that Steve might crap out like this. My mind was racing to come up with something good. Finally I replied, "Hey, there's nothing to worry about, Mahmoud, the guy who sent him to me is someone I've known for years, someone I trust completely. He wouldn't send me anybody that wasn't okay. This guy's just an illegal, he needs a DL and a Social Security card."

Mahmoud looked at me, looked at Kim, looked back at me. Then he turned his head and barked an order in Arabic to one of his men, who nodded and left the office. As I am trying to make light conversation, pathetically, in my imagination I am translating Mahmoud's orders: "Jamal, pull down and lock the front gate, get Mohamed and Abdul to pull the van around the back . . ." I thought about my puny .32 up against two or three MAC-10s and 9mm pistols.

Finally—maybe five-seeming-like-twenty minutes—Jamal returned carrying . . . the DMV and Social Security forms. Survival! As he handed the forms to Mahmoud, I smiled and asked Steve to wait outside. After he left I said, "Listen, Mahmoud, this guy is obviously a real asshole. We'll take him to the cleaners, make as much money off him as possible." Mahmoud nodded and smiled. We were friends again. In the car headed back to New Rochelle, I did in fact tear Kim a new asshole. I yelled at him the entire trip, no doubt due to the fear that I had suppressed during the meet. Steve was contrite, and he should have been, but some of the blame was mine: I had assumed that he had prior UC experience, but he didn't. Nor would he ever. After this maiden voyage, he gave up UC work. He had already had his fill. Fair enough. It's not for everyone. A nice guy really, he ended up as Legat (legal attaché) Seoul, a position of significant responsibility but generally involving limited risk. A diplomat, not a street agent.

Copying my mini-Nagra tape to a cassette—one of my evening chores after every taped meet with a subject, with one copy for the AUSAs, one for Dave and Vicki—I was surprised to realize that a mere second or two had passed between Mahmoud's outburst following Kim's panicked comment and my impromptu response to Mahmoud. In Mahmoud's office, I felt like that passage of time had slowed to a crawl, but in real time it was actually just the opposite. The flow of conversation was almost uninterrupted. A lot of research has proved that this strange slowing of subjective time happens often in gunfights and other high-risk situations. In these Twilight Zones, the brain is actually doing a lot of work and taking action in the briefest of moments.

At the Christmas party in New Rochelle that year, I was talking with a typist from the off-site steno pool who transcribed that cassette audio of the meet with Kim.

"I was so scared," she told me. "I thought that they were about to kill you. I was sure of it."

"Susie, you were listening to it several months later. Don't you think you'd have heard about it, if I'd been killed?"

"I know. But I was still scared."

With good reason. Like I said, that was the most dangerous moment in my career so far. But all for a good cause: That whole sting, with FBI insiders posing as the buyers, would provide real cases against Mahmoud, his employees who processed the work, and the numerous clerks at the DMV and the Social Security Administration.

Alicia and I moved back and forth, back and forth. On a typical day, we'd start at the Yonkers or Bronx DMV. We'd drink some coffee, get a few no-IDs done, get some conversation on tape with a few runners, and if lucky, with a complicit DMV clerk smoking during a break. Then maybe we'd head to the South Bronx for a stop at Holyland, or down to Lower Manhattan to meet Jabes Ortega, the Dominican coyote (illegal alien smuggler) mentioned earlier as the runner with the connections for green cards. With his long, high-end leather trench coat and quality suits, Ortega was operating in a different league from most of the RUN-DMV cast of characters. He was nobody's fool. One day, sitting in the front passenger seat of the red Cherokee (my new UC car), across the street from the Federal Building downtown, Alicia seated in back, Ortega noticed the three beepers on my sun visor. Two real, one the transmitter that could get me in trouble. He reached for the transmitter. I grabbed his wrist.

"That's not yours. That one's for some of my other friends. The one

on the left is yours. You want to see the numbers on yours, no problem."
("Yours" as in "the one you call.") He got the point, and our conversation
about the fraudulent green card I was buying continued. With him—
and him alone, among the RUN-DMV subjects—I wasn't Alex. The Bu
had provided me with a seized Colombian passport in the name of . . .
frankly, I don't remember that alias. I do remember my "legend": I had
fled Cartagena with the Nacionales on my heels, and I was now (as revealed by hints and casual comments over time) reestablishing myself
in the cocaine business. Back home I had been an exporter. Now I was
an importer. Ortega and I spoke only Spanish. Before adopting that legend, I knew from John Sultan (who had been the one to unearth Ortega
originally) and from Vicki's subsequent background checks that Ortega,
in all likelihood, knew less about Colombia than I did.

At a following meet, just as I was making the down payment of $3,000
for Ortega to obtain an "A Number" from the INS (the first step toward
permanent resident status), he said, "You're from Colombia, how come
you speak Spanish with a French accent?"

A sharp customer, this one. I looked at Ortega and smiled and replied,
"I'm impressed." That wasn't a lie. No one had *ever* caught that issue
with the accent. Working on the theory that the bigger the lie the more
likely it is to be believed, I continued, "When I was eighteen, I got into
some trouble. Really big trouble, not just with the Nacionales, but with
some really bad people. The kind of people who mess you up seriously
and permanently. I had to disappear, really disappear, somewhere no one
could find me. I ended up joining the French Foreign Legion. After ten
years in the Legion, almost never speaking Spanish, well now I guess I'll
have the accent forever."

When the meet concluded and Ortega on his way elsewhere, Alicia
laughed and said, "Where did that come from?!"

"I'm not sure. Maybe from watching *Gunga Din* over and over again.
There's no way he is going to buy that story. He's got a few thousand
now. We'll see if he cuts off or comes back for more." Of course, he could
have arranged a "reception committee" for the next meet. The kind that
results in a melancholy outcome. I thought this unlikely.

Two weeks later, back in the Jeep by the Federal Building, Ortega
climbs into the front passenger seat, all smiles, no reception committee.

"I saw some of your friends on TV."

For once, I was bewildered.

"Really? No kidding? What friends?"

"In Iraq. On CNN. They showed the Legionnaires arriving. Tough guys."

"Oh, yeah, I know a lot of those guys who are there now. I miss them, but don't miss being in Iraq. I've had enough of that sort of thing for one lifetime."

Ortega thought of himself as a hard case, and he respected other men whom he perceived to be cut of the same tough material. He believed me because he wanted to believe me. He wanted to be dealing with a man on his elevated plane, a fellow denizen of the shadow world of coyotes, mercenaries, and others who are separate from, and superior to, the sheep that make up the bulk of mankind.

As a rule, all arrests have to be postponed until the end of a case, for the obvious reason: the word of early arrests would spread instantly. The arrest of Ortega did not need to be postponed until the conclusion of RUN-DMV, however, because he had no relation to any of the other subjects, and he had never heard of Alex Perez. There was no possibility of my alias being compromised. In addition to obtaining permanent resident status for myself, alias Colombian drug lord, Ortega had obtained immigration docs for my right-hand man, played by cooperating witness John Sultan. Working with the INS Inspector General's Office, Dave and Vicki had identified the corrupt immigration officials who had processed the paperwork. Their arrests would soon be forthcoming. But Ortega first. He had parked his late-model BMW in a lot on Broadway, up the block from the Federal Building, in anticipation of a meet where I would be bringing yet another cocaine colleague in need of Immigration assistance. He smiled when he saw me and John Sultan, then stopped smiling when Vicki stepped in front, blocking his path, and Dave tapped him on the shoulder, creds in hand. Very low-key, no guns drawn. On this day, Ortega was escorted to a different floor in the Federal Building from the one he was used to visiting. During processing, he told Dave that he had known I was an FBI agent all along.

"Right," Dave replied, "that's why you took nearly twenty thousand in cash and gave him the docs . . . Let's talk."

5

The Daily Grind

Ortega, Mahmoud Noubani, Nair—all qualify as hard cases, by which I mean they weren't particular about the means employed to get what they wanted (generally, money), and would not feel any remorse if others needed to get hurt along the way. The final hard case to earn a reference in the annals of RUN-DMV, perhaps the hardest of them all, in fact, was Santiago Kuris. I met him at—where else?—the Yonkers DMV. He was standing in the lobby, talking to a couple of what I took to be thugs—*his* thugs. A tall, striking figure in a long black leather coat, powerfully built, with spiky black hair and piercing dark eyes, he was laughing quietly as he listened to one of his underlings. Laughing, but with plenty of latent menace and authority. Clearly, this was his posse.

Julio Dominguez, one of my friends among the runners, a small-time but full-time criminal, leaned toward me. "Be careful with that one, Alex," he said. "He's dangerous. Those people who work for him are dangerous." Kuris was, apparently, into whatever could bring in money—guns, drugs, scams, no-IDs, and so forth. This was 1992, and as it happened Quentin Tarantino had just made *Reservoir Dogs,* his super-violent movie about a gang of jewel thieves and their botched heist. One of those thieves—Mister Orange—was an undercover agent, played by Tim Roth. I paid close attention to the scene with Roth looking in the mirror, getting dressed, getting into character before his day's work, which turned out to be fatal. He played it beautifully. I believed him.

Cut to Roth pulling away from the curb in his covert car.

Cut to the two surveillance agents following him, one of whom says, "You've got to have rocks in your head to do that."

He had a point. *Do I have rocks in my head?* I wasn't so sure. I had come to believe that Alex Perez could gain the confidence and engage in criminal activity with *anybody* (any crook, that is). It did not matter what walk of life they came from, their social or economic position in the world, their cultural background. It was a question of identifying and pushing the right buttons. And everyone had buttons. In Kuris's case, I made a point of *not* getting an introduction, *not* talking to him. He would inevitably see me from time to time, eventually would hear chatter about Alex, the formerly Miami-based hood with the lethal fanny pack and the stunning girl by his side. The best possible way for a UC to gain the confidence of a target, for the target to have absolutely no doubt that the UC is a bona fide criminal (and not a lawman, for example) is to ignore him. Show absolutely no interest. To wait for the target to initiate the relationship. Then the roles become reversed: *I'm* the one who has a right to be suspicious, the one who needs to be reassured that Kuris is who he appears to be, not a potential snitch working off a beef with the law. With Kuris, that would be the real concern another criminal could have. No one would believe in a million years that he could be an undercover cop. He was too evil. But he could be a snitch. As on the dark side, who couldn't be?

Usually, Kuris's lackeys would come to the DMV with a couple of Spanish girls to stand on the line. One day, he made an appearance and had too many pieces for his girls to handle without attracting the suspicion of a supervisor. After an introduction from one of the runners, who assured me that Kuris was a "good guy," i.e., trustworthy, I agreed to let Alice do a no-ID for him. And we were off! Within a few months, we, Alice and Alex, developed a good rapport with Kuris, who (as planned) saw Alex as a hard-case fugitive from Metro-Dade, someone whose respect and friendship meant something. One day, he was in his car with a henchman when he saw my car and waved me over. *Alex, you interested in fake bills?* Bills? I thought maybe he was selling bogus Con Ed bills, maybe phone bills, which can be handy for ID purposes. Corroboration. Sure, I said, and he pulled out an envelope stuffed with counterfeit fifties. Counterfeit U.S. currency. I expressed an impressed surprise and great interest in a future purchase, but I would have to ask my people back in Miami, see if there was any interest. Kuris sold me a sample to show "my people." He could have *given* me one. I was mildly pissed-off that he didn't. Looking back, I realize that I was reacting, truly reacting, like Alex. Not like the UC that I was, who should not have cared less whether he sold it to me or gave it to me. Kuris was, after all, taking the game to a whole new level. He understood why I had to show it to my people, to get the okay for a purchase. One of the techniques for success and survival that I developed as Alex, and used for well over a decade, was to always be working, directly or indirectly, for someone else, for a "Mister Big." Alex, like many actual mid-level career criminals in La Cosa Nostra, La Familia, the Crips—whatever—had a lot going on independently and a lot going on not so independently, and for many reasons—for financing, for protection, for support, and to simply belong. The key advantage for me was that by having a boss, I could defer making decisions, commitments, until I checked with Mister Big, who was back in Miami. And I could do so without losing face and without raising suspicions.

I said, "I'll see if he's interested. See how much he wants, how much he's willing to pay."

And that evening I did indeed show the souvenir to my boss, to Craig Dotlo at the Ramada in New Rochelle. And he in turn immediately called his boss, at Headquarters City in Manhattan. And subsequently, the Secret Service, which investigates counterfeit tender. They were very interested—these fifties had recently been showing up at bodegas all over the city, and they had no leads as to the source. But there was an issue: if our sting was a success, Craig wanted assurances that the Secret Service wouldn't take down Kuris and Co. *before* we had wrapped up RUN-DMV. They didn't like this stipulation—they don't like long-term ops on principle (no surprise, few agencies have the means and the institutional patience)—but they understood the obvious rationale—Alex Perez would be toast all over town if they arrested Santiago Kuris prematurely—and signed off on the operation.

Somewhat to my surprise, this QUEER FIFTIES investigation turned out to be one of the riskier ones in my career. Which is to say, it *felt* riskier, beginning one afternoon when Alicia wasn't around for my meet with Santiago Kuris in the Bronx. On the other hand, I did have the luxury of surveillance: Vicki and Dave were watching from the tinted-window minivan parked down the street. I've already noted that backup surveillance may be a day late and a dollar short, even when parked on the next block, but there is some comfort in numbers. When Kuris and I concluded our business and shook hands, Vicki and Dave signed off and drove away. *Then* Kuris returned and asked which way I was headed. Down into Lower Manhattan, I unwittingly replied. So could I give one of his soldiers a lift to Harlem? The drop-off was on my way, I really had no choice. I had to say yes. To refuse would not only have been out of character; it would simply not have made sense and could have planted some seeds of doubt. When the man appeared, I outwardly smiled and inwardly grimaced: he wore the signature "8-ball" leather jacket, at that time a major status symbol on the street and a screaming advertisement to his world that he was a bad motherfucker. The original bad mother-fucker, Jules, whose wallet in *Pulp Fiction* proclaimed him as such, who shot enemies without compunction, had nothing on this guy. Homicides provoked by the desire to acquire these expensive, bomber-style jacket from the current owner were a common occurrence in certain neigh-borhoods in the metro area, though the new owners did take care not to perforate or otherwise damage the jacket in the process. (The police re-fer to these DOAs as "public-service homicides." That's cold, but that's what they're often called.)

I was apprehensive. Had Santiago out-foxed me, with that *belated* re-quest to give his friend a lift? Was this a set-up? Would there be a recep-tion committee? Would they discover my mini-Nagra secreted in its custom crotch carrier, or the remote switch in the right-front pocket of my baggy trousers? If so, it would turn out to be a melancholy day—and my last one. In the car with this guy, I pretended to call my next street appointment to announce that I'd be late and to change the location of the illicit transaction to 125th Street and Lenox Avenue. In fact, I was calling Vicki and Dave, hoping they'd catch on. They would have, but all we had were prototype first-generation "cell phones" (that really didn't deserve the name), consisting of an old-fashioned hard-line telephone handset attached via a coiled cord to a lunch-box size base unit. (No problem being seen with this thing. Hoods had them, too; they were state of the art.) Coverage was spotty. I couldn't get through.

As it turned out, "8-Ball" really did just want a ride and even said thanks when he got out—you can be a hard case and still be polite, Hollywood stereotype notwithstanding—but that was an uncomfortable half hour, and also a lesson learned. I hadn't given this enough thought: never authorize the surveillance to leave *before you do.* I should have learned this lesson from Roger Gomez back in San Juan. Prior to joining the Bu, Roger had been with the Illinois State Police, where he did a lot of UC drug work in the Chicago area. He told us the story about the time he and his confidential witness drove to a meet with a fairly significant dealer who owned and operated out of a garage in one of the seedier parts of the city. After an employee announced that the owner wasn't in, Roger and his associate started to drive off. The surveillance team also broke off and left the scene. Two blocks from the garage, Roger now saw the subject driving toward the garage. The subject gestured for Roger to make a U-turn and follow him back to the garage. When they got there, the dealer asked Roger to come and speak to him privately, behind a Dumpster. Any UC knows—anyone at all knows—that being invited for a chat, alone, behind a Dumpster, at night, is an inauspicious development. And the cavalry wasn't about to arrive, because they had gone home. Sure enough, the dealer didn't waste any time. He drew a large revolver and pointed it at Roger's head, explaining that he knew that Roger was a cop, the second undercover sent by the lieutenant of that particular narcotics unit, and that he ought to blow out Roger's brains on the spot. The final message was that he would let Roger leave, alive, but that any *third* UC would not be as fortunate. Roger had not known that another UC had tried and failed to infiltrate this garage operation. When he now found out, he was standing on the wrong side of a pistol barrel. Back in the office, he went . . . ballistic.

There was no school for undercover operations in my early days. Later, when there was, I would emphasize this point in my presentations at Quantico: The meet may look like it's over, but *it's not over until the UC is out of the operational area. And don't be shy about making this clear each and every time to the surveillance team. In fact, be assertive about setting all necessary ground rules prior to a meet. Because it's your ass primarily on the line, and surveillance knows it. That is, they know it's not their ass.* Alas, we will see the importance of this rule—all too often disregarded—in several later cases. The UC cannot be too careful.

Kuris maintained an office of sorts, on the second floor of a run-down building in Queens. Early one afternoon, I arrived to discuss a purchase and found only 8-Ball in attendance. This was a couple of months after the ride to Harlem. He now looked up to me—a friend of the boss, a fugitive from Miami, a serious felon.

"Alex, you interested in buying any Glocks?"

Bingo! Alex couldn't take two steps in those days without being invited into a new realm of criminal activity. We didn't have to hunt for subjects anymore. My Alex persona was so attuned, so finely developed, and so always-around that I had become a magnet for illegal activity.

"Nine mil?"

"Yeah. Brand-new."

"Sure . . . depends on the price."

He was never able to deliver on the proposed sale. As with many deals, UC and otherwise, it fizzled. But it provided useful intel on the type of characters I was dealing with, and my interest in buying guns—buying *anything* illegal, if the price was right—strengthened Alex's criminal persona.

It turned out that Kuris's associate in the counterfeiting ring was not 8-Ball, but a guy named Paco, also Dominican, bearded and dark-skinned, shorter and stouter than Kuris, and not particularly chatty. Shortly after Paco joined the party, Vicki learned that he was the target of another investigation, this one by the NYPD, for renting machine guns to thugs for use in one-time robberies and drive-by slaughters. Our strategy with the bogus fifties was to progressively increase the size of the buys until the volume and real cash changing hands reached a threshold. Then I would be in a position to tell Kuris and Paco that "my people" down in Florida insisted that I deal directly with the supplier. The two Dominicans would still get their cut—I had no intention of cutting them out—but my boss wasn't about to let me hand forty or fifty thousand in real cash to a couple of middle men who may then evaporate with the buy money. This ploy was the only way to find out where the bills were originating and who the principal distributors were. In order to take down the entire network, I would have to identify the key players and deal with them directly.

I had arranged a new buy, $10,000 real money for $60,000 fake money. Business concluded, I would initiate the discussion to up the ante, paying more real money for more fake money, then bringing up my boss's stipulations. Kuris and I were scheduled to meet early one fall afternoon on a side street on the Lower East Side of Manhattan just South of Houston Street, by the FDR Drive, next to the East River. A quiet, desolate spot, unlikely to attract prying eyes. We had transacted business there once before. Kuris stood by the driver's-side window while I remained in my Jeep Cherokee eating my hot dog from Katz's, the famous Jewish deli a few blocks west on Houston. Pumped on adrenaline, I was not the least bit hungry, of course, but eating the dog as we concluded the deal demonstrated my lack of concern, the naturalness of the situation. It was simply business as usual, routine. But if the situation went rapidly south, I would have drawn and fired my 10mm before the dog hit the floorboard.

I had been driving the Cherokee for some time now. It was a significant upgrade in terms of safety. The Jeep had a transmitter *built in,* complete with a toggle on-off switch under the dash. Hard-wired to the car battery, and not limited in size like a body transmitter, it could broadcast a couple of blocks in the city, even farther on open road. Installing the electronic hardware was costly, requiring some pitching by Craig to his bosses. My other cars—the Chrysler, the Mercedes—already semi-retired upon arrival of the Jeep, were rendered obsolete by this latest electronic upgrade. Plus there was the elevation factor. One of the reasons I preferred SUVs was that they allowed me to talk comfortably from inside the car, without awkwardness. In particularly hazardous situations, I could draw a pistol unnoticed and place it under my thigh, for immediate access.

For this new $10,000 buy, hoping to follow Kuris and Paco from the scene and find out where and to whom they took the buy money, an entire squad of Secret Service agents was conducting surveillance, along with Vicki and Dave in their tinted-out minivan. The van was parked on East Houston, facing east, about a block and a half down. The Service G-Rides (their equivalent to BuCars) were roaming, ready to move in any direction at any speed. Everyone was monitoring my built-in upgraded transmitter (the Secret Service using Vicki's handi-talkie for the day). This was good, but the Service uses a different radio frequency for their own communications, and they had no handi-talkie to loan Vicki and Dave, who therefore could not hear them. This was bad.

So here we were, Alicia and I sitting in the Jeep, facing north and just a couple of car lengths back from East Houston Street, with a good view of the intersection. We waited. Where was Kuris? We waited some more. Not particularly concerned. Patience. A disregard for punctuality seems to be prerequisite for a street criminal. Finally, half an hour after Kuris was supposed to show, my beeper went off. Kuris. I had the lunchbox cell in the car, but there was no coverage down here. I called back from a pay phone on the corner.

"Hey, Alex, sorry, man, I'm running late, I'm on my way . . . still in Queens. I'll be there in about an hour."

"No problem, but I've got another meeting later, and it's something important." On the street, that reads as "potentially very profitable." "So if you're not here by two, two thirty, I'm going. Also, I don't really want to be sitting here all afternoon with you-know-what in my car." A not-too-subtle reminder that if he doesn't get moving both, Alex *and* the $10,000 will no longer be waiting. To kill time and update Vicki and Dave, Alicia and I drove around for a while until I found a block with cellular coverage. I called in. Their cell was working at their spot, so they would stay right there. The Secret Service was, at least in theory, being kept up to date by Vicki, who was in radio contact with their case agent. Then Alicia and I drove to Katz's, where she stayed in the car while I bought us one of their renowned huge pastrami sandwiches. Now I *am* hungry. Amped up, of course, but also hungry. (Another basic lesson in Marc's UC 101—eat when you have some free time; once things get rolling, it may be hours before the next opportunity.) In front of me on line, a long-haired tourist wearing an imitation FBI-blue raid cap smiled at me. Things were beginning to take on an unreal feel, like a bad dream where things don't quite make sense. Back in the Jeep, I flipped on the transmitter's switch and headed to Vicki and Dave's parking spot.

"Hey, guys, radio check, please flash your headlights as we drive by so we know you're picking us up."

No flash of headlights.

"Shit! Let's try again. Kuris should be arriving soon, I don't want him to get there and leave."

Around the block, another radio check, again no response. I couldn't stop and talk to them, I didn't know if Kuris had any of his people in the area. We drove back to our original spot. A few minutes later, Kuris pulled up and parked across the street, walked over, all smiles and apologies, and took up his position next to my window.

"Alex, I'm getting bored." Alicia's signal for possible danger.

I looked up the street. Across the intersection at East Houston, parked by a hydrant, was a beat-up sedan with a dark-skinned Hispanic at the wheel and another in the backseat. Just sitting there.

Kuris spoke first. "Listen, Alex, I didn't have time to go get the fifties. Why don't you come with me and we can go get them?"

Forget it. Not happening. Never get into his car. A few years later in Philadelphia, Bureau UC Chuck Reed would die for violating that cardinal rule of survival. I related that tragedy. "No way. I'm not leaving the Jeep here."

"Okay, okay, no problem, just follow me."

"Follow you where?"

"Williamsburg."

Then he was back in his car, pulling out. The car with the two UNSUBs (BuSpeak for Unknown Subjects) started to move. I pulled up behind Kuris.

I barked to Alicia, "Try and call Vicki."

No luck.

"If anybody is picking us up on the transmitter, flash your lights."

No flashing headlights.

The Williamsburg of the mid-nineties wasn't the reclaimed, gentrified, yuppified neighborhood of artists and coffeehouses. It ranked with Bed-Stuy and East New York for an astronomical homicide rate and all variety of violent crime. Were we headed to the source of the counterfeit currency? Or were we en route, alone, with $10,000 cash—real money, not fake—to a heavily armed reception committee? Alicia was silent. If she had any reservations, she would keep them to herself, but she knew another of my cardinal UC rules: Never let the subject dictate the time and place for a meet. She also knew that six years earlier, UC Everett Hatcher of the Drug Enforcement Agency had been murdered after responding to a beep calling for a meet "right now."

So what was I doing? I was on the verge of violating a cardinal rule, that's what I was doing. Moving slowly along the narrow, twisting streets of Lower Manhattan, we approached the Williamsburg Bridge and the point of no return. The traffic light turned red. I shifted the Jeep into park, opened the door, and strode up to Kuris, sitting at the wheel waiting for the red ball to turn.

"Hey, Kuris, I'm going back to where we met. I'll wait for you to bring the bills."

"Come on, Alex, it'll take two hours, then I've got to go back and forth, and it's going to be rush hour. You can just get them now and it's over."

"I'm not going to Williamsburg. Look, Kuris, I trust you. You're my friend. But I don't know who these guys are, and I don't trust people I don't know."

The other vehicle was clearly also following. I gestured at them. Kuris smiled, said nothing.

"If you want this to go down, you'll have to bring me the bills back by East Houston. I'll wait for an hour and a half, then I'm gone."

I got back in the Jeep. Cardinal rule reinstated. The light turned, Kuris continued straight through the intersection and onto the bridge, I turned right and drove back to our original spot. In the passenger seat, Alicia was visibly relieved. Meanwhile, the Secret Service guys (as I learned later) were not visibly relieved. Instead, they were visibly annoyed. At the post-op debrief, they argued that they'd had me in sight and already had cars crossing the bridge. They were on the verge of finding the source of the fifties. Maybe, I replied. Or maybe they were on the verge of a serious firefight with a Dominican street gang looking for easy pickings on the other side, and two out-of-contact FBI UCs caught in the middle. No, thanks.

Within a couple of hours, after a beep to let me know he was on his way—*please don't leave, Alex* (he did actually say "please"—very surprising)—Kuris returned, alone now, with the bills. He knew I would be pissed by the delays. Had I left, he would have been in an awkward spot with the counterfeiters waiting for their money. We traded our stacks of bills and went our separate ways.

And while it took a little more work, the Secret Service found the source, and at no additional and unwarranted risk. Carefully surveilling Kuris after the next two or three buys, they eventually succeeded in identifying his suppliers in Brooklyn and finding their lair. The next step would be a large-scale buy, one large enough to virtually guarantee that the suppliers *would be on hand* when their middleman, Kuris, returned with the real cash. Or the suppliers might even be somewhere close by to the actual transaction to make sure Kuris didn't have a change of heart about parting with such a tidy sum. And it would be a tidy sum indeed, $100,000 in real USD ("D" as in dollars, Secret Service lingo, of which I'm sure they have more than enough, like the Bu). It would buy one *million* USD, in queer fifties—significantly enhancing the charges that would be filed by the prosecutors.

For a buy of this size, the Bureau (or in this case, the Secret Service) will usually provide "show money." Which, as the name implies, is to be used for that purpose only. It is not intended to "walk." The meet will be a "buy-bust," with no chance that the money is lost. Even concluding the buy and letting the subjects drive two blocks before they're arrested, thus giving the UC time to drive away and establish plausible deniability (*The cops showed up! Thank God I was already gone!*) is against the rules. At no time is the real money out of the UC's control.

So on a beautiful April afternoon, Alicia and I and a knapsack full of $100,000 cash were en route to the same Lower East Side location in my red Cherokee. The Jeep was virtually bristling with weapons. I carried a concealment fanny pack designed for large caliber pistols, a recent acquisition from Guardian Leather, manufacturer of my gift to Alicia (purchased with BuMoney), the pistol-concealing purse. I also carried my "ballistic portfolio," this UC's all-purpose accessory: the sturdy black high-grade nylon portfolio, whose straightforward design made it suitable for both an upscale office and the mean streets. As noted, it featured a level three (virtually impenetrable) bulletproof panel, a Velcro seam concealing a Sig Sauer 9mm loaded with sixteen rounds. In my fanny pack was my Bureau-issued 10mm. It carried only ten rounds (the bullets were so large the magazine had to be single-stacked and thus had a limited capacity), but it was an awesome instrument capable of devastating effect. (I was disappointed when the Bu abandoned it in favor of the new .40 caliber.) The flip-up console between the Jeep's front seats held my old Walther PPK. Alicia carried a 9mm in her Guardian Leather purse, and she had another pistol within easy reach in the glove compartment. And on the rear seat, covered and concealed by a blanket, was an old-fashioned bulletproof vest.

As we drove under the girders of the elevated FDR Drive, passing Dumpsters and abandoned automobile remains, all was quiet . . . until we heard the peremptory *bleep* of a siren and a flashing red light appeared in the rearview mirror. *What the——!* I came to a stop—no need to pull over, there were no other cars in sight—and a uniformed officer approached, his partner standing by their radio car keeping watch. Observing me and my long ponytail driving a nice car and with a more attractive companion than he was ever likely to run across, he was instantly unfriendly. With all the hardware in the car, I didn't want to start off this encounter as Alex. If the situation escalated, it would be impossible to then convince the two uniforms that I was not a hoodlum, but rather blah blah blah . . .

"Hey, officer, sorry to put you to any bother, we're both undercovers, Bureau undercovers, and we're on our way to a meet."

"This is a one-way street. Can I see some ID?" I reacted with barely controlled total disbelief. This underpass was a "street"? I did have my Marc Ruskin creds with me. In the glove compartment. And I should note that BuPolicy prohibits simultaneously carrying the undercover ID and the true ID. Which makes sense in a deep-cover scenario, but the policy can be significantly counterproductive, and even perilous, in routine UC operations. UCs with weapons but without the FBI creds would routinely be subject to the risks and aggravation of being arrested by local police. So was I violating policy, holding both in this scene below the FDR Drive? Well . . .

"Nope," I replied.

"I've got it." Alicia pulled her creds from her purse, handed them to me, and I showed them to the cop. He looked, scowling, more angry now. Probably getting more irritated as he realized that he was about to lose a potential collar—this sleazebag in the sweet Cherokee must be doing *something* illegal. He reached out for the ID.

"Afraid I can't let go of these. Against the rules." This was not what he was expecting. He was fairly young, and fairly short, and no doubt did not enjoy being looked down on by the UC in the SUV with the gelled hair.

"Who are you going to meet with? Where?" Where was this going?

"Afraid I can't tell you." The clock was ticking, and these cops didn't seem about to let this go. Speaking for the sake of the transmitter, I said:

"Can someone drive up and explain to these guys what's going on?"

"Who are you talking to?" asks Short Cop, angrily.

Before I could answer, two G-Rides screeched to a stop, one by the radio car, one by our interlocutor. The Secret Service case agent barked at the cop, who then gave me an I'll-see-you-again look, and they were gone.

A short fifteen minutes later, the Jeep was back at our usual spot, on the left side of the narrow street, facing the intersection at East Houston, about five car-lengths back, when Kuris and Paco arrived together. Kuris passed us slowly, continued toward the intersection, then pulled up on the right and parked. He strode rapidly to the Jeep, but Paco stayed by their car, jumpy, pacing back and forth.

Before my old lady Alice had time to move to her customary back-seat backup position, Kuris had opened the rear door and taken his seat in that location, which was bad enough, but he was also sitting on the body-armor. He carried a satchel. My backpack full of cash was in the footwell between Alicia and the console. I opened it and showed the contents to Kuris, who beamed and handed me the satchel. Full of fifties.

"Do I need to count this?"

Kuris made a what-are-you-talking-about face, and I smiled.

"I didn't think so."

We talked about future business. More counterfeiting, guns, DMV stuff. It goes without saying that I was not very comfortable with Kuris sitting directly behind me, particularly in view of what was about to happen, but there was nothing I could do about that now.

The transmitters were working that day. My code for the Secret Service guys to initiate the arrests was:

"See you when we get back from Miami."

Which I said. Instantly, the scene exploded with sirens, G-Rides, and BuCars speeding up from all directions and screeching to a stop, red balls flashing. In all, the backup force numbered about twenty FBI and Secret Service agents. On the street, Paco froze and was no problem. Kuris jumped out of the car (to my relief) and ran, though not far. Agents grabbed him. Other agents yanked me and Alicia out of the Jeep, pushed us onto the hood and made a show of yelling and fumbling with cuffs. As I had specifically instructed in the pre-arrest conference, we were not to be cuffed until *after Kuris and Paco were secured*. The last thing I wanted was for a firefight to break out with me and Alicia scurrying for cover with our hands cuffed behind our backs. (This is a good example of the kind of detail the UC is responsible for making clear *beforehand* to any and all backup and surveillance teams.)

Federal arrestees are always transported one per car, with one agent seated directly behind the driver, and the subject, hands cuffed behind his back, seated in the right-rear seat (*not* behind the driver). A third agent in the front passenger seat is optional. Two NYPD detectives had been killed a few years earlier when the arrestee sitting alone in the backseat strangled the driver with his handcuffs chain. The car immediately careened off the Grand Central Parkway and crashed into the guardrail. The arrestee disarmed the second detective and emptied the revolver. Yes, the detectives had cuffed him with his arms in front, not behind his back, in violation of policy and common sense. But he'd been so polite and cooperative.

As Kuris was driven away for processing, the driver explained to the other agent—for Kuris's ears, of course—that "the Cuban and his girlfriend" were being taken directly to court for extradition to Florida on fugitive warrants. Thus accounting for our absence and preserving our cover.

Kuris's eventual comeuppance was particularly sweet. Over time, he had grown more conversational, aiming in part to impress Alex Perez, that ruthless Miami expat with the sexy moll usually by his side. As it

turned out, he had talked much too much for his own good, with repercussions beyond what I could have imagined. The damaging (for him)
conversation was in his so-called office about four months before his arrest, when Kuris went off on "faggots and queers." As Marc Ruskin, I
don't countenance such bigotry, but as Alex Perez I had to. No choice.
My role required that I demonstrate as often as possible common values
with my subjects in order to maintain trust. Every culture and subculture has its own markers, if you will, its own rules for inclusion and ex-
clusion. Every culture also deals in stereotypes regarding the markers
of all the *other* cultures and subcultures. These are facts of life, and in
the UC world, we don't have the luxury of taking the high road. The
truth is, we *use* these stereotypes. We have to. Make the wrong first impression, and there will never be a second meet, there will never be a
second chance. Perhaps this sounds politically incorrect, but for UC ops,
especially, ethnicity must *always* be considered for purposes of developing a successful scenario. (The new federal guidelines regarding the
profiling of targets for investigation *in the first place* are a different matter
entirely.) An example is the BLUE SCORE sting, discussed at length in a
later chapter, in which a black UC intentionally answers the phone call
with "Yo!" Our man knew the caller was one of the targets in that
sting—a police detective—and we thought that detective probably
expected *and needed* to hear the stock, clichéd black slanguage, and
our UC was going to give it to him. Just one word, but an important one,
as we will see.

Individuals have their markers, and UC operatives take advantage of
them. Kuris's homophobic rant was a golden opportunity to do just that,
so I made myself complicit: I agreed with him. I identified one of his
markers and then mirrored it back to him. If I had allowed Marc Ruskin
into the exchange and challenged Kuris's bigotry—well, nothing blows
trust more quickly than an ill-timed cultural faux pas that doesn't account for what people are expecting to see and hear.

However, instead of *verbalizing* that agreement I just smirked and
nodded my head in *silent* but vigorous assent. Alicia, who was also present, and knew the drill, smiled and chuckled quietly. The "drill" reflected a hard-learned lesson in the UC trade—any taped conversation
has two audiences: the one in the present and the potential one in the

future, that is, *the jury*. Even if jurors have been told (and they should have been told) that I'm playing the macho role with a macho target, my in-character references to, say, a particularly shapely young lady passing by might not go down well with some jurors. I made that kind of mistake once or twice and thereby made otherwise good recordings aggravating for the AUSA prosecutors (not that I minded aggravating the AUSAs when I thought it appropriate, but I didn't go out of my way to do so). A tape doesn't record hand gestures and facial expressions, and I learned that nonverbal communication could often serve the purpose when on the street, *without tainting the recording*. When lounging with a few runners in the park by the Yonkers DMV when that particularly shapely young lady passes by, I would outline an hourglass with my hands. Julio, Carlos, others might laugh, make some crude remarks, but I would just smile. To future listeners—other agents, prosecutors, managers, finders of fact, judges—Alex had simply been present, an observer.

One day Kuris told me about how the mother of one of his girlfriends had been giving him a hard time. And why was that? Laughing, Kuris explained that the mother was angry because her fifteen-year-old daughter was going out with man in his thirties. "You go out with a lot of fifteen-year-olds?" I asked. At this point, our relationship was sufficiently established that I could ask fairly direct questions without appearing inappropriately inquisitive. With a wolfish grin Kuris said, "They're all fifteen." He was pushing my definition of "villain" to the limit, but I just chuckled, knowingly. I didn't say anything. I couldn't.

Sometimes the chickens do come home to roost. After the arrest for counterfeiting, Kuris's case went to trial after more than a year of preliminary proceedings. (The defense attorney was his third lawyer. The first two had petitioned the court to be relieved from the case, citing threats from, and fear of, their client. I could believe it.) After a proper foundation was established through my testimony as the UC in the case, a selection of the many recordings with Kuris was played for the judge and jury. When the tape of the meeting that included the homophobic rant was played in its entirety (establishing an upcoming purchase of counterfeit bills), the jurors paid closest attention during the long, bigoted rant. From the witness box, I observed twelve disapproving stares from the jury box, with one juror in particular glaring daggers at the defendant. In about the time required to eat their lunch-hour sandwiches, these citizens made the excellent decision to send this felon up the river for a number of years.

The magic number was 50. The prosecutors over at the White Plains office of the U.S. Attorney had determined that this was the ceiling on the number of subjects that could be manageably processed under the umbrella of RUN-DMV. Additional subjects would strain their resources to the point that the cases would be adversely impacted. The Bureau bosses concurred. Fifty, a nice round number, would send a clear message to like-minded corrupt government employees. And the case had to end somewhere. As Alex Perez, I was now operating at DMV offices in the Bronx, Manhattan, Queens, Yonkers, White Plains, and even in New Jersey, as well as at the U.S. Department of Health and Human Services (for the Social Security cards) and the Immigration and Naturalization Service, which provided the green cards. The number of subjects was growing exponentially. I could have made a career out of RUN-DMV.

The last curtain drop was scheduled for Wednesday, November 3, 1993, two and a half years after the first visit to Holyland. Craig Dotlo had arranged with the manager of the Ramada (that housed the New Rochelle office) to rent the entire basement for the day, as the processing center for the mass arrests. Each subject would be taken directly into the basement via a service entrance, searched, property-vouchered, photographed, fingerprinted. Forms would be completed, then he or she would be taken for a detailed interview to one of many hotel rooms rented for that purpose. Some would be interviewed prior to processing, depending on room availability. All FBI business concluded, there followed a short trip to the federal courthouse in White Plains for arraignment, after which the Deputy U.S. Marshals would take custody of the newly minted "defendants."

Fifty arrestees, at least four agents per arrest team, and additional agents for surveillances, tracking down missing subjects, conducting interviews, security, administrative chores—the logistics were intimidating, and nearly a third of the approximately one thousand agents assigned to the New York office were drafted for this extravaganza. On Monday,

Vicki conducted the briefing for all involved in the auditorium at 26 Federal Plaza. I made a brief appearance at the podium, so they would all know what I looked like. *If you see Alex on Wednesday, don't arrest him!* That evening, back in New Rochelle, I had one of only two big arguments Craig and I ever had over the course of what turned out to be a decade's good work. Considering the intensity of most of our cases and the high stakes, operationally as well as personally for me, I think this low, low number reflects the respect Craig and I had for each other. But the disagreement that night was a big one. (The second argument led to a subject committing suicide, as recounted in a later chapter.)

In order to enhance the subject interviews, Craig announced that he wanted *me* to walk into each hotel room to personally confront each arrestee. Seeing Alex Perez, learning that I was an FBI agent, they would presumably throw in the towel and make a full confession.

I was not vehemently opposed. It was way beyond that. I was so opposed I was going ballistic. We already had airtight, locked-down, impossible-to-lose cases, overflowing with video, audio, photos, documents—you name it. Emotions in the hotel rooms would be running high; the results could be nasty. And, as neither Craig nor the others understood, it would be particularly unpleasant, depressing, and emotionally charged for *me*. After all, I'd been bouncing around with some of these guys— Julio Dominguez, Duardo, Carlos, a few others—for a couple of years. But I could not get through to Craig, and he was my direct supervisor, the boss. At 5:00 a.m. on Wednesday I was en route to New Rochelle for the arrests scheduled for 6:00 a.m. The reactions to the "confrontations" ranged from resignation to violent hostility. Duardo, a runner from Yonkers whose son had carved my—that is, Alex's—initials on his skateboard, smiled wanly. *You were only doing your job, Alex. I understand*. Midmorning a true sociopath from the Bronx hit the other end of the spectrum. He and his older sister (a Santería sorceress, also arrested) managed the business in the Bronx that his brother-in-law officially owned. The owner was already serving a life sentence for murder. I've long since forgotten his name, but not his eyes. *This isn't over. This is personal. I'll be coming for you*. I was already in a bad mood, tired and crabby, and this encounter didn't improve my outlook. An hour later, Jack Karst, a New Rochelle organized-crime agent, found me at my cubicle. Jack bore a striking resemblance to Superman, muscles included. He had heard that I'd been threatened. Not to worry, I said, I can handle the guy. Jack proceeded to the basement where the psycho was being printed, grabbed him by the collar, and glared into his eyes. *Take a good look motherfucker. I want you to remember my face . . . Because if anything, I mean anything, happens to Alex, it's the last fucking thing you'll see in this fucking world. You fucking understand?* The loser understood. He was on the verge of tears, pleading, when Jack dropped him back to the ground.

A closing note to the RUN-DMV arrests was the report, which came in late that morning, of the team sent out to arrest Carlos, the runner who had processed my very first no-ID, back in Yonkers. A cheery Puerto Rican about my height, late twenties, with wavy hair, mustache, and a mischievous glint in his eyes. You remember Carlos. Well, he was dead. Two weeks earlier, police had responded to a domestic-disturbance call at his apartment. In the course of that intervention, he had "fallen" down a flight of stairs. That news did not lift my spirits that evening.

6

The Long Arm of the Lie

Put it this way: crime shows on TV almost invariably get one element wrong. At every level of law enforcement in the real world, cases go awry just about as often as the crimes do. Subjects screw up and make critical mistakes—such as trusting my alias—and get arrested, convicted, and serve time. But it is disconcerting how many other subjects go free—and through no good effort of their own. Sometimes the investigation flops or has a near crash because of issues beyond almost anyone's control (such as a UC being on the floor of the NYMEX commodities exchange and being recognized as a former assistant DA by an ill-willed colleague—COMMCORR). Sometimes it's honest human error (for instance, the night I was fooling with the video camera joystick in the predawn hours before BLUE SCORE went down, a major police corruption case described in the next chapter). But sometimes it's because of completely unnecessary institutional infighting and bullshit. That last is what agents in the field find so frustrating, generating as it does cynicism and black humor. One of my few regrets in my Bureau career is not having kept a log of the potentially significant and successful cases that never got going, or did get going but never reached fruition, because of inaction or disinterest or lack of backbone on the part of upper management—the bureaucracy.

Winston Churchill: "Indeed it has been said that democracy is the worst form of Government except for all those other forms that have been tried from time to time." Likewise, the FBI is neither perfect nor all-wise. Its bureaucracy is the worst, *except* for all other law enforcement agencies here and abroad.

The inherent problem at the management level of the FBI is not a mystery. It was explained to me in my early years by an old hand, and in some respects it is virtually universal. The management structure in any organization is a pyramid. The new hire starts at Level 1, rock bottom, and struggles, competes, perhaps cuts some corners and shaves some truths in order to climb all the way up to . . . Level 2. Then onward and upward, with the available positions fewer and fewer at the higher levels. Up there are the best bureaucratic infighters—not necessarily the smartest, but definitely the most competent at this particular endeavor, the most cunning, the most ambitious and motivated, the true believers and the true achievers. But not everyone wants to live that life at the top, or scramble to reach it. Most people in most organizations, whether in corporations or public service, don't have what it takes.

In the FBI and, I believe, in many other law enforcement agencies, the vast majority of the men and women who become special agents seek the excitement and rewards of *working cases*. They want the immediate gratification that comes from saving a kidnap victim, thwarting a terrorist attack, fast-roping from a hovering helicopter, or in my case, gaining the trust of a crooked politician, a cocaine cartel boss, a Mafia capo, a treasonous government official, a Wall Street swindler. The main reward of good casework isn't a lot more money or plaques on the wall, and certainly *not* promotion. It is, besides the respect of peers, *better cases,* those with ever more significance that offer more of a challenge. Together with this increased responsibility comes more independence and less oversight. (I mentioned my dreams of glory and headlines before COMM-CORR fell apart. I called it a potential career-maker. All true, but the result I wanted was not a corner office; it was better cases, *my choice* of cases. As things worked out, I was cut a lot of slack in conducting my UC ops. But that's another discussion.)

The *last* thing most agents want is to sit at a desk, removed from the action. But the higher you climb on the FBI pyramid, the more removed you are from the real world. In the case of the Bureau and the federal government in general, we have to make allowance for a budget item introduced by President Jimmy Carter: "salary compression." This is a euphemism for a ceiling, a cap on salary, and a pretty low one. If the corner office were worth hundreds of thousands of dollars annually, maybe more agents would be interested in living there. But it's not. The extra monetary reward will always be relatively insignificant. In this important respect, the FBI pyramid bears *no* resemblance to the corporate model.

At the FBI, the bottom line is literally where it's at: most special agents want to stay near *the bottom* of the chart. An important side benefit of their lack of interest is heightened camaraderie among fellow agents. Nor do they have to compete for promotion in nasty ways, as is the norm for CIA case officers (the functional equivalents to FBI Special Agents). CIA officers compete fiercely for their intelligence sources, on which they are evaluated. The camaraderie within the FBI and its absence of competition-induced acrimony is a huge benefit, and one that sales people and junior executives in the outside world probably cannot fathom.

There are signs, however, that in the New-Era FBI, this culture is eroding. A more burdensome bureaucracy has changed the nature of the special agent's job. I've mentioned Hoover's "10% Rule"—agents spending more than one-tenth of their workday in the office weren't doing their job. Today, according to an internal study, agents spend 53 percent of each day at their desks, doing what used to be called paperwork. Concerns about political correctness have eliminated most workplace humor, however benign. The good-natured ribbing from the old days may now lead to an EEO (Equal Employment Opportunity) lawsuit. I guess I sound old school, behind the times. Well, when it comes to this kind of PC thing, I am. (Though when it comes to using the latest twenty-first-century tech wizardry, I'm not.)

Raucous retirement and transfer parties, once mandatory, are fading into Bureau history. And in another sign of the changing times, the Bureau's first formal whistle-blower emerged in the early aughts. Mike German, an experienced undercover agent, accused case agents and their managers of concealing and altering documents—offenses unthinkable in the old FBI. Hoover's creation and maintenance of files documenting the activities of individuals on his enemies list, while certainly a misuse of power, involved neither the fabrication of facts nor the destruction of official records. Though an abhorrent practice, the content of Hoover's secret files was nonetheless true fact, and their availability through the Freedom of Information Act attests to their non-destruction. (Despite corroboration of German's claims by a Department of Justice investigation, the managers were never disciplined.)

But some managers *are* necessary. Who are they? Often, they are those who are now certain (if they ever doubted) that they're not really that comfortable on the street. Natural selection during training and on the job is ruthlessly effective. The proverbial "man on the street" wouldn't last two hours on the real street, and some agents learn quickly that they are unable to adapt: they may not have the social skills to develop the necessary rapport to conduct successful interviews; or the street sense to distinguish between fabricators and potentially valuable informants; or the cunning to conduct invisible surveillance of trained terrorists; or the survival skills necessary to handle situations that in an instant can become life-threatening; or the thick skin and sense of humor that *used to be* a prerequisite to earning the respect of your fellow agents. So, if now you're in management, what are your *new* priorities? To climb higher. What's the route? Well, it's not to make waves, or to have any disasters cross your desk, or to take many risks, because bold decisions require taking risks, and should things go wrong in the field a promising career within the bureaucracy can screech to halt. The best route to the top is to make friends in higher places and get your ticket punched.

Are there good FBI managers? Absolutely. Are there managers willing to make bold decisions? Certainly. But are there many others who . . . ? We all know the answer.

After nearly a decade working on the streets and dealing with the bureaucracy (in more detail than I've described here—enough is enough), those BuIssues were already pretty clear in my mind. I was where I wanted to be, and where I could be the most benefit to the Bureau. Everyone understood this.

Every day was a new UC lesson, and I'll just say it: I was a damned good student. Because I loved it. More than once, simply looking the part—the ponytail, the gel, the bling—created new crime-fighting opportunities for me and my employer back in those heady days. Case in point: One afternoon in 1993, I took the Chrysler Imperial to a body shop in New Rochelle for an estimate after a fender bender caused by the (then) newfangled ABS system. (The seized Mercedes had been re-tired.) I found it prudent to periodically cycle covert cars.) I had leased this top-of-the-line white Imperial with the black Landau top and Al-ex's trademark (and invaluable for image purposes) Metro-Dade plates. The vendor was Bud Feeney, a retired agent in a supervisory role in the New Haven division. After a few stultifying post-retirement years as an accountant, Bud had created this niche business, leasing cars to law enforcement agencies for covert use, UC and/or surveillance. Short-term, long-term, high-end, low-end. It was a jackpot for Bud. The unique service brought in tons of business from throughout the North-east. Use any name you want on the lease. Provide any information you want. It was all bogus, all part of backstopping a legend. Only Bud would know. A fellow opera fan, he became a good friend and would always set aside the best cars for Alex Perez. The red Cherokee was another one. There was also the Accord, the Nissan Maxima (totaled on I-684), one or two others, ending the run in '98 with a new Saab 9000 (also red).

In the wreck with the Imperial, I had slammed on the brakes while behind a suddenly decelerating sedan on the Westside Highway. I knew the tires would smoke but the car would stop in time—but the ABS kicked in and overruled me and I ran into the back of the sedan. My Imperial needed a couple thousand dollars' worth of repairs. The shop was practically in sight of the Ramada and the discreet FBI offices therein. As the plates for the Chrysler were covert, I was in character when I drove up in the car. But this was a *new* character I was developing for use as necessary with people not involved in RUN-DMV: alias Sal Morelli. (I already had two Hispanic IDs in use—the reliable Alex Perez and, for some one-off cameo jobs that were becoming more frequent, Eduardo Dean.) I thought a third alias might come in handy down the line, and why not an Italian American handle? Low-level mob guys might relate better to one of their own, I reasoned.

The Sal Morelli ID was almost brand-new, and it was also the first in my experience to take advantage of the Bureau's new Janus Initiative, which was staffed with agents and specialists who could set up virtu-ally any fake background and documentation (AFID, in the now-official parlance: alias and false identification). As I demonstrated in the

COMMCORR chapter, creating and backstopping a legend is a painstaking job. In any large-scale UC op, it is essential that the UC have a
bulletproof fictitious identity. But because that job was labor and time
intensive, in the old days it was not always done right. It is easy to imagine that corners were sometimes cut (but not by me, being somewhat
meticulous by nature). In fact, it just didn't make sense for UCs to be
continuously reinventing the wheel, spending a precious half year
creating a new persona. Janus solved all those problems. It put an end to
those mistakes. These folks are the "backstopping" masters.

The first step on the way to this fully developed program had been
an initiative by a few UCs in Atlanta led by Bob Bettes, a UC with extensive white-collar experience. (That would have been about five years
earlier.) With his finely tailored suits, silver hair, and manicured hands,
Bob played to perfection the quintessential high-level financial consultant with extensive experience laundering cash for cartel bosses and
Mafia dons. As this role became his specialty, he and his partners created
an ongoing Group I op—I'll label it ATLANTA GUARANTEE—as the
administrative framework with which the Bureau could provide money-
laundering services for other Group I ops around the country. It worked
beautifully. Say my own Eduardo Dean or any other UC alias anywhere
in the country was working a subject who needed to launder cash income in order to provide a seemingly legitimate source for the proceeds
of the illegal deal between the two. (I specify Eduardo as the alias because
none of the characters alias Alex Perez had dealt with up to this point
qualified. The denizens of RUN-DMV lived in a cash world.) Before
GUARANTEE, Eduardo would have had to find a cooperative banker
sympathetic to the problem, open bogus accounts, obtain indemnification agreements, and on and on. But with GUARANTEE in place, I could
pick up the phone and call Bob Bettes. Then case agents Vicki or Dave
would follow up with a short written request, and within days Eduardo
was laundering money for his subject. Imagine how invaluable that service could be for the UC.

And for the FBI. That first specialized UC service soon spawned the
idea for the creation of a single dedicated entity to provide operational
support nationwide for ongoing undercover operations. Working out of
offices at FBIHQ in Washington, the new entity ultimately developed

into what is today the National Backstopping Initiative. Initially headed by a fellow UC veteran Pat Geonetta, the initiative manages several regional Janus units that operate out of covert offices (the proverbial "ABC Widgets") scattered around the country. Ironically, I later met Joe Pistone, author of *Donnie Brasco,* when Joe was posted to one of the Janus units and helped out with a couple of my cases.

The agents and support personnel in the Janus offices have developed networks of contacts throughout private industry and government agencies, state and federal. If a UC needs documented prior residences in Seattle, bank accounts in Miami, an extensive history of arrests in Los Angeles, Janus can provide them. A luxury apartment, fully furnished, with each room wired for video and audio, for two or three meets? Not a problem. Janus also served as an informal resource for great retirement jobs. Case agents benefitted, and so did resourceful Janus personnel. On retirement, Pat Geonetta became Global Chief of Security for LinkedIn. A manager of Janus New York landed an equivalent job at Deutsche Bank. Janus also became a good resource for case agents looking for the right UC for their operations, complete with an off-the-record evaluation. *He fits the bill, looks the part, but hard to work with, a real prima donna.* Not the case with me, of course (unless you ask my colleagues in ALTERNATE BREACH, young know-it-alls with whom I disagreed about almost everything and who were ultimately responsible for converting that huge Foreign Corrupt Practices Act Group I into the UC equivalent of the *Titanic.* Full story to come in time).

In the early pre–cell phone, digital beeper days, Janus Miami provided me—Alex Perez—with vital security-related assistance. Janus Miami because, for most street purposes in New York, Alex was mysteriously on the lam from that Metro-Dade region, and of course he had those cachet-loaded Metro-Dade license plates. (My old flame from my San Juan days and through much of RUN-DMV was a lovely Peruvian, an American Airlines flight attendant based in Key Biscayne. I knew Miami well and could easily pass for a longtime resident. And if Julio Dominguez or any other subject were to come up with "You're going to Miami next week, Alex? I'll be there, too. I know a great seafood place . . ." I would simply rejoinder with a new story, a sudden opportunity for some big bucks in L.A.)

For a subject with whom I had developed a relation of trust—beyond just providing my 800 toll-free beeper number—I would provide my local number in Miami. This would show Mahmoud Noubani, for example (Holyland), that I really trusted him, that limiting our means of contact to beepers was no longer necessary. Mahmoud could call the number, which was registered to the cover company in Miami, and either Marie or Denise (sisters who worked at Janus for years) would answer. *Alex isn't around right now, I'll have him call as soon as he gets back.* They'd page me and I'd call back, and Marie, say, would patch me through to Mahmoud, whose caller ID would show the *Miami* number. You can't beat that for validation of a bogus identity. *Sorry, Mahmoud, I can't meet you right away, big real-estate deal here,* you know what I mean, *how about next Tuesday? I have to fly up to Boston, I can stop in New York for a couple of hours.*

I don't think there's any minute detail of backstopping for covert ops that the Janus wizards can't handle, and their work only gets harder as the issues involved in backstopping, and the consequent risks of exposure to UCs, have expanded in direct proportion to the advances in technology. Two decades ago, the risk was that the mob guys or coke dealers would find my mini-Nagra and kill me. Now there are no recognizable recording devices. Any object can be a covert digital recording device, from a designer eyeglass frame to a Montblanc fountain pen. Now the greater risk is a careful Internet search that reveals a defect in an agent's AFID. A fatal defect.

Back to Sal Morelli and the damaged Chrysler. My Sal Morelli AFID was what we called a "shelf-ID," acquired from Janus New York just a few weeks before I took the Chrysler in for repair. These were created by Valerie O'Connell, the Janus expert, and her colleagues with no particular UC in mind, in order to be available on short notice: fictitious identities complete with Social Security card, credit cards, wallet-stuffers such as frequent-flyer cards, and video rental cards (remember those days?). After Val and I exchanged updates on mutual acquaintances in the FBI UC community and shared the usual complaints about management interference in operational affairs, I inquired whether she had anything on the shelf with an Italian-sounding last name. She had a couple. How about Salvatore Joseph Morelli, born in 1950? Close enough. And I couldn't have invented a better name.

Since I was trying to build up my man Sal's credit history, using his Visa card was the order of the day at the local gas stations and at the repair shop. And as my luck would have it, the shop's co-owner was one Frank Lobianco. He took one look at me and my street bling, got my name—Sal—took a second look, paused, then pulled me aside, even though I was the only customer in the place. We were alone. This could be interesting, I immediately thought—and I was right. Lobianco asked if I'd like to join him in making some extra money, compliments of my insurance company. He was blunt about the proposition: He would waive my deductible and give me a couple of thousand dollars in cash if I'd leave the car with him, no questions asked. It would be repaired and ready for pick up within a week. He didn't go into any detail about the scam, but he didn't have to and I sure didn't ask. As Sal Morelli, the mid-level street crook, I wouldn't care—just like, with all my subjects, I never seemed to care where the drugs came from, how the fraudulent documents were made, how the guns were stolen. Real criminals don't care to know what they have no business knowing and don't need to know. No one can accuse you of disclosing information you never had. And because I had the right look, Frank Lobianco correctly assumed that I wouldn't want to know. That I would, however, want the cash. And stealing from insurance companies? That's just tit for tat, right? Like utilities or the phone company. Who cares? Lobianco naturally assumed he and I would share this unspoken sentiment. And as with most of my UC cases, I figured that Dave and Vicki and the team up at the Ramada Inn in New Rochelle would figure out the nuts-and-bolts of the scam and who the players were—but only in good time. Rushing the relationship with a subject is a huge mistake.

Of course, I also had to play for time. I needed some authorization, after all. What had started out as an innocent repair call after a fender bender was suddenly showing promise as an unexpected insurance fraud sting.

"Let me think about it."

"No problem, Sal."

Twenty minutes later, when I walked into Craig's office at the Ramada, our ASAC happened to be on hand, visiting from the big office in Manhattan. I told them what had just happened and asked if I could strap on the Nagra and return to the scene and try to maneuver Frank into repeating his proposition. *Let me see, Frank, I want to be sure I've got this straight, you said I'll get two grand. . . .* The brass said sure, go ahead, give it a shot. No written proposal. No opinion handed down by the lawyers. No background checks on Frank Lobianco. No Dun & Bradstreet verdict on the body shop. New Rochelle was a satellite office in what I could call the "Old Bureau." It couldn't happen like that today. Today, I would be back at the shop two or three weeks later with my still unrepaired car, Frank wouldn't feel safe giving me the time of day and the opportunity for a big insurance fraud case, and its consequential positive impact would have evaporated. All the paperwork would be complete, the appropriate officials notified, the various authorizations obtained—the only thing missing would be a workable case. It's impossible to calculate all the missed opportunities in the New-Era Bureau, even more difficult to document and publicize them. The zeal to regulate has had unintended consequences.

Thus began INFRACEL, a fluke that had fallen into my lap. The investigation ended up targeting a number of body shops in the NYC metro area *and* the insurance adjusters, who are the key component in this racket. They're the ones who have to submit and get approval for the grossly inflated estimates for repair jobs.

It was a strange life—two lives—sometimes three lives—but just the one desk in the office in the Ramada Inn in New Rochelle. Typically, in my desk drawer could be found at least three wallets—one each for alias Alex Perez, alias Eduardo Dean, and alias Sal Morelli. At one point, due to budget issues, I had one SkyPager beeper for both the RUN-DMV subjects, with whom I was Alex, and the INFRACEL subjects, with whom I was Sal. The beeper featured an 800 number, so subjects could call toll-free from the then ubiquitous pay phones. Also, a local area code would not have fit Alex's South Florida persona.

One afternoon, the pager went off, displaying an unfamiliar number. I attached my portable cassette recorder with handset suction-cup mic to the squad's Hello Phone—the BuName for the covert phone maintained by each squad for calls to and from informants and subjects. Whoever answered a call would typically say "hello" (hence the nickname) and take a message. I called the unfamiliar number and, not surprisingly, did not recognize the voice. Kind of a street sound, though.

"Hey. You just beep me?"

"Who's this?"

I could be permissibly evasive, as a real criminal would be suspicious of an unknown number. In my case, not knowing if the beep was intended for Alex or Sal, or conceivably Eduardo, I had no choice.

"I'm the guy you just beeped."

This went back and forth for a bit longer, then finally:

"This Alex?"

Okay. This is better. At least now I knew what case number to write on the cassette. I had to be careful.

"Yeah, who's this?"

"Miguel. I'm a friend of Julio Dominguez . . ."

I was all ears. Maybe Miguel wanted to go to prison. In the end, maybe he did.

Three wallets not to lose, three lives to keep track of, and as for the cameo jobs that came along more and more frequently, I couldn't count all of them over the years. Dozens. A hundred? I never kept track. I was somewhat in demand because I spoke Spanish and French and could pass for all kinds of ethnicities. I was adept at, and had experience with, white- as well as blue-collar impersonations.

Not a waste of time in the one-off category was a bittersweet-favorite episode in Tampa Bay, where the agents working an industrial-espionage case needed a French-speaking UC to meet with two suspects on very short notice. Like the following day. I was busy with RUN-DMV and INFRACEL, but Alicia chipped in with logistical help and I landed in Tampa Bay twelve hours after I got the phone call. The case agent briefed me as we drove to the Marriott or whatever it was, something in that business-class category. The Bu typically reimburses at government per-diem rates unless an upscale abode is pertinent to the UC scenario, which the Bu *might* spring for, given correct paperwork.

For this and most of the other cameos, I didn't need an elaborate false identity. My AFID could be one of the off-the-shelf, ready-to-go packages. In this instance, Janus Miami fixed me up as Pierre (I've forgotten the last name), a French expatriate living in Miami—a straightforward character for me to assume.

The targets were two Belgians, an executive, Stephane, and his partner, Eduard, with the exec claiming to be from one of the largest European fiberglass manufacturers, with valuable trade secrets for sale. I was going to broker this corrupt deal with Owens-Corning, the largest American competitor (and the largest fiberglass company in the world). My corrupt percentage would come out of the half million dollars the Belgians anticipated receiving for their merchandise. The main trick for me as the UC was to get my hands on the actual secrets—an attaché case full of paper documents, apparently—*and* to get the thieves to tell me how they'd stolen these documents.

Initially, the subjects had contacted a local private investigator of French origin, Jean-Claude. He was either honest or realized that this was out of his league, a case with the potential for disastrous consequences, so he had declined the middleman job and tipped off the Bureau. In Tampa Bay, my initial (and presumably only) rendezvous with the subjects, following a referral by Jean-Claude, would be late the next morning. Before then, though, at my request, I met with Jean-Claude and the case agent in my hotel room in Tampa Bay. I wanted to obtain this private eye's impression of the two subjects firsthand, not diluted through the local agents. Heavyset and gruff, with a thick French accent, Gauloise cigarette dangling perilously from the corner of his mouth, Jean-Claude was the French police inspector from central casting. He described the two Europeans succinctly: "Amateurs." Low-hanging fruit.

Early on the next morning's agenda was the meeting with the local Reactive Squad at the FBI office. These particular reactors struck me as an unusually fit seniors club: a dozen white men in their fifties, most wearing Bermuda shorts on this Saturday morning. (Footnote: In any federal building, you see four or five middle-aged men waiting for an elevator, all of whom look like athletes, or at least former athletes, it's a pretty good bet that they are FBI special agents. Four or five middle-aged men from Social Security or any other agency, one will be obese, one will be a toothpick, two will have potbellies.) Oh, yes, and one lone Hispanic female was on hand, just in case the white guys needed someone to ignore. As it turned out, I knew Carmen, who had been an agent in San Juan, where we had overlapped for my last year. She had married another agent down there, and they had lucked out with a transfer to Tampa. Small world, and now I felt somewhat bad for her: the few times she opened her mouth to make a suggestion, she may as well have been talking to a wall. I hasten to add that this had nothing to do with her being female, or Hispanic. It had everything to do with her having less than 5 years in the Bu, trapped with a group each of whom had at least 20 years on the payroll. There must have been 250 years of combined FBI experience in that room. Including Carmen, make that 254.

The prep I received from the local squad was thorough, and I felt pretty comfortable when I met with the two subjects in a room at a hotel. Jean-Claude had told them that I, Pierre, had rented the room for the discreet transaction. I was carrying a satchel with $200,000 cash, show money that was never going to leave my sight. The agents had wired this room with video and audio, and now they were on the other side of the door connecting to the next room, manning the equipment and providing backup, though I had no real concern in that regard. These subjects had just flown in from Europe. They weren't going to have guns on such short notice, and anyway it just wasn't that kind of crime.

Stephane looked the part of a European senior manager: tall and trim, silver hair brushed back, refined. Eduard was his old friend who had his own private investigative business in Brussels; he was short, a bit stocky, owlish eyes behind large black glasses. The moment I met these guys I knew immediately I had yet another major advantage here. They didn't speak a word of English beyond "hello" and "okay," so they were visibly relieved to learn that their contact and broker in the states was this French expat living in Miami, shady as he may have appeared. (I may have been Pierre to them, but it was still the Alex Perez look: ponytail, sufficient bling.) After some initial rapport building, I simply showed the two men the money and said that I had a representative from Owens-Corning on his way over to consummate the deal. This businessman—another UC, of course—arrived in appropriately professional attire shortly afterward. With myself acting as interpreter, he told the two that he had an Owens research engineer with him, waiting in an alcove of the hotel lobby. The engineer would need to look at a sample of the documents to establish their authenticity and value. With the engineer's approval, I would turn over the cash. This was a fair, even mandatory request and procedure, and the Belgians handed over the attaché case without compunctions.

My amazement at what had just transpired was difficult to conceal. These guys had just allowed the *entire* case of documents, the totality of their merchandise, to walk out of the room in the arms of a man they had just met. Had I really been the broker of the stolen property that they believed me to be, I would have made a quick exit, with all my cash, and before they had grasped what was happening they'd have found themselves alone in their hotel room, with no merchandise and no cash and no way to get either one. A clean rip-off by alias Pierre. They would have returned to Belgium empty-handed, but having learned a valuable lesson concerning the risks and consequences of venturing into the dark side. Unfortunately for them, I wasn't a real broker and the consequences of their mistake were to be even worse.

There actually was a real Owens-Corning engineer waiting in a room on another floor, poised to determine if these were legitimate trade secrets. While the documents were being inspected, I had some time on my hands with the Belgians, which I decided to use to enhance the legal groundwork for industrial espionage charges. In general, as we know, asking crooks a lot of questions is suspicious behavior for a UC, if the crooks are at all sharp. In this case, I had nothing to lose. The case was already made. They had proffered the stolen secret documents, and the documents were no longer in their control. There was little chance that they would say anything that could damage the case against them (it could only be enhanced), and if they became suspicious, so what. I primed them by saying how much I admired their initiative, how impressed I was that they had been able to pull this off. Then I proceeded straight to the questions and asked flat out how they'd stolen the documents. Not *did* they steal them. That's important. You never ask "did you . . . ?" questions, which just freak out real criminals who go on red alert. Stephane and Eduard weren't real criminals, in the sense that I was used to dealing with, but I followed my training and experience anyway. Proper craft *as-*

sumes that the answer to the "did you . . . ?" question is "yes" and moves straight to the "how?" Not "Did you steal them?" but "How did you steal them?" Never "Did you have a gun?" (Self-serving answer: "No.") Instead, "Where'd you get the gun?" (Answer: "Jose gave it to me.")

My judgment was correct. These Belgians were clueless and said, in almost so many words, *Oui, on les a volés.*

They stole the documents. The executive, bitter because he'd been passed over for a promotion by the French-owned company, went into great detail about the caper. He had entered the office building on the previous weekend, purportedly to catch up on work. Using his knowledge of the placement of security video cameras, he had been able to access and remove the documents without a trace. The theft would be discovered, he explained, as the documents were too voluminous to copy. The thief would not be . . . until he was, a continent away.

Stephane enlisted Eduard in the scheme because he trusted the PI and believed that his experience would be invaluable in smuggling the documents out of Belgium, finding an American buyer, and negotiating the deal, all without getting caught. In response to my congratulations on how ingenious Eduard had been in carefully orchestrating the consummation of the theft, he explained that they were planning to divide the proceeds 50/50, which for him meant real money.

The audio and video were rolling. In that hotel room in Tampa Bay, the hapless pair unwittingly laid out a great case against themselves. After twenty minutes, the Owens-Corning "executive" returned with the briefcase and reported that the documents were genuine. We had a deal, so I kept the documents and handed Stephane and Eduard the case with the show money, which they eagerly accepted. They had it in their possession for all of five seconds before the dividing door opened and my new colleagues walked in and calmly handcuffed the duo, who turned white as ghosts. The agents handcuffed me, too, just for show—and they handcuffed me *last,* as per my stipulation in the pre-meeting. This is *always* my stipulation, as previously explained. The ruse turned out to be a waste of energy. In some cases, the arrested suspects may never learn that the other guy was actually an undercover agent. In quite a few cases they do find out, it can't be helped: the UC may be the primary, may be the *only* witness to the criminal acts. In this case, the Belgians found out that afternoon, when the case took a queer turn, at least from my point of view. We were in the ultra-modern SAC conference room in the Bureau's division office in Tampa Bay. Stephane and Eduard were smoking—strictly verboten, but there was no management around on the weekend to enforce the rules. (In San Juan, in the mid-eighties when I was there, management didn't interfere: in the office's Squad Area, with its clusters of desks, the blue haze of burning cigarette, cigar, and pipe tobacco permanently suspended in the air.)

It was a Saturday afternoon. Who in this FBI office on a Saturday afternoon spoke French? Who could translate for the suspects during the post-arrest interrogation? Well, I spoke French, so after working these Belgians undercover in the morning, I was translating for them in the afternoon. I explained to them that I was sorry things had worked out this way, but what could I do? I had little choice. (Sorry to be involved in the processing, *not* sorry that they had been arrested.) They just shrugged their shoulders. That was a unique situation, in my experience, and I've never heard of one like it elsewhere. Typically, after a UC case went down, I was out of the picture. In fact, this situation could conceivably have been deemed a problem in a court of law, but the defendants ultimately pled guilty, so the issue never surfaced in court.

In short order, Stephane and Eduard officially confessed and provided full statements. I think they realized they'd been operating above their heads. Another strange Marc Ruskin regret on their behalf: they wouldn't be able to smoke their Marlboros in our politically correct jails, which would be an additional agony for them. A few months later, after their conviction before the federal judge in Tampa Bay, they were deported to Belgium, where I imagine they were prosecuted for theft and may well have done time (but with smoking privileges). I never tried to find out. I wasn't *that* sympathetic to their plight, and anyway it was rare that I would learn the outcome of a case. After the UC phase of an operation, case agents rarely bring the UC back into the loop. (I did learn that Santiago Kuris went up the river, and then there was the SUNBLOCK aftermath, but more on that later.) With these two Europeans, it was over, as far as I was concerned.

Au revoir, mes amis, force doit rester à la loi. Such is the long arm of the lie.

7

BLUE SCORE

Blue as in "police." This was a corruption case targeting the Mount Vernon PD, up in Westchester County, also in the mid-nineties. This wasn't exactly Serpico in its reach and fame, but it was a good case that received widespread press coverage (official corruption always does, when and if uncovered). As it happened—and as reported by all the newspapers—BLUE SCORE was the third major law enforcement corruption scandal in the NYC metro area in a short period of time. A few months before this Mount Vernon case, fourteen cops working out of the 30th Precinct in Manhattan had been arrested on charges of taking bribes and shaking down drug dealers. Then, at the Westchester County jail, ten guards were charged with selling various goodies, including what they thought was cocaine, to the prisoners.

For the previous five-plus years, day in, day out, I had been rolling from one undercover op to the next, originally alias H. Marc Renard, usually alias Alex Perez, sometimes alias Sal Morelli, occasionally alias Eduardo Dean. Craig Dotlo, my longtime friend and supervisor, thought that a spell away from the day-to-day encounters behind enemy lines would be a healthy change. RUN-DMV and INFRACEL had been taken down. And perhaps he was inspired in this decision by a few words from my friends at the Undercover Safeguard Unit down by Quantico. It was their job to look out for the welfare of the UCs nationwide.

The Mount Vernon jurisdiction—its public administration as well as the MVPD, with 176 cops and detectives—was so notoriously corrupt we referred to the town as Mount *Vermin*. In fact, the case had been opened based on complaints from drug dealers, pimps, numbers runners, and the like who had gone to local prosecutors and state authorities. Who would believe such unlikely complainants? Actually, their claims have a reasonable chance of being valid, because such victims don't generally want to bring attention to themselves. But it's true that their credibility is hard to defend on legal, that is, "probable cause" grounds. So they were blown off at the local and state levels. As a last resort, they had come to the FBI and presented their cases to my boss Craig. A veteran investigator with street smarts, Craig would have seen through an attempt to smear honest cops. The detail and specificity of the allegations, along with what was already known about MVPD practices, were enough to persuade him that there might indeed be something there, enough to justify at least initial steps to corroborate or discount the claims.

Craig had names but no ironclad probable cause. He assigned Ed Cugell, who had been co-case agent in COMMCORR, to conduct a preliminary investigation (the initial phase of most Bureau cases). Ed's task was to unearth some hard evidence, if there was any to be found. Tall and portly, salt-and-pepper hair, wearing quality suits (though usually somewhat rumpled), Ed projected the image of a Chase Bank branch vice president. A thorough and bright mid-career agent, he was easily capable of managing complex long-term investigations.

The first break was provided two months later by an unlikely source: a young MVPD street cop who has to remain unnamed (even twenty years after the fact, a police-on-police informant is going to guard his identity closely). I'll call him Rookie. After issuing a double-parking ticket in front of a mob-owned restaurant to an associate of a mob boss we'll call Charlie Sacchi (aka CS, head of a dreaded Westchester crew), Rookie had been ordered by his lieutenant, Philip Valandro, to hand over his summons book. Valandro had then altered an "H" in the plate number to an "A." The young cop soon learned that both Valandro and MVPD Chief of Detectives Robert Astorino were on Sacchi's mob payroll. CS routinely paid off Astorino's gambling debts in exchange for nonintervention in the crew's Mount Vernon operations. Shocked and disappointed by the routine nature of the illegal activities of his colleagues, the disillusioned young cop had approached his uncle, a retired detective, for advice. His uncle happened to be Craig Dotlo's friend.

After persuading Rookie not to simply resign and get a job elsewhere, we had to find a safe way for him to gather credible intelligence. Handwritten notes would not be sufficient, or so said U.S. Attorney Mary Jo White's assistants. We would need audio recordings before we could initiate a full-scale investigation. Of course, a recording device discovered by fellow cops would be Rookie's death sentence. And a police locker room affords little privacy. As was so often the case, Craig came up with the innovative solution. After all, he had dreamed-up the high-tops with hollowed-out soles used in COMMCORR. Now he had a new inspiration, one that Rookie could live with, both figuratively and in the most real sense: a custom bulletproof vest, identical to the body armor used in Mount Vernon, except for a hollowed-out space to conceal a mini-Nagra, the wiring woven into the Kevlar chest plate itself, two mics situated at shoulder level. As Rookie would be wearing the vest through his entire eight-hour shift, a remote on-off switch was accessible by reaching under the vest just over the belt line, as if he was scratching his belly. As had been the case with my mini-Nagra's on-off capability, the prosecutors had to be persuaded. They again complained that defense lawyers would argue that Rookie turned off the recorder whenever the (future) defendants made exculpatory statements. Craig argued that with two hours of tape for an eight-hour shift, most of the inculpatory statements would be lost. Craig won.

Great idea, now to get the vest fabricated. I drove out the offices and factory of Point Blank Body Armor in Westbury, Long Island. (Unbeknownst to me, one of the top executives at Point Blank was Richard Bistrong. Not that the name had any significance at the time, but over a decade later Richard would be the confidential informant in another high-profile long-term operation, ALTERNATE BREACH, aka The Africa/Gabon Sting, one of the more notorious cases of my UC life. Later for that one.) On Long Island, I met with one of the company's sales reps, a retired NYPD detective who was amenable to this intriguing idea, but he would have to work out the technical issues and get a green light from the owners. And come up with a price. I did not mention *where* this vest would be employed. In the end, Point Blank did build that vest, but only after receiving an indemnification letter: If Rookie got shot in the chest, the company could not be sued because the altered vest didn't prevent penetration of the bullet. The invention cost nearly $2,000, compared with the standard $500. Rookie could put on and take off the vest in full view of the other cops in the locker room. There would be nothing visible, no risk. Nevertheless, he was very jumpy wearing it and, for the first couple of weeks, reluctant to draw his colleagues into incriminating conversations. I provided some tips, good questions vs. bad while working a subject, and his confidence increased. Within a couple of months his recordings and information from additional local informants satisfied the lawyers. We had probable cause to go forward.

Three names had surfaced as the likely baddest actors in the MVPD: Robert Astorino, fifty-three, chief of detectives for more than ten years, clean record; James Garcia, forty-six, a twenty-one-year veteran of the department, clean record, at one time assigned to the elite Westchester County DA's detective squad, and ruggedly movie-star handsome; and Frank Lauria, thirty-four, hired in Mount Vernon while facing departmental charges from the NYPD after an acquittal in a criminal trial (the charge: stealing money from a drug dealer's home during a raid). Also implicated was Lieutenant Valandro, a uniformed officer working independently from the detectives. His purported presence on an organized crime payroll would require its own investigation.

To get these guys, Craig, working with the cooperation of Mount Vernon's own police commissioner, Clyde Isley, dreamed up the specific sting. Seemingly simple, yet surprisingly complex and ultimately brilliant in execution, it had a great number of moving parts, all of which would need to be synchronized at the very last minute for the trap to spring and catch the mice. And the final act played out like a finely choreographed and well-rehearsed football scrimmage—although there were a few surprises and unexpected developments, calling for rapid and innovative responses.

The UC action would begin with a *bogus* tip to the MVPD detectives' office from the Hillsborough County Sheriff's Department in Florida, which has jurisdiction for the Greater Tampa area. Craig, who is so resourceful it's scary, had somehow persuaded that sheriff to work with us (their cooperation would be closely held, with only one trusted lieutenant-deputy aware of the sting). The tip would state that according to a reliable local source, a fugitive from justice in Florida was headed up to his girlfriend's apartment in Mount Vernon. An arrest warrant had just been obtained for kidnapping, the charge a result of a botched "home invasion" (in which residents are physically restrained while cash and furnishings are stolen from their homes). This fugitive was also reported to be holding a great deal of cash, the proceeds of a previous armed and violent home invasion. The sheriff would provide MVPD with a copy of the warrant, photographs, the make and model of the car the fugitive was believed to be driving, and additional details as they became available.

In Mount Vernon, the fugitive and his girlfriend would be our UC agents. When the detectives "located" this couple, their search of the apartment would indeed turn up a large quantity of cash. The success of the operation depended on the bet that the crooked detectives would steal some of this money (but not all of it, they were too sharp for that). Generally speaking, when drug dealers, numbers shop operators, and other criminals doing cash business are busted, they expect that a large chunk of their cash will never make it to the evidence room. Sadly enough, they are, on occasion, right. The felons shrug. It's part of their cost of doing business. If *all* their cash, or what they think of as *their* cash, evaporates between time of arrest and arraignment, then the likelihood that they will make a stink increases geometrically, and even jaded prosecutors will start to take notice. The arrestees have had enough experience with the criminal justice system to understand that they might get the money back if the case is dropped or they're exonerated. Depending on the competency of the police agency or prosecutors involved, many cases do fall apart. The FBI botches cases. Everyone does. Also, corrupt detectives in any jurisdiction understand that if raid after raid on lucrative drug operations turned up no cash . . . judges, prosecutors, and their own bosses would be asking questions.

Now, why wasn't this sting also entrapment? After all, if the money wasn't planted in the apartment, the detectives couldn't take it. The key point is that a trap on its own does not necessarily equal the legal definition "entrapment." There was credible evidence that the detectives had committed equivalent thefts before. There were claims that they took payoffs from drug dealers and numbers runners—the tax, or licensing fee, for doing business in their community. So there was plenty of good cause to support the sting. Rest assured that the New York office's Chief Division Counsel and the U.S. Attorney's office had vetted the legality of the whole operation.

As simple as the basic set-up might seem, it took more than six months to set up down to the last detail—*six months* of prep for *two days* of actual execution. And that ratio is not unusual for major Group I ops. BLUE SCORE was a Group I not because it would be a long-term case, but because it involved "special circumstances"—corrupt police officers. Ed Cugell, who had done a great job in COMMCORR, would be the administrative co-case agent for this op, and I would be the operational co-case agent. This would be a new role for me. I was not the UC. I'd have the widescreen perspective. Nor were these detectives our typical street targets. This op would have to be constructed in such a manner as to deceive three highly experienced police detectives, crooked detectives who were well aware that they had to be painstakingly careful. *Professionals*. Who would smell a trap from the least little telltale sign that something was amiss. There would be no room for mistakes, no margin of error.

First order of business: create the fugitive. This wasn't going to be a UC op in the classical sense, as there would be no interaction, no contacts or communications between this fake fugitive and the targeted detectives. It might be more accurate to say that the UC felon from Florida and his girlfriend would be acting in a covert capacity, helping to lure in the targets and set the stage for the sting itself. The scenario for the op (in its three-ring binder, the formal proposal that had been approved by FBIHQ was two inches thick) called for renting two apartments in a mostly black neighborhood—one for the UC "fugitives" and a second to serve as a "perch" to house the surveillance operation, with line of sight to the target. Two agents from Manhattan, male and female, came up to handle the covert duties. Black agents had been selected as the complainants had all been black, and perhaps, in order to play to the subject detectives' stereotypes. Albert, midthirties, athletic, with shaved head and beard, would have no trouble *looking* the part. Behaving like a man on the run was going to be another story. Tina, about the same age, wiry and not particularly communicative, would need to dress down, but seemed otherwise plausible as the felon's Mount Vernon moll. Normally, the UC would have worked with Janus to develop the legend, but Albert turned out to be less than enthusiastic about the paperwork, phone calls, and meetings required. After Craig judged that backstopping progress was proving to be a wee bit slow, those duties fell to me. I didn't mind. I had plenty of experience with backstopping and knew all the people.

Since the fugitive wasn't going to interact with the subjects, we weren't concerned about his level of familiarity with his new identity and history. An appropriate shelf-ID would be sufficient, and I chose one Lester Banks. Even shelf-ID requires additional backstopping. A driver's license and other documents do not, on their own, create a sufficient presence. And particularly in this scenario, of critical importance, the alias would need to have a serious criminal history in the appropriate law enforcement databases. This was vital. The targeted detectives would never actually meet the fugitives, but they would definitely check the cover story that Lester Banks was a dangerous felon. The cooperating Florida sheriff handled that end of the backstopping with Janus Miami, greatly facilitating my task. Our fugitive soon had prior arrests and convictions for assault and robbery and a variety of other violent crimes. Residential burglaries were a major crime problem in the Greater Tampa area—the Mount Vernon detectives needed to understand that this was an important request, one that called for a serious effort.

Surveillance, that is highly professional surveillance, not the case agents' squad-mates getting in a little overtime, was going to be a key element. SO-13, my old squad from pre-UC days, was selected. Thom Nicoletti was no longer the supervisor—he was headed for Guam—but my old buddy Jim Hanstein was now the supervisor. Jim had been a sheriff's deputy in upstate New York and was noted for his sidesplitting comic impersonations of other agents, mostly those in management.

In the field, day after day, Albert and Tina went out to find and rent suitable apartments in a mostly black low-income neighborhood, then returned to Craig with excuses for failing to do so. As the Mount Vernon PD had not yet been put on the alert for Lester Banks, there was no cause for them to show any interest in a new face in the 'hood. Nor any likelihood that they would even notice. Craig finally got fed up and sent me out on real-estate duty. It took a few hours to find a landlord, an Italian guy, who I thought would be sympathetic to the situation of this white guy—alias Sal Morelli for a day—in his neighborhood: I told him the apartments were for "my girls." He knew what that meant, and he had no problem with it, and I carried the leases back to the office in the Ramada that afternoon. We now controlled a one-bedroom second-floor walk-up in a run-down tenement, 30 East 4th Street, and a fourth-floor, equally squalid flat across the street, complete with line of sight. Albert and Tina were now supposed to create a "presence" in the neighborhood among the local residents. Tina would move in, or create the appearance of moving in, spend some time in the apartment, get to know the neighbors a bit, develop a local persona. A couple of months later, Albert would show up, a felon on the lam from Florida. Though he would keep an appropriately discreet low profile, Albert would still make a point of being seen by other residents, shopkeepers, and local street people. Even a fugitive will need his cigarettes, Blue Ribbon, occasional nickel bag. Moreover, when the MVPD detectives got their tip from Florida and showed up, their sources and the ordinary residents of East 4th would need to have something to tell them.

When the time finally came for our Florida-fleeing felon to make his appearance in Mount Vernon, Albert refused to sleep in the apartment. Although the sleepover requirement had been discussed months before, he justified the sudden reversal on security concerns. I had furnished the place with old nondescript items from a Bureau warehouse; it had a phone line and cable TV. Admittedly, it wasn't a doorman building, but we were only asking Albert to stay there a couple of nights a week. Nope. We had to get him a hotel room in Dobbs Ferry (not our Ramada), and he'd come by the apartment and hang out awhile, long enough to get known, as he put it. Tina (who had rebuffed the proposition from the outset) was not as much of a concern; her role was incidental. The detectives would be focused on finding Lester Banks.

Now this was an opportunity to participate in one of the FBI New York Office's most significant police corruption investigations in years, yet these two relatively young agents displayed *zero* enthusiasm. Where was their careerism? Craig shrugged. As he saw it, their role wasn't par-

ticularly demanding, they could do little damage to the case, and with
the backstopping already in the works, looking for two other UCs would
cause excessive and costly delays. There were several experienced black
UCs, but it would be a hassle to free up two of them on short notice.

Next step in setting the stage was a call to SO-7, the Tech Squad,
comprised of technically trained agents, experts in all aspects of communication intercepts, audio and video recording, and surreptitious
entries. Critics of that latter category often condemn such entries as *burglaries* executed by FBI agents. Well, burglary is defined as breaking
and entering into a dwelling *with intent to commit a crime.* Tech agents
only enter when they have an order signed by a federal judge. Sometimes the purpose of the perfectly legal entry is to conduct a search that
the occupants won't be aware of. (One example: in San Juan, my SOG
squad conducted surveillance while tech agents snuck into an apartment
to find the weapons of a couple of terrorists, members of a *Machetero*
splinter group.) More often the goal is to plant recording devices, as per
the judge's authorization. These are not *burglaries,* by any stretch.

As it happened, two of my best BuFriends, Ron Norman and Dave
Swanson, were the "lock guys" for the NYC metro area (and for much of
the rest of the country, for that matter; Ron and Dave were on the road
a lot). Looking like a mole just coming into sunlight, with a way-receded
hairline, blinking eyes behind his glasses, and a frequent sly grin, Ron
could not have looked less like an FBI agent, but he had been the SO-13
team leader who shot and killed two bank robbers in Brooklyn in 1989
(on a day I had taken off to pick up my Key Biscayne girlfriend at JFK).
He knew what he was doing in the field, and then he learned everything
about locks and alarms. He and Dave opened all doors and circumvented all alarm systems so that the audio-video techies could plant their
equipment. All quite specialized and quite demanding. Case in point,
related to me by Ron: entering the Mafia don's home in Staten Island
that had been a near disaster. The usual pre-survey lasting a few weeks
had determined the routines of the residents and recommended the best
time for the installation. The entry took longer than expected because
of the exceptionally sophisticated alarm system. The techs' handi-
talkie squawked: The don was on his way home, his Mercedes just a few
blocks away. My old boss, maniac "Crazy Thom" Nicoletti, who was still

SO-13's supervisor at the time, didn't hesitate. As the Mercedes entered an intersection, Thom raced his Jeep Renegade through a stop sign, smashed into the Mercedes fender, then immediately jumped out of the Jeep and launched into an indignant tirade directed at this don. This was a gutsy, split-second decision. If it didn't work out, Crazy Thom might have faced some repercussions. (Then again, he faced repercussions throughout his career, survived, and even thrived.) This worked out fine. By the time the police reports had been completed, the entry crew was long gone, mission accomplished.

In Mount Vernon, Ron and Dave installed serious locks and deadbolts in both the target apartment and the "perch" with line of sight to that crib. Why? The high-value surveillance equipment in the perch would include parabolic radar antennas, audio and video recording equipment, a high-power telescope, miscellaneous devices and cables, as well as remote controls for the equipment to be secreted in the target apartment. Many thousands of dollars' worth of gear. The second-floor apartment theoretically inhabited by the fugitive and his old lady would eventually house a large amount of the BuCash (purportedly the loot from the home invasions). Locks installed, two SO-7 tech agents met me at the scene. Driving a covert car, these two nondescript tech guys were dressed like a couple of blue-collar working stiffs ready for some maintenance work. First order of business was a comprehensive survey of the target apartment. I was impressed. They suggested building a drop-down false ceiling and secreting several CCTV cameras and audio recorders to provide total coverage throughout the apartment. Another option was to build a faux protruding concrete ledge or corner concealing the lenses and mics. Very cool. Better than a Hollywood espionage thriller. They would send me a written proposal. Back at the Ramada, I recounted to Craig and Ed the sophisticated set-up we were going to be using.

After a polite couple of weeks interval, I called. *Hey, guys, just following up. How's it going on the proposal for the installation?* They were working on it . . . lots of requests were backlogged. I continued working on all the other details, and I started getting antsy about this glitch. When the target date was less than a month ahead, I started to feel really uncomfortable. Group I ops are approved in six-month increments. A renewal proposal is almost as burdensome as the original proposal. And a new budget has to be submitted, and it is subject to new questioning, of course. The Florida sheriff was doing a big favor for the FBI; it would be inappropriate to keep him involved indefinitely. On the legal front, for the prosecutors, probable cause becomes "stale" when too much time has elapsed. Pushing the date back was not an option, absent exigent circumstances. Delay on the part of the tech guys didn't qualify. While not particularly knowledgeable in the construction arts, I imagined that building a new ceiling for the entire apartment, or false ledges, or whatever, would take some time, especially since it had to be done with a bit of discretion, without alerting the landlord or neighbors. I had dark fantasies of the ferret-like, always-suspicious Italian landlord getting wind of unexplained activity on his property, demanding to inspect the apartment and finding an installation half complete, inexplicable wires and cables dangling from a new ceiling he knew nothing about. *That* would be a disaster.

With only a week to go before the time constraint dictated that we roll the cameras and spring the trap, the tech boys finally called. They'd meet me in the perch the next evening, late, to avoid attracting notice. They pulled up in a van, from which we discreetly unloaded cases of equipment. In the perch, they set up the parabolic antennas and showed me and Ed how to work the audio-video recording equipment. But where, precisely, were they installing the all-important recording equipment for the target apartment? In the *unbuilt* drop ceiling? The *as-yet-unconstructed* faux beams? When was *all that* going to happen? Not to worry. Change of plan. Instead of all that labor, two trick table lamps: one for the bedroom, one for the living room. Proudly they demonstrated their inventions. The camera in each was in the base. The electricity provided by the ordinary plug would operate the camera, mic, and transmitter. With no backup battery. The lightbulb could be turned on and off like an ordinary lamp, making the ruse totally convincing. *Wow! Gee, thanks, guys. Appreciate the effort you put into this.* If they noticed the sarcasm, they concealed it well. Why couldn't someone have told us about this change to a much simpler installation? Not wanting to be seen walking across the street from the perch to the crib, Ed and I repacked the lamps and then stashed them in my trunk for later transfer to Albert and Tina. A couple of days later, our UCs arrived home with their new purchases, to be placed in the appropriate rooms *close to a window* and *plugged in*. (I was no longer taking anything for granted.)

Now it was time—at long last—to plant the false tip from Florida and raise the odor of easy pickings for the targeted detectives. The sheriff's lieutenant-deputy in Florida called Astorino (believed to be the ringleader) and reported that a tip from a trusted source put a dangerous fugitive from the Tampa area in Mount Vernon, driving a black late-eighties Camaro, with stolen plates. The name was Lester Banks, and he had apparently stashed some cash in the trunk of the Camaro as "running green" in case he needed to make an emergency departure. Astorino took the call around 6:00 p.m. *Always happy to help. We'll alert the patrol units, and I'll also have a couple of my guys looking.* Of course, we had carefully entered the plate number into the databases, so any inquiry would confirm that they were indeed stolen. The Florida detective also faxed copies of the arrest warrant for Lester and mug shots of UC Albert. Because one of the victims of the home invasion had died from his injuries, the warrant was for murder.

One hour before the bogus tip was delivered, I had parked the vehicle "salted" with $5,000 on a two-way street at a major intersection in Mount Vernon. Not wanting to take *any* chance the fugitive's getaway car could be missed, I had parked it number-one at the corner, with the front aligned with the crosswalk. No cars would be able to park and block the clear view of the plate. And with the absence of functioning streetlights, there was sufficient obscurity at the rear of the car to allow for some of the cash to evaporate if one or more of the detectives took the bait and checked the trunk. Once parked, the car would have to remain under constant surveillance. Not only to observe police activity but to forestall another eventuality: should heaven forbid someone break into the car and steal the cash, I would have had some unpleasant explaining and a load of paperwork facing me.

It was just after sunset. I was accompanied by Bim, the bodyguard and driver of Alex Perez's Mercedes for his first appearance at Holyland, back in RUN-DMV. Armed with powerful binoculars, Bim and I parked the unpretentious covert Honda a comfortable distance from the Camaro. I was accompanied by Bim rather than my co-agent Ed Cugell because Bim was black and Ed was white, very white. In this neighborhood, the combination of Ed and I sitting there would *not* have conveyed the unmistakable odor of easy pickings to the MVPD. *Feds!* more likely. Bim and I could have been rousted, that was always possible, maybe even flaked (that's when cops plant a small amount of weed or coke), but there was no chance of jeopardizing the op. With the tip planted, we were on full alert. A few other surveillance cars were cruising in the area, with alternating cars eyeballing the police department's garage from time to time to give us a heads-up if there was any movement . . . no movement. An hour later, finally, a patrol car rolled out. Which drove through our intersection—the one that counted—without slowing down. Around eight, one of Astorino's detectives drove out of the garage—and returned after a short stop at Pizza King, carrying a couple of pizza boxes—and, no doubt, an envelope for the chief of detectives.

By 10:30, Craig was getting pissed. He and Ed were at the Ramada, a mini-command post. The MV detectives' shift ended in an hour and a half. Craig decided on a last-ditch ploy (last-ditch for that evening, at least) and called Hillsborough County and asked the lieutenant who had passed along the first tip to call Astorino a second time. *Any luck up there? Sorry to bother you guys, but the sheriff is breathing down my neck. He really wants to nail this guy.* Astorino: *We've been combing the whole town and the uniformed patrol officers are looking extra hard.* Craig was livid. These liars might avoid getting ensnared in stage one of this op not because they were suspicious, they were just "too fucking lazy to be bothered."

The detectives' shift was over. We waited an extra hour to be sure nothing was happening. Now the Camaro with the painstakingly registered stolen plates and the $5,000 in the trunk had to be driven through Mount Vernon and five adjacent townships, each with its own police department, to the safety of the New Rochelle office. The obvious candidate for this chore, someone who could take an arrest if necessary, was, of course, alias Sal Morelli. So Bim took the wheel of the Honda, and I pulled out in the Camaro. In an effort to limit the view of the plates to any passing cops, Bim drove directly behind me, with one of the surveillance cars in front. When the lane pattern allowed, such as on the Cross County Parkway, other surveillance cars flanked me. And so we hobbled our way back to the Ramada, where I took the plates off the car while Ed took responsibility for the cash. Altogether, a disappointing night's work. Still, the wheels had been set in motion with the tip about Lester's car, and now it was time to set the stage for the final act. (Albert and Tina were out of the picture. They had never slept in "their" apartment, had never ordered pizza or fried chicken to be delivered. Tina had never cultivated any acquaintances among the neighbors. Whatever impressions they had made in the neighborhood would have to suffice.)

Thanks to Commissioner Isley in Mount Vernon, we knew the shift schedule for Astorino and company. Two days after the car adventure, on a Thursday, the three main targets would pull a 4:00 a.m.–12:00 p.m., then an 8:00 a.m–4:00 p.m. on Friday and Saturday. After that, they would not be regrouped until the following week. Daytime didn't suit our purposes. Police everywhere prefer to pick up a fugitive when his guard is down, ideally sleeping or relaxed, watching TV with a few beers. Alert, in the middle of the day, is not good. So it would have to go down on Thursday, where their shift extended into the dark hours. That morning I did a final sweep of the target apartment before planting the cash, $31,000 in various denominations, stuffed into a large, very expensive gym bag I brought with me. Every single bill had been photographed, every serial number entered into an Excel worksheet.

In the bedroom, I found several unopened packages of men's underwear and the neatly made bed—too neatly. What I *didn't find*, to my very real annoyance, was dirty dishes in the sink, worn clothing on the floor, empty beer cans, trash. So much for verisimilitude. As for anti-verisimilitude, how about the copies of *USA Today* with the Ramada's "Complimentary" sticker that Albert had left lying around? The sticker might as well have read, "Courtesy of the FBI." Clearly, this pair wasn't producing professional UC work. They were either incompetent or simply didn't care. Seeing younger agents not take pride in their work—with ten years under my belt, I was now officially "mid-career"—was a disappointment. Albert ended up in management (surprise). Tina probably continued on the Applicant Squad. Don't know, don't care.

I placed the gym bag on a high shelf in the bedroom closet and tossed some clothing over it. This placement seemed pretty likely as a fugitive's attempt to hide the money and therefore not likely to arouse suspicion that it was a plant. But it would also be someplace the detectives *would* look, if they looked at all. Then I spent an hour doing my best to make the place look as though it had been occupied. And occupied by tenants who had left in a hurry. Once I left the apartment, there would be no going back. Once the Mount Vernon detectives got the final tip, this place would be the operational zone. I turned on the lights before locking the doors.

Late that afternoon, in the perch across the street, Ed and I tested the equipment. For each lamp camera we had a control box with a joystick that could move the lens up-down, left-right. The cables from the parabolic antennas, placed several feet back from the windows, fed monitors that would allow us to observe what was being recorded on the big reel-to-reel. And we maintained a constant eye on the windows and, via the CCTV monitor, the closet. If the cash in the closet were somehow to evaporate prematurely, we would be in a highly unpleasant situation. As for leaving our building for any reason, well, white guys (especially one who looked like Ed) walking around in that neighborhood would be a major tip-off to any observant, even half-sharp local cop that some game was afoot. We were stuck in our perch for the duration.

Everything was ready to go. SO-13's team, with Jim Hanstein at the helm, was discreetly sprinkled throughout the town. Craig Dotlo gave the green light. Astorino took the call from the lieutenant in Florida around 6:00 p.m. *Our snitch just got a call from Lester. Now, ten minutes ago. He's at his girlfriend's apartment. The snitch knows her, she's at 30 East 4th, 2d Floor, in your town, in Mount Vernon.* Standing by the windows of the darkened perch, binoculars in hand, Ed and I waited for the inevitable explosion of police activity. The fugitive assassin had been located. Would the detectives stake out the apartment while a search warrant was being signed by the local on-duty night court judge, or would they simply break down the door?

Neither. Nothing happened. We sat in our folding picnic chairs, the only furniture in the apartment, and waited. Finally, around 8:30 p.m., an unmarked car was called out as leaving the MVPD garage, pulling up directly in front of 30 East 4th ten minutes later. Four men got out, all white. We could make out the stout, tall form of Chief of Detectives Robert Astorino and the bearded James Garcia. Garcia and one of the other two detectives entered the building while the others stood by their car. Through the transmitters inside the apartment we heard loud knocks and shouts, *"Police! Open up!"*

Of course, no one was home. Five minutes later, the detectives came out. All four entered the car and drove off.

"They did *what*?" Craig's voice blasted from my old cell phone's handset. At this point, the real Lester, had he existed and been inside the apartment, would be beating feet for the Camaro and hightailing it for parts unknown.

Craig called Florida. No, the lieutenant down there hadn't heard back from the MVPD. He would find out what was happening.

How you guys making out? Printing Lester yet?

He wasn't home.

And you lazy assholes know that because he didn't come to the door and invite you in? But the lieutenant in Florida didn't actually say that, though sorely tempted. He just thought it. He called Craig back.

They're going to try again in the morning. I pleaded with them to go back now, not to give him a chance to skip. This was the best I could do.

This made sense—from the "what works best for my schedule" point of view. Not from a professional law enforcement point of view. The detectives' shift on Friday started at 8:00 a.m. We were lucky, in a way. They could have been pulling another four to midnight. Now Ed and I would be spending the next twelve or so hours taking turns eyeballing the apartment and, more specifically, the cash. The mood was grim all around, with six months of preparation on the verge of failure, the corrupt detectives about to avoid our sting, and not by dint of ingenuity, not due to a professional sixth sense developed through years of experience, but rather as a result of laziness, disinterest in helping a sister department, and indifference regarding a (supposedly) wanted murderer roaming the streets. The streets of the town they were supposed to be protecting.

One of the many surveillance agents posted around town stopped by the perch with nourishment purchased at a local 7-Eleven. Delicious. Ed and I alternated between reading our one newspaper and watching "TV"—a rather dull show, as it turned out, no characters at all, the set just a crummy uninhabited living room and crummy uninhabited bedroom. Around 3:00 a.m., Ed managed to fall asleep, stretched out on the floor with foam rubber from one of the Pelikan equipment cases as a pillow. Not having the heart to wake him, I stared red-eyed at the monitors, entertaining myself by using the joystick to remotely manipulate the camera in the lamp and explore every nick and cranny of the bedroom. The control box also had a toggle switch for a zoom function, adding another dimension to my diversion.

For an hour or so I fooled around, looking at the ceiling, the worn parquet flooring, the wall on the left, the wall on the right, back and forth, back and—WHAT? I was moving the joystick, but the camera was stuck. Panic now. Back, right, left, up, back—no movement. It was stuck *in the full down position*. The monitor showed me a few square feet of floor, nothing else in the room—the room with $31,000 in cash, the room where, if everything went according to the best-case scenario, the detectives would find and take possession of this loot. All of which would go unrecorded because I had been playing with the tech equipment. Six months of work by special agents, Florida criminal justice officials, prosecutors, financial analysts, confidential informants, and witnesses—all lost, plus a few hundred thousand in expenses. And the reason would be known to Craig, the SAC, the Assistant Director, the U.S. Attorney's office, FBIHQ, and the Public Corruption Division at the Department of Justice. Ruination. Any fears I may have felt over the years in the course of UC ops, lonely meetings with drug dealers and ruthless thugs, paled in comparison. So it seemed to me, in my dazed 3:00 a.m. state of mind. We wouldn't have the video, but *if* lucky would have the money—marked bills—*if* found on the detectives. Some pretty big "ifs," all thanks to yours truly.

Frantically, I manipulated the joystick. With no results. Calming down, I adopted a calculated approach. Small jiggle back. Small jiggle forward. Over and over. Fortunately, Ed continued to snore, oblivious. After about forty minutes, which seemed like hours . . . small jiggle back, and the lens slowly commenced an upward movement. Saved. I raised the lens to middle position with full view of the room, resolved that the joystick would now go untouched until the case was done, whatever the results.

Finally, dawn arrived. May 6, 1994. My handi-talkie started to squawk as our various agents came back on line. At 8:30, the detectives' car pulled up outside the apartment. Garcia entered the building. Of course, there was no response from inside the empty apartment. And off they went. Now, one would think that even the most uninspired of lawmen would obtain a warrant and search for clues as to the whereabouts of a fugitive sought for a cold-blooded murder. And . . . there just *might* be some cash stashed there; if the fugitive has been gone since the previous day, he may still return. But no. These crime-fighters were apparently headed back to the office to call Hillsborough County in Florida to report that the tip from the informant had not panned out. Lester could not be found in Mount Vernon, they had done all that they could do. Sorry. It was over. Handset to my ear, the staticky line of my antique cell phone did not mask the resignation in Craig's voice. We had planned for every contingency—minus this one: that the detectives could not be bothered.

But wait. I had a sudden brainstorm and asked Craig if the New Rochelle resident tech agent, Hal, was around. If so, could he call a contact at AT&T and see how long it would take to call forward the phone in the fugitive apartment to the Hello Phone in our squad area? Then get Bim to stand by the phone with a very simple assignment. Bim was a pro, not the original amateur Albert, who was long gone, having insufficient interest to be on hand for the final act, to see how all of our six-months-plus work turned out.

Hal said this could be accomplished within minutes. Okay. Now Craig got ahold of the lieutenant in Florida and relayed the new plan. Astorino, as hoped, soon called Florida and reported the negative results. The detective down there begged—could the guys in Mount Vernon just try *calling the apartment*, one last, small, effortless try.

All right, but that's it. Then we're done.

Five minutes later, the Hello Phone rang.

"Yo." That was Bim, employing his best version of the stereotypical black street greeting.

The connection clicked off immediately.

Our eye on the garage, cool and professional, almost laconic:

"It's show-time. Three unmarked cars coming out, fast. At least eight guys in plainclothes, some carrying shotguns."

Within minutes, two of the cars had quietly set up at both ends of East 4th, the third car heading to the courthouse. Apparently this was going to be done legally, at least so far as the entry was concerned. Forty-five minutes later, that third car arrived at East 4th and all three cars converged on #30. The cars emptied. Two detectives set up, pointing weapons at the apartment window, using their car as cover. Five ran into the building: Astorino, Garcia, and Lauria—our main three targets—and two we didn't recognize. Through the transmitters and CCTV, we heard shouts, banging, a crash as the lock broke; men with pistols drawn and shotguns at the ready running through the apartment, into the bedroom and. . . . *knocking over the lamp*! Great idea, the lamp. The bedroom monitor (the one that had jammed on me earlier) went dead. Shit, shit, *shit*. Then, a quieting down when they had ascertained that the apartment was empty. Lester had managed to flee.

Now fate intervened. On the living room monitor, we could see Astorino looking around, then Garcia entering from the bedroom carrying the gym bag. Looking at Astorino, pointing at bag, making the "okay" sign, not saying a word. One of the unknown detectives was still in the apartment. Astorino sent him on some errand. Garcia then unzipped the bag as Lauria entered from the bedroom. Astorino looked inside, reached inside, took out a fistful of cash and handed it to Garcia, another fistful to Lauria, another fistful for himself. Each detective stuffing both their jacket pockets. All in the living room. All on camera.

We learned a few hours later from Commissioner Isley that $20,000 was vouchered as evidence. That left $11,000 in the pockets of the three detectives. The arrest warrants were already being drafted, along with search warrants for their homes and office desks and lockers. A few hours later, Garcia and Lauria were arrested at police headquarters, Astorino at his home. Marked bills from Lester Banks's tainted stash were recovered from all three men. That evening, before a Southern District Magistrate, they were arraigned on federal corruption charges and now faced twenty-five years in federal prison. They were done.

As always, I did not participate in the arrests or searches or any other aspect of the postgame cleanup. Concurrently with BLUE SCORE, I was working cameo UC ops around the city, buy-busts and sometimes backing up another UC. It wouldn't do to have my photo taken in Mount Vernon during this public phase of an unrelated case.

Just two months later, in July, Astorino, Garcia, and Lauria all pled out and all went to jail. A couple of months after the convictions, Police Commissioner Isley, in recognition of his integrity and efforts to root out corruption in the MVPD, was fired.

8

SUNBLOCK

At 125th Street and Broadway, I stepped off the uptown number 1 train, walked down the metal stairs, found the old limo waiting at the intersection, and knocked on the window. *¿Estás esperando para Alejandro Perez?* The middle-aged Dominican driver nodded, and I hopped in. With his long sideburns, my man looked as though he had stepped out of a gritty seventies NYC crime film. With the noise of the elevated subway, the dirty snow on the run-down streets and the well-maintained ancient car, there was a sense of unreality to my movements and words. I felt as though I had stepped into a scene from *The French Connection*. I was dressed in full-Alex: three-quarter-length black leather coat, long ponytail and gelled hair, Gucci shirt, sufficient jewelry.

There's a pertinent story behind that leather coat, and that story begins with an ankle holster that was now falling apart, specifically, the one I used (when off duty) for my .40 caliber Glock semiautomatic pistol. And there's a story behind that pistol: Its large caliber yet relatively small size was an inadvertent by-product of federal anti-gun laws from the early nineties. The politicians had decreed that magazines available to non–law enforcement purchasers could hold no more than ten rounds—in the apparent belief that it would not occur to the ill-intentioned to carry additional magazines. The unintended consequence of the restriction was that the engineers at major weapons firms developed new technology, building pistols capable of carrying a magazine with ten very large caliber bullets in a frame half the size. On the street, when not using the fanny pack, I simply stuck this weapon in my waistband. (Bad guys don't use holsters. Cops use holsters.) Only when off duty—*strictly, totally* off duty—I housed the weapon in the ankle holster, for a simple reason: the ankle holster would be the equivalent of wearing a police cap. And due to its difficulty of access (unless sitting in a car), the holster required a lot of practice to draw quickly. Alex Perez would never use one on the street. Mostly, it was for warm-weather use in low-risk off-duty environments. Parties, dinner with friends, blind dates.

So the stitching on my relic of an off-duty holster was coming apart, and a few blocks down from the Ramada in New Rochelle was a cluttered, old-time shoe-repair shop. Inside, the seventyish stooped Italian cobbler was always hard at work. When Alex walked into a legitimate commercial establishment, the reaction was frequently thinly masked hostility, or apprehension, so I wasted no time explaining that I was an FBI agent from up the street, then presented my odd work request. (Was I breaking cover by revealing my real identity? Perhaps. It was a judgment call.) He smiled broadly, introduced himself as Pete Mazzei, reached under his worn leather apron and pulled out a huge revolver, something like the "hand cannon" made famous in *Pulp Fiction*. Robbery attempts had proved seriously unsuccessful in his store, Pete explained.

He solved my holster issue, then came up with a novel solution to another problem. He lined the left pocket of my mid-length black leather coat with extra-thick leather, converting it into a holster capable of carrying a midsize semiautomatic. Quick access to the Glock in midwinter, buried under layers of clothing, was impossible. This had been a pet peeve for years. Peeve now resolved. After that first meeting, from time to time, I would stop in to chat with Pete, a kindred spirit. Several years later, after my New Rochelle days were over, I received a call from his son, who had found my business card in the shop. Pete had died. At the reception after the funeral, I was stunned by his lovely home in upper Westchester County. His sons, his daughters—the children of this Old World immigrant—all had college degrees. An American success story. Maybe this sounds corny, but I always believed I was in the business of helping to protect and enhance this dream. The case I was working at the time, SUNBLOCK, perfectly illustrates how the American Dream can go awry.

In the old limo, decked out as Alex Perez, I was en route to my first-ever drug meet—heroin. I gave the driver the address for the Buccaneer II Diner on Astoria Boulevard in Queens, near LaGuardia Airport. Thirty minutes later, we pulled into the parking lot and I looked through the diner windows. There were four people in the diner, a frumpy couple by the door and the two guys I was expecting to find, and who were surely expecting me, description of the ponytail and the bling in hand, and they would have assumed some equivalent of the Glock somewhere on my person.

Richard was Chinese Malaysian, about five feet six inches, pudgy with a thick dark mustache. His companion, Chang, was younger, leaner, and clean cut, also Chinese Malaysian. Having conducted business with Italians, Hispanics, West Africans, Palestinians, and Wall Streeters (not an officially designated ethnic group, perhaps), I was used to making all kinds of small talk during meets and deals. I'm fluent in three languages, but Chinese was not one of them. But here we were, sitting in a booth, short on language. They didn't want to order anything more than coffee, so I ordered a cup as well. They were smoking Marlboros, and even though I hadn't smoked cigarettes since college nearly twenty years earlier, I accepted Richard's courteous offer when he held out the pack. And smoked it slowly, just to kill time. They started talking in Chinese—Mandarin or Cantonese (or something else, maybe Malaysian, I had no idea), and I was beginning to wonder where this was leading. Wondering, but not particularly worrying. On this day, safety wasn't really an issue. I wasn't there to buy any of their product, so they weren't expecting me to have a lot of cash. And if they got hinky about me for any reason, they could simply have gotten up and walked out the door. (On the other hand, Chuck Reed, the Bureau UC in Philadelphia, had been shot and killed at just such a meet. As was Everett Hatcher, a New York DEA UC who had been working a joint case with the Bu. No, I didn't like all the incomprehensible Chinese.)

After what seemed like a long time, the conversation switched to English and turned to practical matters: a "fish" (whatever that was . . .) of their high-grade heroin would cost me and my people "a dollar twenty" (*that*, I could figure out: $120,000). I nodded and said I would check with my people and beep Richard after receiving instructions.

Richard nodded to Chang, then at me. I put out the Marlboro. Chang stood up and, without hesitation, walked across the dining room and down a narrow stairway toward the men's room. This change of venue had been prepared, obviously. These guys were pros. They had done their homework. I therefore figured they must have at least one guy somewhere outside as a lookout, *counter*surveillance to my own surveillance, which was three blocks distant. Mark Calnan, my case agent on this new Group II, had judiciously placed the cars well out of sight for this critical first meet. The frumpy middle-aged couple eating lunch at a table by the door—they were my immediate safety net, both veteran agents.

Richard looked directly at me and gestured with his head for me to follow Chang. I did so, down the long, narrow, metal stairs. Now my transmitter would be broadcasting nothing but static. As Chang and I faced the urinals (the mini-Nagra in my customized crotch carrier pressing against my hand), he passed me what appeared to be an empty pack of Marlboros, which I slipped into my shirt's chest pocket. We returned to the booth upstairs, where my subjects said a cursory good-bye and left. I lingered for a few minutes and glimpsed a little tinfoil packet inside the Marlboro pack. I picked up the bill.

Once Mark sent the all-clear signal to my pager, I passed the cigarette pack to one of the surveillance agents who had pulled into the parking lot. In the limo, my driver, who had waited for me, realized something was up. As we talked on the drive back to the city, he was clear about being very much at ease driving for a narcotics dealer. In fact, he would be happy to chauffeur me on a regular basis. *In fact,* he was excited about an unexpected and desirable career opportunity. I did nothing to discourage him.

Inside the tinfoil was a sample of Richard's merchandise, which the lab confirmed to be the highest quality, 95-percent pure heroin. I had penetrated a serious hardcore organization with a product intended for major distributors only. SUNBLOCK, as the op had been christened, could be a big one. Very big. My biggest, as measured by a somewhat unusual standard: total years served by the targets in federal prison. And there could not have had a better case agent at the helm. Mark was truly a superior agent, mid-career with C-25, the Asian Drug Squad.

Traditional hound-dog persistent investigator that he was, Calnan had been working this investigation for over a year before bringing me in. The number-one target was a Chinese Malaysian drug lord named Bing Gong Yong, widely known in the industry as Gong. His first job after arriving here from Malaysia had been in the kitchen of a Chinese restaurant in Lower Manhattan, but he'd moved up fast. Within a few years, he was running a major heroin ring. Then Gong repaid the owner of the Chinese restaurant for his kindness by kidnapping his wife. When she died, Gong had continued to collect ransom payments. He was a nasty man. He was also an unusual target for the FBI: he was already serving a life sentence for the kidnapping and murder of his benefactor's wife, in the maximum security prison at Lewisburg, Pennsylvania. He was our target because he was still running his major drug ring from prison. Richard from the diner was his top man on the outside in New York.

The original information about Gong's organization had been developed by Mark from investigation of two of his largest clients, Papo Cancel and Cesar Vega. They ran a narcotics organization operating in New York and San Juan. Arrested and facing the balance of his remaining years in prison, Vega agreed to work for Mark Calnan as a confidential informant. When Calnan mentioned Papo Cancel to me, memories of past encounters flashed through my brain. Nearly ten years earlier in San Juan, Will Godoy and I had been assigned to babysit a federal material witness, Carmen Rojas. Will was my buddy, a man whose laid-back persona ran counter to all FBI stereotypes—he had once showed up at a predawn staging area prior to a raid and asked to borrow one of my revolvers. (Fifteen years later, he was promoted to be Legat Buenos Aires. He is my closest FBI friend.)

Carmen Rojas was the *only* witness who could tie Papo Cancel to the murder of a DEA informant whose torso had been found a few months earlier. It was dismembered, which served two purposes: hamper efforts at identification and, more important, send a message. In sharp contrast to the usual low-rent hotels where I was used to staying at for these babysitting jobs, Carmen was sequestered in a luxurious villa in a gated community near El Yunque, featuring Mediterranean-style stucco and red-gabled houses. No *rejas* (the security gates that adorn virtually every door and window in Puerto Rico) here, instead broad terraces facing the large shared pool, all washed by the sun and fresh mountain breezes.

Carmen Rojas was an excellent cook, and Anna, her fourteen-year-old daughter, being a teenager around grown-ups, kept to herself. Will and I felt like we were on vacation. Almost. Early one sunny afternoon, while lying in deck chairs on the veranda, digesting Carmen's particularly sumptuous version of the Spanish chicken dish *arroz con pollo*, accompanied by delicious Puerto Rican rice and beans, Will remarked that he hadn't seen Anna for a while. Carmen said she'd gone up to her room for a nap. Cautious, Will went to take a peek. The bedroom was empty. The villa was built on a hillside, so walking into and out of the second floor windows unblemished by *rejas* was as easy as walking out the front door.

A quick search did not find her.

Carmen, where could she have gone?

She's been missing her boyfriend, she probably ran away to see him.

Her boyfriend?

Chaco's son. Papos's his godfather.

Chaco was Papo Cancel's right hand. Will made a very embarrassed call to John Navarette, our supervisor. The squad would launch an intensive search for the girl, starting in the vicinity of Chaco's house, but meanwhile Will and I were to get Carmen in the car *immediately* and transport her to the Navy base at Roosevelt Roads, an hour's drive farther east of San Juan. These were the days of Scarface-type cartels, big-money operators who knew no limits—as the DEA informant learned—and Carmen was Papo's one-way ticket to the federal penitentiary. Before we could pack the BuCar, we heard the helicopter. It came in low and hovered over the central pool, as we crouched below the windowsills. Altogether, I had two revolvers and some extra rounds. Will had a shotgun and his five-shot snub-nose. If the helicopter carried three or four lunatics with MAC-10s, it would be a melancholy day indeed. The villas were all more or less identical, and the helicopter hovered over all of them, slowly moving from one to the other. After half an hour—the longest in my history, to that point—the chopper lifted high and departed. The cartel was vicious, but they weren't going to shoot up an entire gated community. Minutes later, Will and I were careening down the narrow access road, Carmen secreted under a blanket on the backseat, screeching right onto the two-lane *carretera* and the safety of a U.S. Navy base. An unrepentant Anna was scooped up by Navarette's agents a few hours later, in a surprise incursion onto Cancel's turf. A risky, but critical play: with Anna in enemy hands, Carmen's cooperation would be over and done.

And so Papo Cancel and, later, Cesar Vega, went to jail. Papo had nothing to gain by cooperating now in the heroin operation. The federal prosecutors were not about to cut a deal with a man who had dismembered a DEA agent. But that was okay, because Cesar Vega knew it all, too, and he developed a good rapport with Mark Calnan. Based on Vega's information, court authorization was obtained for wiretaps on the phones of Richard and other members of Gong's organization: Paul Kwok in Canada, Denise Wei, Kevin Mong. Through subpoenas to the Bureau of Prisons (the BOP in BuSpeak), Mark obtained recordings of Gong's calls. BOP seemed to allow inmates virtually unrestricted phone access, including the right to make collect calls to anywhere. Yes, these calls were recorded, *but they were not monitored*. Mark was stunned by the ease with which Gong (and, of course, the Gambinos, Gottis, various Russians, and others) could run their organized crime organizations from within federal prison walls. It was, still is, a bizarre policy.

Denise Wei served as Gong's principal point of contact with the outside world. He would call her virtually every evening and ask her to patch the call through to one of his subordinates, or to a new client—and thus a new subject for Mark Calnan. Then they would use a very sophisticated code to deceive potential prying ears. Richard would ask Gong how much he should charge the *hēi rén* (black guy) for a fish. At least a dollar ten or a dollar twenty. What about if he wants half a fish? Then sixty-five cents. After about five minutes of this, Mark had concluded that a "fish" was a unit of heroin, which was being offered at $110,000 to $120,000. Unlike cocaine, which was typically sold in "keys," or kilos, heroin was measured in "units," consisting of 700 grams (24 ounces).

After a few months, Mark had Gong's entire network identified: Richard (Kau Hung, technically, but I will stick with Richard) and the Karaoke Club in New York's Chinatown, where he lived and worked.

Denise Wei and her husband, Kevin Mong, a top Gong lieutenant, were located at their Country Club Road home in suburban Bedminster, New Jersey. Their nearby business, The Golden Dragon restaurant, providing a legit front operation. The Kao Yang restaurant in Somerville, New Jersey, operated by Vivian Tsai, Gong's sister, and base of operations for trusted Gong lieutenant, Nanjing Fang, rounded out the nucleus of the heroin smuggling organization. Mark Calnan had it all. His squadmates also started conducting physical surveillances based on information obtained from the calls. Once the date and time and weight and cost had been overheard, the agents would set up on the Karaoke Club and cover the transaction. But as strong as the case was becoming, there was one more investigative technique that Calnan wanted to use. To make the case *airtight,* he needed a UC. Of course.

I've mentioned that the Janus backstopping units also serve as informal clearinghouses for UC assignments. Mark called the New York crew, looking for an experienced sleuth capable of passing for a high-level operator in a Hispanic cocaine trafficking organization, capable of penetrating a major heroin ring. Janus New York had been providing operational support to my UC ops for years. One of the veterans recommended alias Alex Perez, a highly respected, mid-career agent based in New Rochelle, with five years' experience as a full-time undercover. Mark called me, we met, and he laid out the situation. There was also an international angle here, as there is with most drug rings: Canada, prominently, then perhaps Malaysia, from where the drugs were exported. With the prospect of conducting UC ops internationally, not only in Canada, but also in the Far East, I, Marc Ruskin, was excited that Alex Perez might be moving up a level in the world of covert activities. I had never worked a drug case as a UC, but I had developed a conceit that the undercover operation that Marc Ruskin would not succeed in had not yet been conceived, and it never would be. Somewhat obsessively (in retrospect, perhaps somewhat irrationally), I wanted to see how far I could push the envelope. SUNBLOCK would be my answer. This was a big deal for me. On the spot, Mark offered me the assignment. On the spot, I accepted. This was late summer, 1994. BLUE SCORE had recently been brought to a successful conclusion. Pleased with the results of the high-profile police corruption case, Craig Dotlo didn't squawk when I committed myself to this job for another squad.

After reviewing, in painstaking detail, the results of the investigation to date, Mark and I spent a couple of weeks developing a scenario wherein I was still alias Alex Perez, still mysteriously linked to Metro-Dade. Only now I was also the nephew and trusted number two of a convict named Gil Sandoval. Gil was not my uncle, of course, but he really *was* the deposed leader of a Mexican cocaine cartel in the eighties, arrested and convicted in Texas. He was serving "natural life" (that is, without hope of parole) in Lewisburg. He was going to die in jail, period, and he knew it. His was the first life-without-parole sentence ever obtained by the U.S. Attorney's office in El Paso, and they were proud of the fact. They had exploited the sentence for maximum press coverage and had a vested interest, both institutional and political, in seeing to it that the sentence remain unaltered. The U.S. Attorney's office had made it clear that there was only one way that Gil would leave the custody of the Bureau of Prisons—in a cheap pine box. A clearly hopeless situation for Gil. Or was it?

Gil saw another option. Very remote, but . . . it was an option. As the deposed leader of a Mexican cartel, he was, almost by definition of his former status, a bright and entrepreneurial man. In his early forties, he had risen from true poverty to become the CEO of a multimillion-dollar global enterprise. And just as with the Fortune 500, it takes a certain level of intelligence and unique personality traits to achieve the position of number one. In Lewisburg, Gil determined that he could and would make himself useful, very useful, to any government agency that realized what a gold mine he could be. Having developed a level of professional caution necessary to his survival, he carefully developed a relationship with his prison counselor. Once assured that this counselor was trustworthy and wouldn't sell him out to fellow inmates, Gil asked to be put in touch with the DEA—one of his infrequent mistakes, as he would soon learn.

Two DEA special agents arrived at Lewisburg to interview and evaluate Gil's value as a confidential informant. Gil offered to work with them on a long-term basis, and as proof of his goodwill he provided invaluable evidence for what would be a major case. For several years, Gil's organization had been smuggling huge quantities of cocaine from Colombia into Mexico, and then across the border near Juarez into the El Paso region of Far West Texas. He made generous payments to various government officials in order to operate without significant government interference. He understood that occasional, minor losses had to be tolerated so the face-saving officials could boast about their achievements and demonstrate how effective they were in carrying out their duties. Gil had maintained meticulous records of these payments, records that were still in the possession of his former subordinates.

Most important among the public officials on Gil's payroll was the prize he offered the DEA: that very agency's Assistant Regional Director for Northern Mexico. Gil could provide the goods for an airtight public corruption investigation and prosecution. He had ongoing contact with fellow cocaine cowboys who were still making payoffs to this corrupt upper-management official. He could arrange for his friends to initiate incriminating conversations, to be recorded with phone intercepts. He would even notify investigators when payoffs were scheduled. They could get the indisputable evidence on video.

It was a great pitch. Made to the wrong team.

The DEA agents listened attentively. When they returned to their office, they wrote up their report. Gil Sandoval was an obvious fabricator. Desperate as a result of his hopeless "natural life" status, he had provided the interviewing agents with clearly fallacious, wildly concocted, unsubstantiated, anecdotal accounts, many of which were self-contradictory. They closed his file with the DEA and recommended that no future law enforcement agency have contact with him. They also advised the Bureau of Prisons of their conclusions, suggesting he not be allowed future contacts with other government agencies. They did their best to bury Gil Sandoval.

However, Gil had done well in his rapport building with his counselor. After striking out with the DEA—annoyed with himself for his naïveté, he should have known better—he persevered and his counselor reached out to the El Paso office of the FBI. In that office, Rick Getty got the ticket to assess Gil and recruit him, if he had real potential. Rick did his homework. He went through the trial transcripts, the investigative

reports that had led to Gil's conviction, and read the report of the two
DEA agents. Old-timer that he was, he felt intuitively that something was
off. It didn't ring true. Those DEA investigators' conclusions were not
consistent with *every other* document concerning Gil. And Rick shared
the historically mutual distrust between the FBI and the DEA. That distrust is—has to be—denied by management, but it has always existed
and still does.

Rick Getty decided that he would fly up to Lewisburg and see Gil for
himself. The result was one of the great decisions in his career, and I'm
sure there were many. Gil Sandoval became a crucial informant for the
FBI. By having developed a formal relationship with the Bureau, Gil had
overcome a major hurdle. His master plan to *earn* his way out of that
"natural life" sentence was now under way, no longer the impossible
fantasy of a hopeless inmate in whose case they had thrown away the
key. With quiet perseverance he set about developing relationships, cap-
italizing on his pre-conviction status as a cartel boss to establish himself
as a major player with his counterparts behind the big bars in Lewisburg. He soon identified Bing Gong Yong as an ideal target: a global-level
heroin trafficker, a big boss moving large quantities of the number-one
evil drug with a large network of lieutenants and soldiers. Just what the
Bureau would be looking for. By the close of Rick Getty's initial meeting
with Gil Sandoval, they had come to a meeting of the minds. Rick would
"open" Gil as a CI, a confidential informant. Neither he nor anyone else
in the Bureau could make any promises to Gil about an eventual benefi-
cial impact on his tenure in prison. All would depend on the quality and
quantity of cases Gil helped develop. Understood. The paperwork was
completed, which would provide the mechanism for documenting and
keeping track of Gil's contributions, substituting a code name for his
true name, which would be kept secret.

As Gil provided profiles of likely candidates for targeting, Rick would
run the names through the Bureau databases. With Gong's name . . .
Bingo. Rick called Mark Calnan. *I have someone I think you'll want to
meet. If he can help with your investigation of Gong, he's all yours—but
when it's over, we want him back!* In large part, the success of the whole
SUNBLOCK op came to hinge on Gil's information concerning his fellow
inmate at Lewisburg, the still-wheeling-and-dealing drug lord Bing

Gong Yong (and a junkie himself, it turned out, which is unusual for most high-level kingpins, most of whom know better).

Those scenes in *Goodfellas* with the mobsters behind bars but still living large, dining on prime steak, fresh lobster, red *and* white wine were not necessarily an exaggeration. Neither Gong nor Gil lived like that, but both could retain plenty of power, even in the outside world, if they wanted it. Gong did, Gil didn't. He had retired—a change of status he carefully concealed. One might think *all* of the incarcerated kingpins would call it a day, but often they don't. Gil might even be the exception. When the system provides these moguls with the opportunity and the tools, why not keep the operation going? Even when serving a "natural life" sentence, running the gang outside was something to do inside, and there would be no meaningful consequences if caught, at least in terms of extra time added to a sentence. Administrative Segregation (today's more palatable label for "solitary") is a possibility, as we will shortly see. Other kingpins, those not serving life, *could* hope to get out someday, but the elements in their personalities that had motivated them to take the risks to become bosses in the first place were still at work. Some of these guys even risked losing their shot at parole in order to stay in the game from prison.

And other factors were in play. The bosses in prison, as well as their soldiers, were part of tightly knit groups that were more than simply business organizations. Much more. The Mexican and Colombian cartels, the Jamaican posses, the Russian bratvas, La Cosa Nostra: they are extended families, filling many social and cultural roles, providing the members with a system of rules to live (and die) by, with a structure that gives meaning to their lives, and a hierarchy within which they live. Moving in and out of prison is, for them, a fact of life. Replacing a social club with a prison cell need not affect the individual's role in the organization. However, it will certainly be a factor in individual power plays. A rival's incarceration may provide an opportunity for a coup. A jailed boss has good cause to maintain a tight grip on his organization. Particularly, as is often the case, if he has family members on the outside whom he wants to protect and promote.

Gong fell into this category. Pushing fifty, five or so years in prison under his belt, eligible for parole on his life sentence in another fifteen, he was still going strong. He had trusted lieutenants scattered through-out the Northeast, not the least of them his younger brothers Bing Nam Yong and Bing Chun Yong. And now Gil Sandoval offered to help us—the FBI, the federal government, the American people—nail Gong one more time, and for good.

As with all my undercover roles, once I had an idea who the players were, I set about developing the role, coming up with a scenario that would fit the case, would be believable to the targets, and would pro-vide a pathway toward gaining their confidence. In SUNBLOCK, work-ing with Mark Calnan, a street-smart case agent I immediately liked and respected, that creative process became a collaborative one. The more time I could spend with an informant, the better. Many a case agent over the years would tell me, "You can meet and talk with him [the infor-mant] before the meet." A recipe for disaster. The more time I could spend with the informant, the more bulletproof the "vouch." The more I knew about him (usually a him, but sometimes her), the more credible the story I could invent about how we knew each other, and for how long. And the greater the time between developing the made-up relation-ship and meeting the subjects, the more opportunities the informant would have to talk about Alex (or Sal or Daniel, whatever alias I was us-ing) to my future new associates. It bears repeating: most informants want to *minimize* the strength of their fictitious relationship, in order to allow for future plausible deniability. *How could I know he was a cop? I just met him a few times at a club in South Beach.* They would not like it, they would try to balk, when I instructed them to tell their friends *Alex lives with my sister in Miami. In fact, I'm the godfather to one of their kids.*

For Gil, none of this was going to be an issue. He was playing for the highest stakes—his entire future life—and he had every motivation to assure that Alex would have the total trust of Gong and Co. He under-stood what was necessary to maximize the likelihood of success. And he understood the risks. In the penitentiary, he would have nowhere to hide. Mark told Gil to put his nephew Alex Perez on his list of family members who were approved for personal visits. We planned to drive down to Lewisburg on a Thursday and stay overnight. It was June 1994. This would give Mark and I time to get to know each other better, and I would have a full day with Gil. Nor would the prison officials or anyone else with the Bureau of Prisons know who I really was. As far as all of them were concerned, I was Gil's visiting nephew Alex. There was no reason in the world to risk a corrupt corrections officer tipping off whatever criminals had them on the payroll.

Cutting the BOP out of this loop had been a dicey decision. There was no rulebook to follow, it came down to a judgment call by Mark and myself, with a green light from the squad supervisor, Geoff Doyle. If anything were to go bad for me inside the prison—an altercation with an inmate hostile to Gil, or worse, being flaked by a corrections officer with a beef against Gil—there would have been some tap dancing by the Bureau attorneys. And I would have been sitting in custody somewhere, waiting for it to play out.

After signing in with Alex's driver's license as ID, I was led through numerous locked impenetrable portals before entering a huge, brightly lit room with very a high ceiling. Like a combination gym/dining hall, it had rows of picnic tables and benches bolted to the floor, vending machines along a wall, and a high podium at one end, not unlike a judge's bench, from which a corrections officer presided. The COs (corrections officers) were, to my surprise, friendly and courteous (unlike in some state prisons and local jails, I can tell you that; different hiring standards, different cultures). For the benefit of Gil's fellow residents, I was in "full Alex"—the gel, the gold—and had expected, at the very least, long unexplained waits and a certain brusqueness, or grudging responses from the prison personnel. From the way they behaved, I could have been visiting a Courtyard by Marriott.

Inside the visiting room, I took a seat at one of the picnic tables and waited for Gil to be escorted through the door. *Ka-chunk.* The tumblers of the big locks fell into place, the door on the far side of the room swung open, and in walked a short, solid, muscular man decked out in "inmate red." Clearly Hispanic, with chiseled features, broad cheekbones, jet-black hair, and piercing eyes, Gil Sandoval would have been credible as a Mayan ruler or a governor of Sonora. Impressive guy, a leader of men. I instantly agreed with Mark Calnan's assessment, conveyed on our drive to Lewisburg: Gil was smarter than most SACs he had run across. I stood up. From across the room Gil caught my eye, we both smiled broadly as we walked forward, then embraced as would be expected of the close relatives we were supposed to be. All performance at first, but this turned out to be the beginning of a genuine friendship.

Professional that he was, Gil had previously told Gong very little about this nephew who was coming to visit, thus giving the nephew and his uncle time to craft and backstop a convincing and thorough legend. Too often, overeager informants have weaved a complex story about Alex, or Sal, or Eduardo, thereby saddling me with the unnecessary complications and heightened risks of trying to fit into an unlikely scenario. Recall the overly zealous informant Oscar in RUN-DMV, who spontaneously introduced me to the subject (Nair, with the dogs, in Newark) as a Colombian cocaine dealer, because Oscar thought this would sound impressive. His unsolicited contribution could have gotten me killed.

After a good six hours (Gil was fluent in English, though we tended to speak to each other in Spanish), I left his company in that cavernous bullpen in Lewisburg totally comfortable that we could both converse persuasively about each other and about our family, to the limited extent that the subject would come up in dialogue with Gong— and future subjects. The FBI hoped that Gong would be just the first of several targets fingered by Gil. Much of what I had learned about Gil would never be revealed, not to any subjects, and certainly not now, on the printed page. Details concerning his family and personal life, singular in nature and tending to identify him and his family were important for rapport building, but otherwise could only lead to harm. More important, and more likely to come up in our dealings with Gong and his henchmen, were the details Gil and I created that day in Lewisburg concerning the inmate's ongoing cocaine business, and my role in it. We decided on Miami as our base of operations, as I could not converse knowledgeably about El Paso. Occasionally, over the following year and a half, Gil or I would have to invent new details on the spot, in the course of a conversation or meeting with Gong or one of his people. As soon as possible, we would talk on the phone and update each other about the latest backstopping detail. Our stories were always consistent. They had to be. Of course, Gong didn't speak Spanish and Gil didn't speak Chinese, which left English—specifically, Gong's broken English, which didn't allow for much in the way of fine detail. Still, Gil would be able to drop the occasional agreed-upon casual remark about his nephew Alex, adding texture and credibility to our relationship. *That Alex, he stopped in El Paso last week, just to look in on my mom and make sure my brother is behaving himself . . . without him . . .*

SUNBLOCK was a big case for me, and it was a pretty big deal for the FBI: what I call a full-court press. There are six elements at the disposal of the Bureau or any other relatively well-heeled agency embarking on a major criminal investigation: subpoenas, court-approved interceptions of various sorts (mail, wiretapping, and electronic communication intercepts), physical surveillance, interviews, informants, and undercover work. (Informants and UC agents perform pretty much the same function, but the UC is much more reliable and has much greater credibility, in court and out. The downside is the greater risk to the UC agent.) The case agent who is developing a strategy for a new investigation must decide what mix of these procedures are appropriate for the particular type of subjects and the violation being investigated. Interviews may be just the ticket in a mortgage-fraud investigation but are not likely to result in much actionable information when trying to indict John Gotti and his soldiers. Available personnel and financial resources are a factor to be weighed: sending out subpoenas to a bank and going out with another agent to interview victims of a pyramid scheme are at one end of the cost-of-resources continuum (the lower end), while obtaining court orders and wiring someone's home and social club, and setting up a full-time surveillance team are at the expensive end. Putting together and maintaining an operation such as SUNBLOCK, one that employs five of these elements (no interviews here) over many months or, often enough, several years is an expensive, complex, labor-intensive process. But for these investigations, there's no other way.

As Alex Perez, I would work the Gong cartel undercover in the field, beginning with his man Richard. Both Gil and I would work Gong himself, in Lewisburg prison. Language issues notwithstanding—no Chinese for Gil, no Spanish for Gong, just his borderline indecipherable English—Gil had immediate success with the Chinese Malaysian drug kingpin. Sniffing the benefits of a collaboration with Gil Sandoval's organization, Gong was all enthusiasm. The fact that he soon authorized Richard to give me a sample at our first meet, the one in the diner near LaGuardia, spoke to Gil's credibility. That kind of trust usually takes time to develop, definitely in the heroin world. It would not be unusual to have several preliminary meets before the complimentary package of tinfoil changes hands.

Gil was respected as the boss of a large cartel, but Gong was still *Gong*. On the organizational chart (not that we actually had one, pinned to the wall, like on the TV shows) they were up at the top, side by side. Gil's cocaine operations, now based in Miami—El Paso had become too hot—were going strong. After reflection and extended discussions of the practical aspects and feasibility with his nephew during the visit at the prison, he had decided to accept Gong's proposition. We, the Mexicans, would expand into the heroin business, using our existing infrastructure. Gong and his subordinates, the Chinese, would likewise be expanding into the cocaine business. They would sell us heroin, we would sell them cocaine. (None of the conversations between Gil and Gong could be recorded, of course. Their content would be relayed to me by Gil and carefully documented. Later on, when possible, I would recapture them on my cassette recorder, in my phone calls with Gong: *My uncle tells me . . .*)

Gil's reading of Gong (always accurate, it turned out) was that he had no intention of buying cocaine. Gong was only looking for new volume customers for his heroin. The offer to purchase our cocaine was simply to sweeten the deal, make it more enticing for Gil. Later, I would make passing comments to Richard and Chang about selling them coke, simply to maintain a pretense of interest. To which they would reply curtly. *We'll talk about it.* As Gil's nephew, Alex might have some interest in having the Chinese as customers, but as FBI agents, Mark Calnan and I would never be in position to sell cocaine, not unless it was a buy-bust in which it was guaranteed that the drugs would never leave our possession. Not the scenario here. Cocaine was just something to talk about.

Within a month of our meeting in Lewisburg, I gave Gil the green light to pass alias Alex's beeper number to Gong, while requesting a contact number for Alex to use with Gong's people. After doing a little research on the mechanics of call forwarding, I devised a very useful ruse to mask my true location. Contacting the Florida telephone company as Alex, I obtained a local number, with all the optional bells and whistles. Then, I set up the call forwarding so that when I placed a call, on the recipient's caller ID would be displayed a number with my 305 South Florida area code. Two weeks after Gong had been given my beeper number, late one evening when I was at the office in New Rochelle, my new SUNBLOCK 800 number beeper went off. I checked the list of known numbers Mark had given me. In the preliminary stages of the case, methodically, painstakingly, he had developed much intel regarding Gong's organization, their names, addresses, phone numbers. This beep was from the Karaoke Club operated by Richard, believed by Mark to be one of Gong's chief lieutenants. Gil had already passed me his name. From the case agent's perspective, this was a major step forward. Corroboration of the intel already developed, and more important: First Contact.

From the New Rochelle Hello Phone, I returned the call.

"Hello . . . is this Alex?" The man on the other end of the line had a heavy Asian accent. "I'm calling for my brother in Lewisburg."

This was Richard. I said I was planning to be in New York in two weeks and would give him a call a few days before, then beep him to set up an initial meet—the one at the diner at the end of which he slipped me the small sample of his product. After receiving that sample and confirming its 95-percent purity, I filled in Uncle Gil on the meeting. He was going to tell Gong that both of us were very pleased with the quality of the sample, that he had instructed me to make a small buy on my next swing through New York. Just five ounces. A test run, just to see how things went. Then we would move up to the serious level. After some de rigueur haggling, we set the price at $4,300 an ounce, $21,000 altogether. With heroin on the street having a purity no higher than 10 percent, the 90-percent product we would be purchasing could be cut and produce a very respectable profit margin. It's important to note that, operationally, Mark did not have an unlimited budget for SUNBLOCK evidence purchases. He had asked me to stretch the allocated budget as far as I could without compromising my credibility. I was to cast a wide net, meeting Richard's associates in New York and his counterparts in other cities, while keeping costs under control. The initial proposal had been approved with a six-month budget of nearly $200,000, of which 75 percent was allocated for purchasing evidence, i.e., buying wholesale heroin. An impressive sum on paper, perhaps, and a fair amount of money for the Bureau to let "walk," but at the level we were dealing with, it could be burned through rapidly if care was not applied. Ultimately, Mark would have to request budget enhancements, which always involved internal haggling with the Bureau bean counters. (Gil and I weren't the only ones who had to haggle.) Mark got more money. I don't remember how much. Knowing the Bu, I'm guessing an additional fifty thousand. Gil's professional caution with regard to the heroin purchases, as exhibited to Gong by making initially modest buys, served multiple purposes. In the first place, Gong would expect it, and in the mirror world of covert operations, it is often the case that there are several layers of "reality," where behavior is tailored to the perceptions of the targets while actually serving the practical exigencies of the investigators and prosecutors.

Within a short couple of weeks after the agreement about quantity and price for my first modest purchase from Richard, the phone rang one night at the New Rochelle office on my 305 area-code number. I wasn't expecting this call. Gil hadn't advised me it was coming because he didn't know, either.

"Alex?" It was a high-pitched foreign voice. "This Sonny from Lewisburg. You know me?"

"I know you." It was Gong, and this was to be the first in a bizarre series of conversations that would stretch through the following year.

"So you want to open Chinese restaurants? You want . . ." The rest of the sentence was unintelligible. Now I had to ad-lib. Gil and I had not known what code Gong would be using. "Fish" was all I knew about. Almost half of what the man said was so garbled and accented as to be beyond comprehension, but not wanting to piss him off, I responded to the tone of his utterances with a concurring *huh huh* or *ah ah* or *yeah yeah* or whatever utterance seemed to keep the conversation moving.

"Sure. My brother in Lewisburg. He owns many Mexican restaurants. He wants me to open Chinese restaurants."

"How many menus you want?"

"Well, that depends. It depends on how much the menus cost." I had no idea what quantities he was talking about. Is a menu a unit? Maybe an ounce?

"You can have menu for four and half dollar." Yes, a menu must refer to an ounce. (This code may seem kind of silly and definitely not something that would fool anyone listening in. However, the transcripts were indeed full of such absurd transparent attempts at concealing the true subject matter.) "My brother wants me to buy four menus. It's the same dishes as last time, right? The same food as I had at your brother's restaurant in New York?"

"[gibberish] . . . same food . . . [more gibberish] . . . you buy four and half menus, okay?"

What the hell? So much for the code. I came to believe that its use was simply pro forma, obligatory for any self-respecting drug dealer. Or perhaps, absorbed by the negotiations and the importance of getting the details straight, the price and the volume, these targets mental focus shifted, drifted from the underlying purpose of using codes in the first place. Could it be a product of their poor English? That they didn't realize just how tortured the conversations appeared? Unlikely. I've seen equally twisted use of code words from drug dealers born here in the United States.

And why was this boss of bosses calling me directly? Gil for his part, never called Richard or Kevin Mong. The three of us—Gil, Mark, and I—surmised that as a micromanager and a junkie still fixing in federal prison, and with a seriously twisted mind, Gong required direct communication with not only the buyer he knew in Lewisburg, but the buyer in the field. And we had no reason to discourage the calls. They could only strengthen the case against the man. I had once seen an arrest photo of Gong, glaring and scrawny, but I could not erase from my mind the mental image of Fu Manchu, only in prison garb. (A stereotype, admittedly.) Even at the end of a phone line, I found Gong menacing, and I had dealt with more than a few menacing types. I could only imagine the effect of Gong's frequent implicit threats on his subordinates.

After each call with Gong, except in an emergency, I would wait for the call from Gil, who would have learned from Gong himself about the call in short order, and he and I would work from the notes I had scribbled. It could take us an hour or more to figure out the ten-minute conversation. Seriously. But Gil and I had to do it, because as my uncle and boss, he had to know everything that was going on. How else could we plan our next moves—when to make a buy, what quantity, what price, who should conduct the final negotiation, him with Gong in Lewisburg or me on the outside with Richard? As Alex's uncle and boss, Gil could always approach Gong and, visibly annoyed—*my nephew sometimes forgets his place*—overrule my decisions, providing me a useful safety valve.

I ended up having umpteen phone calls with Gong, each quite a chore, due to his tortured English, and we were using a code on top of that. It was a little easier for Gil, sitting there with Gong in the big dining hall. Inside the prison walls there was no fear of electronic eavesdropping, thus no need to speak in code.

In his conversations with Gong, it had to be clear that Gil was firmly in control. And Mark Calnan and the prosecutors certainly needed to be aware of the substance of the conversations. Not least in importance, yours truly very much wanted to know what, if anything, I had agreed to. So Gil and I persevered, but sometimes we never did figure out what Gong was talking about. His reference to "starting a union" stands out in my memory.

"A union?" I repeated. "You mean for the people who work for me?" That would be a first in the long history of drug dealing.

"A UNION!" Now he was loud, angry, and, of course, garbled. Maybe he needed a fix.

"You want to start a union?"

"Right, right, hey Sonny, it's not up to me. I just do what I'm told. I got to talk to my brother."

My "brother" (Uncle Gil) had no idea what this union might be, and he couldn't ask Gong outright without appearing unprofessional. Gil's advice was to wait and see if unions came up again. They didn't. Gong dropped the new code word, whatever it meant, and we stuck to our menus.

After receiving and approving the first little sample inside the tinfoil in the pack of Marlboros, I made two small purchases of heroin from Richard's associate Chang at one of the hotels near LaGuardia airport. My latest BuCar, procured under the auspices of another op (juggling multiple UC cases at the same time was old hat by now), was a late-model beige Acura. Great car, but of course I wouldn't be driving it to a meet with Chang or Richard or anyone else in SUNBLOCK. I *might* drive the Acura to the general vicinity, then get to the meet some other way (probably a cab). For that first get-together in the diner I had hired the old limo. I could have come up with a plausible explanation for having a car in New York, but it wasn't a part of the scenario.

The basic set-up: Richard would call me at the 305 number in Florida, I'd fly into LaGuardia (so he believed), maybe just laying over for a few hours on my way to another meet equally important as this one, maybe more important. I'd then page Richard from whatever hotel I ended up in. Mark Calnan and I would have booked adjoining rooms the previous day, one paid for with one of Alex's credit cards, one with an AFID credit card Mark maintained for just such instances. By the time I beeped Richard, all of the technical surveillance equipment complete with video, had been set up and tested. He understood that I wouldn't be telling him which hotel in advance. As a professional, buying from people I had no track record with, I would not want to provide him with the opportunity to arrange for a welcoming committee. And who knows who might be listening in on my calls, or on his. So I waited until the last minute to reveal my hotel. Basic drug-dealer tradecraft.

With everyone still happy, a larger purchase was set up. Beforehand, I met up with Mark in the parking lot at LaGuardia, as usual. He and his squad had already briefed at a staging area a healthy distance from the airport. Squad supervisor Geoff Doyle was with him, an indication that this was no ordinary meet. (Geoff always reminded me of the lieutenant in *Miami Vice* played by craggy Edward James Olmos.) Supervisors rarely leave the office, their administrative duties being so onerous as to discourage direct involvement in operational activities. They only turn up if there is a high possibility that events can quickly turn bad, very bad, in which case upper management would be asking, in the post-critical event review, why there had been no on-site commander for potential "critical incident" management. Very reassuring. Adding to my growing feeling of unease, Geoff told me the entire Task Force was present, FBI agents, specially selected NYPD officers, around twenty-five total. I would have been better off with three. Truly, I would have felt less stressed if it had been just Mark and a couple of guys in a minivan. But that's just not the way it works with significant drug buys—not even then, much less now. Now there might be the same number of guys and gals on the scene, but a lot more paperwork, and several additional layers of approval.

Inside his BuCar, Calnan handed me the cash, 1,050 twenty-dollar bills, $21,000. I had brought along a large manila envelope for the cash, which would sit in my portfolio next to another manila envelope—the one with the Nagra. Richard would have no interest in the second envelope. He knew it was none of his business. In the first two purchases, his sidekick Chang had carried a men's leather handbag. To all appearances, I never paid note, and I certainly did not inquire as to its contents. It was none of my business. Even if it was ideally suited for carrying a .38 caliber five-shot revolver . . .

I left the Acura in the lot, walked over to the terminal, and grabbed a cab to the Courtyard, where my room had two double beds to the left, and a round table straight back by the sliding-glass doors that gave way to the balcony, with its cheery, unobstructed panoramic view of the parking lot and Grand Central Parkway beyond. I placed my portfolio on the table and removed the not-yet-activated Nagra, which was, on this occasion, purely for backup and to record any conversations that might take place outside the room, which had been carefully wired for video and audio. (Under these "set piece" circumstances, there was no need for the mini-Nagra secreted on my person.)

Using the touch-tone phone on the night table, I paged Richard and entered the hotel phone number followed by the hotel room. I knocked on the locked dividing door to the next room, which was opened by a smiling, young lanky police investigator wearing a Yankees T-shirt. He was excited to have a key role so close to the center of the action in a big drug deal. Fine, I didn't care. He was accompanied by a C-25 agent adept at technical equipment, Jeff Lum. Jeff would go on to become the supervisor of SO-7, the NYC metro area's premier tech squad (and would help me out in a Genovese Crime Family Group I, a decade later). I surveyed their room. It was littered with open Pelikan equipment cases, a tripod with parabolic antenna, monitor, recording equipment. On the bed were a shotgun and MP5 submachine gun.

Back in my room, I turned on the TV and sat on a bed, leaning against the headboard to wait for Richard's call. Twenty minutes went by, no call. Ten more minutes and I called Mark's cell phone. He agreed that I should page Richard a second time. I did. More TV, as I reviewed the possible scenarios that could be playing out, and how best to play them in turn. How long would *Alex Perez* wait? How long would *Gil Sandoval's nephew* wait? Those were the questions, not how long Marc Ruskin aka Alex Perez would wait. After a certain indefinable point, the scale would tip and further waiting would appear odd, would set off mental alarms for Richard.

Mark was rotating the surveillance so that there would not be anyone in the lobby area long enough to appear unnatural. An agent would descend from the elevator, look at his watch, and take as seat and "wait" for a companion. Ten minutes later, a male-female agent couple sitting on lounge chairs would get up and walk into the bar for a cocktail. On my next call to his cell, Mark said that an unknown Chinese man had been observed walking through the lobby. He was now gone. A third page to Richard—this would be the last one—went unanswered. Then, Mark and I decided on a gamble.

Long before, Gong had given Gil the number to Denise Wei's hard line at her New Jersey home, *but* with specific instructions that he *not* pass it on to Alex. Mark was worried that calling Denise would piss off Gong and throw a wrench into their evolving relationship. I thought it through. Gil was my uncle and cartel boss. Would he pay any attention to Gong's restriction? Could he care less? No. Of course not. So, from the hotel phone, I placed the call to Denise Wei. She had been patching through calls from Gong to my Hello Phone, and would know that I was a business associate. But I had never talked with her directly. A female with a heavy Asian accent answered. I told her I had a message for Richard. She didn't know any Richard. I said that it didn't matter, just listen. *My brother is a very good friend of Richard's brother. I'm waiting for Richard. If I don't hear from him in twenty minutes, I will be leaving. My brother will be very angry. Richard's brother will be very angry. Do you understand?*

Yes, she understood. Nevertheless, half an hour later, Mark called. It was over, he was breaking off the surveillance. I should check out and take a cab back to my car. Fine, but just one thing. I asked Mark to tell the various squad and Task Force members to *stay put* until I was out of the area. This was one of my cardinal rules: surveillance doesn't leave until Ruskin leaves. I still had bad memories of my drive into Harlem with 8-Ball, Santiago Kuris's henchman, after Vicki and Dave had departed the scene back in the Bronx during RUN-DMV. And years before, UC Roger Gomez had ended up staring down the barrel of a gun after his backup had made a premature departure over a drug deal that likewise appeared to be a non-occurrence.

Not possible, responded Mark, their antsy feet were already hovering over the accelerators. He had already been dealing with much griping about the perceived waste of their time. I was adamant. They agreed to stay put. At the front desk, I turned in my key card, crossed the lobby, and was almost through the door when my pager beeped. A 917 number. Richard's cell. I called him back from a pay phone. Very sorry, he was running late and would be there in five minutes. Angrily, I complained that I would now have to recheck into the hotel. Which he no doubt knew. Using the same degree of caution as myself, he must have had a confederate running countersurveillance. Had I been approached in the lobby by white guys in baseball caps after the operation was "over," maybe with handi-talkies in the back pockets of their FBI standard issue cargo pants—it would have been a grim day for Marc indeed. And then for Gil back in prison.

Back in my room, I quickly called Mark, told him the buy was a go. All hands on deck! I draped my three-quarter-length black leather coat over a seat by the table with the views. In the left "holster" pocket was my Glock .40 caliber pistol. My Guardian Leather portfolio, with its bulletproof panel was propped against a leg of the table. Behind the hidden Velcro seam was my Bureau-issued Smith & Wesson 10mm cannon. An awesome weapon. Now it was time to activate the Nagra, place it in its pinpricked manila envelope, seal it with masking tape, and return it to the portfolio. Alongside the cash. The guys in the next room were hustling to reassemble their equipment. I leaned back and breathed deeply. Show-time.

A knock on the door. Richard and Chang walked in. And a third man, early twenties, a Bruce Lee clone. Gong's organization used a Chinatown street gang, the Grand Street Dragons, for enforcement and security. This must have been a Dragon. Visions of an invisible flying sidekick to my head whipped through my mind as they entered the room. Richard sat across from me at the table, as I had anticipated in arranging the chairs. Chang to his right, on the foot of the bed. And Bruce Lee on the first bed, near the door, and outside my field of vision, of course.

After the obligatory cigarette and exchange of polite inquiries regarding our respective inmate bosses, Richard nodded to Chang, who removed a paper bag from an old-style zipper-top airline travel bag. Without comment, Richard took it and placed it on the table as I slowly— while closely observed by Bruce—removed the manila envelope from my portfolio and slid it across the table toward Richard. I opened the bag. Inside was what looked like a small brick wrapped in aluminum foil. I folded the bag closed and placed it in the portfolio. Out of professional courtesy, as a sign of regard for Gong, I did not take any steps to weigh the product or examine it. Likewise, and for the same reason—a demonstration of respect for Gil—Richard simply picked up the envelope without opening it and passed it back to Chang, who placed it in his Pan Am bag and zipped it shut.

"My uncle will be pleased. He appreciates working with serious businessmen."

The mood was tangibly lighter. We all smoked as we discussed our next transaction. Richard's pager beeped, he checked the display and smiled. "All Clear" message from his lobby man, I gathered. And they were gone. With a loose tail by Mark's squad-mates, not close enough to risk compromising Alex in the future. Mark also had cars set up at Richard's club, and there was an eye on Denise Wei's house in New Jersey. If the surveillance agents lost the car, one of the other sets of eyes would probably be able to call it in when Richard put down.

In the airport lot, I gave an ecstatic Mark the paper bag of what proved to be a slightly generous weight of 95-plus-percent pure Asian heroin. Geoff Doyle wore a satisfied smile. SUNBLOCK was now a major going concern. That night, I decompressed big-time, after a long and pleasant chat with a very contented Gil. My (carefully concealed) fears preceding the meet replaced by a post-adrenaline euphoria. The next day, after an extended workout, I completed the minimal paperwork resulting from the meet and went home early. Mark obligingly drafted the bulk of the reports, including those relating my activities (the essential details derived from listening to the Nagra recordings). Starting with the SUNBLOCK case, I entered into an understanding with all the case agents. I would do the undercover work for their investigation. They would do the paperwork.

Two weeks later, on a Saturday night, I joined my mother at the opera—the Met, where we made do with the balcony and enjoyed a performance of *La Bohème*. Opera was a family passion. *Ebbene no, non lo son. Invan, invan nascondo la mia vera tortura. Amo Mimì sovra ogni cosa al mondo, io l'amo, ma ho paura, ma ho paura!* My father had enjoyed belting these lines from this particular Puccini triumph with gusto, dramatically lifting his arms to emulate Pavarotti or Carreras playing one of the star-crossed lovers. But now it was just my mother and her oldest son as the opera lovers in the family. For this occasion, I had the Alex Perez ponytail but paired it with a sharp blazer, to all appearances a curator at the Metropolitan Museum of Art across the park. Refined, no gel, Alex the hard case replaced for the evening, forgotten—but for the constant reminder, even at the opera, the Glock .40 caliber in a concealed-carry holster over my left hip.

My SUNBLOCK pager vibrated. (Annoyingly, I now always carried at least two: one for each active case and one "real" pager, for anyone trying to reach the real me.) Because the new sting was just starting to take shape, I had to check this out. It could be Richard . . . It *was* Richard. Why was he calling at ten o'clock on a Saturday night during the third act of *La Bohème*? Then again, he didn't know I was at the opera. Maybe he was just checking me out, making sure I really was Alex Perez, making sure I wasn't at the opera, say. At intermission (*La Bohème* has four acts), I stepped onto the outdoor terrace, took in the cool crisp air of the winter evening, gazed at the architecture and fountain of Lincoln Center, then hustled to the pay phone in the dark velour alcove by the entrance to the balcony and called Richard. From Miami, of course, using the 305 area-code patch-through. We chatted for a moment, to no real purpose. I was right. He'd just wanted to make sure I didn't keep a banker's hours—or an opera lover's hours. He wanted to confirm that I was indeed a drug dealer whose Saturday night on the town wasn't even under way at such an early hour. As payback, I should have waited until two in the morning to return the call.

I slipped back into my seat just in time for the curtain. My mother glanced at me. She knew something was up, but by now she had made her peace with my profession. I squeezed her hand, and we settled in for the wonderful tragedy about to transpire on stage.

Mark's wiretaps picked up a call from Gong to Denise Wei, which she had patched through to Richard's club. Richard's only comment regarding Alex and the $21,000 buy was a complaint that the quantity was too small to waste the time for a trip to Queens. This elicited an angry response from Gong, with a few Chinese insults, and reminders about who was in charge. And the future sales would be for appropriately significant quantities. Half a fish, at the least. With the phone conversations placed by Gong through Denise Wei's line, compounding his calls made directly to me, the AUSAs and Bureau management were pleased to see the noose tightening. Mark also intercepted a call between Kevin Mong and Peter Li that featured the same complaint. Mong had asked how "the one from Miami" (that would be me) had obtained Mong's home number (which was also the number of Mong's wife, Denise Wei). Li mistakenly blamed Richard, and the two grumbled about Richard's stupidity and lack of trustworthiness when it came to coughing up the cash due the higher-ups in the organization. Then they shifted their focus of annoyance to include the one from Miami, agreeing that the quantities this small-timer was buying were insufficient to justify the time of Richard and his crew.

By that time, I had handed over close to $35,000, which isn't chickenfeed, but their complaint goes to show the incredible amounts of money generated by the drug trade in literally every corner of the globe. Since the plan had always been to incrementally increase the size of Alex's purchases, Mark and I now agreed that it was time to push the volume to the next notch. The intercepted phone call indicated the timing was right. We had no concern that Peter Li might think *Hmm, we complain about small buys and the buys immediately increase*. It was too remote a connection. In all my prior ops, I had relied on intuition, my

feel for the subjects, to make tactical decisions. With Mark's web of telephone intercepts and informants, we could virtually read these guys'
minds and react accordingly. We knew they would just be happy to see
the increased cash flow. Over the next two or three or four calls between
me and Richard—given the necessary haggling and the necessary con-
currences from Gil and Gong, respectively; it was always a matter of
several calls—we reached an agreement for me to buy a half unit, "twelve
fish" (twelve ounces) at $4,100 per ounce, for a total of $49,200.

On a chilly early spring morning in March of 1995 I beeped Richard
and provided the ID of the hotel (the Ramada) and my room number
therein. A few minutes later, one of Mark's squad-mates assigned to
"wire duty" picked up a call to Richard at the Karaoke Club from Chang,
a request for marching orders. *Go to Alex's hotel room "right away . . .
take care of it."* Sitting in the hotel room with nearly fifty thousand, I
would ordinarily not have been thrilled to learn that the soldier had
been ordered to "take care of it." While Chang was no killer, this was
still the heroin business. I wasn't buying auto parts. Gong was in jail for
murder and complacency in undercover operations is not a particularly
desirable attitude . . . I had never seen Chang without the revolver-sized
leather handbag.

Mark had already posted a surveillance team at Chang's place of
residence in Chinatown, (as well as at Richard's club, just in case). They
watched as Chang hailed a cab and arrived at the Ramada at about
twenty past noon. Moving surveillance of a subject in a taxi is particularly easy—no rearview mirror concerns, no hinky driver. With Mark
keeping me abreast of the evolving scenario, I turned on the TV, watched
the news, and waited, knowing what to expect. Or so I thought. Chang
was somewhat too deferential, not business as usual. Sure enough, a
minor inconvenience: he did not have the product with him. If I would
be so kind as to let him have the money, he'd be back shortly with the
agreed upon half unit.

You want me to front you fifty thousand dollars?

Richard returned Chang's beep within minutes. The yelling over the
receiver was clearly audible, though the Chinese was not comprehensi-
ble. Then I took the line. No can do. No fish, no cash. Against company
policy. Nothing personal, but my uncle would take an extremely dim

view of my losing that kind of cash. Next for Chang was a cab ride home, three minutes inside the apartment, reemerging, now carrying what appeared to be a toiletries bag, and a cab ride back to the hotel. This meant an additional hour of CNN for Alex, who switched to Spanish language Univision when word came of Chang's imminent return. With only eight ounces, not the full twelve. As agreed in the call with Richard, this would be a two-stage transaction. I made no attempt to hide my continued annoyance with the change in plans, for which he babbled apologies. I paid him $32,800. He left with more apologies and promises for a short wait. Another hour and a half of CNN, and a call from Richard. Chang was on his way. One minute earlier, Chang had called Richard and reported that he had given Alex the "eight people," and now had "the four." Chang must have called Richard from the hotel lobby. I just had time to switch to Univision before the knock on the door. Another aluminum brick, smaller this time, in exchange for the remaining $16,400. Done deal, finally.

A dozen mind-twisting conversations with Gong later and I was back in a hotel at LaGuardia. This time the Marriott, and again only the delivery boy, Chang, represented the other team. Their comfort level was rising. They never asked what seemed to me to be an obvious and potentially troublesome question. *Why was Gil's number one, the top lieutenant, still making the buys personally and not sending a soldier to handle the high-risk task?* Perhaps they decided it wasn't any of their business. The money was coming in, and all was going well. That was enough. But if they did ask, Mark and I had scripted my answer: *Professional courtesy.* Gong had been sending his top lieutenant, Richard (at least until now). Gil was responding in kind. Chang had brought a "half-menu," and my manila envelope contained $50,000—a special price for Gil. When I asked Chang about the quality, he looked at me, puzzled. With the language issue—his facility with English was somewhat limited—the question had perhaps lost or gained something when translated in his mind. His response nearly caused me to fall off the corner of the hotel room bed where I was seated.

"I just sell this"—nodding toward the aluminum foil brick with a look of disdain, disgust—"I don't *use* it." The implication was that if others wanted to poison themselves, it was no concern of his, particularly if it resulted in a large tax-free cash flow. Until that very moment, I had believed that such a reply was something only a UC, an *amateur* UC, would say. But if *a real heroin distributor* could say it, I could as well. And I did, years later, in 2010, buying volume oxycodone from a Dominican in the Bronx while adding, with a chuckle, derisive remarks about the *tarados* (knuckleheads) who actually swallowed these poisoned pills. As with everything I said and did, the idea was to enhance my Alex Perez persona as a legitimate hard-case professional criminal who would use and discard addicts as easily, as heedlessly as he would tissue paper.

I've mentioned that one of the first confederates that the earliest physical and electronic surveillance of Gong's troops identified was one Paul Kwok, of Toronto, Canada. (This was many months before Mark Calnan recruited me for the UC job.) As it turned out, Gong's heroin originating in Malaysia was smuggled first to Toronto, ultimately arriving in New Jersey and New York for coast-to-coast U.S. distribution. Other shipments went elsewhere. This was a global network. From the beginning, therefore, the Canadian angle—Canada and *beyond,* all the way to Malaysia, ideally—was a major attraction for the SUNBLOCK investigation.

I would discuss with Richard my Uncle Gil's intention to expand our Canadian operation by starting to distribute heroin as well as cocaine through our existing network, which was based in Montreal and Vancouver. Of course, Gil and I could not openly know about the Canadian connection. As experienced professionals, we had never asked, nor did we care about, the source of the heroin. What we cared about was price, quality, reliability, and security. All of which Gong's organization could provide to our satisfaction. It would be up to Gong, or Richard, to suggest that I meet with and start doing business with Paul Kwok, and ultimately Kwok's associates, in Toronto. With time and luck, if the volume justified it, Gong or Richard might even put me in touch with the exporters in Malaysia. As the buys became significantly larger, Gil would have the leverage to insist on dealing directly with the principals, using his own (purported) cocaine network to securely transport the product. Gong would not object—Gil would assure that he still received his percentage.

The Canadian connection dictated that SUNBLOCK therefore become a joint investigation with the Royal Canadian Mounted Police. At one of the "all those involved" planning sessions, I met the two principal Mounties who would be handling the Canadian end of the op, which they had codenamed PROJECT ORDAIN. (In this narrative, I'm sticking with SUNBLOCK.) Their case was being developed using traditional investigative techniques. They were conducting physical surveillance of Paul Kwok, Gong's Toronto source for the heroin, and other players in Canada, and they had set up a number of phone intercepts. Important early questions for the Mounties were how Kwok and his minions got the heroin past Canadian Customs, and what the organizational chart looked like. What the Mounties could use in the worst way, but did not have, was an undercover agent in place. Not due to lack of highly skilled UCs in their service (as I would learn personally a decade later in the TURKEY CLUB sting against the Italian Mafia), but rather due to lack of a means to penetrate this tightly knit, professional, closed group of drug-dealing confederates.

Without divulging that his goods in fact came into the United States from Canada, Gong had told Gil that he had reliable people in Toronto, and suggested that Gil have Alex travel there. Richard would be there as well and personally make the introductions. During my next call with Richard, made to his office, the Chinatown Karaoke Club, I relayed the news that my brother had been speaking to his brother about new restaurants—Richard knew the code—and we needed to meet. I'd be passing through New York in a few days. I'd book my flights to allow a few hours to get together. As per our now-established routine, I'd page Richard as soon as I had a room in one of the hotels by LaGuardia. As usual, Mark Calnan and I would have booked adjoining rooms the previous day, and by the time I beeped Richard, all the technical surveillance equipment complete with video, would have been set up and tested.

Fifteen minutes after I sent the beep, he was knocking at the door of my hotel room. Unusual alacrity—impossible alacrity. He must have already been in the area. As I later learned from the wiretaps, Gong had made it clear in his call to Richard's club the night before that this meet was going to be important, and he wanted to hear good news afterward. That is, he had better hear good news.

Chang stood by Richard's side in the doorway. I invited them into the hotel room, and after the obligatory cigarette—I was beginning to look forward to them—I told Richard of my uncle Gil's plans. He wanted to open Chinese restaurants in Florida, California, and Canada. I explained that we already had a number of Mexican restaurants in Miami, L.A., Montreal, and Vancouver (code, obviously), and as we were making so much money with the Chinese menus that we were buying in New York, it just made good sense to follow the same pattern at our other existing franchises. Richard said he just happened to have a friend who managed Chinese restaurants in Canada and could provide us with menus there, and at a good price. Coincidentally, he was planning to travel soon to meet with his friend, and it would be his pleasure to arrange a dinner where we could all meet and discuss the ins and outs of running this kind of restaurant in Canada. Miami would also work. They had people in place to cover the southeastern U.S. market. Unfortunately, they wouldn't be able to service us in California. (Gong later explained to Gil that he had agreed to remain out of the West Coast, so long as his California Chinese heroin boss counterpart stayed out of the East Coast.) Gong would personally vouch for Gil's organization—and for Alex Perez as its number-one man on the outside—to Paul Kwok in Toronto. Richard, Chang, the other guys—they didn't have the authority or credibility to handle the task.

By vouching for a new customer, Gong was putting his own credibility and reputation on the line. Whenever a confidential informant (or a subject, unwittingly, as in this instance) vouches for a UC, he is bestowing his entire credibility on that UC. He is saying *you can trust Alex as much as you trust me*. In a world where misplaced trust can lead to prison or worse—when perhaps the customer pays not with cash but with gunshots—this Vouch, with a capital V, is a matter of no small import, and Canada was now an open door. It just remained for my case agent Mark Calnan and his Royal Canadian counterpart to work out the details and draft an operational plan to send to the corner offices in D.C. and Ottawa.

This is where I came into the picture: everyone wanted me in Toronto, meeting with Kwok and Co. I agreed, but raised two preconditions. First, FBI agents would participate in the surveillance of the UC meets. Second, I would be authorized to carry a firearm. In the United States, of course, a weapon is a given, but this is not the case for UCs in Canada. Especially foreign UCs. No problem on either count, replied the Canadians. They would obtain the necessary approvals. But their approvals were just the beginning. An international UC op would require all kinds of approvals, including the FBI Legal Attaché office (LEGAT in BuSpeak), the special agent liaison officers assigned to the U.S. Embassy. We would need a little time. Possibly a problem, if the approvals dragged on too long, but we caught a break: Gil called with the news that Gong had been caught with heroin in his cell and would be in Administrative Segregation for the next three months. Gil expected me to be upset. Not really. The bureaucracy might need that much time. Richard and I therefore kept the Canadian date loose, agreeing only that the meeting in Toronto would be after his "brother" got his phone privileges back.

Over a month later, Mark heard back from the Canadians. Regrettably, the Mounties' management could not (or would not, who knows?) obtain authorization for American participation in the surveillances on Canadian soil. Not to worry, their teams were highly experienced, knew the terrain and the players, were accustomed to covering UC meets, and would take all necessary steps to assure my safety. Do we see where this part of the SUNBLOCK saga is headed? I have to admit, when I thought of the Royal Canadian Mounted Police in action, I did not visualize the FBI Hostage Rescue Team fast-roping from helicopters onto rooftops with full auto MP5s slung over their back and flashbangs strapped to their web gear. Nor did I visualize the Israeli Shin Bet crashing into Hezbollah safe houses. Nor the Argentine National Police or French CRS. Rather, the image I conjured was of a more . . . diplomatic . . . nonconfrontational agency. It's Canada, after all. I started to imagine a nighttime meet with Kwok, Richard, and others yet unnamed, in an unknown suburb of an unknown city in a foreign country, its crack surveillance team—keeping careful distance to avoid being burned—*losing me*. Or, worse, one of the Mounties doing something that did in fact burn me, inadvertently compromising my covert identity, and then the rest of that team *not* rushing in to save the day, but rather seeking a "peaceful" resolution, while the Chinese narco-traffickers opted for the other kind.

Does this sound too U.S.-centric of me? My enthusiasm for this gig was diminished, and then a few days later, with one additional phone call from Mark, it was extinguished altogether. Profuse apologies from our friends up north, Mark reported, but I would not be allowed to carry a firearm. No exceptions, foreign lawmen can't be armed while in Canada. Not to worry, their teams were highly experienced, knew the terrain and the players, were accustomed to covering UC meets, and would take all necessary steps to assure my safety, blah, blah, blah.

That was it. I wasn't going. The Mounties could try to complete their case without a UC. And that wasn't all they could do with their case. Clearly, they had known full well that they would not be likely to obtain the authorizations they had promised. Like true bureaucrats, rather than telling us the truth upfront, or making the effort with the hope that they just might succeed, they chose the disingenuous and lazy route. Expecting, no doubt, that I would be swept into the operation by the tide of events, by the momentum of the extensive preparations that were well under way, and by pressure from FBI management. They were wrong. Mark and C-25 Supervisor Geoff Doyle backed me up. I never again raised the topic of Chinese restaurants in Canada with Richard, and when Gong returned from Administrative Segregation to the general population in Lewisburg and raised the subject, Gil told him that the timing no longer worked, that for now he wanted to concentrate on opening more restaurants in the United States, a territory he was comfortable with, and would look into expanding his Canadian operations later. In this way, Gil skillfully shifted the onus of the lost Canadian opportunity to Gong. It was now *Gong's* fault that the expansion into Canada was no longer viable. In the world of crime, as in real estate and finance, timing is everything.

Behind bars in Lewisburg, Gil understood that one major investigation, albeit targeting a global narcotics operation like Gong's, would be just the start of his *just barely conceivable* long journey home ("home" being out of prison and secreted somewhere in the Witness Protection Program). He had by now developed a useful "friendship" with another Lewisburg inmate, Carl Abbot Armstrong, a West Coast free spirit convicted for importing marijuana from Mexico. By the ton. And beware to anyone who stood in his way. Even though he was behind bars in Lewisburg. Armstrong, like Gong, was still in business. Gil and I brainstormed how we could credibly pitch our desire to get into Armstrong's business. For us Mexicans, who grow so much pot ourselves, to be *buying* pot—like selling ice to Eskimos, the true salesman's greatest mythic challenge. What we came up with was typical of our synergistic teamwork, what made Gil and me a seamless pair. And, as time rolled by, and the weeks became months (then years, long after SUNBLOCK was closed out), we would talk about personal matters, his daughter's college applications, his mom's health. I gave my opinions, advice. Sometimes I even talked directly with his mom or daughter or brother in El Paso (after Mark had obtained the necessary approvals). Gil and I were developing a relationship that to all outward appearances truly was that of an uncle and nephew, with close professional and family ties, mutually dependent. A dependency that was enhanced by a never-articulated truth, the consequences of which we both fully understood: we each held the other's life in his hand. An error on my part, revealing my true occupation, would inevitably result in a shiv between Gil's ribs and a premature completion of his natural life in prison. A slip-up by Gil when talking with Gong or, now, Armstrong, an overheard telephone conversation, and I would encounter a very unwelcome surprise at the next meet. A bullet, presumably. Not a shiv. No need for homemade daggers outside of the federal penitentiary.

After receiving the green light from Mark and his supervisor, Geoff, I told Gil the Armstrong initiative was a go. He then expressed his interest in expansion to Armstrong, who had a complex and effective transport system in place that involved cargo ships, secret ports, and specially adapted tractor-trailers. *You have the infrastructure. We have the pot. We need you.*

Armstrong bought it. Gil's trusted nephew Alex Perez would handle the day-to-day operations. Just as RUN-DMV had spawned spin-off UC cases that remained under the same umbrella, SUNBLOCK had begun to beget offspring. Armstrong was the new Santiago Kuris.

Like Gong, Armstrong was paranoid and a lunatic in his own way. (To improve his health, he bought into a prison-specific urban legend and for a while was drinking his own urine, a practice that Gil politely declined to follow.) Armstrong maintained contact with his chief lieutenant on the outside through (incredibly) his mother. A cool professional, she also handled much of the cash. Armstrong instructed her to accept calls from Alex, and set up an introduction with his right-hand man. Now we had the Jewish white guy working UC as both a Mexican cocaine dealer and as a marijuana dealer in league with middle-aged white hippies with a violent bent. It was a new twist. With Gong and his frequent calls, preparing for and executing the heroin buys, the nightly calls with Gil, and now Armstrong and a few others, SUNBLOCK had evolved into a full-time job and more, despite the now-forgotten assurances from Mark's supervisor to Craig Dotlo that I was on part-time loan from Squad C-21—*just a few UC meets, now and again.*

However, I was always available for a cameo, pursuant to my still-in-place, never-say-no policy, and one evening while I was duping tapes of a call with Gong, an agent from the Organized Crime Squad stopped by my cubicle in New Rochelle. He was the case agent on a long-term investigation of one of the La Cosa Nostra (LCN) families in the Bronx. Their primary meeting place was a social club/restaurant in the Bronx. The agent had an unlikely confidential informant for a mob case, a Puerto Rican guy named Angelo, aka Angel. He knew all the players, having insinuated himself as a compliant and reliable errand boy. What the sting now required was a perch for him to sit in on Arthur Avenue, with a direct view of the club. This neighborhood was a colony of Little Italy in Lower Manhattan: all inbred Italian, a closed society. Today, of course, Manhattan's Little Italy is now a pitiful remnant of the thriving community of the good old days. Chinatown has fared better. The agents on the case had been trying to rent an apartment, answering classifieds from neighborhood papers, equipped with their AFID driver's licenses and credit cards. And they had been met with blank expressions. *It's no longer available . . . I've rented it . . . I've changed my mind . . . Followed by a slamming door.*

What we had here was clearly a task for Sal Morelli. I needed a few hours break from SUNBLOCK to clear my head and was grateful for the low-stress cameo role—UC Lite. I drove to the informant Angel's apartment building on the Grand Concourse. And was truly surprised. In the midst of the still devastated, graffiti-ridden South Bronx, his apartment was pristine. Behind the deceptively battered front door with the obligatory multiple locks was a sanded and polished parquet floor displaying antiques that had been carefully, lovingly restored. Angel also proudly showed me his collection of classic watches. (I still take my watches to the then-already-old Dominican watch repairer Angel recommended.)

We took a drive down Arthur Avenue, in order to get a feel for the area. The old style delis were filled with imported foods. I bought some excellent, hard-to-find Sicilian cheeses and olives, value added to the expedition. Angel pointed out the pertinent sites, the LCN families' boundary lines, the gathering places. Then it was a matter of minutes for Sal Morelli to talk up the landlord of a walk-up studio apartment unearthed by Angel, virtually across the street from the social club, and make the down payment. Happy to do it. As New Rochelle's resident UC, performing such small favors kept me in good graces with the various supervisors and agents. Consequently, little attention was paid to my comings and goings, and I led a remarkably unstructured work life. The public perception of the FBI as a highly regimented, nearly paramilitary organization is a fiction to begin with, particularly so for the full-time UC.

No sooner was I back in the New Rochelle office from Arthur Avenue when Gong checked in. After the usual indecipherable exchange and menus, half-menus, and maybe unions (they occasionally still came up), we reached accord, such as it was. As usual, Gil and I required forty-five minutes to decipher what I had just agreed to. As it turned out, the next meet would be one of my last ones with the Malaysian heroin distributors. My role in SUNBLOCK had been running for a year and a half; soon it would be time for the last curtain call. Mark Calnan's net was nearly ready to be gathered and pulled in. For one thing, he was just about out of buy money. And the case was ripe, ready to be taken down. Assembling all the pieces, the UC buys, the telephone intercepts, the CI information, a solid prosecution of the entire organization was nearly ready to initiate. The full-court press had worked almost to perfection.

The final, final negotiation took place in Lewisburg. *My uncle says you're good with four dollars a menu, with us buying twenty-four Chinese menus.* Gong had made it clear that $96,000 was a special price for his Mexican friend. White clients, black clients, never paid less than one ten, one twenty, regardless. Richard and Chang both showed up to the LaGuardia Marriott, this time accompanied by a new Grand Street Dragon. Knowing there might not be a future opportunity, Mark and the AUSA who would be handling the SUNBLOCK prosecutions had asked that I push the envelope as far as I comfortably could. After the cash and heroin had been exchanged, Richard and I puffed on our obligatory Marlboros and discussed future transactions, expanded delivery sites. I turned the conversation to Canada, to sources, to ways in which our organization and networks could facilitate those used by the Chinese. Discretion being the better part of valor, I exercised restraint. With the criminal case complete—the conversations taped, the buys on video, the heroin in evidence vaults—I still wasn't eager to be on the receiving end of a flying sidekick from the aloof Dragon hovering in the background. And there was Gil's well-being to think about. By this time, it was very important to me.

Leaving the hotel, I felt the oncoming blues, the end-of-story lassitude that accompanied the end of every long-term undercover operation. Starting with RUN-DMV, the anticipated elation at the end of a successful case seemed to elude me. The adrenaline rushes were over, replaced by a cold-turkey, low-level depression and thoughts focused on the missed opportunities: the buys never consummated, the subjects who had not been developed, and, in this op, the travel to the Far East that never materialized. (But like a junkie looking for his next fix, I already had the groundwork set for my next UC op.)

As soon as the prosecutors had drawn up the warrants, Mark, his squad-mates, the NYPD Task Force, and four SWAT teams swept up Gong's entire organization. Mark had arranged for Special Operation Group surveillance teams to maintain observation of all the subjects, guaranteeing that their whereabouts would be confirmed on the scheduled arrest date. Thanks to Mark's elaborate preparations, none slipped through the net. Gong was "arrested" in prison and escorted (politely, of course, because this was the BOP!) to solitary.

A few day later, Mark called me at my desk in New Rochelle. The Canadians had successfully rounded up Paul Kwok and his organization, at least those they had identified and built cases on. Our excellent neighbor's PROJECT ORDAIN was not as rock solid as SUNBLOCK. For one thing, they hadn't been able to introduce a UC. After reneging on their assurances to me, ready and eager to work both sides of the border . . . whom did they have to blame for that?

Of course, Gong's people—Richard, Chang, Denise Wei, Kevin Mong, Peter Li, and on and on, eighteen targets altogether—all categorically denied any involvement in businesses other than Chinese restaurants and karaoke clubs. Until they were shown a few videos and listened to a few phone recordings. *The guy you're talking to there. With the ponytail? He's an FBI agent.* Guilty pleas followed shortly thereafter. As to those who were arrested, there were no trials. I never testified. Gong got an additional twenty-seven years, to run *consecutively* with his current life sentence. The judge ordered that he be delivered to INS for deportation upon completion of his sentence . . . Gong will be well over a hundred years old before he's eligible for parole. Richard, Peter Li, Kevin Mong—the top lieutenants—received sentences ranging from twenty-two to twenty-eight years. They're still in prison. (Most states lop off one third of the time for good behavior. Not so in federal prisons, where 85 percent of the sentence *must* be served before parole eligibility.)

Among Gong's minions, Chang, with no priors, received the shortest sentence, ten years. When the time came for his release, ten years later— no reduction for good behavior—hound-dog case agent Mark Calnan gave me the heads-up. *Marc, beware, the SUNBLOCK subjects are beginning to hit the streets.* This was the *only* such courtesy heads-up I have ever received in my two-plus decades' career as a UC. Yes, I'm a big Mark Calnan fan.

But what could I do, really? Not live in a cave in Timbuktu. If Gong's men found me, they found me. At that time, I was back working UC ops in New York, after a seven-year hiatus managing undercover operations nationwide from FBIHQ, and tracking down terrorists, fugitives, and others on the ground in South America.

As for our play with Armstrong and marijuana, communication with that target rapidly decelerated due to an unexpected development. Fol-

lowing a request to be lodged closer to his family, Armstrong was transferred to a federal prison in Texas. The routine conversations with Gil
were replaced by infrequent, coded telephone calls. As a result, progress
toward a meet was now at a snail's pace. With the arrests of the Gong
gang, the Armstrong spin-off case was reassigned to Los Angeles, where
his top lieutenant resided. The investigation was in an early stage, to say
the least. Other than the initial intel developed by Gil and a few contacts
by me with Armstrong's mother and one of his henchmen, no concrete
steps had been taken. Los Angeles would have to start from scratch.
Inevitably, Gong would learn that Alex was an FBI agent, Uncle Gil was
no uncle at all, and the word would spread throughout the penitentiary,
and then throughout the entire chain of federal prisons.

Gil Sandoval was moved to the Bureau of Prison's own internal Witness Protection Plan at an undisclosed facility—segregated incarceration
for cooperators and convicted law enforcement officers, inmates whose
longevity in the general prison population would be rather limited.
He was alive and relatively safe, but Mark Calnan and I wanted more.
We pushed hard for a resentencing hearing for Gil. Rick Getty, Gil's
original contact agent in El Paso, had retired, with the file assigned to a
rookie two years out of the academy. While very pleasant, she had really
nothing to gain from what promised to be a significant amount of work.
The El Paso U.S. Attorney's office had no interest in conducting the legal
research and drafting the requisite affidavits and motions requesting
a resentencing hearing. They ultimately agreed, grudgingly, to file the
documents—if someone else prepared them. In the end, it was two grunts
in New York, a busy undercover guy—fortunately for Gil, a former
assistant district attorney—and a narcotics investigator who put it all
together. When, after many years, the U.S. District Court for the Western
District of Texas, presiding in El Paso, granted a motion for a resentencing hearing, Mark Calnan and I took the highly unusual step of testifying
on his behalf—in El Paso, at the Bureau's expense. To any readers who
may still question the FBI's commitment to its informants and the extraordinary investigative results that this commitment yields, this passage
is self-evident in its significance.

Eight years after the Gong gang's indictments came down, Gil was
finally released from Lewisburg into the U.S. Marshals Service Witness

Protection Program. He was no longer serving a natural life term in a federal prison. He was now serving a different kind of natural life term, the same one as yours and mine. Before disappearing over the horizon, Gil called to thank me and say good-bye. Now *he* was headed undercover, in a way. I hope and believe that he has made a good life for himself, somewhere out there.

9

Starlight Lounge

The Rastafarian stood in front of the dingy social club, his dreads bundled into the traditional multicolored knit cap, his shirt half unbuttoned to reveal the taut muscles beneath. Drinking a beer, the Rastaman was deep in conversation with a middle-aged stocky wiseguy, with silver hair brushed straight back, a cigar in his thick right hand next to the oversized jeweled ring, his suit sharkskin—nothing but the best. Out of the shadows slipped an outlaw biker, muscular tattooed arms exposed by the sleeveless black leather vest. The cruel smile on his bearded face exposed stained teeth. This odd trio turned together to greet the banker, elegant in his finely tailored suit, his silver hair carefully groomed, his manicured hands holding a leather portfolio. By his side, a blond, blue-eyed man with an icy stare—he would have been the perfect poster boy for the Hitler Youth—stood guard with an insidious smile and military bearing, the twin lightning bolts pinned to his shirt collar betraying his neo-Nazi affiliations.

As I approached, those ten eyes, even the Nazi's, fixed on mine: an intimidating crew, to all appearances—but they were only appearances, because I was in on the deal. All of us were simpatico, part of the FBI team, the UC team, enjoying a few beers in the Starlight Lounge after an evening of practical exercises in Hogan's Alley, the simulated city at Quantico utilized by all manner of agents, including SWAT teams perfecting their hostage-rescue skills, surveillance teams, and us undercover specialists. (The neo-Nazi was Mike German, the key guy for working the Aryan Nation and white supremacist militias. Five years prior to German's whistle-blowing and departure from the Bu.)

At the Starlight, I was Marc Ruskin, not H. Marc Renard on Wall Street, not Alex Perez buying fraudulent government documents and kilos of dope, not Sal Morelli scamming the insurance companies. Gone were my long ponytail, the gel job, the T-shirt, the bling. I was in "business casual" mode, because I was now management—yes, management, of all things—but a different kind of management, I hasten to add (considering the prior discussion). This was 1999, and I was assigned to the Undercover Safeguard Unit, which had been created in the early nineties to "address the needs of UCEs . . . throughout the six phases (selection, training, operational planning, deployment, decompression, and reintegration) of covert activity" (FBI Law Enforcement Bulletin, August 2008, p. 2). It was an anomaly within the BUREAUcracy—an HQ entity dedicated to cutting through red tape, rather than adding to it. More recently, the formal training curriculum for wannabe undercover agents had been initiated, replacing the OJT (on-the-job training) that had sufficed for the older generation of undercovers. As we have seen in some detail, for my first decade working undercover, everything had been OJT (trial and error, monkey-see-monkey-do, learn-or-leave-or-worse). Now, finally, the undercover craft as practiced by the FBI was being codified, and not just the paperwork, in the field as well. We were actually changing the conditions for undercover work with major consequences.

This was all to the good, but my decision to get deeply involved in the new program had not been an easy call. One of the hardest, in fact. Being a street agent was in my blood. I'd had real doubts about leaving it behind as I stared at the FD-638, the form to submit to management in order to compete for a slot in that management. It was still blank. After fourteen years of disparaging managers and management, ten of those years almost exclusively undercover, I was having a hard time pulling this trigger. Did I really want to go over to what amounted to the Bureau's own dark side? Because that's how I thought of it. That's how many special agents in the field thought of management in general, and Headquarters in particular. Since BuTime immemorial, field agents have viewed FBIHQ, as it is known to all who have never served there, as an unfathomable source of aggravation and interference with ongoing and proposed investigations. An incomprehensible zombie factory, from where once-normal agents emerge somehow altered: remote, aloof, rule-driven, obsequious to those higher up. There is much truth in the perception. And also some exaggeration, the suspicions naturally bred by ignorance—an ignorance that agents are more than happy to maintain, if the cost of enlightenment is an indeterminate sentence within the concrete walls of JEH, as it is known to its denizens and to all who *have* ever served there, the J. Edgar Hoover Building at 935 Pennsylvania Avenue, N.W., in our nation's capital.

The big building had always evoked images of an oversized military bunker, a large blot to the landscape, particularly hideous since situated in a city of majestic monuments and landmarks. And what's with those hideous concrete walls? The explanation is an interesting and not irrelevant story. In the cavernous garage, spanning an entire city block, I had observed (years before) ceiling-high stacks of unknown content, draped in dust-imbued old canvas. Many, many stacks. What were the mysterious contents? From friends in Facilities Management, sitting in their windowless offices in the basement of JEH, I now finally learned the story (or perhaps the urban legend) behind the concrete walls—and the mysterious stacks of . . . white marble panels. Huge panels of beautiful, valuable marble. Marble that had been destined to cloak the new headquarters, provide the finishing architectural touch, and allow the building to take its rightful place in the panoply of Washington's awe-inspiring structures. And then came ABSCAM, a group I mentioned earlier. It had been a big deal in the years when my desire to join the FBI was germinating. The large-scale public corruption investigation had rooted out some bribe-takers from within the ranks of Congress. A laudable, inspiring event, only possible in a true democracy. Unfortunately for the FBI, however, it later emerged that there would be a price to pay for unearthing the rotten apples from among those who control the purse strings. And among the budget disasters that followed, an initiative that fell victim to ABSCAM was the marble-ization of JEH. The marble is still stacked down there, unused, and in the nearly forty years since the stone was first delivered, there have been no further investigations seeking to uproot corruption on Capitol Hill. (*American Hustle,* the mega-popular movie disliked by many of my retired colleagues for its wildly inaccurate depiction of FBI agents, missed an opportunity to capitalize on Congress's notorious double standard: exempting themselves from the rules applied to all others.)

The Ramada in New Rochelle wasn't JEH by a long shot, but it was a lot closer to the spirit of the place than the streets on which I'd been working with great satisfaction for about a decade. And that's where I was sitting (specifically, in my cubicle) as I stared at that blank FD-638. I stared at the form in my daydreams . . . and then in my nightmares. Steve Salmieri, chief at the Undercover Safeguard Unit, had a vacancy for a Supervisory Special Agent, a slot reserved for highly experienced UCs. Steve had said, "There's no one more qualified, Marc. You've been out there long enough. Down here, you can make a contribution to the program nationally."

And he continued with more of what I took to be stroking. *You— only you—know what UCs need, operationally and emotionally, blah, blah, blah.* True enough, I agreed on that point, but Steve had been infiltrating the Weathermen and La Cosa Nostra while I was still in law school, and I knew to take his praise with a few grains of salt, and I wasn't surprised to learn a few years later that he was using the same blandishments with Mark Pecora, an agent with extensive UC experience infiltrating outlaw biker clubs, the Pagans, and the like. Mark was the other main candidate for the opening.

As I turned the 638 over—and *over*—in my hands, literally, and in my mind, figuratively, I attempted to persuade myself to submit it . . . then to tear it up . . . back and forth. The truth was, after ten years of nonstop full-time UC work, I had recently been taking some risks on the street that I knew were unwise. On the (somewhat) unconscious assumption that I was invincible, I had been preparing less and less for UC meets. Winging it, bluffing, ad-libbing. (*Some* ad-libbing was almost always called for, of course, but not as a substitute for adequate planning.) It had floated to the surface of my perceptions that this could only lead to a not very happy ending. But I loved the work. This was my calling. I had found, in this arcane vocation, the one job at which I could truly excel. I thought I could have been a good—even very good—tinker, or tailor, or soldier . . . but I was a *great* spy. One of the best. (Yes, an undercover is a spy; the terms are synonymous. Whether in the criminal world or in my next UC decade, the world of counterespionage, the job is to cross enemy lines, gather intelligence, report it, and try to get out in one piece.)

I knew that the timing for a change was right—the cartoon hook was poised to yank the obsessed actor off the stage—and the headquarters job *was* virtually custom-tailored for me, but there was another issue, another way I might be able to convince myself and Steve that the timing was in fact wrong: I was in the middle of a Group II investigation (bizarrely, perhaps, this op's official TITLE has faded from memory, and I now think of it as simply "The Fort Lauderdale Case").

Steve heard me out . . . made some phone calls . . . haggled . . . then called back a few days later. *My section chief will authorize a waiver. If you're selected, you come down here and start the new job . . . and you continue working the Group II. But, when it's over, that's it. No more UC roles!* I would be the only supervisor in the FBI, now or ever, also working as an active undercover agent. No minor concession that. I was out of excuses. I said okay, if I'm selected, I'm your guy.

A final factor in this decision: Despite my love of UC work, my *dream* assignment —a dream that coexisted side by side with my love of the mean streets had long been a posting overseas, preferably to Paris or Madrid or Buenos Aires, intended to cap off my career—it had eluded me for four years. Application after application had been turned down in favor of less qualified (from my perspective) candidates. Often candidates whose linguistic skills were limited to English. What they did have, however, were . . . positions in management. They were GS-14s or above—supervisors. In order to go home to Paris—the city of my birth—or to get to any other U.S. Embassy job, I would have to bite the bullet and join them in the labyrinthine bureaucracy. (The Hoover building itself is literally labyrinthine—an actual labyrinth, with countless elevator banks leading to innumerable halls, many of which suddenly come to a plasterboard dead end. The design seems deliberately calculated to foster the corresponding mind-set.)

Three months after I had agreed to apply for the Safeguard Unit job, it happened. Steve called again. *Congratulations, Supervisor Ruskin!* Steve meant well, but the words fell somewhat flat, grating as they did against my inherently anti-authoritarian inner self. I got the nod thanks to the diversity of my UC experience, from Wall Street to heroin dealing and a lot in between. Damn that diversity! The thought of turning down the promotion did cross my mind, but I really did believe I could make an overall contribution to the Bureau's vital UC program. What's more, the ongoing sting would significantly ease the transition. It was a good case that required me, case agent Joe Buzcek, and my UC girlfriend Christine Ridless (whose role also encompassed being my cute and bubbly blond administrative aide and secretary) to fly down to Fort Lauderdale once a month. That schedule would continue as promised.

On the Bureau's organization chart, Safeguard was slotted under "Headquarters," but we didn't actually work out of JEH. Knowing this made taking the job easier. Another factor that made taking the job easier: Although in practice this unit was operational—a subsection of the Operational Support Section—it was technically "management" and I would therefore receive credit for "Headquarters Time," thus possibly furthering my ambition to land a job overseas. At the same time, I was working day-to-day in a pleasant commercial space, reasonably far from the palace intrigues and onerous upper-management oversight of JEH. Yet, as my duties called for liaison with many of the entities based inside the walls of JEH, I had ample opportunities to visit, network, and familiarize myself with the beehive, without being chained to one of its myriad cubicles. While on the one hand assuming a role where I could impact the FBI's undercover operations nationally, I was simultaneously penetrating the opaque walls of the FBI nerve center, its central nervous system, if you will.

At Safeguard, I was initially one of six supervisory special agents, three veteran UCs and three psychologists. Then, after a year and a half, Acting Unit Chief. There were several motivations for setting up a more accountable framework for UC operations, of which this unit was a major component: a few operational debacles, some lawsuits, all finally prompting the Attorney General's office to issue new guidelines for UC work.

Comfortably ensconced at the covert off-site, I focused on the Unit's mission: vetting prospective UC agents and then training the lucky few chosen for the job; supporting individual undercover agents nationwide; and enhancing the FBI undercover program itself. As the unit's name reflects, it was created to safeguard undercover agents in the field—to serve as their safety net and to provide a source of last resort. And as to training, the recently inaugurated Undercover Certification Course was rigorous and serious.

My friends at the Starlight Lounge, all veteran UC agents in full covert disguise from attire to facial expression, were guest instructors in that course, now enjoying a beer in the faux social club in Hogan's Alley after a night of practical exercises. Whimsically recounting anecdotes from the streets and meets, the way other professionals on the outside might describe landing a big sales contract or negotiating a real-estate deal. Casual observation— and my casual description—of these guys in the Starlight Lounge might imply that UC work is playacting. Not quite. It is *acting*, but by this point in my career I had decided that the agent's scam on the street works best if it touches something real in his or her makeup—method acting, if you will. (Some years earlier I had met Michael Dennehy, the primary UC agent who played the sheik in ABSCAM. His brother is Brian Dennehy, the gruff character actor. The thespian streak runs in that family.) Nor is UC work *playing*. Some of those whimsically recounted tales were about life-threatening situations.

UCs tend to have big egos. Perhaps it's even mandatory, this conviction that we can put on and take off the mask on a moment's notice, that we can penetrate and then infiltrate any criminal enterprise, up to any level, with "controllable" risk and little psychological exposure. In film and fiction, UCs work long-term deep-cover investigations, develop seemingly close personal relationships with terrorist masterminds, Mafia bosses, cocaine cartel leaders. And then they are back home, sleeping soundly, satisfying healthy appetites, even-tempered, all's well that ends well . . . So the big ego is mandatory but also dicey, because events may crack the façade on a moment's notice, and there we are, hung out to dry.

The Bureau learned the hard way. Following a successful two-year UC op targeting the mob's pornography business in Miami, UC Pat Livingston was arrested for shoplifting. He was fired. The denouement? A well-publicized and embarrassing—for the Bu—segment featuring Pat on *60 Minutes*. Following on a lucrative—for Pat—lawsuit against the Bu and BuManagement. His was one of the related lawsuits that motivated the chiefs to set up Safeguard.

Hoover was not fond of the undercover technique. He foresaw what few others did: the personal toll that such work would have on the individual agent. Not simply the physical risks of injury from violent action—they are part and parcel of the lawman's occupation—but the mental anguish, the contamination from overexposure to diseased minds.

So there *is* a need for careful vetting and recruiting and training for UC work, and then there's the need to monitor UCs in the long-term cases, operationally and psychologically. The driving force responsible for moving Safeguard beyond the "good idea, someone should do something" stage was Steven Band, a Special Agent with a doctorate in psychology and a true believer in providing a helping hand to undercover agents floundering behind enemy lines. Steven and a small team of psychologists conducted research to identify the risks inherent in working undercover, as well as to develop a profile for the personality traits associated with the "ideal" undercover. To identify those individuals who could successfully perform the arcane and unique tasks, and then egress unscathed.

One can imagine a fictitious Performance Appraisal Ratings System: *Rate employee's ability to perform the following tasks: Lie to strangers. Gain the confidence of individuals in order for them to make self-destructive decisions. Work irregular hours in the company of hostile and ruthless individuals, perhaps with limited contact with family and friends* . . .

Steven's team highlighted the psychological hazards inherent in such UC work, developing a "process [that] challenges the myths promulgated by popular culture portrayals of undercover operatives and inoculates, or protects, UCEs against the adverse impact of undercover stress" (*FBI Law Enforcement Bulletin*, August 2008, p. 2).

For the personality evaluations, the Safeguard creators used standardized psychological tests, the FIRO-B, MMPI, etc., but developed their own scales and ranges to identify what they had determined would best suit the prototype of the "ideal UC."

The *preferred* personality traits included the following: extroverted, even charismatic; comfortable in social environments; a facility in earning the trust of others while at the same time cautious and somewhat skeptical in evaluating the motives of others; requiring *minimal positive feedback*. Overall: lots of characteristics associated with the ability to operate independently, a respect for rules (without an obsessive dependence on them), tolerance of stress, a reasonable degree of cynicism. Just because you're a bit paranoid doesn't mean you won't be a "normal" UC.

By the time I was assigned to work at Safeguard itself, I had been "safeguarded" (as it came to be referred to in UC agent slang) almost twenty times. By retirement, UCs such as Jack Garcia and myself had volumes of files, the weight of which made for a running joke whenever we showed up. (Steven Band had conducted my first assessment during the start-up of COMMCORR. This was before they had the covert office I was later to occupy. Steven flew up to New York and grilled me in the back of a van. When he took off his suit jacket, I was bemused. Imagine, a psychologist with a 9mm and two spare magazines in the belt pouch.)

Undercover agents being undercover agents, the challenge became how to conceal any issues that could result in an unsuccessful "safeguarding." For the "regulars," the hundred or so full-time FBI UCs nationwide, Safeguard assessments were perceived as having significantly dissimilar outcomes: providing a helping hand in a time of need, *or* an obstacle to continuing in covert roles. The recommendation of "time assigned to routine agent work upon completion of the current Group I" would have been a dreaded result, to be avoided at all costs.

Perhaps this is the time in my story—ten years into UC work—to discuss my personal dark side, as I have encountered it. On a level of which I was not consciously aware, the personally taxing consequences of the previous decade may have put me on the road to Safeguard. In San Juan, pre-undercover, I had undergone a transition that set the stage for the rest of my FBI life. Initially overwhelmed at being a "combatant" and potential target of the *Machetero* terrorists, frightened at what would be the lot of an FBI agent taken prisoner, I developed a stress level sufficient to provoke strong doubts about my recent career change—assistant DA to FBI agent. And then I arrived at the critical determination, come what may: *I will not be taken alive.* The conviction released me from the stress. One fine moment, three months into my assignment in San Juan, I came out of my cocoon for good. I've described the scene: when I advanced, revolver drawn, on the shadow men in the cul-de-sac. That nighttime confrontation sealed the transformation. "Epiphany" is an overworked term, but that's what this was. My usual equanimity returned. I had a calm confidence that I might die fighting but I would, at all costs, remain in control.

It was in this same spirit that I received the counsel from my San Juan buddy Mike Castro some years later. A former Green Beret and big-city cop, the five-foot-six, hardcore UC projected the strength of a six-foot-five heavyweight. I was surprised when Mike told me he used his BuPistol, registered to the FBI, in UC ops (not a covert, untraceable handgun, such as my old Walther PPK).

What if the bad guys see the serial number? Run it by a crooked cop or someone?

"If they're reading the serial number," he replied, "you'll already be dead."

Alas, that conviction not to be taken alive and the equanimity it conveyed couldn't cover everything. Couldn't come close. I don't have *nothing but* rocks in my head! The moment in San Juan provided the mental and the emotional foundation for a uniquely hazardous career, but laying a foundation is only the first step. In COMMCORR, working deep cover in the stress of the chaotic exchange floor (even given no real perceived physical risk), taking on the chin the hostility of my employers, juggling the long hours consumed by working two jobs, in effect, as well as the sense of isolation—frankly, Jameson's Irish Whiskey became an all-too-regular friend. Less than a week following the fifty-subject takedown of RUN-DMV—an episode particularly loaded with the emotionally charged confrontations with the subjects, as mandated by my supervisor Craig Dotlo—I arrived at my girlfriend's house in Paris. Half a bottle later, I awoke long enough to fall down a flight of stairs. No injuries, miraculously, but after that: no more whiskey. Ever.

Of course, my desire to succeed as an undercover, to prove myself, to be the *best,* was still immeasurable. Those who are not cut out for covert work, yet try it regardless, are pushed by this urge into making *operational* errors—they simply make too many mistakes, a little slip in preparation for a meet, unconvincing haggling, an impromptu slip of the tongue, an unconvincing reaction to an unexpected turn, sheer panic (remember Steve Kim, who froze at Holyland and could have gotten both of us killed on the spot). Any of these will almost certainly dead-end the case, at the very least.

With me, it was different. With me, the greatest risk of all was emotional entanglement, an occupational vulnerability of which I was, at the time, totally unaware. No one had ever warned me, but regarding which I subsequently counseled innumerable rookie UCs. Regardless how high one scores in the "Strong Independent Character" trait on the Safeguard tests, the emotional ties that evolve day-to-day behind enemy lines take their toll. And I'm not talking about falling in love, which really would be catastrophic, either personally or for the op, or both. I'm talking about *ordinary* emotional ties. That's what happened in RUN-DMV, which eventually featured (thanks to my zeal to succeed) a core of subjects whom I would see on almost a daily basis for two and a half years. And I allowed—no, I encouraged—bonds of friendship to develop. In my narration of that op, the name Julio Dominguez came up briefly. Julio was an easygoing Dominican runner with an understated sense of humor, a pleasure to be around. Almost anyone would have that reaction to Julio, he was just that kind of engaging guy. His feelings toward me were such that he invited me to his wedding. One doesn't invite casual acquaintances to a wedding. Close friends, yes. It wasn't a big wedding, and I didn't go. I knew it would be inappropriate: I had gone well beyond gaining his confidence. *I have to be in Miami that week, Julio, I'm really sorry but I can't make it.* That was fine, no hard feelings, we'll miss you.

Then there was Duardo, or more specifically, Duardo's son. Duardo was a close friend of Julio, and he was helping me with frequent no-ID registrations at the Yonkers DMV. He would sometimes bring his son, who must have been seven or eight. We adults don't really know how kids see us, but I knew I was a familiar face to the boy. Then one day he showed me the skateboard on which he'd embossed my alias's initials:

"AP." That really touched me. Late that afternoon, as I drove off, I had some real misgivings. Sooner or later, the boy's father was going to be arrested, along with his Tío Julio, both as a *direct* result of their friendship with me, Tío Alex. When we arrested Duardo that dramatic morning less than a year later, I thought about that skateboard. Memo to Marc: Avoid emotional ties with subjects.

No, I didn't twist their arms to break the law, I definitely did not entrap them in any way; their fraudulent documents were a good business long before I showed up. But I resolved almost then and there that with new subjects in all future ops, it would be all business. The excessive friendship didn't threaten the ops, but eventually it took a toll on me. Henceforth, I engaged in only as much socializing as needed to gain the subjects' confidence, and that's not much. The subjects in most cases didn't really care if I was the friendly sort. They just wanted me to be competent and dependable in my crookedness. My new attitude: *We've got friends already, who needs more; let's just make money.*

And finally, on this subject, there was a major public corruption op, not long after the BLUE SCORE success in Mount Vermon in Westchester County. This time we were in Dutchess County, due north of Westchester. This was late 1997, about a year before I headed south to FBIHQ. William Paroli, the de facto boss of Poughkeepsie, and a number of other top county officials were suspected of pervasive extortion, massive shakedowns. In the course of the investigation, I had developed a valuable relationship with Basil "Bill" Raucci, Poughkeepsie Town Property Assessor, a senior official who had accepted a number of bribes (from me) on behalf of my father-in-law's construction company. Phony father-in-law, of course, but a real construction company upstate whose actual CEO was exceedingly tired of being hit up for bribes as a cost-of-doing-business and set this investigation rolling. Originally, this CEO agreed to wear a wire, but second thoughts arose as the date approached, and he backed out. He was willing, however, to send a trusted subordinate (i.e., an undercover agent) to manage his Dutchess County projects. In order to account for my lack of expertise in the construction field, I suggested the role of son-in-law (nepotism being a practice these subjects should understand). After two days at the CEO's office, I had acquired sufficient vocabulary to get by and come across as, well, a pampered (and underqualified) son-in-law.

With this branch of the investigation well in hand, Craig Dotlo, once again my excellent supervisory agent, and Jim O'Connor, the case agent, decided to flip Bill Raucci and bring him in as a confidential witness. *Wait a minute, Craig.* Why risk the guy saying "Fuck you," accepting the prospect of prison, then tipping off all of the other targets? What would be the benefit of that? The guy was *already* working for us unwittingly. Big argument with Craig—the second one ever, and we went back and forth for a couple of weeks. His point was that as a CW, Raucci could be given specific instructions and closely managed. Such a full debrief would provide valuable intel on all the players, the main one (William Paroli) in particular. But I was the one who had been meeting with him, and I was better placed to evaluate his character. In my judgment, flipping Raucci was a long shot.

I lost that debate. After my next UC meet with Raucci at the Fishkill Holiday Inn, Craig and Jim walked into the hotel room as I walked out. I glanced back. I still remember his startled look. They gave him until Monday to sign on, or be arrested.

Over the weekend, October 4, 1997, the man decided on a third course of action: After carefully placing his wallet, keys, and jewelry on a dresser at home, he walked into the Hudson River. I was upset, really upset. Bill Raucci died as a consequence of his interaction with me. So I felt at the time. If I'd had my way, he would have been arrested at the same time as the other targets, and they would all have gone down together. I was convinced this would have worked against any suicidal impulse. And he would have had plenty of company. Along with Paroli, who was convicted in February 2000, a half-dozen others were caught in the net, with charges ranging from conspiracy to commit extortion to murder.

I had a hard time caring about the case's success, frankly, even though my anger over the suicide was not the result of having gotten too close to Bill Raucci "operationally." I had not done that, so this was not a situation where . . . *If I'd kept my distance from him, I would not have cared so much.* It was just another by-product, an unintended consequence, of working the dark side, where all manner of dire consequences are always possible, barely discernible in the shadows. Where emotions will often be near the surface—or, worse, buried . . . It's not coincidental that within a year I was on my way out the door of the Ramada in New Rochelle and posted to the Safeguard Unit at the covert site in the D.C. suburbs. It was not coincidental that I needed Safeguard.

10

Never the Same, Never Again

By noon on September 11, 2001, I knew—everyone knew—that the FBI would never be the same. For the foreseeable future, it would have, if not quite a new mission, a totally recommitted one. On Monday morning, I was in the office. From this perch at the epicenter, as a Headquarters supervisor plugged into the Bureau's nerve center (even though my physical base was Safeguard's covert off-site), I would have a firsthand view. Within days, I was assigned to supervise a team of support personnel at the Victim Assistance Center on one of the Hudson River piers. This surprised me. I was an undercover agent (and, now, for the time being, supervisor). What were the chiefs thinking? Not much, really. The assignment resulted from a bureaucratic anomaly. On the Bureau's organizational chart, the Victim's Unit happened to be in the same section as Safeguard, and the assistance center near the World Trade Center needed bodies.

Mayor Rudy Giuliani had set up this complex, and every government agency with any excuse whatsoever—local, state, and federal—set up a presence somewhere in the vicinity of the Towers that fall. As the War on Terror geared up, with almost unimaginable funding and corresponding chest-pounding, no agency could afford to be left behind. That's not a cynical statement, not at all. It just states a truth about institutional behavior—that is, human behavior. And don't forget: every agency, every individual wanted so much to help, to *do something*.

The telltale odor from Ground Zero lingered for months. It was a surreal environment, as everyone who was in the city knows. Mark Mason, a friend and fellow agent based in New York, was my host for my first tour of Ground Zero. Despite having seen the devastation endlessly repeated on cable news, I wasn't prepared for what I saw. Words failed me then, and they wouldn't be any better now. Despite my thoroughly cosmopolitan background and life, I can be an old-fashioned patriot, and what I saw was a battlefield—a terrible defeat in a real war on American soil. The attack had claimed the life of John O'Neill, whom I'd known in the course of one of my temporary duty assignments to the U.S. Embassy in Paris a few years earlier. In the late nineties, John was chief of the Bureau's counterterrorism operation. After he retired—and less than three weeks before the attacks—he had assumed his duties as chief of security at the WTC. For everyone who knew him, the irony was brutal.

My new assignment was not a chore. I did not resent the time away from the UC world. Like everyone, I wanted to *do something*. I didn't want to be on the sidelines. And here I was, one of the soldiers. My assignment, in theory, was to oversee the FBI's team of victim-assistance specialists in the Victim Assistance Center, but as it turned out, I didn't do much actual supervising. Each family wanted to speak to an FBI *agent*, and I was the only actual agent on hand. I served as their repository for nightmare scenarios come true—one after the other, twelve hours a day, seven days a week, until further notice. (Those were everyone's hours.) I listened as family after family described the details that precipitated the death of their father . . . mother . . . brother . . . sister . . . child . . . only child. I still see—often—the dignified, aging black man whose son had gone to the World Trade Towers that day for a job interview. For some reason, his grief in its quiet, infinite magnitude, struck a unique cord . . . But, truly, every story was heart-wrenching.

The anthrax scare added another layer of fear and uncertainty and affected my work in an unforeseeable way. Official bulletins warned that the most significant threat came from airborne dissemination of the deadly virus. Given this danger, the NYPD director of security for the pier and myself decided that no aerosol bottles would be allowed into the tightly packed, enclosed area. Well, we two men had no idea how many women carry some form of spray bottle or other spritz in their purses. A comic counterpoint to the oppressive and pervasive gloom, our precautionary prohibition caused a near riot. For women with nerves already approaching threshold breakdown levels (which was also the case for many if not most New Yorkers), this was an intolerable imposition. The repercussions reached the Police Commissioner's Office and the deputy mayor. In true bureaucratic save-one's-own-backside form, my NYPD colleague, a senior official, told his bosses that he had been *ordered* to impose this security measure by the FBI, in the form of one Marc Ruskin, Special Agent. And against this official's advice and better judgment, of course. While absurd on its face—NYPD Inspectors are not known for meekly taking orders from the Feds—the accusation was sufficient to win me a (by this time welcome) ticket back to Headquarters, where I would be available for an *operational* assignment, my forte and better suited to my temperament. The weeks in ravaged Manhattan had served as a good education, an eyewitness introduction to the horrors, physical and emotional, wrought by cruel, implacable enemy forces—forces with which the Bureau had been at war for more than a decade, at last taken seriously by the public at large, and by politicians and talking heads as well.

The Bureau, and every law enforcement entity anywhere, no matter how remotely connected to the attacks, was flooded with leads and tips and hunches and rumors and allegations about suspected terrorists but woefully short of *verifiably good sources*. I knew one reason why.

Three years earlier, I had signed up an informant to help in a public corruption Group I op targeting administrative law judges in New York City who were accepting bribes funneled their way by equally indiscriminate lawyers. For this sting, we had used the fictitious law office developed for a previous investigation. But the targeted judges would not nibble at the bait proffered by this new face, alias Mark S. H. Ruskin. Lesson learned from COMMCORR, Craig and I reasoned that posing as a crooked attorney in New York, I ran a pretty good chance of running into an acquaintance. For my alias, besides the minor changes to my name, I obtained a fictitious Social Security number, based on a new date of birth, along with the usual credit cards, driver's license, and wallet filler. The one catch: I could not obtain backstopping for my credentials as an attorney licensed to practice in New York. The responsible authorities in the courts, in the bar associations, refused to cooperate. They protect their own. Cagey subjects, these. Not ordinary. This was perhaps the only case in which I failed to penetrate the criminal network and gain the confidence of the subjects.

Our informant in the case with the judges, David Almasi, had extricated himself from a legal situation (violation of a city ordinance) with such a bribe to one of the judges. He then doubled down on his jeopardy by recklessly mentioning the incident to an acquaintance. Who happened to be an FBI source. Bad break. Aware of the Bu's interest in public corruption, that source had relayed the information to his contact agent, which led to an interview of Almasi—a nonconfrontational interview. The agent was interested in the bigger fish, the men and women behind the bench who accepted bribes. He introduced me to David Almasi, and I formally "opened" him as a CI.

Almasi was forthcoming from the start, and without any subtle threats of prosecution he agreed to work with the Bu. Short on cash, however, he would not refuse a little spending money. The bad break was suddenly a good break! A native of Tehran, in his midforties, with steel-wool hair and bushy mustache, Almasi struck me as particularly well suited for counterterrorism work (CT, as it is referred to in the profession). This trustworthiness vis-à-vis the jihadis gained further credence from the fact that Almasi was Jewish, having arrived in the United States following a few years in Israel after leaving Iran.

Yes, he was willing to infiltrate Hezbollah cells in the United States, or at least try to. Here was the dream CI for the War on Terror, a once-in-a-lifetime find. I was certain of this. In any event, I felt that the least the Bureau should do was to find out for sure. But, maddeningly, I could not find a counterterrorism agent to work him. I was able to set up a few interviews between agents and Almasi—*Marc, this guy's great, we'll get back to you*—but the expressed excitement was always followed by . . . nothing. This was a couple of years before 9/11, and the lackadaisical attitude I encountered in the matter of David Almasi was not unusual in the nineties, despite the wake-up call from the Blind Sheik in the first WTC bombing.

Now recall John Sultan, the contractor originally from Bangladesh who was so instrumental as a cooperating witness in RUN-DMV and numerous other operations. John had a list of Bureau-botched opportunities for the development of good CT cases. In one instance, he had insinuated himself to the point that he worked "Security" at an Islamic (read *jihadist*) conference. Assigned by CT agents to gather intel, John attended services and meetings at mosques in New York and Newark, identifying radical Imam guest speakers and reporting back on the vitriolic and violent content of the sermons. "Death to the Great Satan" was a popular and *already* well-worn theme before the planes struck the Towers. But not much happened within law enforcement and CT circles. John's value was woefully underappreciated and undervalued *until* 9/11, when the counterterrorism scene became, overnight, barely controlled chaos. *Now* frantic calls from CT management poured in.

Marc, your Jewish Iranian guy, would he still be willing to work for us? No luck. David Almasi was nowhere to be found. After a couple of years' good service, he had dropped off the radar and moved on. As for John Sultan, he now had a lucrative career and young family, and his past experiences had left a sour taste. He would not be coming back. A significant loss to the CT cause, I believe, but at least the FBI and everyone else now understood the gravity of the jihadi threat and the necessity of inside information. As I wrote in the Introduction, this is especially true at a time when terrorists and criminals are becoming ever *less* likely to trust any kind of recordable or traceable medium. As noted earlier, the bad guys' expectation of privacy is already approaching zero (and ours isn't much higher). The National Security Agency could announce that it is unilaterally shutting down its entire electronic surveillance operation, or the debate over the constitutional legality of such snooping could be settled in favor of privacy (a political impossibility, at the time of this writing), and the bad guys would *still* scoff. They know which way the wind's blowing—and they also know how to employ the newest, commercially available encryption technology. As the effectiveness of the traditional methods of electronic investigation decreases, the importance of UC work necessarily increases. Even if the NSA does collect every single communication generated in every corner of the globe, where's the value without a basis for evaluation and corroboration?

One reason legal cases against terrorists are so hard to prosecute is the difficulty of planting undercover agents in those environments. The ill-fated Detroit Sleeper Cell case, coming right on the heels, literally weeks, after the destruction of the WTC, confirmed the need for undercovers. Informants may not be trustworthy; their information has to be corroborated. The bottom line: in the era of electronic surveillance, undercover work is *not* passé. It is not obsolete. Just the opposite, in fact. It enforces accountability. It prevents mistakes.

That said, there's no doubt that CIs have a critical place in counterterrorism cases, but they have to be handled with extreme caution and care. The infamous Whitey Bulger episode in Boston was as bad as it gets, but the opportunities for out-of-control CIs in CT investigations are almost self-evident. High-caliber CIs and CWs such as John Sultan and David Almasi being few and far between, institutional pressures for positive results immediately after the Al-Qaeda attack led to a lowering of the bar in the CI recruitment process. With dubious results. In the case of the Newburgh Four, for example, an informant had apparently offered the targets of a CT case huge quantities of cash, a late-model sports sedan, and a barber shop in exchange for firing a Stinger missile at an air force plane and bombing synagogues. Yet Federal Judge Colleen McMahon, who presided at the trial of these four men, complained, "The government did not act to infiltrate and foil some nefarious plot; there was no plot to foil . . ." In other words, these guys in Newburgh were more *aspirational* than *operational,* a distinction the Bureau itself has drawn. The judge lamented: "I believe beyond a shadow of a doubt that there would have been no crime here except the government instigated it, planned it, and brought it to fruition . . ." Nevertheless, she felt obliged to uphold the jury's guilty verdict and imposed the mandatory minimum sentences required by federal law: twenty-five years hard time.

Mike German, successful infiltrator of the Aryan Nations, my fellow UC instructor and a fixture at the Starlight Lounge, now a fellow at the Brennan Center for Justice at NYU Law School, commented in a *Huffington Post* blog, "What I find problematic is when the defendant has no connection to real terrorists or access to weapons . . . There are real terrorists out there, and all of the resources used on these manufactured cases should be devoted to those real cases."

I concur, and add that all of these issues and obstacles should serve to demonstrate the *enhanced* post-9/11 imperative to utilize the gold standard in investigation and then prosecution: the undercover.

After 9/11, there was also a universal call for extensive counterterrorism training to enhance the capabilities of all FBI agents to effectively wage the belatedly acknowledged war against Al-Qaeda and all the other jihadi cells. Few agents were familiar with the operational techniques utilized by the various IT organizations and the optimal investigative approaches. Naturally enough, my instinctual response to the crisis was to utilize undercover operations to identify and ultimately arrest the key players. However, the *direct* approach, trying to have an agent actually become a member of a terrorist organization, would be virtually impossible. (Confidential sources like John Sultan were difficult enough to find and trust.) An agent would not only need to speak the properly accented Arabic, but also have an intimate familiarity with the geographic area from which the group originated, acquaintances in common, and so forth. The appropriate UC scenario for the environment immediately following 9/11 was not to become a member of the group, but rather to provide an essential service. I hasten to note that in current times—the second half of the second decade post-9/11—close-knit terrorist cells have evolved into international armies, welcoming new recruits from the West, which should facilitate the introduction of UCs. But don't forget: a jihadi organization overseas is the *ultimate* high-risk operational environment. I still believe that the operation that provides an essential service to the jihadis is still much more likely to succeed. It would also be much safer for the UCs.

Terrorists hoping to operate in the West would need fictitious ID, as they had obtained from Mahmoud back in the nineties. They would need secure means of travel, such as untraceable cars, secure means of communication, such as advanced encryption programs. They would need explosives and detonators. A suitably experienced UC, with the right introductions could provide all of these and more. And then the Bureau would know where the jihadis were going, what they were saying—and to whom. And the Bureau could be certain that the bombs would be harmless. The training for the UCs, for the case agents, for the analysts, for all the pertinent Bureau personnel would be time-consuming and costly, requiring in-service courses at the academy in Quantico—but highly worthwhile.

Following 9/11, however, that was the road not taken. That was the training that was not implemented. Instead, some committee at JEH had a brainstorm, and the FBI Virtual Academy was developed. Thanks to this invention, we could all sit comfortably at our desks, click through the twenty-minute modules followed by multiple-choice test questions, and in a couple of hours complete *all* of our training in international terrorism. But I exaggerate. It didn't need to take two hours. The questions were so easily within the grasp of a high school student with a moderate familiarity with current events that it wasn't even necessary for us college-educated FBI employees to actually read the modules. Nor did the virtual courses track the time spent on each module, only the duration of the entire course. You probably see where this is going: agents soon figured out that they could open the program, minimize the window and maybe work on their actual cases, get in a good workout, and/or grab a bite, then return to the program, click through the modules without paying much attention, correctly answer the questions for each module, and complete the training. Maybe the program recorded two hours of study, but in fact the charade had been finished in under half an hour.

Thanks to the Virtual Academy, the Director of the FBI could now testify before Congress and the American people that *every single FBI employee* had now received invaluable counterterrorism training.

Unbelievable, but true.

By November 2011, I was back at Safeguard's covert headquarters, nosing around JEH for an appropriate role—but not UC for the time being. I was still in management, and that door was still closed—absent exigent circumstances, my bosses were not about to let me work undercover. Supervisors aren't supposed to get their hands dirty. The state-of-the-art command post at Headquarters had the atmosphere of a NASA launching, only ratcheted up to peak level, every minute of every day, co-coordinating leads between agencies both CONUS and OCONUS (intel-speak for within and beyond the continental United States). At the International Operations Unit, I learned that many of the LEGATs (Legal Attachés, the discreet name for FBI offices in U.S. embassies) needed support. In particular, LEGAT Paris. I had maneuvered into a three-month assignment there a few years earlier, thanks to my native French proficiency. That experience made me the ideal candidate to ship out to Paris to lend a hand for three fascinating months.

Those twelve-to-fourteen-hour days flashed past. Working with the *Direction de la Surveillance du Territoire,* the *Police Nacionale,* and the *Gendarmerie* proved revelatory. Reluctant as Bureau upper management might be to acknowledge the fact, the French counterintelligence operation knew whereof it spoke. As the former colonial rulers of most of North Africa, the French CT establishment had a long history of managing CT investigations to deal with the various insurrections. And sporadic fatal jihadi bombings in Paris over several years were more than enough motivation to enhance the already well-developed intelligence-gathering network, with numerous productive sources and sophisticated management of the collected information. And pragmatic, deceptively simple countermeasures as well. Example: The casual tourist may not realize the rationale for the design of Paris trash receptacles, those steel hoops holding a colored but *transparent* plastic bag. Any bomb would be visible. Okay, but a bomber could simply put the bomb in an ordinary package of some sort, and put that package into the transparent garbage bag. Yes, but *any* appropriately sized package will trigger alerts, particularly in times of heightened awareness.

Also revelatory: French authorities were not limited by an equivalent of America's Constitutional protections of individual privacy (requirements for court-ordered warrants and the like). I was stunned to learn the French CT forces, at any given time, were listening in on seventy thousand ongoing phone intercepts.

Approaching Christmastime, three months after 9/11, the work in Paris slowed down. The holidays provided an excuse to recharge my batteries after the exhausting fall months. A very short recharge, however, because Legat Enrique Ghimenti called my cell phone on the evening of December 22. Soft-spoken and controlled—even in times of unspeakable pressure—Enrique asked if I would be so kind as to come into the embassy. It seemed that there had been a bombing attempt on an American Airlines flight that had originated in Paris, bound for Miami. LEGAT Paris was immediately flooded with leads. The Director wanted the facts. All the facts. Right away. Theories about coordination with other, potential bombings were everywhere. We were all concerned that this attempt was just the first of a series of Al-Qaeda Christmastime airline bombings, and were taking all imaginable steps to prevent the anticipated catastrophe.

The entire world knows that the hapless Richard Reid was subdued before he could blow up that AA Flight 63 to Miami with the explosives hidden in his shoe. And we also know from the exhaustive follow-up investigation that the concerns at the time were valid: Reid had been selected as the first of several Al-Qaeda operatives to blow up *a series of U.S. carrier flights* over the holiday period, in a coordinated attack matching 9/11 in scope and calculated to shatter the collective Western psyche.

Having worked on the investigation from its inception, I have my own thoughts as to why he failed. First, like any terrorist bureaucracy, Al-Qaeda was reticent to use (and therefore *lose*) their top talent. Way, way down from the top of the chart were Richard Reid and the projected second bomber, Saajid Badat. Reid had been ordered to board the flight on the 21st of December, but he had bungled his simple task, arousing suspicion by his frazzled looks and absence of luggage. After that failure, he was operating on his own. The planned scenario had taken a twist, and the plot now required its principal operator to take independent action, to use his judgment, to make decisions. And that is when it started to go south, because Reid was not the sharpest nail in the coffin. He checked into one of the airport hotels. With a full day before he could again attempt to board AA Flight 63, he would have felt his stress levels rise. He had much to occupy his thoughts. He had bungled the early stages of an important mission—already the leadership would no doubt be grumbling. And tomorrow he would be dying. That's no minor matter for a long night's consideration. On his first attempt to board the flight, all through the final steps leading to his arrival at Orly, Reid would have been accompanied by comrades, constantly reminded of the importance of his martyrdom and his impending euphoria upon arrival in Paradise, and kept busy with the execution of last-minute details and checks. Busy work. But now, one day later, all of that support structure was gone. He had no comrades, little to do, and plenty of time to reflect on what little remained of his future. Perhaps, a little weed was called for. A short walk through the hotels, maybe chatting with some service staff, and he could retire to his room with enough marijuana to carry him through to the next day. One joint, now relaxed. Maybe another one, for good measure . . . and another. All lit with the same disposable butane lighter he had been given to light the fuse of the bomb in the heel of his shoe.

The next morning, rising late, still half-stoned, he rushed to the gate. Checking his pockets while hurriedly striding through the terminal. *The lighter! Did I leave it in the hotel room?* A quick stop at a newsstand, cigarettes, and a couple of books of matches, and boarding time. Seated on the plane, wasn't the mission nearly accomplished?

No. The mission was already a failure. Reid no longer had the requisite tools to destroy the airliner and murder those within. The detonator cord. In order to light the fuse, the cord required uninterrupted exposure to a source of intense heat. Hence the butane lighter. The cord *could not be ignited with a match—or even matches, plural, frantically lit one after the other*. Reid sought, over and over again, to light the fuse. The cord would not light. Finally, passengers reacted and won the struggle. It was over. Richard Reid had bungled the operation and was now just uniquely a loser.

Security measures at airports worldwide skyrocketed. The Al-Qaeda masterminds immediately realized the entire, meticulously planned operation would have to be scrapped.

I wasn't the only temporary duty agent with LEGAT Paris in those months right after 9/11. The office had required a steady supply of temporary duty agents to supplement the permanent staff. However, a permanent vacancy was also imminent, Enrique had confided: ALAT (Assistant Legal Attaché). The assignment was for three to five years. There would be a beautiful office in the chancery, the classically designed embassy building, next door to the supremely elegant Crillon Hotel, walking distance from the Arc de Triomphe. I believed that my UC career was in all likelihood behind me. I was very wrong about that, but that was my feeling. And the ALAT posting was quite attractive in its own right. As a senior law enforcement diplomat, one of the three special agents assigned to represent the FBI in France, I would be working day-to-day with the highest level officials in the Ministry of the Interior, the French National Police, and the Gendarmerie. At embassies throughout Paris, I would be networking with my counterparts from across the globe. Periodically, I would be attending conferences at Interpol (in Lyons, culinary capital of France) and across Europe. Finally, Paris was the city of my birth. Uncles, aunts, cousins, childhood friends resided there. I knew instantly that I *wanted* that job. I wanted Paris.

So did Marc Beauchemin, also on temporary assignment in Paris, with only a week remaining prior to his return to JEH in Washington. A supervisor in the Finance Division (yuck), he had less than five BuYears under his belt. Though generally suspicious of those who enter management with minimal street experience—he had clearly applied for a hard-to-fill vacancy to wedge his way into the mainstream—I suppressed my instinctual reaction to Marc's position. We had much in common, after all: two less-than-hulking skinny guys, both born in France, native French speakers, with many relatives and friends living nearby, both aspiring to a permanent assignment in Paris. Beauchemin had served as a paratrooper in the French military prior to moving to the United States. (*This* impressed me.) In evening chats while leaving the U.S. Embassy, walking down the snowy boulevards, we exchanged plans and goals. I talked of perhaps one day living in retirement in a country house in southern France. He wanted to pursue his career and raise his family in his native France.

Marc had been required to renounce his French citizenship as a precondition of joining the Bureau (though his children retained their French nationality). He was surprised (and then some) to learn that I enjoyed dual-nationality status, entitled to hold both French and American passports. (In my time, nearly ten years before Marc's, the question hadn't come up. The box on the application form asked a simple yes/no question, *Are you a citizen of the United States?* Yes, and assistant DA that I was, I knew better than to answer unasked questions.)

Given his short tenure—just five years of combined street and management time—in the Bureau, I counseled Marc not to get his hopes up. Time was on his side. There would be plenty of opportunities in the years to come. Both of us returned to the states early in 2002. It was springtime in Virginia. I could ride my Honda Valkyrie 1500cc touring bike to work and on Sunday cruises through horse country. During the week, I was back at Safeguard, where, now four to five months after 9/11, we had resumed our work supporting the Bureau's undercover agents and operations.

Finally, the call came from International Operations Unit I, responsible for Europe. Out of the eight applicants for the ALAT job in Paris, the Career Board (the Bureau's best-attempt mechanism at ensuring fair and impartial promotions, and it does work pretty well . . . when left alone and not tampered with) had selected me for permanent assignment to Paris. Sixteen years in the Bureau, thirteen of them in the field, had come to fruition. Five years in Paris as ALAT would presumably be followed by five years as Legat, the big (Camembert) cheese. Imagine: a large and beautiful paid-for-by-Uncle Sam apartment would allow me to accumulate sufficient funds to buy the apartment I would occupy while working at my retirement job with some global corporation with a presence in Paris. By which time, I would have met a cosmopolitan beauty and started a family. Delightful dreams.

My orders were cut. As with all intra-BuTransfers, I had ninety days to report to my new duty station. A global relocation company received the contract and contacted me to initiate the move. Even my Honda Valkyrie would cross the ocean. A vacancy was posted to fill my place at Safeguard. By midsummer, I would be sipping a crisp and chilled white burgundy at a familiar café overlooking the Seine. Then, one morning while I was at home preparing to move into a furnished apartment for my last few months in the States (I had canceled the lease on my Virginia residence), I received a second call from the International Operations Unit. My orders had been put on hold. The Unit Chief didn't know why.

The rest of this tale could have been written by Franz Kafka. Here's the short version, but it still says a lot about ponderous government bureaucracies and their knee-jerk reactions to crisis. The Bu's feared and generally despised Security Division (SECDIV) had inexplicably intervened in my transfer. Why? Well, Robert Hanssen, an FBI agent who had been spying for the Soviet Union since 1979, had finally been arrested slightly over a year earlier, in February 2001. This was on top of the fiasco with Aldrich Ames, the now-infamous CIA intelligence officer, who had been spying for the Soviets for nearly a decade before his arrest in 1994. For years undetected at the center of their respective agencies, Hanssen and Ames had been selling secrets of enormous value to our enemies. Covert intel-gathering operations costing multimillions of dollars had been exposed. The identities of Russian generals and officials secretly working with us had been exposed. The two traitors were responsible for at least a dozen deaths, some (intended as object lessons) were particularly gruesome. One betrayed high-ranking KGB officer was tossed alive into the Lubianka furnace, while his colleagues were forced to look on.

Ames was bad enough for the Washington-based law enforcement bureaucracies. Hanssen was the last straw. In the post-Hanssen Bureau, the upper-upper managers were determined to avoid another such disaster, and the consequent public humiliation. SECDIV bureaucrats were no longer a bunch of back-office benchwarmers. They were now cleanup batters with disproportionate influence, almost all-powerful, given a free hand and a blank check with which to clean house.

And SECDIV had received an anonymous report. Allegations had been made which necessitated thorough investigation. Concerning a certain Headquarters supervisor: Marc Ruskin.

What the hell was going on? If there was to be any possibility of salvaging my transfer (and career, for that matter), I needed information. Bimonthly trips to JEH became biweekly, visiting all my acquaintances, looking for rumors, overheard conversations, anything that could shed some light on the source and contents of this anonymous report. And I had a head start in this regard. Unlike many, actually most of my fellow GS-14 supervisory special agents (despite the title, the lowest rank of agent at HQ, the grunts), I had never limited my networking to those at the next higher rung. Over the four years (much longer than anticipated) of my Headquarters tenure, I had befriended inhabitants of many hidden corners in JEH: phone operators, freight handlers, electricians and mechanics, supply clerks, analysts. The permanent staff of the building. Those in a position to provide *real intelligence of value, real favors*. Who is talking to whom, who is coming and who is going, what's available and what isn't. UC techniques, though not UC.

The first break: Denise Wong, a senior analyst at International Operations Section, had learned the identity of the anonymous complainant who had accused me of "divided loyalties" and sparked the ensuing SECDIV investigation that had resulted in the *revocation* of my already-cut orders to LEGAT Paris. One condition, Denise said. I could not disclose my knowledge of the anonymous complainant's identity, as the information was "singular in nature," that is, my possession of the knowledge would lead SECDIV investigators directly back to Denise. I agreed. (She is now retired—the story can be told.)

The complainant was . . . Marc Beauchemin. The little rat! I was stunned. And not simply by the betrayal. I would never have expected true camaraderie from an FBIHQ supervisor assigned to the Finance Division with virtually no time on the street. But not this. Not a dagger between my shoulder blades. And it was my naïveté that angered me. How had I managed to let my defenses down? Where was my UC-honed sixth sense about people?

The Section Chief at the International Operations Section was burly and gruff Mike Pyszczmuka, former Legat Moscow. Mike was supportive and said, "The big stumbling block at SECDIV is Alan Levy. He is the Unit Chief overseeing this mess, and is adamant. Why don't you go talk to him? Can't hurt." Why not indeed? Hoping to catch Levy off guard, I arrived at his nest unannounced. Though a special agent, he was permanent staff at JEH, part of the subculture of managers who had never managed their way upward and out to management jobs in the field. Short, chubby, face shiny with perspiration—the mutual animosity was instant. He agreed to discuss the allegations. As I sat there, he read aloud from the complaint. *Apparently you have plans to retire in southern France.* This confirmed to my satisfaction the anonymous author's identity. I had told Beauchemin of this dream of mine. Levy continued. Having been born in France, with family and friends there, I would be a ripe target for recruitment. By the *French* Intelligence Services. The French. Not the Russians, not the Cubans, and certainly not the Iranians. The French: A friend would ask me for something innocent, maybe to write an essay on the U.S. legal system, which might be followed by a request for something a bit less innocent, perhaps the phone directory for the embassy.

I've been an FBI agent for over fifteen years. You don't think I might recognize a recruitment attempt?

Aldrich Ames didn't start until late in his career.

Kafkaesque.

Remember Steve Kim, the Seoul native who had served one day as my client at Holyland and froze up and almost got us both killed? The Bu posted his ass back to Korea. No divided loyalties there. Mexicans in Mexico? Not unheard of. Legat Warsaw was Polish. But Marc Ruskin in Paris? A security risk for America. Sitting in Levy's office I saw red. Clenched fists. *I* had "divided loyalties"? While I had risked my life buying heroin in Queens and counterfeit on the streets of the Lower East Side, this fat slug had been flying a desk at Headquarters. And he dared to compare me to Aldrich Ames? And wait a minute—last name *Levy*— Alan, dude, aren't you a fellow tribesman? Thanks for nothing, *schmuck*. The mounting urge to punch his greasy nose, to hear it crunch and for the blood to spurt across his desk, was barely suppressible. There was nothing further to be gained here. The instantaneous decision to be made: break Levy's face and throw away my career, or not. I walked away.

With the battle lines drawn, I sought allies. FBI Director Robert Mueller's right hand, Mike Mason (now Chief of Security for Verizon), lobbied on my behalf. As did the Executive Assistant Director, Kathleen McChesney. But the fix was in. A few long weeks later, McChesney called me in. There was a vacancy in Buenos Aires. My lucky day. I guess SECDIV didn't know that my mother, as well as most of my aunts, uncles, cousins, and a host of nefarious friends, in and out of government, were Argentine. Levy would have had conniptions at the thought of recruitment attempts by those vaunted, insidious, Argentine intelligence services. I could take Buenos Aires now or wait for the inevitable cancellation of Paris and—and what? Back to Safeguard?

• • •

As my flight and personal effects winged southward to the land of Tierra Del Fuego and grass-fed beef, rather than eastward toward the land of Provence and haute cuisine, I reflected on the fortuitous timing of my departure. As a result of internal forces, such as the Hanssen embarrassment, and external forces, most significantly the WTC attack, the huge cogs of the BUREAUcracy's grinding machinery were at a crossroads (if I may be allowed a mixed metaphor). Is there anyone on the globe not aware of the FBI, who does not respond (maybe with admiration, maybe with loathing), to the three-upper-case-letter "brand" (in the old sense, a mark burned on the side of a cow, not marketing newspeak)? Well, this world's premier law enforcement entity could now either sharpen its focus and mission and become an *enhanced* FBI, or it could meander aimlessly in a vain attempt to "redefine" itself.

The earlier discussion of the Bureau hierarchy provides clues as to which path it chose, although "chose" isn't quite right, because there wasn't much volition going on. Mostly political buffeting and inertia. Despite the well-meaning Director's best intentions, the political pressures were enormous. What happened next may have been inevitable: It wasn't just SECDIV that was being transformed. The policy makers in upper management commenced relinquishing FBI jurisdiction over key areas of criminal activity to other agencies, much to the chagrin of agents in the field, the world's foremost experts in investigating those domains. Much of the work corralling fugitives was farmed out (forever) to the U.S. Marshals. (Think "FBI Ten Most Wanted List" to gauge the significance of this move. The phrase won't have quite the import in a few years.) Credit card fraud went to the Secret Service (yes, the Secret Service), narcotics to the Drug Enforcement Administration.

The FBI, though by necessity very strong in intelligence gathering, had been, both by definition and in J. Edgar's realized vision, a law enforcement agency. *The* law enforcement agency. The CIA is *the* intelligence-gathering agency. (Its initials are pretty well recognized as well. So far as professionalism is concerned, it is in steep competition with the Mossad, French DGSE, and Russian FIS, formerly the KGB.) But fearing that the politicians would create a new and independent *domestic* security agency, à la British MI-5, the post-9/11 Bureau immediately initiated a shift. Mirroring the CIA's twin hierarchies—Case Officer and Intelligence Analyst—the Bu converted its old analyst position (previously a stepping stone to Special Agent) into a career-path Intelligence Analyst, with its own distinct course of training at Quantico. Following the true bureaucrat's intuitive belief that additional levels of administration and complexity create a more effective organization.

And of course there's the inevitable drift toward bureaucracy and paperwork. I have already explained Hoover's TIO (time-in-office) rule, aka the 10% Rule: TIO should never to exceed 10 percent. Today's ratio is 53 percent, and this does *not* include supplementing fieldwork with online or telephone or database investigation, but simply complying with administrative requirements. Just doing paperwork. Precisely what Hoover had sought to avoid, presciently aware of the inevitable consequences.

As to the implications for individual privacy rights arising from shifting a law enforcement agency with police power into domestic intelligence-gathering . . . *initially* not a concern. Critics will no doubt snicker and make reference to the 1950s blacklists, disregarding the lead role played by the U.S. Congress, *Senator* (not FBI Director) Joe McCarthy, the *House* (not Bureau) Un-American Activities Committee. Virtually all FBI special agents I have known over three decades have had significantly more respect for the Constitution (that we are sworn to uphold) than politicians, prosecutors, and journalists. But as the vulnerability to political (particularly executive) pressure increases, and as the institution evolves, so does the culture, and so do the hiring criteria. The old-school agents retire, and the stage is set for an Orwellian shift. Or not. Taking into account the voluminous data-gathering of the NSA, the shift across the board appears inexorable. However, long service does reveal the cyclical nature of government agencies and political entities, similar to booms and busts in the economy. If the will is there, the pendulum will swing back toward the Bill of Rights. Meanwhile, here's a public-service tip learned from many hours of listening to telephone intercepts as a young agent, and from subsequent reliance on all variety of eavesdropping in my UC ops: Never utter a word or compose a phrase, over the phonc or in a digital message, that you wouldn't be comfortable seeing in your local newspaper the next morning. And you'll be fine.

Postscript: The ex-congressman Anthony Weiner sexting scandals, the Clinton server debacle, the WikiLeaks email disclosures, and resultant high-profile publicly and/or privately shattered careers all serve to confirm the worth of my admonition.

All in all, 2002 was a good time for me to leave JEH behind. To go OCONUS. To try to forget what I knew would be the case: The mutual suspicion between myself and SECDIV would be a leitmotif until my BuRetirement in 2012.

11

But First, That Shootout in Buenos Aires

The tires squeal—really, they do—as I spin my gray Ford Focus hatch-back in a hard U-turn, putting the front of the car between me and the Honda speed bike up ahead, using my engine block for cover. The wheel is in my right hand, my gun (in Buenos Aires, the .40 caliber Glock M27) in my left. Why the precaution? Moments before, the bright red bike has screamed into my story. The passenger with shoulder-length black hair and no helmet has dismounted and aimed his large-frame pistol at the head of the driver of the car directly in front. When I react to this threat, the gunner shifts focus and aims his weapon at me.

I am on my way home from a late Sunday brunch with my cousin Eduardo, followed by some casual shopping in downtown Buenos Aires. Driving up four-lane Libertador Avenue in the heavy evening traffic, I'm thinking about which movie to put on the VCR, which excellent Argentine wine to uncork. Suddenly, there is a gun pointing at me. Holy shit. This is for real. In my seventeen years with the FBI, routinely hanging out with all manner of criminals, pretending to be one of them, never have I been face-to-face with the wrong end of a firearm barrel—not in Puerto Rico, not undercover. Nor have I ever fired my weapon except on the range. In the field, I've drawn it many times, mostly during those years in San Juan, on raids and while making arrests, but I've never shot anyone, or tried to. And now here I am, off duty on a crowded avenue in this cosmopolitan foreign capital, with this armed robbery or attempted murder, possibly an assassination, happening right in front of me.

Glock in hand, I throw open the door, using it and the windshield frame for cover. Then . . . what? . . . what happened? . . . It's a blank in my mind, a hole as my synapses fast-forward, leaving three, four, five seconds unaccounted for. Until my car is spinning, barely in control. After the emergency spin, my right tires are on the sidewalk. Now the gunman is seated on the Honda, his back is to me, the bike just yards ahead of the Ford. His upper torso twisted to the right, his face twisted in fury, eyes glaring. Right arm outstretched, a flash from the muzzle as he fires a single shot right into my windshield. I hear nothing but have the truly idiotic thought that *this isn't fair*. I still have the distinct memory. He's shooting at me! *Why?* I return fire, the Honda's engine screams from the immediate application of throttle, and the bike tears off. The driver of the other car, the original target for the crime, also speeds off. Total elapsed time, thirty seconds, maybe less.

Then time slowed back down. Within minutes, the police were on hand. On the tarmac fifteen yards in front of my car, they found a fully loaded magazine for a Glock 9mm—*not* my .40 caliber, therefore the shooter's pistol. He had not properly seated the magazine. In my mind (still operating a bit below capacity), I reasoned that this find would corroborate my account that the guys on the Honda bike were in fact armed. And that prints might be lifted. But the all-important, overriding significance of this gift from fate, from our Father, from my father looking out for me, did not surface until the next day as I recounted the incident to a couple of the DEA agents at the embassy. This magazine on the tarmac was the explanation for the inexplicable *single* shot from the shooter. He could fire only the one round that was initially chambered. If the magazine had worked, he would have sprayed my windshield and I probably wouldn't be typing these words right now.

I had fired one shot, or at least that's what I remembered, but a couple of weeks later, when I picked up my weapon from the *Policia Federal de Argentina* forensics shop, it had only eight rounds remaining. Interesting, because the fully loaded capacity of the Glock is ten shots. Had I fired the second bullet during my memory blank-out? Perhaps. Had the thug fired a round when he first saw me? Vast experience (not mine; law enforcers' in general) has proved that when the bullets are flying, eyewitness testimony from the immediate vicinity is often contradictory and pretty worthless. Sensory perceptions are distorted in a variety of forms: everything happening in slow-motion, tunnel vision, flashes of amnesia, high volume or no volume (but I *know* the tires on my Ford were squealing). Aim is also seriously affected. Bullets fly everywhere, even those shot by trained officers. This time in Buenos Aires, thank goodness, no bystanders were hurt. I don't know about the shooter or his driver. They were never found. Neither was the driver of the other car. The motive for the original confrontation was never established.

The rest of that evening was spent not watching the movie with the glass of fine wine but sitting in the dingy police station, answering questions and signing paperwork. However, the process was courteous, thanks to the presence of the number-four man in the Argentine federal police, Director of Counterterrorism, my friend Jorge Alberto "Fino" Palacios, the first person I called after the shooting. No, the hassles came later. Any shooting incident, in any law enforcement agency, is always considered a major event with potential legal repercussions. (In reality, gunfire is not that frequent. Most law enforcers of any kind go through their entire careers without firing a shot outside the range.) My incident in Buenos Aires had other exacerbating circumstances as well. I was a foreign national with diplomatic status in a sovereign nation. In the history of the FBI, no agent OCONUS—on assignment outside the United States in any capacity—had ever fired his or her gun, on or off duty. Hard to believe, but true. It's still true. (Not officially, at least. It's not too difficult to envision this scenario: FBI special agent, after firing the fatal rounds in a remote area in a foreign land, hands the weapon to his partner in the local constabulary, the National Police of Wherever, with a comment to the effect of "nice shooting, Jose" (or Tadej, or Hassan), and a wink.)

It would be only a slight exaggeration to state that FBI agents have nearly superhero status overseas—in sharp contradistinction to the perception domestically, particularly in New York and on the West Coast.

With every introduction overseas, you can see—you can *feel*—the eyes on you, *hoping* to be impressed by your authoritative FBI presence, your implicit FBI confidence, your penetrating FBI sagacity. You do *not* want to let the team down. At least I didn't. At the American Embassy in Buenos Aires, my transition from UC meets with heroin dealers (although it had been close to four years since those days on the streets) to ALAT meets with cabinet ministers and provincial governors had been smooth enough. Two agents in my office, assisted by the spectacular raven-haired Nilaya Vargas, the three of us responsible for all liaison and investigations in Argentina and two of its neighbors, Uruguay and Paraguay. All the agencies that handle information no one else was supposed to know about—the ones referred to by their initials in upper case—were bunched together in a special area in the embassy. The FBI team was cramped, with less privacy than a cubicle would have provided. Access to this redoubt was reminiscent of the clanging steel doors and secret passageways utilized by Agent 86 in the old *Get Smart* television show. We didn't have the Cone of Silence but came close.

FBI agents from throughout the United States would contact us directly with requests for local investigation on cases they were conducting in the States.

"Setting leads," in BuSpeak. The leads covered any and all domains. A suspected Hezbollah operative in Minneapolis is believed to have lived for ten-plus years in Argentina, please provide all available intel: more than a third of the leads were terrorism-related. A New York financier is being investigated for a complex Ponzi scheme, swindling millions of dollars. Eight potential victims have been identified as Buenos Aires residents, please interview. The leads flowed in both directions. Miguel Angel Galassi, Subcomisario, in *Delitos Economicos* would give me a call. Marc, we have a case against Julio Jimenez for mortgage fraud. We have source information that he has a secret bank account in Miami. Can you help? I—we—could sure try.

Interpol was of substantial assistance, but not as the general public would expect. There is, in fact, no single law enforcement agency named Interpol. Rather, almost every national police agency in the world has an office dedicated to international cooperation, staffed by its own officers. These offices are coordinated by a purely *administrative* (not operational) agency in Lyon, France—the Interpol General Secretariat. The Interpol office in the United States, situated in Washington, D.C., is made up primarily of FBI Agents. The Interpol office in Paraguay is manned by *Policia Nacional de Paraguay* officers. There is no such thing as an agent of Interpol.

The way it worked, if I did not already know a certain agency's chief regarding a certain subject matter—extortion, say, or blackmail, two popular choices—I would stop by the office of Luis Fuensalida, Comisario Inspector with the PFA, the *Policia Federal de Argentina*, and therefore— *Jefe*, Interpol. Tall and lanky, with a close-cropped gray beard, Luis would sit back, slowly draw on his pipe, and listen carefully. After I had filled him in on the case, he would either assign one of his officers to assist or call the *jefe* of the relevant division, and we would all work the matter together. Fuensalida's boss, overseeing Interpol, as well as Kidnapping, Complex Crimes, Terrorism, SWAT, and more, was Jorge Alberto "Fino" Palacios, introduced above as the friend whom I called immediately after the shooting, and who raced to the scene. (Not many years later, after I had returned to the States, my old San Juan era friend Will Godoy, now Legat Buenos Aires, informed me that Fino had been jailed on orders of First Lady Cristina Fernandez de Kirchner. He had refused orders to arrest judges and politicians from opposing political parties. In the end, after a year and a half, he was released but is still being dragged through the courts on spurious charges.)

As a temporary legal attaché in Paris (twice) and Madrid (a thirty-day stint in late 1998, right before starting at Safeguard), my relations with the local officials had always been clear-cut, the exchange of information following established patterns. At my office in the embassy in Buenos Aires, it didn't take long to realize that performing the identical tasks throughout the southern half of South America was akin to finding one's way in a thick fog. A fog of politics and intrigue, a subtext that ran through all exchanges. *All* of the local officials were functioning in a complex cnvironment, where their professional survival often depended on forces well beyond what we in the United States were used to. Admired as the institution may be, the initials FBI also often carry a political overtone. For certain locals, being identified as having close ties with the FBI could be of uncertain value. The initial task, for me, was to evaluate the degree of integrity and goodwill of the various officials, and proceed accordingly. It made for a fascinating and absorbing work environment, sufficiently challenging to fill the void left by UC operations and Safeguard.

The Legat himself, Augie Rodriguez, was an odd duck, not unlike an insurance salesman: he liked to talk incessantly and without interruption to people who didn't want to listen and weren't paying attention. While there was no love lost between us, we managed to maintain a relatively functional working relationship. That's where matters between us stood on March 25, 2003 (a year before the shootout). I was sitting at my desk one afternoon when Augie walked in. *You're going to need to fly out to Asunción on the next flight. There's been a kidnapping, high profile. The Ambassador wants the FBI on the scene. Right away.* He handed me a fax from the Asunción RSO, the State Department's Regional Security Officer responsible for embassy security. It was a clipping from a local tabloid. Mariángela Martínez, former Miss Paraguay—twenty years former— had been jogging in a secluded park that morning when she was abducted. And that was it.

During the three-hour flight on TAM, I reflected on my experience handling kidnapping cases. Overall, the Bureau is particularly well renowned for expertise in this area, but as for me—my reflection was a short one. One time I had acted as Spanish interpreter at the victim's family home, monitoring phone calls from the drug-dealer kidnapper to the drug-dealer father of the victim.

More worthy of reflection: Why was I on this flight, and not the Legat? His decision to pass up an opportunity for high-level praise could not have been taken lightly. Unless . . . there was significant potential for high-level *condemnation* instead. Success in this mission would be followed by discreet exit as the major *local* players took all the credit to demonstrate their astute use of all useful resources. Maybe there would be a side note that an FBI agent had been present. Failure, on the other hand, would be *entirely* the fault of the FBI agent on the ground. Me. *We shouldn't have listened to him . . . our plan was to . . . but he was FBI . . .*

TAM's touchdown in Asunción was close to 10:00 p.m. Two marked police cars were waiting for the flight, then sirens and flashing lights as we sped to the ancient building housing the Ministry of the Interior. The uniformed officer ushered me into a large, reception-hall-size office, with high ceilings to match, fans above slowly circulating. The room was full. My entrance noted, the loud buzz of conversation came to an instant stop. Total silence. All eyes turned to me. I got the picture loud and clear. I—the FBI—was the cavalry.

Victorino Fernandez, Deputy Minister of the Interior and former Chief of the *Policia Nacional de Paraguay* (PNP), strode forward, introduced himself, and then introduced me to the principal attendees: the Minister of the Interior, the Attorney General, the Director of the PNP, the Director of the *Departamento de Investigaciones* (their FBI), the Chief of Staff of the Army, the Chief Justice of the Supreme Court and several Justices, senior legislators from the *Congreso Nacional and Camara de Diputados,* and some also-rans. All looking intently at Marc Ruskin, former FBI UC turned very visible savior (if not publicly acknowledged) . . . or scapegoat.

Projecting (I hoped) the air of calm self-assurance expected from the representative of the world's preeminent national police, I made my first contribution: *Have you set up a command post?* The Minister turned and barked orders. My next contribution: *We'll need a bank of dedicated phone lines, manned twenty-four hours a day. Do we have investigators at the victim's home?* More barking. Drawing further on my vast expertise on kidnapping from watching movies and TV shows, I provided sufficient fodder to get everyone started. And had myself thoroughly briefed. Finally installed for the duration at the Granados Plaza (where the doorman carried a double-barreled shotgun), I made a late call to the duty agent at JEH in D.C. Could he patch me through to Chris Voss? Chris was the Bureau's top expert on kidnappings. I knew of his exceptional skills from mutual friends at Quantico, though we had never met. He spent the next couple of hours educating me and recommending the next logical steps to take, warning me of the potential pitfalls. Chris was to be my new best friend, holding my hand telephonically for the next couple of weeks.

Paraguay had its own standard of "normal" whose parameters were just short of bedlam. Which may account, in large measure, for why I felt a deep affection for the country and its highly eccentric populace. This was not my first voyage here. For the past two years in Buenos

Aires, I had been assigned the "road trip" to Asunción, with primary responsibility for liaison. (The Legat himself handled the road trip to Montevideo, Uruguay, a forty-minute flight from his office, though it was not unusual for either one of us to cover for the other. We maintained overlapping networks of contacts in both countries.)

Distinguishing Paraguay from all other countries in both Americas is the fact that *everyone* is bilingual, speaking fluent Guarani, the true native tongue, and Spanish, the colonial language. It was not uncommon for officials to switch languages when discussing a point they preferred for me not to be aware of. The extent to which the native Guarani Indian culture makes up a part of the modern Paraguayan culture is a matter of unsupported speculation for a non-anthropologist such as myself, but it is clearly significant. The vitriolic and warlike nature of the political debate may be an example, with figurative throat slashing and backstabbing having replaced the physical utensils. The women are generally beautiful, a blend of Spanish and native Indian, slender, raven-haired, with almond-shaped eyes. One was a *Policia Nacional* sergeant, Sofia Oviedo, with whom I had developed an acquaintance of sorts, but it was difficult to maintain, because Paraguay had perhaps the worst communications infrastructure in Latin America, always on the point of collapse.

The first morning in Asunción, and every subsequent morning, the Deputy Minister would fetch me at the hotel. Victorino Fernandez— almost everyone's name being a subtle variation from the common usage—became a friend. On future trips to Asunción, Victorino would always be at the airport. Later, I would be a frequent visitor at his farm in Coronel Oviedo, situated in the rural, desert-like eastern district. Since he was a grizzled bear of a man in his early fifties, I had anticipated a matronly plump grandmother for a wife. How presumptuous of me. Maria Helena was about thirty years old and a woman of average looks for Paraguay. That is to say, stunning.

On the way to the hotel, in the marked police car, Victorino handed me a large-frame, fully loaded .38 caliber Colt revolver for use during my stay. Not official, by any means, on his part or mine. Had the U.S. ambassador known that an FBI agent was traipsing around the wilds of Paraguay, armed, without any authorization . . . I would probably have been PNG'd posthaste. (That's *Persona Non Grata*'d, officially ejected, with a one-way ticket home.) The revolver, clandestine as it might be, served a real purpose. In the most economically advanced First World countries, the work of a Legat is formalized and rigidly limited, with requests for assistance—and reports on results—exchanged on paper and through formal meetings. *Would Scotland Yard be so kind as to locate and apprehend John Smith, wanted in the Eastern District of New York for the crime of mortgage fraud?* But the greater the distance from First Worldism, the more *operational* the Legat. In the field, with a gun, taking risks. *Jefe, we're looking for a fugitive, Juan Esmith, we think he may be hiding out with his family at a ranch in the Triple Frontera.* That's the border area where Argentina, Brazil, and Paraguay meet, divided by the narrow Parana River and a true "badlands," as we will see. *No problem . . . take Inspector Santana with you.* (In the old days, with respect to our border with Mexico, "extradition" might have consisted of a shove by the Mexican police official, with the fugitive falling directly into the arms of awaiting federal agents. He would then be arrested while attempting to surreptitiously enter the United States.)

In Paraguay, in 2003, the seismic reaction to the abduction of Mariángela Martínez cannot be overstated. Subsequent to her reign as the beauty queen, she had advanced to become the wife or lover of every major politician and magnate in the country (and many out of the country, according to *Zeta*, a local news magazine). She was a *major* celebrity, and she had better be rescued pronto.

Directing the investigation on the ground for the Paraguayans should have been *Comisario Principal* Aristedes Cabral, *Jefe del Departamento de Investigaciones de Delitos.* Cabral had come up through the ranks and was, as I quickly perceived, remarkably well qualified for the job. But he was restrained from doing so because Minister of the Interior Osvaldo Benitez, the politico in charge of the police, with no relevant experience, took the reins of the operation and micromanaged every step. Young for the role, midthirties, thin, with heavy mustache and dark hair, Benitez projected to his subordinates the generosity of spirit exhibited by a famished falcon cruising intently for prey.

The intrigue in Asunción was so thick and so layered it could have been cut with a knife. Really. As I worked my way through interviews with whomever I could, generally in the chilling presence of Benitez, I was beginning to wonder who, in fact, was the victim here—not at all clear—and what the real crime was—not all that clear, either. The facts, as they stood on the first day: Mariángela had been kidnapped during her daily *caminata* (power walk) around Parque Ñu Guazú at 10:30 in the morning. Forty-five minutes later, her *ex*-boyfriend, handsome and wealthy politician Juan Ernesto Villamayor, received a cell phone ransom demand for $300,000. An hour and a half after that demand was made, Mariángela's thirty-year-old eldest son, Hugo Talavera Martínez, made a public statement offering to switch places with his mom and rejecting any assistance from the police.

I immediately interviewed Villamayor and found him surprisingly charismatic and frank, not the least bit arrogant. He told me he would consider paying the ransom. Someone would have to, because Mariángela was broke, in large part because her son Hugo had been swindled out of $500,000 of her money (nearly all she had) in a fraudulent investment scheme. I was pretty convinced—and my co-investigator Cabral privately agreed—that in all likelihood this purported kidnapping was primarily an *extortion*, with the victim being the ex-boyfriend.

Was Mariángela also a victim, or was she one of the extortionists, maybe even the mastermind? And her son, who had volunteered to take her place? Hugo was lying low and wouldn't speak with me.

After three or four exhausting days and nights, I turned off the light at midnight. Finally a full night's sleep . . . The phone rang. Minister of the Interior Osvaldo Benitez.

"Hugo is willing to talk to you. Since you're FBI."

"When?"

"Now. We're in the lobby."

Hazy as my sleepy brain was, I didn't at first grasp the significance here, but by the time I reached the lobby, I had. The swindled son had not changed his mind about and arranged to meet specifically with the FBI agent—and with no Paraguayan police present—in order to exchange late-night pleasantries. This could be a break in the case. For the next couple of hours, I interviewed Hugo, my short questions answered with long, rambling, free-form stream of consciousness replies. When I returned to my room, I believed to a moral certainty that he was a participant in the crime—extortion—and would in fact be getting a cut of the $300,000 ransom. The next day, accompanied by Cabral, I went to see Mariángela's house, get a feel for the staff, inspect the equipment and personnel set up by the PNP to monitor any calls from the kidnappers. It was one of the smaller houses in a high-end gated community. A smiling female officer standing in the diminutive front yard greeted us. In the techno-modern living room, Hugo introduced us to his kid brother, Chachito, and his nanny, the maids, and cook. There were no cops anywhere inside. In his loft bedroom, Hugo proudly displayed the large-frame 9mm pistol he kept under his pillow. Mariángela's ne'er-do-well son clearly had several screws loose. A heavy cocaine user, Cabral later confirmed.

The only PNP officer present, therefore presumably the one charged with monitoring calls from the kidnappers, was standing outside in the front garden. What was going on here? I turned to Cabral, who was somewhat discomforted even before I framed my question. Hugo assured me that the policewoman could enter the house at any time. To use the bathroom, even the kitchen. It had been arranged—with Minister of the Interior Benitez. The selective implementation of my recommendations— such as having an officer *inside* the house, monitoring *all* incoming communications—inspired in very large part by Chris Voss at Quantico, and by my own observations and interviews, left me with a growing sense of being manipulated to serve ulterior motives. This was beginning to irk.

By late in the first week of the affair, we had (at my insistence) recorded roughly a half-dozen ransom demands delivered over the phone to the house in the gated community. Efforts to triangulate those calls, made from cell phones, pointed to their origination in Los Bañados de Asunción, one of the city's large, run-down barrios. Late one evening, an informant working for one of Cabral's men relayed bodega gossip concerning an odd new customer from a nearby rental, a dilapidated one-story shack, typical of the homes in the area. Speeding in an unmarked car through the darkened, poorly lit (of course), potholed backstreets of Asunción, accompanied by other unmarked cars, Victorino's revolver in my waistband—well, undercover work Stateside had been exciting indeed, but this wasn't a poor substitute by any means. The targeted house was desolate and empty, but only recently so: the mattresses on the floor, littered food containers, cigarette butt-brimming milk-carton ashtrays were all the indicia of a makeshift hideout. Even an old FBI undercover agent turned diplomat, working beyond his area of expertise, could put that two and two together.

The next morning, heavy-handed busybody Osvaldo Benitez called a meeting at his Interior Ministry. Exactly two weeks to the day from the abduction date. Most of the players previously introduced were on hand. Benitez announced that the extortionists, bending to reality, had modified—lowered—their demand to two-thirds the original amount. Ex-lover Villamayor had agreed to pay the $200,000. I had no idea why. No explanation was provided. The drop-off instructions, seemingly inspired by Hollywood, were to be followed meticulously, on pain of death for Mariángela. Her son, the ne'er-do-well Hugo—and only Hugo, the abductors insisted—would drive the delivery car, alone. Perhaps they believed this would assure no double-cross.

That evening, around 9:00 p.m., we were all assembled in the command post of a high-tech private security firm, at Villamayor's insistence. It was *his* money and his confidence in the public authorities was limited. Hugo was given an additional cell phone. He would keep this line open for communication with the command post. We watched him drive away in his BMW (no surprise in his choice of automobile) with the $200,000 in a shopping bag by his side. He did not have any kind of "loose" tail. A botched surveillance would have been fatal for Mariángela.

The first call from the extortionists, made to Hugo's personal cell, instructed him to proceed to a large mall after removing the batteries from any *other* cell phones in the car. He did this, even though he didn't have to . . . how would they know? Again, no surprise . . . but was his compliance an indication of complicity? Regardless, the command post was now deaf, though we still traced his location by triangulating his personal cell. Arriving at the mall, Hugo received a second call. He was told to pick up a small KFC paper bag from a stall in the men's room. This bag contained a new cell phone, with a note. He was to throw his own phone in the garbage, with the battery *not* removed. Any electronic babysitters would therefore believe Hugo was still in the mall. The kidnappers hadn't missed any angles.

After a couple of tense hours of radio silence, with the large crowd of investigators, politicians, and hangers-on waiting anxiously, Hugo called the command post. From his home. Claiming that he had followed a series of instructions received on the new cell, driving from one Asunción destination to another, here to there and all around, before finally being instructed to toss the bag with the money off an overpass by a dark and deserted stretch of road on the fringes of the city.

A few more hours later, shortly after dawn, a disheveled Mariángela, wearing the same jogging suit as on the morning of her abduction more than two weeks earlier, waved down a pickup truck and was soon back home—and back in a brighter limelight than ever.

There were no arrests. No one *dared* interrogate Hugo. My gentle suggestion that such would be the logical thing to do engendered only chuckles from my new pal Cabral. Should he attempt any such thing, one phone call from Mariángela to Minister Benitez, and Cabral and his people would be running a jungle outpost, if they were not fired outright. They made it clear: Mariángela's reaction to the merest hint that her darling Hugo may have been complicit would have been frightful to behold. As I packed my carry-on after those couple of weeks in Asunción, Minister of the Interior Osvaldo Rubén Benitez Galeano and Attorney General Oscar German Latorre Canete held the big press conference. Cabral and others in the background wearing their dress uniforms added color to the spectacle, but make no mistake, citizens of Paraguay, the true saviors of Mariángela were at the mic.

A few months later, Attorney General Oscar Latorre in Asunción called me in Buenos Aires. Mariángela wanted to make an official statement. To the FBI agent. *Now* Augie Rodriguez, the Legat, was willing to assume the burden of spending a few hours with the ex–Miss Paraguay. But no, she wouldn't have it. Not *an* FBI agent, *the* FBI agent, the one who had been so helpful during her ordeal. So I returned to Paraguay and was soon sitting in the short, stocky Attorney General's enormous office. He sat there, dwarfed by his oversized Louis XIV desk. Mariángela and I sat at a distance on a couch. Of course, I would have preferred hearing what she had to say while alone with her, with no Paraguayan ears to inhibit her disclosures. But that was never in the cards. A remarkable beauty, Mariángela was in her late forties but seemed ten years younger. Clearly, she breathed the same air as the world's supermodels and film stars. Her description of the abduction, the imprisonment, the overheard conversations, the blindfolds, the hygienic accommodations, the gag-inducing food—none of her story was playacting. I was certain of that. She had been kidnapped, and she had been in genuine fear for her life. In response to some gentle, delicate questions: yes, her son had lost a small fortune, but he was an entrepreneur, who would eventually make his mark. She trusted him. Case closed.

Not long after the kidnapping, counterterrorism officials at JEH determined that on-site intelligence was needed from a remote area covered by our Legat office. Two prominent magazines—*The New Yorker* and *Vanity Fair*—had featured pieces on Hezbollah training camps and major terrorist fundraising initiatives—but not in Lebanon or Yemen, the usual suspects, but in and around Ciudad del Este, Paraguay—the main city in the region known as the Triple Frontera, the border zone with Argentina and Brazil, delineated by the Parana River. Following a flurry of leads from JEH, I boarded a flight to Puerto Iguazú, twenty miles from Ciudad del Este, on the Argentine side of the border. My Argentine Federal Police contacts would provide my initial introduction to the region. (Although I had previously visited the spectacular waterfalls of Iguazú, I was now returning to visit the area's dark side.) The city was formerly named Ciudad Stroessner. Then the nearly simultaneous death of the long-term, iron-rule dictator Alfredo Stroessner and the collapse of Paraguay's infrastructure necessitated a change of name. Since its foundation nearly a century earlier, this town, whatever the name, has been the black-market capital of Central and South America. Yes, for that entire massive area and economy. Ciudad is a virtual no-go zone for every pertinent law enforcement agency in all three of the bordering nations: stolen and counterfeit goods are the foundation of the economy. As dusk falls, launches large and small move cargo back and forth on the Parana and various waterways between and among Paraguay, Argentina, and Brazil—all unmolested. Day and night, traffic (much of it illicit) is bumper-to-bumper across the Puente de la Amistad, the only bridge between Ciudad and Foz de Iguaçu, Brazil.

From Fino Palacios, top chief of counterterrorism in Argentina, I had learned of all the measures and operations taken to protect the country from the Hezbollah and Hamas operatives—some official, some not so official. The Triple Frontera was the black-marketers' utopia, requiring law enforcement attention. Although it was getting plenty of attention, there was little in the way of enforcement.

But terrorism was a different matter. Palacios's *Departmento Unidad de Investigacion Antiterrorista, Sección Triple Frontera* had stretched a tight net across the frontier. Heading the Sección was Roberto Salvador "Toto" Ontivero, one of Fino's most trusted lieutenants. Toto had an unofficial network of informants in Ciudad—very unofficial, since they were running sources in a neighboring country, which is just not done officially. No bad guys would be crossing *his* border. Profiling? *Of course, profiling! Are we idiots?!* Toto and his people didn't have time to waste on elderly couples returning home with heavily discounted large-screen TVs.

Dressed in T-shirts and jeans, three of Toto's shaggy young officers drove me in an old Jeep Renegade from their outpost on the Argentine frontier, across the border into Brazil, first, and then onto the bridge that would take us into Paraguay and Ciudad del Este (there being no border crossing directly from Argentina into Paraguay without a long detour). Bumper-to-bumper traffic on the bridge, of course, but lane splitting moto-taxis whizzed by with their helmeted passengers. At the border, our driver shook hands with the customs officer, as did the drivers of virtually every car and van. Those who, through ignorance or avarice, failed to make the discreet cash handover would be waved toward a side ramp for a thorough inspection. Passports? Who needs passports?

An *American* FBI agent riding around with three *Argentine* covert anti-terrorist officers in Ciudad del Este, *Paraguay*? As an old UC, with an understanding of the need for flexibility in conforming to rules when operating in a foggy environment, I was not concerned. I was unarmed, but my companions packed adequate firepower and would have loaned me a spare pistol should the need have arisen. Six thousand miles from home, I was feeling right at home. This liaison-work thing was proving to be not too dry for my tastes after all. Toto had assured me that I would *not* be traveling in the vicinity of the terrorist training camps, for the simple reason that they did not exist. Toto's men and their sources had made an exhaustive search. There were no informants, natives, merchants, or anyone else who had seen or heard any sign of such a camp anywhere in the Triple Frontera. The magazine stories had been fed to eager journalists in search of a big story, willing to put the accounts to paper without corroboration and without personally venturing beyond Ciudad del Este into the bush to make personal observations. I don't know where those reporters traveled in-country, but they didn't actually see any training camps . . . Not that the articles were without significant elements of truth.

I was astonished to hear from Toto that residing in the vicinity of Ciudad, situated on the edge of nowhere, jungle on one side and the Parana on the other, were *sixty thousand* Arabs and nearly as many ethnic Chinese. They were not terrorists, nor even sympathizers. They were merchants, participants in the famous black market where all transactions were in cash, lots of cash, and with virtually no rules and no taxes (other than the "tax of doing business," the barely unofficial contributions to the retirement funds of poorly paid local officials). In recent years, however, and just for the Arab merchants, a new tax had materialized, administered not by Paraguayan authorities but rather by Hezbollah authorities. No forms to file, no deductions, no exemptions. The hardworking proprietor of a stall in a bazaar might gross two million dollars (yes, an enormous sum for a stall in a Third World bazaar, but this is no ordinary bazaar, as we'll see shortly)—10 percent went to Hezbollah. Failure to pay? Old Aunt Alima back in Beirut—wouldn't it be a pity if she was run over by a bus. A bit short on the percentage? Little brother Iqbal, what with six little children at home, he may have difficulty working with both legs broken . . . or a cracked skull . . . or blinded by a glass of acid. Everyone paid.

For Hezbollah, this region of South America had long been a comfortable soft-target zone for terrorist attacks. Fino and Toto were particularly aware of this reality. In 1992, Hezbollah operatives had blown up the Israeli Embassy in Buenos Aires, and then in 1994, the Argentine Israelite Mutual Association building (the Jewish cultural center), killing hundreds. The Jewish community in Argentina numbers several hundred thousand. (Juan and Evita Perón's version of fascism had been *light* on anti-Semitism, but that was fifty years earlier.) Several of the operatives in the bombings were believed by investigators to have been using

Iranian diplomatic cover. They had genuine diplomatic passports bearing fictitious names, though unlike RUN-DMV documents, they had probably not been fraudulently issued. The Iranians knew with what sort of political leaders they were dealing. Over several administrations, Argentine executive leadership had been notoriously open to barely concealed, surreptitious inflows of cash. Closed-door deals involving sale of Iranian oil to Argentina were believed to have been an influence.

The bottom line: a decade after the bombing, all charged in the crimes were found not guilty. Prominent among them were a number of the provincial police accused of accepting bribes in exchange for turning a blind eye to evidence. Investigating magistrates and prosecutors were either discredited or persecuted, or, as was the case with Juan Galeano, the judge in charge of the bombings case, impeached. Before Galeano's impeachment, he and I and the Legat enjoyed lunch from time to time in Puerto Madero, overlooking the Rio de la Plata waterfront. We discussed progress in his investigations of the two bombings and what assistance we, the FBI, could provide. Discreetly. A timely footnote to this narrative about the bombings was the involvement of Cardinal Jorge Mario Bergoglio, aka Pope Francis, of course. The clergyman was the first public figure to sign a petition demanding justice in the bombings. A decade later, in January 2015—more than two decades after the Hezbollah bombings—Argentine prosecutor Alberto Nisman, *still* investigating the now-ancient bombings, was assassinated in his Buenos Aires apartment the evening prior to providing evidence to the Congresso Nacional of a Casa Rosada cover-up. (The Casa Rosada is the Argentine White House. The trail had led to the very top.)

That was the brief background for my journey into the bowels of the Paraguayan black market. My three *compadres* and I drove through the steep, winding streets of Ciudad del Este, with countless dark passageways, sidewalks packed with vendors, panel trucks operating as makeshift shops as boxes marked with the Gateway computer logo passed into the arms of eager buyers. Those workstations had no doubt taken a wrong turn while en route from Seattle to wherever. Then we proceeded into the residential areas of Ciudad and Foz, where I was shown the mini-mansions of the more successful traders. Palaces in the jungle. That night, back across the bridge and into Argentina. In Misiones's rustic steak house, an outstanding *bife-de-lomo* (filet mignon of the world's best beef), a few glasses of the local Malbec, and the good company of Toto and his soldiers, eager for fresh conversation in their isolated northern outpost.

Early the next morning, after crossing *officially* from Argentina into Brazil, complete with a stamp on my diplomatic passport from the smiling customs guard, I was handed over to a broadly smiling Victorino Fernandez, Paraguay's Deputy Minister of the Interior, whom I had met and come to admire not long before, during the kidnapping. My Paraguayan host wore unofficial garb. Our driver sat behind the wheel of a discreet faded black pickup, and we were closely followed by a dusty SUV whose tinted windows concealed the four well-armed men.

At my request, Victorino dropped me off on the Foz de Iguaçu, Brazilian side of the Puente, before we had crossed into Paraguay. I walked up to the group of rangy young *moto-taxistas*, smoking and waiting for fares. One U.S. dollar to cross. My man handed me a full-face helmet, I hopped onto the two-cylinder bike, and he flew onto the bridge, cutting lanes, racing over the white lane markings, a few inches to spare between both knees and the slow-moving (and contraband-laden, in many cases) cars—ancient Argentine-built Ford Falcons to late-model BMWs. Then past the customs men and around a corner. He smiled as I commented favorably on his racing skills. Any doubts I might have had about the ease of terrorists traveling across border were now resolved. Without any documentation, my features fully concealed, I had illegally crossed the border from Brazil into Paraguay. Cost: $1 U.S.

Our hotel, built half a century earlier to resemble a small French château, and punctiliously maintained, was situated in a gated community. Really, *the gated community of gated communities*. With the wealthiest of the many expatriate black-marketers as residents—many with good cause to entertain credible security concerns—entry was controlled by paramilitary armed guards (read mercenaries), professional and well-paid. The cleared kill zone around the outer-perimeter fence was regularly patrolled. Inside, there was an oasis: palm trees, flower gardens, the chirping of birds and trickle of brooks; villas with small bicycles lying on lawns beside open garage doors; the rear panels of BMWs, Mercedes, Audis glinting in the setting sun.

The next day, my little group explored the dark passageways leading into the galleries that constitute the primary shopping sources of Ciudad. Shopping malls from hell. Down decrepit halls, up a few broad flights of chipped and cracked stairs, are endless labyrinthine passageways, with endless shopping stalls and stores, small and large—the previously referred to bazaars which form the Hezbollah tax base—where the four thousand vendors *average* grossing two million dollars per year, many several times that figure.

For purely professional purposes, Victorino and I stocked up on Polo sports shirts, Gucci dress shirts, Ralph Lauren windbreakers, Hermès ties, counterfeit DVDs. My only disappointment was finding later that *The Lord of the Rings* was dubbed in Portuguese. Departing the Triple Frontera, we drove the rutted roads inland toward Asunción, then joined the traffic on a two-lane "highway" through arid red earth. Along the way we drank chilled maté, a concoction prepared from yerba leaves. In an expression of Paraguay's peculiar form of populism, the drinking of maté crosses all social and economic lines. In a country where temperatures are routinely hovering at 100 degrees year-round, the constant hydration with this beverage is mandatory, and the caffeine charge never hurts. The national beverage is transported everywhere in a Thermos (maybe small, maybe very large) and sipped through a metal, often silver, straw. One Thermos is shared by everyone in a given group—officials, officers, soldiers, drivers, FBI guests, it doesn't matter. Everyone drinks, no one wipes the silver straw. I diplomatically took a visibly long pull, then passed the Thermos for another round. (The morning maté is blended in a tea-shop-like establishment to address any one of many distinct conditions, including fatigue, headache, constipation, dizziness, and so on. The afternoon maté, however, is universal, always the same beverage. And delicious.)

Our destination was Victorino's farm, where his wife, Maria Helena, had prepared the guest bedroom. I spent the weekend reading on a hammock, while Victorino tended his bees and looked after the farm. The steak, from the rugged and scrawny Paraguayan breed of cattle, required a particularly sharp blade and much chewing. The wine, however, was Argentine, and the company could not have been better. When I asked Victorino how he felt about the bribe-taking by customs officials—it was he who had pointed it out—he smiled, shrugged his shoulders, answered with resignation in his voice. *Their salaries are very low . . . And they are far from Asunción.* He was a pragmatist. As to the flagrant illegality in all directions, I said not a word, certainly asked no questions. He would have thought me naïve.

My reports from the field (minus the shopping spree) filtered upward. Three months later, I was traveling up the Parana on a large launch, accompanying John Pistole, then number two in the FBI, Director Mueller's top executive. Pistole had risen through the ranks but still remembered what it meant to be an agent. Accompanying the only SA with firsthand knowledge and personal experience of the Triple Frontera, John was game for the adventure. Connecting with Victorino's men, I gave him the Cook's Tour, something to talk about back in JEH. And he may have purchased a few Polos as well. He definitely revved up with the yerba maté.

12

Back to New York

Nearly five months after the May 2004 shootout on Libertador Avenue in Buenos Aires, during which the shooter's failure to seat the magazine of his 9mm Glock may well have saved me from termination with extreme prejudice, the Inspection Division's Shooting Incident Review concluded that my discharge of my firearm was "justifiable and proper under the circumstances." Bummer, in the eyes of Augie, the Legat (later Chief of Security for the NBA). He was visibly disappointed. His recommendation had been for a negative determination, arguing in a memo (which had not been intended for my eyes) that I had acted recklessly by firing a pistol in a public area, in the vicinity of innocent bystanders. (The Legat did *not* carry a firearm, sparing himself the inconvenience of intervention when present during the course of a violent felony. And depriving him of the capability of defending his family, should they be the target of the violent felons with which Buenos Aires was, and still is, burdened: a staggering level of robberies, kidnappings, burglaries, all enhanced with an abundance of weaponry.)

The shootout turned out to be a turning point. Enough of that good life overseas. Let's get back to what I do and like best—real operations, real crime-fighting. I was fifty years old, with nearly twenty years of FBI service behind me, ten years undercover, six months before possible retirement. Generally speaking, ten years of full-time UC work was and is considered all one agent can or should handle in a lifetime. Generally speaking, I agreed—except when it came to me. My plan was to become a tech agent. I've described them earlier: that select group who conduct surreptitious entries to plant bugs in the homes of mob capos and terror cell leaders (all sanctioned by search warrants, of course). I also thought that learning to use all the latest gadgets and technology would be a great augmentation of my UC skills. And a valuable addition to my CV. I had long ago abandoned any ideas about LEGAT Paris. The battle with SECDIV (FBIHQ Security Division), back in my Safeguard days, had firmly sealed shut that door.

The boss of the New York Special Operations empire, which included tech agents, was my old mentor, Mike Pyszczymuka, former head of International Operations at JEH. Mike had counseled me when SECDIV exposed my vulnerabilities as a potential double agent for . . . France. I suspect, though I have no evidence, that it was Mike who had salvaged my Legat career by arranging the transfer to Buenos Aires. We met in his corner office at 26 Federal Plaza. He'd be more than happy to put me on a tech squad. But it never happened. Unfortunately for me, the Security Unit based in New York was understaffed. That unit works FBI internal investigations, background investigations for the issuance of security clearances, and is responsible for the physical security of the NYO. Andy Arena, the agent in charge of such matters in New York, knew that I wouldn't be thrilled with this assignment, so he made me a promise: one year with Security and then I could have my pick of assignments. Usually such promises are worth as much as the paper they're not written on, but I had been in the Bu long enough to know the unwritten rules. If I wanted back in the world of covert ops, as a tech agent or whatever—and I did—I had to do this other thing first. Any saber rattling with the bureaucracy, even with a good guy like Andy Arena, and I would have found myself back on surveillance, shift work, and I hadn't done that since my early pre-UC days working for Crazy Thom Nicoletti on SO-13.

The irony that I was now assigned to Security was not lost on me. What had happened to SECDIV's grudge and accusation, the one that had cost me the full-time posting in Paris? The agent formerly deemed so vulnerable for recruiting by that notoriously hostile intelligence service (the French) was now a member of what amounted to the equivalent of SECDIV in New York. Only in the FBI! Recall Jack Karst, the Superman look-alike who had threatened the subject who had threatened me ("This is personal.") during the RUN-DMV arrests: he was now Chief Security Officer for New York, my new boss.

Naturally enough, as word that I was back circulated through the Bureau's UC community, Safeguard, and the various Janus offices, calls for UC help started coming in, despite my "day job" with the Office of Security. As soon as those first opportunities trickled in, any reticence I might have had about returning to UC went out the window. I stopped trying to fool myself. It was in my blood.

First in line with an offer was an agent in Chicago, Louise Riley. Would I be able to help out on a terrorism investigation? Finally, my first official terrorism case! Low-key, yet significant, the sting would all take place over the phone. The twist: this wasn't Al-Qaeda or Hezbollah or Hamas. No, the targets were from the other end of the spectrum, disciples of Meir Kahane and ultraviolent members of the Jewish Defense League, widely known by its acronym, JDL. Domestic terrorism is a brand of violence utterly anathema to the teachings of the Jewish faith, but for a small number of fanatics, the moral principles that define their very existence can be explained away. Responsible for several bombings and assassination attempts, key members of the JDL were already serving lengthy prison sentences.

The JDL, and its bloodthirsty successor, Kahane Chai came to be recognized by the United States as a Foreign Terrorist Organization. After the assassination of Israeli Prime Minister Yitzhak Rabin on November 4, 1995, Kahane Chai chairman David Ha'ivri told Israeli television that Chai had celebrated upon hearing the news. "Every dog has its day," he said, and toasted the killer. "It wasn't a Jew who was murdered. It was a traitor who was executed."

The group's high-volume hate speech, punctuated by sporadic attacks, continued to the end of the century and beyond. In April 2002, Kahane Chai operatives planted a trailer loaded with explosives, fuel, and nails in East Jerusalem. Their target: a Palestinian girls' elementary school. The attack was thwarted by alert police officers. With its blind adherence to violence directed at civilians and its fanatical ideology, Kahane Chai was the mirror image of Al-Qaeda—and, to me, somewhat reminiscent of the *Macheteros* back in San Juan—tough talk, accompanied by courageous attacks—against unarmed civilians. Targets that don't shoot back—the thread that runs through all terrorist organizations, left and right.

On February 12, 2003, JDL's chairman, Irv Rubin, successor to Meir Kahane, and his top leadership held a secret meeting with other, lower-ranking JDL activists, including a recent convert, Steve Levine. The agenda was to plan the group's next operation: simultaneous explosions at a New York City mosque and in the office of a U.S. congressman in Chicago. But this murderous ambition was more than Levine had bargained for when he signed on with the JDL. He went to the FBI.

The plot was derailed, though prosecutors had insufficient evidence for arrests. Levine had agreed to cooperate as a confidential *informant*, not confidential *witness*—he would not be testifying. Soon thereafter, Aaron Glick, a Rubin lieutenant, visited Levine's Evanston synagogue on two occasions, purportedly seeking assistance with a JDL recruitment initiative, but more likely to feel out Levine, searching for the FBI source, suspicious perhaps that Levine was the betrayer.

Now we move ahead twenty months, to November 2004. As a result of internal bickering (maybe in part a consequence of the intensified FBI investigation), the JDL was in chaos. One morning, Steve Levine attended a Bar Mitzvah with his wife at their Evanston synagogue. Afterward, as they walked through the parking lot to their car, a beige Chevrolet followed slowly, then pulled alongside. Levine recognized the driver: Aaron Glick, the JDL lieutenant who had been snooping around the synagogue a year earlier. As the car came to a stop, the middle-aged man sitting alongside Glick got out and approached Levine. Close, in his face. *You fucking traitor, you asshole . . . You call yourself a fucking Jew? Hey Levine, you're not going to live very long, motherfucker. You scumbag. Bo-ged!* (traitor). The man glared at Levine, then with calm deliberation got back in the car. Glick slammed the accelerator and they were gone, as Levine hurried his terrified wife back to the safety of the synagogue.

From a photo array, Levine later identified the other man: Ari Ben-David, a Miami-based JDL operative with a military background. His threat had to be taken seriously.

A few weeks after the confrontation in the parking lot, at case agent Louise Riley's direction, Levine called Glick's home and left a message. Louise needed tangible, independent corroboration of the threat. Even without Levine's testimony, it might be possible to use a recording against Glick and Ben-David. A recording, say, that had been intercepted from an FBI wiretap of JDL operative Steve Levine's home phone. Alternatively, Louise could try and persuade Levine to agree to testify after entering the Witness Protection Program.

But Glick had not returned the call. Levine's stress levels were sky high; he could not make any more calls. Someone else would have to. Thus Louise Riley's recruitment of me for the job of the disembodied voice. She anticipated that the investigation would be concluded with five or fewer "substantive" contacts, thus not requiring a formal Group II Operation, with the requisite substantial paperwork and approvals. Given this lower-level designation and the likelihood that the covert activity would in all likelihood be conducted entirely over the telephone, I failed to attach to this op the level of significance it merited. Not that my commitment to the role was in any manner diminished—on the contrary—it was simply that there was not the personal risk to myself inherent in face-to-face UC meets. I would accomplish all the UC work as I sat alone in the safety of a dimly lit office in a nearly deserted corridor of the aging Federal Building in Lower Manhattan. Louise, however, understood the importance of this op (as would Aaron Glick and Ari Ben-David). She understood that any failure to respond to episodes of retaliation against informants and potential witnesses in domestic and international terrorism cases would have a disastrous impact on future such investigations. (The crime carries a potential sentence of twenty years.) A swift and certain response was required. In this particular instance, covert intercession was a prerequisite. Over the telephone, it was all the more difficult because of the limitations of contact made over a faceless line. No ruses, no disguises to deceive, no winks and nods. Just my disembodied voice.

Because Ben-David had never met Levine except for the parking lot, Louise believed, and I agreed, that he would be unlikely to recognize, much less remember, his voice. Still, I would need to familiarize myself with Levine sufficiently to avoid telltale gaffes. Which I did. Glick's failure to return Levine's phone call would be my opening. I dialed Ari Ben-David's home phone. Louise, who was patched in from Chicago, was taping the call.

"Hello?"

"Ben-David?"

"Who's this?"

"Steve. Steve Levine. I called Aaron Glick last week and—"

"—You motherfucker, how did you get this number? How dare you call me, you traitor—"

No doubt now. We had the right man.

"Listen, Ari—"

"—Why should I listen to you, you motherfucker—"

". . . my wife, she was terrified, you have no business frightening her, she has nothing to do—"

"—Fuck you and fuck your wife. She should have married a real Jew, not a *goy*."

I sensed that Ari Ben-David was about to slam down the receiver. The plan was for me to direct the conversation to the encounter in the parking lot and the threat of retaliation against Steve Levine. We needed actionable threats. I had to improvise.

"Hey Ben-David, I'm beginning to understand why the JDL is such a chicken-shit outfit, with losers like you—"

"Traitor! You, you with your friends at the FBI! You're going to pay for it, we're coming after you, you—"

"—You and Glick didn't scare me in the parking lot"—*I had to get that scene in somehow, maybe I would be rewarded with a response*—"and I'm not scared now. You can threaten me all you want. You're out of your mind, Glick knows it, everybody knows it, that's why the JDL is falling apart." *Keep him on the line. Anything to keep him going.*

"You're dead . . . I'm talking to a dead man, you motherfucker. You call yourself a fucking Jew."

"You don't know what you're talking about. And if you think that I'm afraid of you and Glick, forget about it, just leave my wife out of it, you—"

"—You're done, you're not gonna get one night's peace or rest you scumbag traitor."

"Just keep away from my schul [synagogue], from my wife."

"Fuck you!"

None of that really surprised me. What *did* surprise me was that he hadn't followed up on how I had obtained his phone number. If he had, I would have said Glick gave it to me. When Glick denied it—who would Ben-David believe? (More fodder for infighting.) From what I had learned about Ben-David, he may indeed have been a handful as a field operative, with his own ideas on how to serve the cause.

Louise Riley and the prosecutors were pleased. Ben-David had neither denied the incident in the parking lot, nor Glick's presence there. The new threats, arguably provoked by yours truly, would not be sufficient on their own, but linked to the parking-lot incident, they *would* serve to corroborate the testimony of Levine and his wife, should they agree to testify. My instructions were to wait a few weeks, let the dust settle, then call back with a more conciliatory tone. If I got the machine, I would hang up without leaving a message. I didn't want him to *expect* my call. I called late one evening when he might be a bit tired, less on edge. In a near-pleading tone I said:

"Ben-David, please listen to me, this is Steve. You need to know, I didn't do what you think I did. I promise, please give me a chance to explain."

Silence, but at least he didn't hang up.

"I had nothing to do with the FBI busting up our plans for the congressman's office. They set me up. It's a frame. They want to set me up. Get us fighting against each other."

"What bullshit. Now you're fucking scared. You're no Jew. You whiny Yitzhak Rabin." (He was referring to the Israeli Prime Minister's "betrayal," the signing of the Oslo Peace Accords. Rabin was murdered days later.)

"Listen to me, Ari, blame the FBI. Can't you see what they're doing? By threatening me you play right into their game!"

"So why are you calling me, you scared little shit?"

But I could sense a change of tone. His insults had less conviction.

"I want—I need to straighten this out, I can't sleep at night."

"Serves you right, scumbag."

Click.

This time, again, there were no denials from Ben-David, no "What the fuck are you talking about?" or "What fucking parking lot?" or "What fucking threat?" or "What fucking Glick?" Practically everything Ben-David said in our every conversation implied confirmation of the Levines' accounts. Sitting in my office at 26 Federal Plaza, I made two more calls to Ben-David, both featuring more of my whining and his foul-mouthed contempt. He was toast.

As investigation of Ben-David and Glick continued, the Jewish Defense League continued to come apart, dividing and subdividing like a cancer. Which became a new problem for the rest of us.

Regarding my one-year commitment to the Security department, my supervisor Andy Arena was *better* than his word. I didn't have to wait a year to return to face-to-face UC work. After six months (the highlight was vetting Mayor Michael Bloomberg), I got a call from an old friend, Kevin White, a former UC supervisor at headquarters, now supervisor of the Organized Crime Squad working Long Island. Kevin explained that his primary undercover operation, code-named TURKEY CLUB, had become more important and demanding on his personnel than initially anticipated. The targets were "made" members of the Genovese family, one of the Five Families that had controlled organized crime in the Northeast for decades. One of the Lucchese crews, a rival family, was the subject of *Wiseguy,* Nicholas Pileggi's gripping book, a true story, adapted by Martin Scorsese as *Goodfellas,* a very realistic (as I was soon to learn), harrowing movie. Henry Hill, who narrated the story, was a low-level mobster with tainted blood (i.e., not 100-percent Sicilian), so he was free to run his own guys and make a ton of untaxed money, but he could never enjoy all the privileges of being a made member of the family. In the end, every one of Hill's featured partners, made or otherwise, ended up dead or imprisoned when he flipped on them in open court ("ratted out" is the more pejorative term preferred by the tabloids) and then took cover in the Justice Department's Witness Protection Program. Those violent events predated my story by several decades, but make no mistake: in 2004, the Genovese, the Lucchese, all the LCN families, they were still a dangerous crowd to run with.

The initial UC on TURKEY CLUB was a young guy whose name I have changed to Kamal, who was good, no doubt about that, but also a beginner. Kamal had been an agent for only four years, and this was his first big UC op. He had been introduced to Genovese "made man" Nicholas "Nicky" Gruttadauria and had developed good rapport. But as a young UC, he was in somewhat over his head. Aggravating the inherent risks, the case agent, last name Holmes, had only a couple of years' agent time. Could he possibly have the breadth of experience to manage a complex investigation targeting highly professional, wily, and seasoned mobsters? And other members of the team averaged only two years FBI experience. Kevin White, their supervisor, saw the problems and asked whether I could step in as Kamal's partner and help out on a case in which I'd have almost as much time on the job as everyone else put together. This would be my first foray into the world of traditional, big-time organized crime, La Cosa Nostra. Andy Arena and the managers in New York had given their consent. What can I say? It seemed like a good idea at the time.

I needed an alias. Maybe a new one was called for. Both Alex Perez and Sal Morelli had been out of circulation for several years. They seemed stale, but I checked in with Janus. Valerie O'Connell was still there—felt like old times—*good* old times. So, Val, can I get away with resuscitating Alex's AFID? *Don't push your luck, Marc. Alex has way too much history as it is.* She knew me all too well. Her seasoned perspective, expressed with a kind laugh, settled it. Besides, Alex's background, credit history, etc., wouldn't provide the best legend for my targets in TURKEY CLUB. Google had gone public the year before, but its search engine was already changing the world, and backstopping in this new era was a whole new and much more complicated ballgame. And I didn't have the time. The TURKEY CLUB principals wanted me available as soon as possible. Dedicating the six months that it still took (and still takes) to develop an alias from scratch was a luxury I didn't have. A shelf-ID was called for. Val walked over to her filing cabinets (metaphorically speaking) and pulled out a few possibilities . . . No, I couldn't use the one with a date of birth from the seventies (youngish as I may have liked to believe I appeared), not if I wanted to survive . . . No, the Italian surnames were definitely out. I wasn't about to try and pass for an Italian among real Italians . . . Maybe . . . age midforties, surname could be European . . . Okay, it's a deal. Val filled me in on all the paperwork procedures, which were, to my surprise, almost unchanged from fifteen years earlier. I filled out many of the same forms, and within a matter of a few weeks I was a new me. Name: Daniel Martinez, international jewel thief and vendor of stolen jewels—in effect, an upscale fence. In this identity and capacity, my presentation to the targets' world was just about the opposite of Alex Perez's. I was now a sophisticated cosmopolite with expensive clothing, manicured nails, and no bling beyond the Rolex Presidential. And no ponytail. And don't call me Danny. I don't appreciate that. Where does Daniel Martinez live? Don't ask. In the underworld, it's inappropriate. It's something *a cop* would ask. Wiseguys are vague with their answers. But when push comes to shove, I enjoyed the comforts of a sweet little pied-à-terre on Manhattan's East Side, in addition to my cribs in Paris and Buenos Aires. Not backstopped at all, not even crudely. Was that risky? I didn't think so, they weren't likely to ask for addresses. If they did, the right (moderately pissed) expression combined with a vague, though polite reference to an affluent neighborhood would have sufficed. Might they check surreptitiously? High-end jewel thieves don't leave a great many tracks. My local knowledge would be my backstopping.

Over the next nine months, Kamal and I met with a shifting ensemble of the Genovese guys in Queens, on Long Island, and down in Florida, maybe a dozen times total. One night early in the story, we had dinner with four of them, maybe five, at the classic, old-style baroque Park Side Italian restaurant deep in Corona, Queens, the heart of mob country. This was the new FBI era in which most UC encounters are covered by surveillance, but there was no way we could have any kind of close surveillance in that restaurant without being burned. Everyone in the place was Italian, part of the neighborhood, many of them presumably tight with the family, if not made. A couple of new, square guys sitting alone at a table would never have passed muster. When I went downstairs to the men's room, one of my new associates escorted me. Then Nicky Gruttadauria joined us at the base of the stairs. He was about sixty, and short, in good shape for his age, exuding Italian bonhomie. As we came back up, he put his arm over my shoulder. We had hit it off right from the beginning, but this was still totally out of character. Then his hand moved up and down by back, the beaming smile never leaving his face. We sat down at the table. Evidently he was now satisfied that I wasn't wearing a wire, and he had good reason to be. I wasn't wearing a wire. It would have been foolish to do so. The risk was just too high, given the venue and the fact that Kamal and I were still establishing trust, and we didn't anticipate any major evidentiary conversations anyway. It was too early for that.

As we ate pasta, drank our Chianti, talked, and laughed, the thought crossed my mind: these guys have slaughtered other guys (no doubt including snitches, rivals, and worrisome business associates) with baseball bats . . . I'm over fifty and eligible to retire . . . what am I doing here? *Do I have rocks in my head?*

I didn't have a car for the TURKEY CLUB meets. I was using a late-model BuCar for routine noncovert getting-around-town (aboveground, at least), and I did not need the hassle of caring after two cars. But no car was no problem, legend-wise, because Daniel was supposed to be out of town most of the time anyway, traveling all over the world on big deals. Sometimes I used a limo to attend a meeting. Uncle Sam could foot that bill. Once I was short of time and needed to meet Kamal and Nicky at the Garden City Hotel in Long Island, which was owned by other mobsters. Case agent Holmes suggested that one of his squad-mates drop me off. *In front of the hotel. In his BuCar!* No thanks. The agents in that room just didn't understand why that plan was a patently terrible mistake. In fact, they were wondering what was *my* problem. So we were off to an inauspicious start. This was my first clue (in what was to become a series) that the first word of the *TURKEY* CLUB code name might have been unwittingly appropriate for this investigation. The agent ended up dropping me at a nearby coffee shop, which I entered from the rear parking lot. I sat there for twenty minutes sipping espresso and reading the *Times,* then hailed a cab for the short ride to the hotel where I met Kamal and Nicky, who pulled up in a Jaguar. Also present that day was another key player in the UC op: François, Daniel Martinez's Canadian connection who was bringing us some merchandise of interest.

François worked UC for the Royal Canadian Mounted Police. We had met the night before at a hotel in Manhattan. François was traveling with Jean-Pierre Petit, his "cover agent." Belying his surname, Jean-Pierre was tall, thin, with shaggy blond hair accenting a good-natured smile and calm demeanor. I learned that all Mountie UCs work in a two-officer team, consisting of a professional full-time UC and a professional full-time cover agent. The cover is *always* in close proximity to the UC, running interference with the case agent, surveillance team, managers, any and all who might place the interests of the investigation above the safety and well-being of the UC. The cover makes sure that all the necessary gear is provided, handles administrative matters, and is the UC's lifeline and mother hen. Pretty sweet for the UC, in my estimation, leaving him free to do his job. Score one for the Canadians—though they were still losing the game with me, thanks to the performance of their bureaucracy in the ill-fated SUNBLOCK collaboration. These two fellows had little in common with the Mountie officers I had met during that otherwise very successful op. But this was not a surprise. Covert operators are a subset of whatever organization they belong to, having more in common with each other, even across jurisdictions, than with other members of their home entity. In the eyes of the case agent and management, the UC is simply another investigative tool: the most expensive, resource intensive, and trusted, the most reliable asset in the courtroom—but also the *least* trusted by much of management. Our hobnobbing with the criminals can't help but result in some cross-contamination, or so the upper managers believe. Nor are the UCs fully integrated into the squad culture. Most other agents who can't imagine talking to a drug dealer, mobster, terrorist (other than on the other side of a bolted-down table in a locked interrogation room) often have difficulty comprehending and relating to the UC who *appears* to easily while away the time of day with the denizens of the dark side. At the Mounties' hotel, we were old hands (Kamal was not present) at an arcane occupation whose actors were few and far between, spending the evening together, exchanging anecdotes over a room-service dinner—a pleasant and instructive experience.

The large windows of the grand dining room at the Garden City Hotel overlooked a parking lot. As a sophisticated cosmopolite wearing an elegant blue suit over a dark gray pullover, I thought that eyesore diminished the panache of the place—this wouldn't happen in France, that's for sure—but whatever. I didn't allow it to come between me and Nicky. By this juncture in the investigation I'd been with him quite a few times. We liked each other. Waiting for my Canadian friend, we drank San

Pellegrino and chatted about his home in Florida (shared with his very attractive, very young, very blond wife) and his Jaguar (his favorite topics, all three, as I had already ascertained). When my cell rang, on schedule, a brief conversation in French confirmed that my man François would arrive shortly—while also reconfirming my authenticity as a native French speaker. A few minutes later, François's entry into the dining room was dramatic, as he's about six four, with wall-to-wall shoulders, a long, jet-black ponytail, dark beard, and piercing blue eyes. His English is thickly accented.

After minimal pleasantries, I asked François to show Nicky what he had brought us by way of a sample. He casually reached into his jacket, produced a small pouch of rolled burgundy velvet, and handed it across the table. The nearby tables were unoccupied; there was no real concern of prying eyes. Nicky untied the lace and unrolled the velvet on the tabletop. We were looking at a dozen, maybe fifteen glittering diamonds. Also glittering were Nicky's eyes.

"No problem," he said immediately. "I have a jeweler on 47th Street, he can handle them. No matter how hot."

François and I had a quick exchange in French and agreed to leave one jewel with Nicky, to show our good faith. François then rolled up the velvet. True to form, the mobster accepted the diamond and didn't make much of an effort to pick up the tab, small as it was. But Kamal was happy to pay. We were in good shape. Our bona fides were firmly established. The fix was now in.

For all of five minutes. Then . . . after shaking hands and making arrangements to call and set up the sale after Nicky had vetted the merchandise with his jeweler, François and I walked out the front door of the Garden City and walked to the parking lot in front. Kamal and Nicky stayed behind in the restaurant. As François started the engine of his covert red Jeep Cherokee (awakening memories of *my* covert red Jeep Cherokee, from years before), a group of maybe ten earnest-faced, clean-cut young men approached from different directions. Some wore T-shirts and baseball caps, a few carried handi-talkies. *What the—!* My mother could have ID'd them as some kind of law enforcement or military personnel. In fact, they were our colleagues: the FBI case agent and his squad-mates.

"How'd it go?" one asked.

François and I stared in horrified disbelief. This was so pathetic I was embarrassed for the FBI. François immediately bellowed, "DO YOU THEENK MAYBE WE CAN TALK ABOUT ZEES SOMEWHERE ELSE?"

"Oh, gee. Sure. Sorry." They ran back to their BuCars and drove off to regroup somewhere.

Had Nicky seen the show from the dining room that overlooked this parking lot? Maybe one of the doormen? Or valet guy? *Hey, boss, guess what I just saw?* Had Kamal and François and I been burned? We'd know soon enough. As François and I drove off, I bemoaned the state of the new Bureau, specifically the missing street smarts of the new generation of agents who couldn't shoot straight. This was my first long-term UC role since the start of the new millennium, since 9/11, and after a five-year hiatus from the world of covert ops.

Or was it just me? As an old-time UC, had I become a bit of a prima donna, adamant that all my operational requirements be met, reasonable or not? During my first Safeguard assessment since my return, back on the examinee's side of the desk, the psychologist was alarmed. On the standardized test, I had spiked, maxed out, in the "Needs to exercise control" measurement. I called around to full-time UCs who had been continuously operational in the course of my passages through JEH and OCONUS. The feedback was not encouraging. One of them, Zhang Lu Yi, a native Chinese UC with a thick Mandarin accent, said he was now a tech agent and explained, "No way will I do a UC now. These agents won't listen, they know everything. Learned it from TV. I'm not going to get killed, at this point, for no good reason. Listen to me, come out here to the tech squad, then retire in one piece." Which was to say, retire, *period*, as opposed to, say, being dragged off the stage in a body bag.

Sound advice. Budget issues resulting in a long hiring freeze had produced an unforeseen (at least by me) problem. There was a dearth of mid-career agents. That meant few mid-career UCs and few mid-career case agents, field agents, surveillance agents. The bulk of the twenty-first-century Bureau was made up of old-timers and rookies. And the new generation were patterning themselves after the special agents of Hollywood and the STARZ network, rather than the other way around. For the time being, however, I was stuck. Deeply entrenched as Daniel "Don't

Dare Call Me Danny" Martinez, the refined jewel thief, it would have been impossible to extricate myself from TURKEY CLUB without losing face. I could only mitigate the risks, up to a point. However, I was significantly irked to find myself with hard-case professional assassins on my left, amateurs on my right, all the while holding the hand of a good-natured neophyte UC, full of enthusiasm and still-unrealized talent.

We got lucky that afternoon. Neither Nicky nor any of the doormen or valet guys had spotted the FBI rubes, so we got away with that dangerous error in the parking lot, but the TURKEY CLUB mistakes piled up. After each one, I called supervisor Kevin White.

"I'll talk to them," he said.

I'm sure he did, but nothing came of it. Still, the sting progressed, despite everything.

For the meet with the jeweler who would fence the diamonds, Nicky called Kamal the day before and suggested an address in Manhattan. One block from my mom's apartment! Why not have the meet *at* her apartment and save me the trouble of watching over my shoulder for the next twenty years? *Kamal, tell him it won't work. Say that Daniel's got to meet someone all the way on Wall Street just before. That we'll all have an expensive lunch in the Financial Center. Explain the situation to Holmes for me.* No word back from Kamal. The next morning, late, I got a call from Holmes. Could I help out Kamal with the meet? In an hour—*one hour* to prepare for a meet with members of the Genovese LCN family. Where? At the original location a block from my mother's building. I stared at the handset, not certain as to whether to merely hang up, or . . . Instead, I politely declined. Holmes conceded that he had been informed by Kamal of my problem with that address, but from his tone it was clear to him that I was simply not being a team player.

From my perspective, it was increasingly clear that for the case agent and his squad-mates, this whole thing was no more real than a film or a video game. As soon as the players were off the set, they no longer existed. They were no longer a threat. The meet with the fence from 47th Street went ahead as planned, without Daniel Martinez, whose absence was of no concern to the other players. Kamal had the diamonds. The fence studied the stones, hemmed and hawed, and all parted company without reaching agreement. With that deal still pending, Kamal and I had told Nicky that we had a volume of cash coming in from various deals and needed to have it laundered through some "legitimate companies" and then taken out of the country. We could work something out, Nicky assured us. The Genovese had an "interest" in the Café by the Sea, a restaurant in Freeport, Long Island. Nicky would bring along Kim Brady Land, the owner. The meet was set for the Garden City Hotel once again, 9:00 p.m.

In the lobby, Kamal and I were met by two of Nicky's soldiers. With long black leather coats and greased-back hair, they were unlikely to be mistaken for tourists. As my comfort level with the TURKEY CLUB squad was about zero, I was equipped with a .40 caliber Sig Sauer in my old portfolio, as well as my Glock M27 (the one I had fired in Buenos Aires). The rationale for carrying the portfolio: it contained $15,000 cash for the first laundering transaction. In the unlikely event that Nicky's men were to pat me down (maybe not so unlikely, after the friendly hug in the restaurant), well . . . I was carrying a gun. So were they, without a doubt. Their concern would be for a wire, some sign that I might be an informant—fatal—or a UC—*probably* fatal. (Some traditional La Cosa Nostra mobsters, the bosses in particular, understood that killing a fed would result in catastrophic repercussions.) They didn't pat me down.

Earlier in the afternoon, Kamal had been provided with two miniature digital recording devices—the latest thing. With a four-hour capacity, there would be a backup, should the need arise. Resembling a cell-phone battery, they added no risk. Even if found, carrying spare batteries was not uncommon in lower-tech 2005. With Kamal doing the recording, I would be doing the transmitting—and transmitters could now be easily detected by commercially available scanners. Was I being overly cautious to imagine that made members of the Genovese LCN organized crime family, with long experience of FBI intrusions into their business affairs, with long experience with betrayal by trusted colleagues (Salvatore "Sammy the Bull" Gravano is one turncoat who comes to mind) might take some inexpensive precautions when dealing with these two relatively recent, non-Sicilian, not-even-Italian acquaintances? No matter, I would wear the damned transmitter. The contact agent handed me the box with the transmitter and extra batteries (real batteries, thank you very much). Kamal got the latest thing, I got a 1970s-era vintage beeper.

One of the large ones. *One of the cheaper ones,* which did not have real beeper functionality—just the series of dashes painted on the display, as I've described and derided much earlier in this narrative. With the handy belt clip. Just to make sure that everyone could see that in 2005, cash-rich international jewel thief and fence Daniel Martinez carried not a BlackBerry, for example (they'd come out a couple of years earlier, while the iPhone was still a couple of years in the future), but a pitiful fake beeper with the series of dashes painted on the display.

It was laugh or cry. I did a bit of both—then took action. At the first opportunity, en route to the hotel, the beeper went into the portfolio. The quality of the transmissions might suffer, but at least it would not be in plain sight. Following the pattern from SUNBLOCK, I was picked up by the Dominican limo driver at 125th Street in Manhattan. (Yes, the same driver used for many of the trips to meet with Gong's man, Richard, at one of the hotels near LaGuardia.) He was, a good driver, with a sense of humor, and he still did not mind the obviously shifty nature of the passengers we might pick up and drop off in the course of the night, nor the evolving itineraries. Actually, I was more comfortable with my driver than I was with Holmes's squad-mates on Long Island. At least the driver had no capacity to compromise Daniel's identity (which he didn't know) and leave me walking into a lethal reception committee.

Daniel would be footing the bill that night at the Garden City. The Leather Coats remained in the lobby. Nicky was already in the living room in one of the luxury suites, drink in hand, when Kamal and I strode in, flush with cash. Kim Land, the restaurant owner, greeted us enthusiastically, with dollar signs almost flashing in his eyes, and why not: a significant infusion of cash was imminent. A few of Nicky's colleagues sat around the large coffee table, and we shook hands warmly with Fat so-and-so, Crazy whatever, Trigger-happy first-name-ending-in-a "y"—all middle-age men who could have been warming up for a Knights of Columbus lodge dinner. No surprise. They would always be gruffly friendly, in their avuncular style—up to the moment when the mask dropped and the nightmare would begin. (In *Goodfellas,* the made men are amiably chatting with Tommy DeVito (Joe Pesci) until one second before the bullet hits the brain.) Kim Land did not appear to be Italian, though I guess his grandparents could have arrived at Ellis

Island as the Landinis. Tall, with medium-length curly hair, he had the easy smile and bonhomie that are the prerequisite to the management of a successful restaurant. Kamal and I sat down at the coffee table, sipping the Chianti poured by Nicky, paid for by Daniel, and soon the conversation turned to dollars and cents. I had spent a few days reading up on the restaurant business and had talked to a chef friend, owner of a popular Manhattan eatery. Enough to ask a few probing questions and comment knowledgeably on Land's responses and claims. The assembled mobsters nodded knowingly, approvingly, and grunted almost on cue. I was making the intended impression: I was nobody's fool when it came to placing the hard-earned proceeds of my shrewdly successful schemes. A thief like me—of my obvious caliber—had choices. I wouldn't patronize just any laundromat. I'd be careful. My new friends would have been suspicious if I had *not* asked such pertinent questions.

Kamal and I passed the test. By some prearranged sign, the other mobsters gave Nicky the green light to proceed. He suggested a drive to Land's restaurant. We would eyeball the place and have a leisurely dinner. Or so it seemed. Going with the bad guys to an unexpected, impromptu destination—I would be violating at least one of my cardinal principles of UC work. A quick judgment call had to be made. This was not a controlled street buy (as with Kuris and the counterfeit fifties, for example, with covering surveillance galore) or the floor of a financial exchange. Insinuating myself with serious mobsters would require serious risks. Any contrived reason for backing out of the next step would have stretched credulity with the subjects. It would have been an embarrassment to Nicky. He was vouching for us. In all likelihood, bringing the case to a rapid end . . . And, more importantly, ending any hopes for my renewed UC career. Holmes and his squad would conclude that I had "chickened out," and my explanations about security measures would have elicited barely concealed skepticism. Word would soon spread. *Ruskin doesn't have it anymore. Okay, he was a great UC in his day, but that day has passed. May he retire in peace.*

And so I went for it. All in. With no plausible reason for taking two cars, I left the limo at the hotel. Kamal took the wheel of his UC SUV, with Nicky riding shotgun, providing directions, Land and I sitting in back. It was a long drive, first on the highway, then along secondary roads, followed by a dark, two-lane blacktop along the coastline of the South Shore. The Leather Coats were in the follow car, its lonely headlights bouncing and illuminating the rear window. If the squad agents conducting surveillance had been with us as we left the hotel, their headlights were now nowhere to be seen. An *experienced* Special Operations Group would certainly have been there, two or three units tailing at a prudent distance with headlights off. Highly trained and experienced drivers, using the brake lights ahead to keep track of the road, can pull off some amazing feats. We used to do this in Puerto Rico fairly often. *I* used to do it. At age thirty, the eyes are a lot sharper. Now, at night, headlights are the least of my requirements. I need eyeglasses and still have to drive below speed limit. But then I'm no longer dealing with Nicky Gruttadauria and his associates. The rest of the experienced team would have vehicles racing along parallel routes to find discreet observation posts *ahead* of the two targeted vehicles, the team leader hurriedly reviewing maps and calling out instructions over the encrypted BuRadio. Dicey and complicated? Of course, but at least it might have given Kamal and me a fighting chance, should trouble break out. As it was, we had no chance of such coverage, nothing resembling a safety net. We were alone.

The atmosphere in the SUV was all bonhomie, what with the wine already consumed and the prospect for profit enlivening Nick and Kim Land. When the lights of the Café by the Sea came into view, my concerns were alleviated. Though the adrenaline always flows, particularly with high-risk subjects, it is invariably reassuring when all indicators turn positive, with none of those subtle, almost indefinable indicators that set back-of-the-neck hairs to rise and for the mind to race, searching for a safe exit strategy. We pulled into the parking lot and entered the airy, deliberately ramshackle seafaring-design structure overlooking the waterfront. The ride had taken nearly an hour (it felt much longer). This was a brisk early winter night. Just the right weather for my black three-quarter-length black leather coat. The one with the holster pocket sheathing my .40 caliber Glock, stitched by Pete the Cobbler, years ago. The muscle stayed in their car.

A respectable trout, accompanied by a pleasantly surprising Long Island Sauvignon Blanc, was followed by a tour of the facilities. A clean, well-run kitchen, introductions to the staff. Winks and smiles from Land accompanying the presentation of the beach-bunny waitresses. In his private office overlooking the beach, more serious talk. In due course, I removed the 15K stack from my portfolio and passed it to Land. Large denominations, hundred dollar bills, some fifties, were mandatory, because we were jewel thieves, not drug dealers aggregating multiple sales. Land in turn handed me four postdated checks drawn on the Café's account at a local bank, totaling $12,600. (I had been adamant about bringing down the 20-percent commission that Kamal had agreed to—without haggling, at least by a token amount. Sixteen percent was still too high, but so be it.) Land made some entries on his workstation, then silently read off figures from the screen. Two sets of books. *Aren't you concerned about keeping all that on your computer?* Good question. One that smart, careful Daniel *should* ask, because the answer affected him directly. By implication: *I'm a little concerned.* And Land should have his answer ready—and did, and smiled.

"Daniel, all I have to do is hit these two keys at the same time"—he pointed at them—"and the entire hard drive will be wiped clean. Same result with a failed login. For that, I paid nearly as much as I did for the computer. Beats going to jail."

We all chuckled appropriately, and I made a mental note to make sure the arresting agents would have a heads-up and then pick up the duplicitous restaurateur at a safe distance from his workstation keyboard. Then again, given the squad I was working with, what good would my suggestion do? All of us then hopped into the vehicles and proceeded to our next stop, an upscale home in East Meadow owned by the Manhattan jeweler who had agreed to fence François's diamonds at a respectable price. Or so Nicky claimed. We entered by the front door— always a good sign. Had we entered through the garage or walked down to a soundproofed basement, I would have had some trepidation. (Remember the *Goodfellas* scene: Joe Pesci and the two made men who killed him entered the house through the garage.) The front door was good, but the jeweler was apparently caught by surprise and not particularly eager to entertain these midnight visitors. However, after we were seated in the den and Kamal unrolled François's velvet pouch for a second inspection, the jeweler's attitude improved. He agreed to fence the stones, and we left the merchandise with him. Those diamonds were worth something in the range of $120,000. Stunned, I tried not to show it.

Back in the car, Kamal confirmed to Nicky that he would receive a third of the proceeds from the diamonds as his commission. Nicky smiled. My eyes widened. This was the first I had heard of it. Worse, Kamal then reached into his jacket pocket and removed $5,000 in hundreds and fifties, handing it to Nicky as a down payment. Before Kamal and I had seen one cent. In the course of the evening, we had passed to LCN members and associates a satchel with all those diamonds and a total of $20,000 in cash, and received in exchange . . . four pieces of paper purportedly worth $12,600. Very professional for a pair of worldly scoundrels with business all over the globe.

We were back in the hotel suite by 1:00 a.m. Time for a nightcap, but Nicky was tired and soon announced that he was going home. Finally. I was exhausted. The Leather Coats were in the lobby lounge, paws wrapped around glasses of Scotch, with a group of chums. All good cheer, they waved over Kamal, who returned and said, "They want to buy us a drink. I think we should accept. At least one." Was this friendly drink prearranged? Always a possibility. Was a more exhaustive search in the offing? Or worse, had Kamal or I inadvertently done something that compromised our cover? Or had the squad agents somehow burned themselves and set off a chain of suspicions? However, the smiles of these *Soprano* look-alikes seemed genuine, and we were in the very public lobby area, and most of the squad were stationed in darkened surveillance cars scattered through the lot outside, should things go south and the goons insist on taking us for a ride. Reluctantly, I agreed with Kamal. He was right. There was nothing to be gained by offending these Genovese soldiers, and building rapport with the troops could only help the case.

The alcohol went down without a hitch, and an hour later I emerged from the hotel. Kamal had booked a suite, he'd have breakfast with Nicky in the morning. I walked through the very quiet parking lot to my Dominican's limo, in which he had by now been patiently waiting for close on seven hours. My oversized transmitter was still on, with its numerous batteries presumably still working, so I said to the surveillance agents, "I'm headed home, you can break off now. Can one of you flash your lights to acknowledge . . . (*pause*) . . . whoever's got me in sight, just flash once so that I know you copied."

Nothing. They had broken off, left the scene. There was no one there. I was stunned. *I was furious.* It was Friday night, or very early Saturday, actually. If things had gone bad, it would have been Monday morning before anyone became aware that I was missing. At least my trusty Dominican driver was still there. I tapped the window, woke him, and we headed west toward the city. As the limo cruised the nearly deserted Long Island Expressway, I stretched my legs and reflected on the course of this op, weighing the benefits against the risks. I was back on the streets, working one of the most challenging cases yet. This was all good, but for the first time in my UC life I was also feeling in danger. And not due to the Genovese mobsters and their soldiers. I was confident that I could survive them. If—and it was a big if, growing bigger—I wasn't undone by my own side. How I pined for case agents like SUNBLOCK's Mark Calnan.

The following week, the monster beeper-transmitter still in my possession, I called Jeff Lum, who had been very active in SUNBLOCK, which seemed now a lifetime ago. Jeff was now the supervisor in charge of SO-7, the NYO Tech Squad, the most highly trained, state-of-the-art sophisticated technical team in the FBI. After a long laugh—he wasn't aware that such museum pieces as this beeper were still in existence, much less in use—he provided the solution. "We call them rat-phones," he explained. "They're cell phones that can record or transmit, depending on how we set them up. And they're encrypted. Best of all, they can send and receive calls. That's your ticket. Just have the case agent send me a request and we'll send it out.

Holmes sounded underwhelmed when I relayed by phone the positive results of my call to Jeff Lum. *I'll talk with our tech agent here in Long Island and get back to you.* Perhaps that tech agent had issues with Lum's squad in Manhattan. In any event, his answer was contrary to what I wanted to hear. *We have all the equipment we need as of now.*

Inexplicable. From long experience with seasoned case agents, I had come to take it for granted that a UC op proceeds as a collaborative venture. And distinct from a theatrical production not just because it really is "for real," that the bad guys were still bad guys when offstage, but also because this script had not yet been finished, these closing scenes remained a mystery until actually enacted. And in these productions, the leading man—myself, the undercover—necessarily holds the additional position of coauthor. This scenario should be fine-tuned as called for by the flow of events, enhancing the likelihood of success and maximizing the leading man's likelihood of surviving to participate in future productions. In TURKEY CLUB (and soon in ALTERNATE BREACH), the twenty-first-century Bureau case agents, supporting personnel, contact agents, tech agents, surveillance agents—virtually everyone—viewed the role of the UC—correctly—as an investigative tool, but *incorrectly* as a tool to be used just like any other tool. In the new FBI, the UC would have no more input into the operational scenario than would the electronic devices used to intercept and record telephone calls. With the primary distinguishing characteristic being that the UC was more annoying, having a tendency to express differing opinions and having unreasonable expectations, such as modern and secure digital recording devices. The case agents had written the script, and that's the way the story would go. It was up to the UC—*and the bad guys*—to conform to expectations. With this approach, disaster would be avoided only as a result of the UC's experience, and despite the case agents' and the desk agents' best efforts. (ALTERNATE BREACH, as we will see, with its twenty-plus subjects, all arms dealers, crashed and disintegrated exclusively as a result of the neophyte Bureau and Justice personnel. I was the only participant to emerge unscathed.)

Before I had signed on to TURKEY CLUB, Kamal had spent a weekend with Nicky Gruttadauria at his place in South Florida. After the successful laundering caper and completion of the diamond deal, Nicky invited Kamal to fly down for another visit, this time accompanied by Daniel. Were this a Hollywood film, in the next scene I'd be sitting in a lounge chair by Nicky's pool, sipping a cocktail, as his bikini-clad wife looked me over from behind a pair of Chanel sunglasses. As it was, I saw no reason to violate another of my cardinal rules for UCs, the one about getting too close to the subjects. Kamal and I *already* had Nicky's confidence. Nicky knew he could "earn" (for obvious reasons, a popular mob term) off us. He already had. Nicky wasn't active professionally in

South Florida, so the likelihood of meeting local mobsters was nil. Turning down the invite would have no impact on my UC reputation; no one would care if I chose not to spend a weekend at a luxury home in sunny Florida. In the middle of winter.

Holmes was not happy. Kamal would be there, and my presence would boost his credibility. He could use my support. But the guilt trip was not going to work on me. I didn't see any significant benefit from Kamal spending the weekend with the Gruttadaurias, but that was his call. I suggested a compromise. Kamal would explain to Nicky that Daniel has important business to conduct in Buenos Aires, regrets that he can't spend the weekend with us, but he'll be flying through Miami on Thursday and will change his connecting flight in order to join us for dinner.

It worked wonderfully. Kamal spent a long weekend with Nicky, which he seemed to enjoy (though no new business was discussed, no new subjects introduced). Daniel's reputation as an international wheeler and dealer was enhanced by the (purported) business travel to Argentina, and the Gruttadaurias had enjoyed a very expensive Italian (of course) dinner in Miami. Daniel's treat, *bien sûr*. All of which led to the next act in TURKEY CLUB, written by Holmes and Co., and accepted without question by the eager-to-please, compliant Kamal. It was relayed to me as a fait accompli via a phone call from Kamal:

"You'll be flying down to Miami twice a month. With twenty-five thousand for laundering. I've talked to Nicky."

"That's nice. *I'll* be flying down. Did it occur to you to maybe talk to me about it first? *Before talking to Nicky?*"

No, it had not occurred to Kamal to confer with his fellow UC about operational covert travel, meets with LCN subjects, carrying large sums of cash. Issues that I might have some small interest in.

"Oh . . . Tom Holmes told me to set it up, to call Nicky."

"How much are they charging us?"

"Twenty percent."

"That's a bit high. A bit *very* high. Especially for the volume we're moving. Normal is eight, ten, maybe twelve. Did you negotiate at all?"

I knew the answer to that one. Kamal, with case agent Tom Holmes's okay, agrees to a ridiculous price, without haggling, giving off the scent of something fishy, and Daniel Martinez—me—makes the deliveries. To

Nicky and friends of his with names like Fat Tony, Crazy Pete, Jimmy the Barber, and Vinny the Trigger. And, of course, security for Daniel in Miami would be worked out later.

"To fly down to Miami twice a month, it's going to take up nearly half my time. Pre-travel planning, testing tech equipment, making travel plans, the actual flying, meets, hotels, travel back, vouchers, reports. I'm working other cases. I can't be Daniel Martinez and Leonardi simultaneously." (Leonardi was Mario Francis Leonardi, a role I was developing for a domestic terrorism UC op.) "What I *can* do is fly down once a month, with *fifty* thousand. It'll accomplish exactly the same thing."

Good idea. They hadn't thought of that. This was now four or five months after the initial close call with François the Mountie in the parking lot of the mob-owned Garden City Hotel. And as the covert side, the dark side of the op progressed, the overt side with the Long Island squad deteriorated. I made plans for an important family function on an upcoming Saturday. Knowing that the first money-laundering trip to Florida was about to be scheduled, I told Kamal not to schedule anything with me that weekend. I couldn't and wouldn't make it. I was serious.

On the Friday afternoon before the Saturday of the family function, Kamal called to say a meet was on in Long Island for the next day. Nicky was expecting me to be there.

"No, it isn't happening," I said, "call and tell them Daniel's not available. We'll do it next week."

Kamal pleaded.

"Absolutely not," I repeated. "I told you about Saturday."

"Please, I can't go alone."

"I'm not asking you to. Cancel the meet. Reschedule. Real criminals do it all the time. Real businessmen who aren't criminals do it all the time."

This went on for an hour. Kamal did not cancel the meet. The case agent would not budge. Kamal went alone . . . But that was the last straw for Daniel Martinez and the TURKEY CLUB op. By mutual implicit agreement, my colleagues would henceforth have to get along without the cosmopolitan crook who was now too busy fencing jewels in Europe, in South America, in Asia. No problem. My former colleagues soon harvested a bunch of indictments and convictions anyway.

And Kamal? What happened to him? Four or five years later, I flew into an unnamed city to conduct a presentation at a UC school on one of my False Flag cases (related in the next chapter). At that evening's Starlight Lounge, among the usual assortment of faux villains, was Kamal chatting up a couple of cute UC wannabe agents. I walked up and he gave me a broad smile and introduced me, "Meet Marc Ruskin, without a doubt, one of the best UCs in the FBI, ever."

The compliment I accepted with several grains of salt, coming as it did from a now-experienced and professional BS artist. That is, a fellow UC.

"That's right, I'm a legend in my own mind."

Kamal smiled sheepishly when talking about TURKEY CLUB. *It was my first Group I. You put up with a lot, and I learned a lot.* I left him to continue to regale his ripe-and-ready audience with tales of heroism, but I was comforted to see how he had grown, and that he had sufficient perspective to assess critically his earlier experiences. Approaching my mandatory retirement, it was refreshing to observe the maturing of a next generation of UCs.

13

False Flags

The best way to catch an individual—specifically, an American—known to have classified information or materiel for sale is to pose as a spy from a foreign country interested in buying it. However, posing as a spy and setting up an elaborate sting is also an effective way to waste a lot of resources on a wild goose chase. Going in, you can't be sure how it will turn out, but in this regrettable day and age you have to find out. Establish trust and slowly but surely approach the truth. These are called "False Flag" operations, and following TURKEY CLUB, which truly soured me on criminal UC investigations as they appeared to be conducted in the twenty-first-century Bureau, I was recruited for what became a series of these short-term espionage cases that stretched almost until my retirement. Aware of my disenchantment with criminal UC ops, a manager in the counterintel side of the Bureau opened this new door and I walked through without hesitation, migrating from the world of criminal UC to the world of FCI UC: a long-term Group I Foreign Counterintelligence operation. My commitment would be three to five years. Fine. This would be my longest UC op to date, replacing RUN-DMV, which ran for two and a half years. For the foreseeable future, I would inhabit the world of intelligence officers, spies, and counter-spies. A new dark side ruled not so much by violence and intimidation, but by cunning, ruse, and methodical planning and execution.

I would live in New York—home of the United Nations, with the presence of foreign missions from the entire globe (friend and foe alike), the new Vienna, the world capital of espionage and counterintelligence—but my new bureaucratic home base was a small office lost in the depths of JEH. These few men and women, a dozen or so, in the FBI's espionage unit were responsible for uncovering and rapidly apprehending the most reprehensible of evildoers, those who would sell out their country and its people. Traitors. The U.S. Constitution makes special mention of the crime—"The Congress shall have Power to declare the Punishment of Treason"—a federal statute singles them out for the harshest treatment—"Whoever, owing allegiance to the United States, levies war against them or adheres to their enemies, giving them aid and comfort within the United States or elsewhere, is guilty of treason and *shall suffer death, or shall be imprisoned*. . . ."

The issues that surfaced as a result of the substantial press coverage of many of my False Flag ops are thorny indeed. Spying between hostile sovereign powers is expected, even *encouraged* by their constituencies. How often is the CIA criticized for excessive intelligence-gathering over-seas? Never. Just the opposite, in fact. The loudest cries from legislators and the media are reserved for failures to provide actionable intelligence: for *not* knowing more about WMDs that may or may not have been se-creted in Iraq, about reliable resistance fighters in Iraq and Syria, about impending conflicts here and there. But espionage *between allies* is an issue, lacking moral clarity and unanimity of condemnation or even consensus among those who drive public opinion. The Edward Snowden leaks, taken at face value, suggest that it has happened, and if current news reports are to be credited, it is still a common practice by many world powers. Publicly condemned but tacitly taken for granted.

Some ops were morally unambiguous. An engineer from a nuclear research lab, believing me to be an intelligence officer working as a proxy for a hostile Middle Eastern power:

Alejandro, I can provide a blueprint for building a dirty bomb. Complete instructions, ingredients, parts, processes, everything. Can you find out for me what they would pay?

Rafael, Just to be sure that I understand this clearly. You mean radio-active. That is correct, no?

It certainly was. A U.S. citizen was putting up for sale the recipe for mass destruction and terror, for use at the local mega-shopping mall situated in Anywhere, U.S.A.

I'm sure they will be very interested.

And they *were* very interested. I never learned what happened next. With my UC job completed, I almost never did. (Best guess: Leavenworth.)

Many details of the Group I op, my primary assignment during this period, starting with its name, were and still are classified. Any detailed discussion is strictly forbidden, and with good reason. There are two categories of classified materials: those that are reasonable and necessary to legitimate national security concerns, and those that are ridiculous and excessive, the product of mid-level bureaucrats erring on the side of C.Y.A. Working at U.S. embassies, I had been exposed to large volumes of both. Standard coffee-and-breakfast reading for "cleared" personnel is all the cable traffic, relaying news and analysis from around the globe, much of which is marked "Secret." (The "art" of classification is an arcane one, fully understood only by true devotees—not by flummoxed bystanders such as myself.) Much of what was marked Secret could be read with coffee and breakfast a few days later in *The New York Times*. The legal nicety, and an important one, is that even after the news has appeared in the *Times*, the information is *still* classified. Which means that even with security clearances, you'd still better not talk about that tidbit of information, regardless of whether it was picked up by *Nightline* and discussed the previous evening. Therefore the following narratives leave out all classified details. Corroborating facts are derived from FBI and DOJ press releases, court documents, and other public records. And there are some sanitized, quasi-fictional elements that convey what happened but with false specificity.

The most notable episode by far featured one Roy Lynn Oakley, an employee of Bechtel Jacobs, which had been the prime contractor at the Department of Energy's East Tennessee Technology Park. Their business was uranium enrichment. As a supervisor in facilities maintenance,

Oakley had virtually unlimited access to the physical plant (though not to files and documents). He put out the word that he wanted to sell some kind of classified equipment or materiel, presumably something to do with uranium enrichment, stolen from the facility. When the Bureau got wind of the offer, the reaction was immediate and from the highest levels. The risks posed by whatever was in Oakley's possession could only be imagined. Was it radioactive? If so, what was the extent of the potential damage if deliberately or accidentally mishandled? Detonation? Widespread contamination? Would evacuations be called for? Or just the opposite, quarantine and roadblocks? The science-fiction nightmare scenario, the Stephen King page-turner brought to life. Lack of knowledge breeds fear and spurs the imagination. FBI Director Mueller wanted the facts. Now.

Jonathan Sarno, senior analyst within the espionage unit, reached me late on Friday afternoon, January 19, 2007. Over an encrypted phone line he provided sketchy details. As in all False Flag ops, I would pose as an intelligence officer from another country—in this case, France. Flash back nearly a decade, when SECDIV cancelled my orders to LEGAT Paris because a particularly obnoxious desk-jockey had feared my recruitment by intelligence officers working for the French espionage agencies. Now here I was being recruited to *pose* as an intelligence officer from France. I was over that outrage, though the irony did not escape me. Sarno and espionage supervisor Michelle Levens were leaving for Reagan National to catch a shuttle to New York. Could we meet me at my cubicle in New York the next morning? (Though infrequently used, I maintained a desk in my squad area.) Chris Day, the case agent in Knoxville, was waiting for confirmation of the appointment. He'd get on the next flight out and join us.

On that midwinter Saturday, the floor was quiet, a few agents scattered around, catching up on paperwork, maybe preparing for some kind of op or just coming in from one. Jon, Michelle, Chris, and I settled down by my cubicle with coffee. Chris was a mid-career agent with a military background. With goatee and longish hair, he had the demeanor of a Special Ops veteran—somewhat offbeat, and very bright, very tough. He filled me in on the details. A confidential source in Houston, a contractor with significant overseas experience, had received a call from Oakley, with whom he had worked at the facility a few years earlier. Oakley claimed to have something of great value to sell. He did not want to describe it over the phone, but hinted that it would be "worth millions" to any country seeking to develop or enhance its "capabilities"— and there was only one kind of capability that could have a connection with Oak Ridge. Oakley's old friend understood. Would he have any contacts from his overseas construction contracts? Preferably a European country. Preferably France (*France?*). Oakley was adamant that he did *not* want to be helping the North Koreans, who were up to no good, or any Middle Eastern countries, which were even worse. So here was a potential traitor with principles! If the good friend could help, there'd be "something in it" for him. His friend said he could help. Oakley then concluded the call after providing his friend with the phone number to an "untraceable" TracFone (the sort of anonymous cell phone available at any Best Buy), and his friend agreed to put this number in the right hands. And he kept his word, though not in quite the anticipated manner. He called the FBI.

Chris Day's initial investigation in Tennessee had confirmed the information provided by the source. Oakley *had* worked at Oak Ridge, and he *had* had access to valuable, classified materiel. The untraceable TracFone had been traced back to a local Walmart—and video surveillance cameras had recorded its purchase by Roy Lynn Oakley. Chris had also obtained the number to Oakley's "real" cell phone, as well as his home number. Even his wife's cell-phone number. And his home address, employment history, banking information, DMV records, firearms licenses—of this I made a mental note—everything. He was pretty thorough. My appreciation of Day's professionalism moved up several notches with every detail. I was immediately on board with this investigation. I could work with these people. I wanted to.

In the course of that Saturday, the four of us developed an approach and a script for my initial call. As in all False Flags, the initial call would open the door or shut it forever. The first call with a subject in such an op is particularly critical. I would have *one* opportunity and one only to persuade the traitor that I was indeed a French intelligence officer. The slightest doubt in his mind, and it would be over. By the time we had worked out what I could and could not say when talking to Oakley (and then the Department of Justice attorneys would have final word on every variation in the script), it was after 9:00 p.m. Director Mueller and Attorney General Alberto Gonzales were briefed on developments.

Then and there—my cubicle at the FBI offices in New York—I used the TracFone provided by Chris Day and punched in the number for Oakley's TracFone. His phone was not powered up. I was diverted directly to voice mail and left a message. My name was Jean-Marc. We had a mutual friend in Houston. He sends his greetings. *We are very interested in the product that you have.* In the event that Oakley was not sophisticated enough to bring up the number of the missed call on his machine (unlikely, but possible), I spoke it out, slowly and clear, asking that he call back at one the following afternoon.

The next day, Sunday, our team of four gathered back at my cubicle. No return call. Another call to Oakley, but his TracFone was still off. I didn't leave a message. He would see that there had been a second missed call. *If* he ever turned the phone back on. Time was not on our side. We had to make contact, and soon. Chris had the other phone numbers, but there was the obvious problem all of us saw: Jean-Marc could not know any of these numbers, because Oakley had not passed them to his friend, the source in Houston. I suggested that I go ahead and call Oakley's personal cell. If he asked how I had obtained the number (and assuming we even got that far without a hang-up), I would say *we have ways of obtaining all sorts of information . . . it's what we do for a living . . .* After all, he wouldn't know what we—French intelligence— are capable of. And I would be simply "Jean-Marc." If Oakley asked about my last name, I would say, "It's safer for you not to know."

Sunday, early afternoon, I made the call. To Oakley's personal cell. He answered.

Oakley: Hello.

MR (in his heavily French-accented English): Hello . . . my name is Jean-Marc. A friend sends his greetings, a friend from Houston. We are very interested . . . you know what I am talking about?

Oakley: I know . . . but I don't need to talk on this phone.

We agreed that I would call him back in an hour on his TracFone. Five minutes later, my TracFone rang.

Oakley: Hello, Jean-Marc. I'm on the phone I bought so that I could talk to you all.

MR: Very good, very good. Tell me, what name do you want me to use?

Oakley: Why don't you call me Paul Collins? [Chris Day later researched Oakley's alias: A Paul Collins wrote a conspiracy-theory-laden far-right blog. The disconcerting choice might provide some insight into Oakley's mind-set.]

MR: Yes, yes, very good. Can you pleese tell me, what it ees, that you have to sell us.

And he did. Fuel rods (as later described in a DOJ Press Release). Classified. From Oak Ridge.

MR: Pleese tell me. What is eet that you are looking for, precisely?

Oakley: Two hundred thousand dollars.

MR: That is a lot of money . . . I will need to talk to my chiefs, back in my country. I will call now, eet is six hours later een my country. [Lest there be any doubt down the road that he was dealing with an agent of a foreign power.] You understand?

Oakley: Yeah, yeah, okay, I do. Just call me back on this phone that I got . . . Just forget about the other number.

MR: Yes, yes, of course, I have already forgotten eet. Tell me Paul, thees phone, you must buy meenutes for eet, yes? You have eenough meenutes?

The surveillance team that was covering Oakley 24/7 reported that he jumped into his pickup and raced off. Destination: Walmart. Purpose: purchase additional minutes. A real pro. Still, we had progressed from initial contact to active negotiations. Following a number of agitated calls between JEH and DOJ, Jean-Marc placed another call to Paul Collins and we sealed the deal.

MR: Hello, Paul?

Oakley: Hello!

MR: Paul, my superiors, they may be eenterested. But Paul, they have talked to our engineers. The say that a fair price, one hundred and twenty thousand dollars, that would be thee correct price.

Oakley: Jean-Marc, if it's worth one twenty, it's worth two hundred. You can tell your boss I ain't going to argue about price.

MR: Paul, I will need to know more about what thees rods are used for, to tell my superiors in Paris, eef I can persuade them to pay thees much.

Oakley: If you're interested, you're going to have to come down and look at them yourself. There ain't too much I can tell you on this phone, in case somebody could be listening. What I can tell you is that they're used with uranium. For gaseous diffusion.

MR: For gaseous diffusion?!

Oakley certainly knew which words to use in order to ratchet up the already stratospheric frenzy level at JEH and Justice. I told Oakley that I would call the following evening to finalize arrangements for a likely purchase later in the week.

We booked a flight for early the next morning, Monday, to Knoxville. Not being much of an early riser, I joked that arrival at LaGuardia at such an hour might not be a feasible accomplishment. Chuckling, Chris responded that if he didn't see me at the airport, he'd be at my Manhattan apartment posthaste, dragging me out of bed if need be. *You will be on that flight.* He was not being humorous. I could see it in his eyes. (Urgent as the case may have been, there was no call for using the Director's personal BuPlane. Arrival a few hours earlier would not have advanced my communications with Roy, alias Paul.)

At the FBI's Oak Ridge Resident Agency, an RA out of the Knoxville Division, my first impression was that of an ants' nest that has just been kicked. Hundreds of agents and higher-ups, Justice Department officials, SWAT teams, and Temporary Duty Assignment Special Operation Groups were brought in to maintain twenty-four-hour surveillance on Oakley and his residence. Special agents and engineers from the Department of Energy had been brought in. Other than when Oakley was known to be asleep, Bureau surveillance planes were flying donuts high overhead. (This was still the pre-drone era.) In my experience, the attention to detail in this National Security Op was off the charts.

A state-of-the-art CP, Command Post, had been set up in the Oak Ridge Resident Agency. The CP, with banks of phone lines, computers, video monitors, all the technical gadgetry, manned by duty agents round the clock, would be the nerve center of the op. Next door, Special Agent in Charge Rick Lambert, ordinarily based in Headquarters City, Knoxville, had established an office in order to personally manage the op—a first in my experience.

Trim and athletic, in a crisply pressed dark-blue suit, with steel-gray hair, bright eyes behind wire glasses, Rick projected a calm confidence belying the controlled chaos of the satellite office. Not merely a manager, a true leader. He greeted me warmly—he was to prove very supportive throughout the week—and introduced me to the brass from JEH. These included managers from the WMD (Weapons of Mass Destruction) Unit, and any other unit that had any conceivable connection with the subject matter. Essentially they were observers, relaying developments to their respective bosses back in Washington.

Initially, the powers that be wanted the deal to go down within a couple of days—midweek—but Oakley wanted a little more time, and it soon became apparent that a slightly later date was more realistic. A number of teams, all with critical tasks, needed to be in place prior to the meet. These people are the best, but there are limits. So we ultimately scheduled for Friday. The SWAT guys were planning the operational details. How to deploy the teams. Where to set up the vehicles. The execution of the arrest. The engineers would be handling risk containment, HAZMAT, procurement of specialized radiation-related equipment, radioactive material handling protocols. Tech teams were bringing in state-of-the-art equipment to record the meet from a variety of locations, accounting for all possible scenarios. The SOGs were glued to Oakley. The CP, coordinating all, pulling here and tugging there, serving as liaison with JEH, doing all to assure that everything would come together at show-time Friday morning. It's important to note that all this activity, intense as it was, would *not* have been observable to the keenest eye. All was conducted with the utmost discretion—to all outward appearances, Oak Ridge was, as always, a tranquil backwater town.

Meanwhile, the UC team . . . well, I had plenty to keep me busy. Chris Day and Jon Sarno were my "handlers," with Chris acting as my link to the RA, funneling all requests and scheduling all the preparatory activities, protecting me from an inundation of conflicting orders, requests, suggestions. Jon ran interference with JEH and DOJ. Michelle floated around, keeping track of what was happening all around, and keeping us up to date. In a rapidly evolving near-crisis environment, what you don't know is the prime cause of stress—and I knew next to nothing about uranium enrichment. It was critical that Jean-Marc be familiar with the contraband to be purchased. While I did not need to be an expert on the mechanics of the tools used in the enrichment process, I would need to be sufficiently conversant with the subject matter to be a credible middleman. French intel would hardly have sent a senior officer totally nonconversant with the nuts and bolts of nuclear material to make such a purchase. On a personal but no-less-significant note, Marc Ruskin wanted to know exactly what the radiation exposure might be. Over the years, I had handled heroin, stolen cars, fraudulent documents, all variety of contraband. None of which had been carcinogenic. I would need to be pretty damn sure that whatever transpired on Friday, whatever might go wrong, I would not develop leukemia ten years down the road.

The first afternoon in Knoxville, I received a briefing from a nuclear engineer: Uranium Enrichment 101. Centrifuges for Dummies. By this point, based on Oakley's access and the phone conversations, the pros had a pretty good idea of what he was offering for sale. They were "fuel rods . . . tubes and other associated hardware items . . . pieces of equipment known as 'barrier' . . . which play a crucial role in the production of highly enriched uranium. . . . through the gaseous diffusion process." In a highly simplified manner, the engineer explained how it all worked, and why it was classified. Very classified. The technology was the product of years of *very* secret research, not known or shared with even the closest of allies. If this material were obtained and reverse-engineered by a foreign power, the savings would be a few hundred million dollars in research costs. I was paying Oakley $200,000, a bargain indeed.

The nuclear engineer's agenda included reassuring me as to the *de minimis* risks. If the materials were unused, as Oakley claimed, they would pose absolutely no risk. Right. *And if he just happened to be lying?* Well then the likelihood of there being any residue was really very small. I just nodded. He wasn't the one who would be fiddling around with the stuff. I kept asking questions.

On Monday night, dinnertime, I placed a call to Oakley's TracFone. Jean-Marc was supposedly in New York. His superiors had agreed to Oakley's price. I would fly down to meet with him on Friday. There was one issue. *To finalize everything . . . they want to see pictures.* He could perhaps buy a disposable camera? (The rube!)

"I've got a digital camera . . . I could put it on a floppy, and just get you the floppy, how is that?" Served me right. "How am I going to get it to you?"

"For us, thees is very easy . . . you put eet in an envelope . . . I give you a name, an American name, and you leave eet at the airport, at the Hilton Hotel and I arrange to have eet take . . . to have eet shipped to New York. If you can arrange to do this tomorrow or Wednesday . . ."

"I'll do it . . . I'll do it Wednesday, I'll, I'll take off early from work and do it Wednesday."

"Yes, write Robert Ford and then write New York City. New York. Just like that, and I will arrange, uh, to have eet—how you say—Federal Express to me. You just . . . at the front desk, just leave it there . . . like you say, Wednesday." I would call him Thursday evening to make final arrangements for Friday morning.

All in my best Inspector Clouseau.

Midafternoon on Tuesday, the tech agents were setting up the recording equipment in the hotel lobby. One stood on a ladder, attaching a camcorder to a ceiling lamp. Others installed the wiring. They were almost done—when Oakley walked through the doors and entered the lobby. He had said he'd deliver the package on Wednesday! This had been and would be a superbly run op, but it was all happening on the fly and on this second afternoon in town it could have collapsed then and there. The installation could have been executed at 2:00 a.m., rather than midday. But it wasn't. But they got away with it. Oakley failed to notice the five "maintenance men" wearing ordinary blue-collar work clothing, blue Dickies pants and worn button-down canvas shirts—one of whom nearly fell off his ladder. Any kind of pro would have casually taken a closer look, sat in a lobby armchair and observed, sniffed a problem, turned around, and walked out. Instead, Oakley walked directly to the front desk, FedEx envelope in hand. This constituted his first overt act arising from his contacts with Jean-Marc, the intel officer representing a foreign power. Oakley was crossing a line—the line of no return. He could still turn around and walk away. And providing the motivation to do so, if he had been alert, were the five FBI tech agents just yards away. After a brief exchange with the concierge—a real one! On Wednesday there would have been a BuAgent in his place—Oakley was gone. Minus one very incriminating envelope. The photographs confirmed the engineers' grim predictions as to the significance, the *nuclear significance,* of the stolen items offered for sale.

Many had wondered, after the collapse of the Soviet Union, how it was possible that better care had not been taken to keep track and safeguard the building blocks of doomsday machines. Yet here in East Tennessee . . . but for the FBI's widespread criminal information-gathering network and efficiency, the disappearance of the "hardware items" would have gone unnoticed. The Department of Energy would have to revamp and revise its security protocols—in an ideal world. In all likelihood, in the tradition of large bureaucracies worldwide, the DOE probably pinned the fault on one or two mid-level managers, fired them, and moved on.

While the tech agents at the airport hotel were busy almost blowing the entire operation, Chris took me on a shopping trip. Oak Ridge having a limited supply of French haberdashers, we had to make do with J. C. Penney. I had been uncompromising: I would not wear any of my own clothes to the meet. Chris had checked with the HAZMAT team—they would be briefing me on Thursday—and they had concurred with my caution. Anything worn by Jean-Marc would be checked with a Geiger counter, bagged, and incinerated. The clothing chosen was generic, dark slacks, a Polo shirt, three-quarter-length lightweight blue wool coat, driving gloves—to be worn as an extra-layer of protection, direct from the nuclear-testing labs at Totes—Fruit of the Loom undergarments (Oakley was not likely to be reading the labels). Astonishingly, we found a French-style short-brimmed cap, the sort that Jean-Paul Belmondo would wear pulled down to his brows. Chris then paid for my classy new wardrobe and passed it along to the tech agents, who would make the alterations necessary to secrete the audio and video recording devices. This was not Holyland or Mount Vernon or Tampa. There would by multiple layers of review. The equipment would be tested and retested by the tech SAs, then by myself, with Chris, on Thursday evening. Everyone understood that any equipment failures traceable to human error would be dimly received.

Chris had, in his role as point man, effectively communicated my not insignificant safety concerns to management, and the HAZMAT briefing was meticulously prepared. Hal Levine, top HAZMAT engineer/ supervisory special agent and two of his engineers had flown in from Quantico to direct the effort. Short and stout, Hal's demeanor projected bulldog assuredness, rather than any softness of character. I had met him in the course of my frequent visits to Quantico while stationed at Safeguard. His credibility was already established, now what mattered was the substance. While Hal's responsibilities at Oak Ridge were broad, this particular briefing was strictly focused on Jean-Marc. My interest in what exposure, if any, existed to the population at large, what containment protocols and evacuation procedures needed to be established, was peripheral at best. My tunnel vision limited the breadth of interest to number one.

Hal and two assistants spread the equipment on the conference-room table. There were two plastic items the size and weight of key fobs. Passive radiation detectors to be carried in my pockets, they would be analyzed later—and would Lord willing provide negative results. A device that appeared to be a post-shampoo blow-dryer was an ultrasensitive Geiger counter. With which Jean-Marc would scan Oakley and his merchandise—a reasonable enough demand, considering the singular nature of the contraband.

On the table were also three plastic-enclosed coins, the size of silver dollars, spaced two feet apart. Hal turned on the faux blow-dryer and pointed it at the first coin, about six inches distant. One slow *click*. So you know that it's working. Then, he moved to the second coin. A medium response. . . . *click* . . . *click*. Mildly radioactive, he explained, no risk. Then to the third coin. An explosion of loud, rapid *click click clicking*.

"Gamma rays. Very hazardous."

"Right. And if I hear that clicking, then what?"

The briefing had thus far served to inform me that I would be carrying a machine that would let me know I was being poisoned and two key chains that would later confirm my sorry state.

"It's not going to happen."

Once the final op plan was in place, the HAZMAT team would establish a "choke point" through which Oakley's car would have to pass. Strategically parked would be a nondescript panel truck that was, in fact, an ultra-high-tech response truck with high-sensitivity external monitors. Inside the truck would be a five-operator SWAT team, all wearing HAZMAT suits and standard ordnance, to include submachine guns. Any detection of gamma rays—and Oakley would not be arriving for the meet with me. Good, but I still wanted a HAZMAT suit. I was worried.

As the army of lawyers at DOJ and JEH continued to debate what I would and would not be allowed to say on D-Day—none of whom were likely to have had any real-world experience that might inform them as to what a UC can and cannot say to a subject without sabotaging the entire op—my preparations continued. One of the high points of the week was the tour of the lab the following morning: a visual familiarity with the devices found in a nuclear facility being a prerequisite to an informed discussion, even with a relatively ill-informed conspirator. Jean-Marc should certainly appear to be as familiar with the machines as Oakley. Chris, Michelle, Jon, and I all stared at the huge high-tech machinery. The engineer, accustomed to providing VIP tours to budget-approving legislators, provided the enthralling details in layman's terms.

The SWAT commanders, in an indication of true professionalism, had requested that I participate in their operational planning sessions. It is not uncommon for SWAT team leaders and their "operators" (as the individual commandos are called) to resent input from outsiders. These self-assured veterans knew better. The decisions made here could be determinative as to whether I would still be around, alive and kicking on Saturday. They laid out their thinking and their planning.

Adjacent to the Knoxville Airport Hilton is a four-story stand-alone garage. Then, farther out, is a large, surface-level parking lot. Initially the SWAT chiefs were inclined to select the large lot for the meet. With unobstructed views, a number of observation posts could be established. Ben Templeton, the overall SWAT commander, pointed out that the area was not enclosed, thus difficult to secure and also offering numerous escape routes. His suggestion: the rooftop level of the garage, with clear line of sight to the upper floors of the hotel proper, and a single ramp in, a single ramp out. The HAZMAT truck could be parked the evening prior by the second-story ramp, to screen Oakley as he came in.

On the hotel side of the lot, there was an enclosed stairwell. Jean-Marc's car could be parked alongside that stairwell. Adjacent to my car, a spot would be saved for Oakley with one of our vehicles. Once Oakley's approach was called in by surveillance, our car would pull out and free up the space for Oakley. I pointed out a flaw, and a solution.

"If our cars are parked side by side, Oakley may not even get out of his car, just open the window and start to talk. You guys won't have a good view, if the sun is reflecting off the windshields, you won't see what's going on. He could have a gun in his hand, no one will know. It'll be too tight, there'll be no room to maneuver . . . Why not save him a space across the lane from my car? Then we both need to get out of our cars."

Templeton did me one better. Directly in front of the stairwell door, the lane was blocked out by diagonal yellow lines. Jean-Marc's car would be parked to the right of the stairwell, Oakley's "reserved" space would be to the left, with the yellowed-out lane in-between. Perfect.

Throughout the course of the meet, a SWAT team would be waiting in the stairwell. Hearing my prearranged signal that the meet was over—or earlier, if demanded by circumstances—the twelve commandoes would emerge for the arrest of both Oakley and myself. I added my usual caveat: The arrest of Jean-Marc, accompanied by the appropriate level of verbal abuse and manhandling, would *not* be brought to completion until Oakley (and confederates, if any) were cuffed and the area secured. Cardinal principle of UC work.

On Thursday—D-Day minus one—a real conflict arose. One of the DOJ attorneys came up with a change in the scenario, designed to enhance the evidentiary strength of the case. A videotaped sale of stolen, classified nuclear materials to a foreign intelligence service wasn't enough for him—selling secrets to the French wasn't sufficiently sexy. His suggestion—his requirement, in fact—was a short addendum to the closing scene. Once the cash and materials had been successfully exchanged, I was to say that the contraband was destined for Sudan.

For Sudan! Oakley had unequivocally stated that he did not want to make a sale to "Arabs." He owned handguns. Read extremist right-wing blogs. How would he react? Perhaps in a very unpleasant way, and I had no intention of finding out. A phone call with the attorney ended in a heated exchange. *And what am I suggesting that they use it for? That they reverse-engineer it in a stone pot?* He in turn "required" that I include the addendum. I outright refused—a bluff. Were FBI upper management to side with the DOJ and order the change, then so be it, but with everyone of authority I could corner, I made my case. In addition to the operational concerns, I suggested a legal rationale. Adding the "Sudan postscript" would essentially fabricate an additional charge. The defense would certainly so argue, claiming (accurately) that the FBI and DOJ were overreaching, thus diverting attention from the rest of the charges, and ultimately weakening what was already a rock-solid case. They agreed, went to bat for me, and convinced the bosses at JEH, who—to their credit—drew a line in the sand. DOJ backed down. Late in the afternoon, the SAC gave me a call. Forget about Sudan. (Gladly.)

Thursday evening I placed the last call.

MR: Hello, Paul, how are you?

Oakley: Hello! I'm just okey-dokey. Are you down here?

MR: Eet does not matter. But I will be tomorrow morning. My superiors were very happy, very happy, weeth thees peectures. They have agreed to thee two hundred.

Oakley: That's just super-duper. When?

MR: At nine a.m., we will meet at the airport, on the roof of zhe garage. Thees way, I can leave quickly, after. I will be alone. You will be alone, no?

Oakley: Yeah. I'll be alone, for sure. How do I know who you are?

MR: I am a skinny man, I will be wearing a dark coat and a dark blue cap, holdeeng a black briefcase.

Oakley: Okay, I'll see you tomorrow.

MR: Paul, one more theeng. The product. Put eet een baggies or ziplock bag, something so I can see.

Oakley: Okay. Okay. I'll see you tomorrow morning.

MR: Okay, Paul, I weel see you in thee morning.

After the call, Jon Sarno and I checked out of the Oak Ridge Embassy Suites in the afternoon and relocated that evening to the Airport Hilton. Management wanted me safely on site. Two rooms facing the garage, upper floor. One was to serve as the on-site command post, the other as the Surveillance/SOG Command Post. Jon would have the use of one room for the night, myself the other.

Arriving just before 8:00 p.m., I crossed paths with the SWAT and tech agents who were on their way out. Friendly smiles, wishes of good luck, *be careful Marc*. I checked out both rooms, which were replete with all manner of law enforcement gear. There were large ballistic nylon duffel bags, black Pelikan cases of varying sizes, tripods with high-power binoculars, with telephoto-lens-fitted cameras, with parabolic antennas. Recording equipment. Communications' equipment. Weapons cases. I had seen many such set-ups before, but nothing this elaborate. Second place in my experience would have been the one for the mass *Machetero* arrests in WELLROB, years ago, back in San Juan.

Five minutes later, I was at the front desk to get *my own room*.

"You'll have to call Hilton's 800 number to reserve a room."

"I'll what? I can't get a room at the front desk?!"

Not being disposed to entering into a ridiculous argument, I called the number and ten minutes later had a large room on the Hilton Honors Members' Floor. I let Chris know where I was and settled in.

At 7:00 a.m. Friday morning, after a quiet night's sleep, I was joined in my room by Chris, and a frazzled, bleary-eyed Jon. *What happened to you?* Starting at 4:00 a.m., there had commenced a steady procession of tactically uniformed, heavily booted agents entering and exiting the room, radios crackling, orders being barked. Tech agents making final adjustments and tests of equipment. Phones ringing. Coffee runs, shared jokes. I glanced around my quiet, cozy room—no doubt, one of my better tactical decisions. As we ate breakfast in this superior room, Chris conducted last-minute checks on my recording equipment and transmitter. The audio was the primary concern, both for evidentiary purposes and security. My videocam would be supplemented by telephoto-lensed camcorders in the SOG room and by a camera secreted in an empty pickup truck already parked in a space across from the planned meet location.

My faith in the efficacy of transmitters had not appreciated significantly since RUN-DMV, nearly two decades earlier. There would, however, be plenty of eyes fixed on Jean-Marc and Oakley. Chris ran through the checklist. Both audio and visual "danger signals" confirmed. The visual signal I had selected was clear, unequivocal, unmistakable. I would take off my short-brimmed French cap and toss it to the ground. Then the sparks would fly indeed. As always, I had limited confidence in the audio danger signal. (I've forgotten what it was.) The "take down" signal (deal completed, move in, please): *I salute you for helping my country*. I wasn't particularly concerned as to whether they could be heard or not. Everyone would see Oakley and myself complete our exchange, break off and approach our respective cars, and know the deal was done.

Continuing down the list. My trusted ballistic panel portfolio with concealed weapon. Check. The Geiger counter that looked like a hair dryer (battery-powered), clearly visible in the portfolio, zipper deliberately open—no chance of Oakley's mistaking it for something lethal. Check. A nylon flight bag containing 10,000 twenty-dollar bills in two sealed, transparent plastic bags. Check. (Chris pleaded: *This is the way I got it from the bank. Please try to avoid Oakley tearing them open.* Intact, they could be returned as is. Opened . . . well, he and a bank employee would have to count the entire $200,000. I would do my best, I promised. Chris had done right by me all the way.) Passive radiation detectors in pants and jacket pockets. Check. Car keys. Cell phone. Cap and gloves. Electronic devices activated. Check. Check. Check. Check.

And then they were gone. 8:30 a.m. Fifteen minutes left prior to my scheduled five-minute walk to the meet. Looking out the window, listening to my own breathing, no point in thinking about the meet. As with the last moments before a heavily prepared exam. Even with Sudan deleted, the DOJ attorneys had come up with a laundry list of questions and topics they wanted covered. Of course. With the focus and review that would follow what transpired today, it would not be judicious to follow my usual MO and blow them off. Reviewing my crib sheet was out of the question. With the video running, I had my reputation to uphold. Whatever was going to happen would happen. There were no options left to explore, no additional preparations, no fine-tuning.

Picking up the portfolio and flight bag, down the hallway, elevator, side-door exit, crunching the gravel as I approached the garage stairwell and up the four flights to the roof. The SWAT operators were not yet in place. They weren't supposed to be. I emerged on the roof just as the car holding Oakley's space pulled out and proceeded down the exit ramp. Perfect timing. The command post was moving the pieces like clockwork.

Opening the trunk of my standard-issue midsize rental sedan, pre-parked by Chris in the designated spot, I set the flight bag next to an open attaché case, which had been placed there at the instructions of Hal, the HAZMAT team leader. I was to tell Oakley to place the materials in the case and close it. Jean-Marc and the nuclear hardware would never come in physical contact.

Portfolio set on the closed trunk, I leaned against the car and looked toward the hotel. Listening to the roar of planes at the adjacent airport. Conscious of the multitude of observers, watching me in real time. In the hotel, instantaneously relayed to the offices in Oak Ridge, in Knoxville, in our nation's capital.

A large gray Lincoln Town Car tore up the ramp, Oakley at the wheel, alone. Big and burly, he got out of the car. No greetings or pleasantries at all, straight to business as I approached with the Geiger counter, explaining the need to check him and the merchandise—there it was, on the front passenger seat—for radiation. Oakley scanned the area and then looked at Jean-Marc. What he saw and, maybe more important, *didn't* see—confederates, lawmen, sources of danger—seemed to conform to his expectations. Astonishingly, he handed over a business card with his true name. I told him, in my heavily French-accented English, that I didn't need to know it. He was unconcerned: "It's all right as long as you don't get caught before you get out of here."

Quite matter-of-fact, Oakley proceeded to detail the safeguarding provided to the stolen "product" by Oak Ridge. Upon entering and leaving the facility, he was obliged to change clothes. So as not to remove *the dust*—dust so secret that mere motes were capable of revealing the extraordinary nature of these highly prized materials he was selling Jean-Marc. Waving toward the zipper-lock bag containing his merchandise, he went on. The uranium enrichment fuel rods and tubes, originally twelve to fifteen feet in length, had been broken up by the team of laborers that he supervised. *Twenty-two tons of tubes.* Could he obtain more? Not any longer. *Now,* it was guarded: his men had been pulled out, armed guards brought in. To watch over tons of pulverized secret bits and pieces. The other buildings all had metal detectors.

"Where they had the most sensitive stuff . . . no metal detectors."

This was progressing better than expected. Oakley had already convicted himself. Fully immersed in the role of Jean-Marc, I picked up the zipper-lock bag, holding it high as I examined the contents, providing my audience back in the Hilton and elsewhere with a clear and unobstructed view. *What the hell was I doing?!* Hubris. Rapidly, I dropped it back into his car.

Was he sure the hardware was secret?

"I know it was classified." There had been briefings to that effect. Even talking about the materials outside the facility was forbidden.

The sound of a car in the background caused Oakley to spin suddenly, abruptly departing from his narrative, aware of his surroundings. Keeping the conversation moving, I assured him that there were just a few more points "my superiors" wanted me to clarify—information we would need to maximize the utility of our purchase. I removed the list of questions. That was a judgment call—but by this point, why not? We already had him dead to rights. . . . *And how are they used?* . . . His answers may not have been worthy of a physics professor, but they would certainly impress a federal judge. The Uranium 237 was converted to 235 (it may have been the other way around, neither one of us was an expert). The resulting product being radioactive, the stuff was used in bombs. How had he known "my country" would be interested? He said that the plant security people had told him, *the French would love to get their hands on it.*

Seeing the cash, Oakley visibly relaxed. Any thoughts of a rip-off firmly put to rest. If possible, he became more loquacious. At one point, he had second thoughts about the authentic business card he had presented and asked that I not hold onto it "for too long." By letting the meet continue, I simply allowed him more opportunity to bury himself. Lest his future attorneys entertain thoughts of denying essential elements of the crime, I emphasized the high points. Having drawn from his own lips his very pronounced awareness of the contraband's classified status . . . were there any concealment issues I should be aware of—such as setting off metal detectors—as I would "smuggle them . . . to my own country."

We had been on the garage roof for over half an hour. The transaction had been concluded. Every conceivable incriminatory statement had been either volunteered or extracted. Also covered: when he stole the hardware, how he had concealed it, the absence of co-conspirators. The time had come to close the curtain.

"I salute you for helpeeng my countree."

Shouting and rapid movement as the flurry of ninjas magically appeared. Indignant shouting by Jean-Marc. *I am a tooreest! You have no right . . . I want to call the quonsulatte!* A little over the top—it had been a long week. Chris: "Be quiet!" Silence.

Once I was "arrested" and inside the tinted-window SWAT SUV, Chris scanned me with the Geiger counter. I was now particularly concerned about my hand, but *no clicking.* One of the SWAT operators stuck his head in. *He's all secure. We found a pistol. In his right coat pocket. Looks like a .380.* Ah, the pocket his right hand had been in throughout most of the meet. Until he saw the cash.

My Geiger counter didn't pick up a single bad atom that afternoon. Oakley was arrested, detained, *and then released.* The judge, to the surprise of most, had set bond. The indictment itself didn't come down for six months, in July. A public record, it states that Oakley, "having possession of, access to and having been entrusted with sections of 'barriers' and associated hardware used for uranium enrichment through the process of gaseous diffusion . . . having reason to believe that such data would be utilized to injure the United States and secure an advantage to a foreign nation, did communicate, transmit and disclose such data to another person."

"Another person" was Jean-Marc. The "barriers" were devices "that play a crucial role in the production of highly enriched uranium . . . used in the manufacture of atomic weapons." Oakley's lawyer dismissed some of the material in question as "pieces of scrap" and downplayed the whole case as much ado about nothing. Which, after plea bargaining, translated into seven years federal time. The official redacted video of the meet on that garage roof is public record. In fact, I used it in presentations at Quantico as a case study in carefully orchestrated, successful undercover operations and apprehensions.

14

ALTERNATE BREACH

In late 2008—almost two years after the January 2007 takedown of Roy Lynn Oakley in Tennessee—the full-time gig with the Foreign Counterintelligence squad came to an unexpected conclusion. Without a word other than vague references to dollars and cents, the entire Group I op—well established, thoroughly backstopped, and consistently successful—was deep-sixed. I was astounded. In addition to the assortment of part-time False Flag cases like Roy Lynn Oakley's (if less notorious) that were successfully concluded, my primary assignment had been this long-term op. Three UCs (two women and myself) on that detail were providing intel of value (or so we believed, and were *led* to believe) on a regular basis. For over three years, I had inhabited the FBI's deliberately less-public side, the world of counterespionage, identifying foreign spies and foiling their plans. My activities must be related in the vaguest of terms. In the course of my (covert) workday, and in the evenings, I would cultivate relationships and build rapport *with* foreign nationals in order to gather information *from* them, which would later be documented and distributed to those within the Bureau who would be interested. Unlike the criminal UC work, a certain degree of socializing was acceptable, even encouraged in this very different arena. The people I was interacting with would never be arrested, never learn of my true identity. As with real-life professional and personal relationships, I would eventually drift out of their lives, simply moving on.

Specifically, I developed an acquaintance with an executive from a country historically hostile to the United Sates. Code name Victor, this executive engaged in two jobs: a cover job that I (and everyone else) was meant to believe was his true occupation, and that true occupation, which was intelligence officer. Over a period of six months, I had seen this gentleman frequently, maintaining a courteous but distant relationship. I waited for *him* to make the first move. Which he did. First with small talk, working up to occasional lunches (for which he invariably picked up the tab) and later, exchanges of personal confidences. The classic steps taken by an intel officer assessing a potential recruit. I was a "dangle." A double agent pretending to take the bait. Once recruited, he would be my control officer, directing *me* to develop relationships with those in the know, collecting intel useful to his country. As a double agent, I would indeed provide intel. A careful blend of apparently useful (but insignificant) true information, salted with apparently useful (but false) information.

This one relationship continued after the counterintelligence op was officially shut down near the end of 2008. By early summer of 2009, we believed the "pitch" from the foreign intel officer was imminent. I was ready. I was stoked. From UC in heroin and Mafia cases in the dark side of the criminal world, to becoming a UC double agent on the dark side of espionage and counterespionage? I would have done it all. And then, on a beautiful Sunday afternoon, on July 9, on a country road in Connecticut, that case, too, went kaput. Where and how? On the back lanes of southern New England, while riding my classic Honda Valkyrie 1500cc touring bike.

I loved those New England backcountry byways that manage to retain all the charm and resonate with the tranquility of a less complex era. (I realize that some, maybe many people consider the big bikes outrageous offenders of peace and quiet, but *most* of the bikes have mufflers that make them as quiet as cars. Those bikers who substitute aftermarket exhaust pipes without baffles, simply in order to make a lot of macho noise, are jerks, to say the least.) Past village squares bordered by red-brick Federal-style buildings and balconied colonials, passing dairy farms and stables, I cruised with deep pleasure—for years, this had been my antidote to the world of crime, corruption, avarice, deceit—the zone whose parameters defined my day-to-day existence. On this sunny July afternoon, I crested a hill southbound on rural Route 202 heading toward New Preston, Connecticut, the two-lane, shoulderless road curving to the right, limiting my field of vision. At the approach of a northbound Harley, I turned my head to the left to exchange salutes. A slight turn to the right—and the impact was instantaneous. The face shield of my helmet ripped, my chest tearing along the trunk of the car that was stopped dead in the road at the end of the curve. Then the impact as my body hit the asphalt, landing like what I was, a bag of bones. Immobile, as the Harley driver—an EMT, who had heard the crash and immediately turned round—asked if I knew my name, what day it was, all the diagnostic first-responder questions. Never losing consciousness as the faces streamed past, wondering only if my ticket had finally been punched, not by a felon with a 9mm—*that* I could almost have accepted— but as a civilian motorist, inanimate, in the middle of the road. A banal traffic statistic.

Was this how I was going to die, alone amid strangers? The responding state trooper ascertained I was a lawman—gun and creds were in my fanny pack—and made sure they pulled all the stops. I was medevaced via helicopter to a trauma center in Waterbury, where it was soon established that I would likely pull through. The butcher's bill: two broken—shattered—elbows, a lacerated kidney, right knee damaged, upper lip torn open, miscellaneous abrasions and bruises all over. When I met the angel-of-mercy trooper, he explained. The car had stopped while waiting for a car in front to make a left turn. As there was no shoulder, that driver had not been able to pull around. After skidding and banging over the trunk, then the roof, I was airborne for twenty-five feet. When the momentum dictated by the laws of physics came to an end, I landed, plopped to the ground like that aforementioned bag of bones. No sliding along the asphalt. Even better—amazingly—my flight was not interrupted by a guardrail, lamppost, tree, or second car. To that good fortune alone did I owe my survival.

It would be four months, November, before I could return to work.

Nor was that counterintel sting the only one disrupted by the motorcycle wreck. I was also right in the middle of ALTERNATE BREACH and

OXY BLUE, two ops I had been invited to join following the Bu's abandonment of the counterintel op. When that decision came down at the end of 2008, I initially feared that I might now be assigned to "real cases" as an ordinary case agent, no longer the full-time undercover guy. Hoping to fend off any such development, I scoured Janus for UC roles, but my fears were largely unfounded. It turned out that I was now essentially the New York office's éminence grise of undercover agents, enjoying upper management's *sub voce* carte blanche to work any UC ops, whether in New York or elsewhere. With a highly unusual twist. Historically, I had worked cases arising out of the squad to which I was assigned— COMMCORR, RUN-DMV, INFRACEL, BLUE SCORE, and others not recounted in this tome—while being "loaned out" to other squads and field offices on an ad hoc basis. But now, going forward, I would be assigned for administrative purposes to the same counterintelligence squad for which I had been working. But my UC cases would have no connection to the squad. This was a significant gesture, because managers were allotted limited numbers of special agents, from whom they were expected to receive tangible, measurable results. The managers' own performance evaluations were dependent on the stats generated by the agents under their supervision. That's the way all bureaucracies work.

With me, that counterintel squad was utilizing a valuable SA slot but with no return for their squad. The Bu might benefit, the NYO as a whole might see enhanced results, but for my specific chain of command, zip. I was truly a freelance UC, free to work any UC op that came my way, whether in New York or elsewhere. The only caveat was to keep myself busy, to periodically provide my supervisor with a rundown of the cases I was working. I owed this unique position to the benevolence of Phil Romano, my boss's boss. Formerly the Chief Division Counsel, top lawyer for the New York office, he was now an Assistant Special Agent in Charge of that office. And for me, a guardian angel. The only other FBI UC agent I have known with similar freedom of movement and accountability was my pal Jack Garcia, the 350-pound New York UC (author of *The Making of Jack Falcone*). Once Jack retired in 2006, it was just yours truly.

The agents on ALTERNATE BREACH and OXY BLUE recruited me in early and late 2009, respectively. In both instances, I had accepted even though I was somewhat ill-informed. In fact, I had not performed *any* due diligence—a recurring error, no doubt a personality trait. As admitted earlier, I always assumed I could handle any case, and I always assumed that I *should* handle it because I was probably the best man for the UC job. Leaving TURKEY CLUB (the La Cosa Nostra op) before its final (positive) resolution was an aberration, brought on by internal conflicts and what I considered simply egregious errors of surveillance, backup, communication, and more, as related.

ALTERNATE BREACH, an international case featuring corrupt international arms dealers was much more involved and requires and deserves much more attention here, but OXY BLUE had its smaller-scale moments of interest and lessons learned. My alias was a reincarnated Alejandro, organized crime captain controlling a New England drug distribution network from his home base in Danbury, Connecticut. This was a sudden reversion to the Alex Perez–like world of the mid-nineties, of SUNBLOCK and QUEER FIFTIES. In charge of this op (a health-care fraud Group II) were Mimi Forester and her future husband, Bill Shaughnessy. The scenario initially seemed somewhat below my skill set. Mimi and Bill were looking for a UC to visit the offices of predicated doctors (that is, targeted for a good reason, as per AG guidelines) who had been identified by reliable informants, and obtain prescriptions for Oxy-Contin, Percocet, and other pills for which there is a booming market on the streets of our American cities and towns (and farming communities, I wouldn't be surprised to learn).

A somewhat over-the-hill pill popper? I could do that. Especially as I had few other cases going, and especially as Mimi and her squad of young agents were very professional and enthusiastic—going a long way to rehabilitating my perception of New-Era Bureau special agents. Her operations plans, drafted for each meet, were composed *after* consultation with the primary UC (that would be me), and incorporated my suggestions for security enhancements, surveillance, communications, all tactical issues. The most successful UC ops are fluid; they evolve to encompass new opportunities. They require flexibility in approach, and the capacity for adaptability by the entire team. This team had these attributes, in sharp contradistinction from the TURKEY CLUB and, as we shall soon see, ALTERNATE BREACH teams.

Most of the targeted quacks operated out of run-down clinics in run-down neighborhoods—and in one case, remarkably enough, out of a home office in Staten Island. That was an octogenarian MD with a few screws loose. I once sat in his waiting room as he chased off a cashless patient with an ancient shotgun. So what "tactical issues" could possibly arise out of visits to such bent MDs? Initially, the term seemed melodramatic for what I took to be a garden-variety health-care fraud. Then I learned better. Take Dr. Diana Williamson, for example. She had been a rising star in the medical profession, treating the needy out of her Harlem clinic, she seemed the role model for the caring physician, mindful of her roots, providing services to the community from which she had arisen. Until she started to sell OxyContin (the brand name for oxycodone), with South Bronx drug-dealer Lenny Hernandez, aka Dominica, as her partner in crime. This duo had devised a system for aggregating quantities of Oxy through the use of fraudulent prescriptions and "straw" patients. Dominica moved the Oxy on the streets the way he knew best—as though it were *manteca* (heroin) or *perico* (cocaine).

On the surface, I was all enthusiasm with OXY BLUE. Old enough to be the father of any agent on the squad, except only their supervisor, I had an image to sustain. But I had also married less than a year earlier, and my wife was expecting, and the thought of once again buying illegal *whatever*—drugs, guns, stolen merchandise, pills—on the streets of Spanish Harlem or the Bronx—*Oy vey*. This scenario was less than appealing. How to mitigate the risk? A flash of inspiration. What had worked in the nineties would no doubt work again. If—a big if—I could find the right partner. Brash and pretty, Linda Nemeck and I had worked together intermittently over the past few years. She was about fifteen years younger. We would hit the streets together. Linda agreed. Mimi and Bill (and Dorothy, the new co-case agent) agreed. All of their supervisors agreed. Two weeks later, aliases Alejandro and Linda Huertas Vega drove their seized late-model white Benz across the Third Avenue Bridge, northbound into the Bronx. Recording devices activated, weapons secreted, Linda ready to hop into the rear passenger side seat at meettime, prepped to blow Dominica into eternity if I called her "Honey." Just like old times, only with a different old lady. And just like those old times, my old lady and I hit a series of home runs. In the parking lot of a South Bronx McDonald's, we watched as Dominica hopped out of a dark-colored SUV, and walked toward the Benz. Linda jumped in back, he took her place in the plush leather bucket seat, and . . . forty-five minutes later we were almost old pals. Four or five buys from Dominica led to convictions for both him and the good doctor in Harlem. And for others in Brooklyn, Staten Island, and one in New Jersey, convictions for passing the bad scripts.

The lesson learned: sometimes you can go home again.

At the opposite end of the operational and "repercussional" spectrum was ALTERNATE BREACH, which overlapped with OXY BLUE. As OXY flourished, BREACH . . . well, it didn't flourish. In fact, it went down in flames. Quite a saga. Made the papers. Sabotaged a few careers (*not* among the subjects—rather, among the good guys in the FBI and the DOJ). And it started so great. The case agents promised me the moon. As initially described, the Group I op had all the elements of a fast-paced action film: those despicable arms dealers; a Third World dictator; and a certain so-phisticated, international, globetrotting undercover agent. A role virtu-ally custom-tailored for me, I accepted on the spot. I imagined interacting with targets like Sarkis Soghanalian, the infamous "Merchant of Death" who had supplied arms for three decades to national military forces, as well as rebel troops, in Third World conflicts around the globe. (He was an inspiration for the 2005 film *Lord of War*.) I was a mite disillusioned when the BREACH targets turned out to be roughly two dozen senior executives, sales managers, agents, consultants, and even a general counsel—U.S., U.K., and Israeli citizens from established military and law enforcement suppliers, small and large companies, privately held and publicly traded, Smith & Wesson among them. It was quite a menagerie of the accused. Important targets, no doubt. But not quite as glamorous as the Lear Jet globe-trotters I had imagined, but no matter. If they were violating federal criminal statutes, I would provide the evidence. And the job would turn out to be unlike any I'd ever undertaken.

First thing first: Who was I? It was not a trivial question. Even though my targets in ALTERNATE BREACH would not be denizens of the street like Mahmoud in RUN-DMV, or drug dealers like Richard in SUN-BLOCK, they would be suspected felons with plenty to lose in this operation— their entire businesses, plus federal time. I couldn't see taking a bullet in the Four Seasons in Washington, but some "payback" elsewhere? Not likely, but not impossible, so I wasn't taking this matter of an alias lightly.

For a couple of decades, of course, I had maintained three, sometimes four wallets, each fully stocked with aged documents, functioning credit cards, and filler, ready to go at a moment's notice. (No bogus family photos, however. I haven't mentioned this: in twenty years, no subject had ever shown me a family picture. It simply isn't done, not between criminals, not between spies.) However, aliases Alex Perez, certainly, and Sal Morelli didn't match my new career in the international arms business. The most minor doubt on the part of the targets might initiate a certain degree of due diligence by any of them, and the op would soon be kaput. Daniel Martinez had been an international jewel-thief type, ideal for this new op, but TURKEY CLUB had led to high-profile prosecutions. The AFID would not withstand scrutiny, not since the advent of the Internet. What about Henri Marc Renard, from COMMCORR? Although nearly two decades had elapsed, and the name had never gone public following the Wall Street sting's infuriating demise, I considered the name jinxed.

My logic was sound, but a brand-new AFID designed and then created from scratch would take four to six months, as I explained to Chris Forvour, the lead case agent. No problem, he replied. Just try and get it moving as soon as possible. I puzzled over my name: something unequivocally, unmistakably, instantly recognizable as French. I reviewed the Paris white pages online. Legrand? Too generic, the French equivalent of Smith. Lafayette—ridiculous. Lasalle—maybe. Latour—perfect. Unusual without being remarkably so. A touch of class without the pretensions of a hyphenated surname. Then, a search of my personal phone book and I found "Pascal." Thoroughly French. Armed with a new name, I reached out to Val and my other good and invaluable friends at New York Janus to get the ball rolling in the matter of this French fellow approaching fifty (funniest thing, as I grew older, my aliases started growing younger) who would need to have *verifiably* lived in a variety of venues in and outside France. And complicating everything was the issue mentioned earlier: In the age of Google, it would not do for Pascal Latour to have popped into existence just two months earlier. So in mid-March 2009, I submitted the sheaf of required documents to Janus—FBI authorization memos and assorted bureaucratic paperwork. It was time now to turn to backstopping my brain—to acquire the knowledge and vocabulary consistent with an international financier with experience in the complex international arms trade, as well as high-stakes money laundering on a global level. *And* a faux personal relationship with Pascal Latour's close friends and principal source of income, Ali Bongo's family, the ruling dynasty of Gabon. Many minute details required, ignorance of which would be disastrous. My usual flights between Paris and Libreville, the capital of Gabon. My usual hotel (or did I stay at the palace? At Ali's compound?). The exchange rate, euro and dollar to CFA francs (Communauté Financiére Africaine). The source of funds to be laundered: *Banque Gabonaise de Developpement*. I would need a week in Nairobi. I would definitely need a week in Gabon to provide sufficient familiarization for credible conversation on that score. I would need time in Paris to establish the necessary residence, office space, phone lines, bank accounts (all this in addition to the backstopping by Janus).

Case agent Chris and my assigned contact agent, Dave Rauser, promised to meet all of these operational requirements. But none of it happened. Interacting with subjects who would be quite familiar with Nairobi and Gabon, I would have to wing it. I didn't have to wing it about Paris as a city, but French phone lines for backstopping purposes? An outrageous expense. Real French bank accounts? *Non.* LEGAT Paris was not even contacted to ascertain the feasibility of backstopping this UC op within its jurisdiction. It was all out because in an operation costing hundreds of thousands of dollars, if not seven figures, they chose to cut costs (and save time) through inadequate backstopping. They were prepared to jeopardize this entire Group I op by failing to address easily avoidable vulnerabilities. My suggestions, later undisguised *complaints*, were brushed off. Instead, Chris Forvour provided a basic scenario and timetable, and it was now up to me to create the role and the legend, pronto. As for Janus's backstopping, the BREACH team did not realize, or did not care, that the processes could not be rushed, absent *truly* exigent circumstances.

The link between the twenty-plus subjects in ALTERNATE BREACH and Pascal Latour was Richard Bistrong, president and co-owner of Point Blank Body Armor, the company on Long Island that had manufactured the Nagra-concealing bulletproof vest used by our informant—the Mount Vernon street cop—back in BLUE SCORE. Since that case, Richard had been arrested and charged with violations of the Foreign Corrupt Practices Act (FCPA), which makes it illegal to pay foreign officials to get business. Facing a significant prison sentence, he had agreed to be the confidential witness in what would be the largest (there have only been two) FCPA undercover operation since the enactment of the legislation in the mid-seventies. Of course, Richard did not require a new AFID—he would be introducing me to targets he had known for years. He was, however, now president of The Bistrong Group, Inc., a totally bogus firm as deeply rooted in the real world as Latour Conseil, and its Directeur Général . . . Pascal Latour.

Richard was tall, elegant, fit, every bit the cosmopolitan executive, projecting more of the image of a senior manager at L'Oréal than a vendor of the tools of war. Ironically, he was the most savvy of the individuals I worked with in ALTERNATE BREACH. And he had the most to lose. With a taste for Hermès shirts and ties, Rolex watches, Montblanc accessories, and Cuban cigars, Richard was singularly ill-suited for federal prison. He was therefore highly motivated to make this sting work. Unique in my experience with confidential witnesses, Richard had developed an elaborate legend connecting our two lives. Intertwining his true background with my fictitious one. Dating back to the year I had (supposedly) spent pursuing graduate studies in international affairs at his alma mater, the University of Virginia in the fall of 1984. The dates and details of our early arms transactions after my return to France. Purchases of armaments on behalf of Gabonese President for Life Omar Bongo dating back twenty years. Leaving nothing to chance, Richard coached me in the subtleties of negotiation and execution of arms deals. I learned the vocabulary, the argot of the true insider.

As to the how and the why of Gabon as the unwitting centerpiece of ALTERNATE BREACH—to this day, the question is a mystery to me. Had some friend of my case agent's at the State Department come up with this African backwater? Perhaps the country's remoteness, its relative isolation from the mainstream, was believed by the case agents and federal prosecutors to be an impediment to corroboration of the entire scenario. Not that I was complaining. From Pascal Latour's perspective, Gabon was ideal. As with all African nations with a French colonial history, the Gabonese are francophone and fierce francophiles, proud of their ties to the "homeland." My homework revealed that the Bongo family had huge property holdings in France. Who better to have arranged the purchases and currently manage the estates than Pascal Latour? As to the initial contacts leading to a relationship of deep trust spanning decades—Minister of Defense Ali Bongo, President Omar's son, was roughly my age. *Bien sûr*, Ali and Pascal had met as university students in Paris. As an extroverted, somewhat strapped-for-cash neophyte play-boy, Pascal had a large social network—lots of pretty girls, late-night parties. Ali was wealthy. We made a great team. By the time Ali graduated and returned home, we had developed an enduring friendship.

So, yes, from my alias's perspective, Gabon was great. But from *my* perspective—Marc Ruskin, UC agent—those same attributes of remoteness could backfire in an instant. If just one of the numerous subjects had an acquaintance with just one member of the internecine ruling elite in Gabon, much less with Ali Bongo, my alias would disintegrate. End of op, certainly. End of a certain UC's story? Not impossible.

In early April, I received an email from Chris, announcing that he had instructed our confidential witness Richard Bistrong to contact a number of subjects for meetings in mid-May. They would fly into D.C., where we would all have rooms at the Mandarin Oriental or the Four Seasons. Then, following a week of preperation, phase two would be a series of equivalent meets in Miami.

Mid-May? I had joined this op less than three months before this pronouncement. My *AFID* had been in the works for maybe six weeks. I didn't have any of the documents back yet, and I knew I wouldn't have all of them by mid-May. I answered immediately. *Chris, what are you doing? I don't have a driver's license yet. I don't have any ID yet. We can't set up UC meets until after the AFID is in place.* This point was so obvious that it would not have occurred to any instructor of UC seminars to even state such a self-evident procedure. (Not that it would have mattered in this op, because the ALTERNATE BREACH team had not bothered to attend these seminars, presented by the good people with the

FBIHQ UC and Safeguard Units.) Now I envisioned TURKEY CLUB all over again, with surveillance high-fiving in the parking lot after a meet in the hotel. But Chris and the team had their schedule and they were sticking to it, come hell or high water. To mix the metaphor: it was seemingly etched in stone. Richard, our informant, had been instructed to reach out to the subjects, *all of them,* who were already booking flights and hotels.

My inclination was to let events take their course, and let the professionals running the show develop a strategy to deal with the fact that their UC alias, Pascal Latour, was unequipped to check into a hotel room or pay for a meal, much less board a plane. (I believe we're all familiar with Homeland Security and have patiently endured its excesses at the airport. The "security theater" may be absurd, but it is a reality that Pascal would need to deal with.) Case agent Chris and contact agent Dave called Janus NY directly and begged for special treatment. Which they received, after Janus obtained my concurrence—I didn't want to facilitate the case agents in sabotaging their op. (As events would reveal, they were fully capable of doing so on their own.) And at the end of the day, inadequate backstopping (resulting from the unnecessarily tight timetable) would have created additional difficulties for me as I sought to finagle my way through the upcoming meets. Maybe I would have ended up riding Amtrak all the way to Miami. But Val from Janus burned some accumulated goodwill at NYS DMV, and I wasted a day on a round-trip drive to Albany, to obtain Pascal Latour driver's license. I still didn't have—and I would never have—my French backstopping, the bank accounts, verifiable office, residence, and more.

As a poor substitute to visiting Gabon itself, I received a ninety-minute country-background briefing at State.

But give Richard Bistrong a lot of credit. With his input, Chris and his supervisor had put together an impressive list of subjects, major and not-so-major players in the international arms trade. As noted earlier in my story, the AG guidelines require that the targets of UC ops be "predicated," thus countering a defense attorney's potential countercharge of entrapment. Even the body shops—all of them—in INFRACEL had been predicated with reliable source information. At the two or three meetings with the investigative team, held at DOJ in Washington, prior to going operational, I asked pointed questions about targets in BREACH, some of whom appeared to be unlikely candidates for scrutiny. As the UC, the primary, pivotal point of contact with the targets, *I, Marc Ruskin,* did not want to be ensnaring any who did not belong in the net. With a discomforting lack of specificity, Chris assured me, *we have sufficient PC on all of our subjects. The DOJ attorney concurs.* And the attorney nodded and smiled in confirmation. In the course of certain meets, my doubts resurfaced and were afterward expressed. To be quickly brushed aside. Fine. It wasn't my concern. But two years later . . . I'll get to that in due course.

We would be meeting with representatives of each company in Bistrong's suite at the Mandarin Oriental. Back-to-back UC meets, all day, every day, for an entire week. A schedule developed with no concept of the reality of undercover operations: At a UC meet, adrenaline is pumping full force, every word a calculated lie, a minor gesture capable of revealing the truth. There would be no opportunities for fine-tuning, for damage control—the next client would already be knocking at the door. I have emphasized time and again that the first UC meet with a subject is always the most important, and the most difficult. Without preexisting rapport, first impressions are key. This schedule, devised without my input, promised to be exhausting. Several months' worth of meetings crammed into two weeks. Whoever heard of such a thing? In the UC world, no one, believe me. This was new.

The pitch had all the trappings of an elaborate confidence scheme, reminiscent of a David Mamet scenario in *House of Games* or *The Spanish Prisoner*. Undercovers and con men are mirror images of each other. An undercover takes on the appearance of a criminal in order to gain a criminal's trust and cause him to take actions that are ultimately not in his interest—leading to a criminal conviction. A confidence man takes on the appearance of an honest person, in order to gain an honest person's trust and cause him to take actions that are ultimately not in his interest—leading to significant financial loss. In the process, the UC and the con man use the same tools—ruses, props, lies. For ALTERNATE BREACH, current events had fortuitously provided me a perfect opportunity to employ a panoply of ruses, props, and lies. While researching my legend. I'd learned that a few months earlier, there had been an assault on the president of Equatorial Guinea, one of Gabon's neighbors. This attempted assassination provided Pascal Latour with the perfect bogus story: For President Bongo, this had been the tipping point. Vague plans to enhance his military capabilities needed to be translated into concrete action. Defense Minister and presidential son Ali Bongo got the ticket: Refurbish the elite Presidential Guard. Money was no object for this oil-rich, mineral-rich nation. The refurbishment might require a temporary diversion of national treasury funds from their principal purpose—funding the Bongo family's overseas accounts and holdings—but so be it. Some sacrifice would be required to protect the nation and the family's vast wealth—and to maintain power.

Richard Bistrong's Presidential Suites at the Mandarin Orientals (D.C. and Miami) were wired for video and sound, with Chris, Dave, and company in the adjoining room monitoring the proceedings. I had asked Dave to call Pascal Latour's cell about ten or fifteen minutes into each meet, giving me an excuse to chatter a bit in my native French. The ruse had worked to enhance many of my aliases for nearly twenty years, and was still as effective as ever. For the benefit of those targets with some understanding of the language, I would throw around some numbers (*mon vieux, it's twelve million as agreed, or we'll have to walk away*).

By Sunday evening before the arduous week ahead, we would all be in place. Monday morning I would take a cab from the Four Seasons, elegantly decked out in my James Smart (a high-end Argentine haberdasher) suit and Hermès tie. There was *no* money budgeted for case-appropriate clothing, I ended up borrowing from Richard—*from the CI*—a Montblanc wallet and portfolio. My handgun was back in my desk at the New York office. Pascal could not board a plane with a bottle of water, much less with a pistol. In the past, when traveling covertly, I would borrow a gun from the local case agent. For ALTERNATE BREACH, I judged it to be unnecessary. It was unlikely that the targets, most of whom were flying in themselves, would be carrying weapons.

Richard's suite periodically received well-stocked trays from room

service (primarily for the benefit of the subjects). We would help ourselves to breakfast as we waited for the first targets to arrive. And then
the show would begin. All day long, throughout the week.

As Richard and I established in the opening of our dialogue with
every subject, the entire one-thousand-man Presidential Guard in Gabon
was to be re-equipped, from head to toe, literally. New boots, uniforms,
body armor, holsters, gloves, and insignia-bearing black berets. Machine
pistols (a translation of the German term *maschinenpistole*, a handheld
automatic firing pistol cartridges, fully automatic or in burst fire, such
as the MAC-10, a favorite of gangbangers for use in drive-by shootings),
handguns, sniper rifles, scopes, night-vision goggles, armored vehicles,
missile launchers, ammunition. Lots of ammunition. Every vendor would
get their respective slice of the project.

On one condition. With the completion of the negotiation phase of
each meeting, *after* the price had been established, Pascal raised "one
last point." In order for Ali Bongo to sign off on this deal, he required a
10-percent commission. So did I. Richard and I had our own private arrangement (no one asked for details). Therefore it would be necessary to
enhance the negotiated sale price by 20 percent. The illicit nature of this
"commission" was clear enough to frighten exactly one team of vendors.
No sooner had I completed my pitch than these citizens pulled out. Too
risky, *a violation of the FCPA,* not worth the aggravation just to make a
few dollars. Unfortunate, as they were by far the most obnoxious of the
targets I dealt with. And they were the *only* targets to walk away. The
others were fine with the "commission," though some agreed in terms
that were not utterly damning. A manufacturer of military-grade goggles, with whom Richard and I "met" via Skype, said that as long as his
price was met, he wasn't interested in what happened to the money. Such
statements were arguably "complicit," implying assent to the illicit payment, but before a jury they might detract from many of the stronger
clear-cut cases. They were prosecuted nonetheless. (Due to the high
number of indictments, the prosecution was broken down into four or
five separate trials. By what criteria, I was never made privy.)

We explained to the subjects that the project would be concluded in
two stages. Initially, there would be a "First Article," an initial phase in
which one hundred members of the guard would be equipped. This

would allow for inspection of the products, assure that all export mechanisms were working, and as I articulated clearly to each subject, confirm to Defense Minister Ali that he was receiving his agreed-upon percentage. From an operational perspective, this first phase would be the *only* phase of the op. Larger bribes would not be needed for prosecution under FCPA, but the prospect of the much larger sales—ten times larger—was intended to whet the appetites of the targets. They would not have flown in from points all over the United States and Western Europe in order to equip a paltry one hundred soldiers in Gabon.

On the first night of the first week of meetings, Richard and his "assistant" Raul (actually a young UC on his first Group I) invited the assembled subjects to an upscale D.C. steak house. The community of international arms dealers is not large; they all knew each other. Many would inevitably be dining together anyway, and it was better to know what was being discussed. Certainly the deal with Gabon would be a prime topic. No doubt, they would want to build on the new acquaintance with the elegant French financier—a useful contact for future business. There was no concern as to Pascal being a new player on their stage. I was a money manager of sorts, so there was no reason for any of them to have run across me in the past. Pascal was not an arms merchant—that was the reason I had enlisted my old friend Richard Bistrong to bring the project to a successful (and profitable) conclusion.

The original plan had called for me to be present at the dinner, but Chris announced late in the afternoon, after the last meet had come to a (successful) conclusion, that I didn't need to be at the dinner. I could order room service at the Four Seasons. Fine with me. In my view, Pascal might have been able to elicit conversation about past "commissions" paid by these businessmen (and they were all men, with one exception), corroborating the probable cause for the prosecutors and further deflecting future entrapment defenses. On the other hand, from Chris's perspective, Richard and Raul would be easier to micromanage, more compliant. With a Mark Calnan (SUNBLOCK) or a Dave Clark (RUN-DMV), I would have discussed the strategy. Not here. This put a lot of pressure on Bistrong, an amateur, and Raul, a raw rookie. Not my call. I was relieved to have the evening free. I'd rarely been able to enjoy meals with active subjects, regardless of the degree of luxury. A workout, hot shower, an excellent dinner on the balcony wearing my plush Four Seasons terry-cloth bathrobe, some TV, followed by a good night's sleep. Much more relaxing. Then, for the remainder of the week, evenings were free time. I would either stay "home alone" or, after a little dry-cleaning, have dinner with local friends.

Living at the Four Seasons was fine, but by Friday morning of the first week in Washington, I was spent. I had lost count of the meets, all blending in my drained mind. I think the reader can understand. We had two meets scheduled for that morning, be done by lunch, then the shuttle back to LaGuardia. When my taxi pulled up to the Mandarin, the doorman opened the car door, smiling.

"Good morning, Mr. Latour."

How the blazes does he know my name? Does the concierge at the Four Seasons call ahead to the Mandarin? Is this how the other 0.01 percent live?

"Good morning to you!"

The noon meet was for tactical vests—more tactical vests, we already had plenty. But Richard was confident that these subjects, local vendors who had not been at the dinner, would not be aware of the deal with one of their competitors. The owner of the company, J.M. Consulting, a family business, called Richard. He couldn't make it, but his sister, Magdi, would represent the company and had his authority to commit.

Shortly before she arrived, Chris and Dave came into the meet suite from the adjoining surveillance room.

"Marc, when Magdi Habesha arrives, you don't need to lay it on so thick . . . the Latour shtick. Let's just get it over." (Was this what Monday's dinner cancellation had been about?)

So now Chris was a movie director. He was going to teach me how to play an undercover role. After all the Gabon study, the drive to Albany, the past week of successful meets. Any response would have necessitated the use of crude vocabulary, so I kept quiet. And when this woman arrived, she enjoyed the same performance as her predecessors, with the same result. Agreement to the felonious cut for Ali. (Her brother was implicated through subsequent communications.)

Before the flight to New York, I turned in my receipts to contact agent Dave. The next Monday, he called.

"Hey, Marc, we've got a problem . . . the dinner in your room Monday night. It was over a hundred dollars."

Was he pulling my leg? Not likely. To date, he hadn't displayed a capacity for humor.

"For an appetizer, main course, and three beers. Nonalcoholic beers. It's the Four Seasons, not the Courtyard."

"Right. But the per diem for D.C. is forty-three dollars. That's all we can pay. I checked with my supervisor."

Un-fucking-believable.

"This was *operational* travel, Dave. I was there as Pascal Latour. Should I have taken a cab from the Four Seasons to find a McDonald's? That might appear a bit odd. I paid with the Latour credit card. If you want me in Miami next week, you figure it out." A week earlier, it had been Marc Ruskin who had entered the cab headed to LaGuardia Airport. It was Pascal Latour who paid the driver upon arrival in Washington. From check-in prior to the flight through luggage retrieval upon return, I was Latour. Twenty-four/seven. Wiser case personnel would have written it up thus, and it would have been approved, all expenses paid, no question. I was not used to dealing with a contact agent in such dismissive terms . . . but after TURKEY CLUB . . . and now BREACH . . . Was this today's New-Era Bureau the one that another old-time UC turned tech agent had warned me about? Was the excellent OXY BLUE team the aberration? Did I still belong in the FBI's UC world? I was beginning to have real doubts.

The following week, Pascal Latour kept his reservation at the Four Seasons, Miami. I never inquired as to the resolution of the per diem issue—perhaps they took up a collection on the squad to cover the balance. A little research, including calls to fellow old-time UCs—primarily intended to elicit sympathy and concurrence—had revealed that *technically*, reading the rules as narrowly as possible, my contact agent's interpretation was defensible. Idiotic, but defensible. So long as budgeted, all UC operational costs are paid for by the Bureau, no problem. A suite at a luxury hotel to project a big-money image while entertaining subjects—done. A few thousand dollars for dinner with high-roller targets—done. The parameters of "operational" are a gray area where the meeting of minds between bean counters, no-street-sense office agents, and UCs can be impossible to reach.

Predictably, Miami proved to be a repeat of D.C., with the addition of palm trees. The extensive white sand beaches and alluring bikini-clad volleyball players were visible from the balconies. The BREACH staff had packed our schedule so as to guarantee that there would be no need to unpack bathing suits and flip-flops. No precious minutes wasted on beach time. On Friday, having firmly set the hook on an additional baker's dozen of subjects, the Group I team—about eight agents from the squad, Richard, Raul, and myself—boarded our return flights to D.C. and New York. Further evidence of the "operational" nature of my travel: as Pascal, I passed through the interminable and intrusive security checks. Meanwhile, Dave and Chris and Co., traveling overtly, sailed past these crack units at the airport.

Back home, tensions within the team continued to escalate. In furtherance of one of the crooked transactions, Dave sent me an "Agent Agreement" to sign as Pascal Latour, in my capacity as Directeur Général of Latour Conseil, along with instructions to mail the originals to Protective Products International (PPI), one of the subjects in the sting. Those executives would in turn sign and mail an original to Latour Conseil's P.O. box in New York. Of the many C.Y.A. BuLessons learned over the decades, one of the foremost was to *never* sign a legal document, under true name or covert name, creating a legally binding agreement, without review by the appropriate BuLawyer (in this case the Chief Division Counsel (CDC)) and approval by management. Otherwise—in this specific case—should the day arrive that PPI sued the Bureau for loss of millions as a result of its reasonable reliance on a contract signed by an FBI employee, I would be in a highly unenviable position. I dropped in on the NYO CDC, an old acquaintance.

Make sure the D.C. agents send you documentation that their CDC has signed off. Otherwise, of course you don't sign it.

I called Dave.

Hey, Dave, did your CDC approve the contract? . . . cough, cough on the other end. *Did anyone approve it?*

The AUSA said it was okay for you to sign.

The AUSA isn't going to defend me when I get sued. Let me know, when you've got all the approvals.

Which they never did. I found out later that one of them had just made up a name and signed as an employee of Pascal Latour.

In the course of my accelerated backstopping of Pascal, I had created a .fr Yahoo account and Janus had obtained a French cell-phone number that forwarded to the covert New York number on Pascal's BlackBerry. Two weeks after Miami, I sat alone, at night, in my black UC Jeep Cherokee on the rooftop of a garage in Jamaica, Queens. This was a cameo gig, a few meets to be followed by a buy-bust. (Not OXY BLUE, another short-term op I was squeezing in.) At about nine, waiting for the target to pull up, the ALTERNATE BREACH BlackBerry rang. (Whenever feasible, I have always carried all my covert communications devices (beepers, then cell phones, then smartphones), maximizing my accessibility. Active professionals—journalists, lawyers, financiers—often carry a BlackBerry for email, an iPhone for Web-browsing, maybe a flip phone for that arcane practice, phone calls. Criminals may also carry several. In one recent case on which I provided a bit of assistance, a kidnapper in San Juan carried a knapsack-full, rotating between phones to elude tracking (yet another consideration for the UC as well). This was not an unusual hour for BREACH-related calls, particularly for the West Coast–based arms dealers. But the screen displayed a 202 number—Washington, D.C.—and it seemed vaguely familiar. Not familiar enough, however. Otherwise I would have turned off the phone (just declining the call would not have sufficed, because a "missed call" would have hit the log).

"Hi, Marc? Couple of quick questions." A cheery Dave was calling.

"Hey, Dave. Say, what phone are you using to call me?"

A long pause. Then with a hesitant, questioning tone, "My BlackBerry."

"Your *Bureau* BlackBerry?"

"Yeah, why, is that a problem?"

It was TURKEY CLUB all over again. I have laid out the added difficulties the Internet imposes on backstopping a new AFID. (In the mid-1990s, there was little risk that Yong Bing Gong's henchmen in SUNBLOCK would Google Alex Perez. Google didn't exist, and none of the predecessor search engines were worth a damn.) The unforeseen and newly evolved risks of exposure necessitate a heightened awareness, caution, and some common sense. If something compromising is on the Web, the UC has to assume that it can be found. If *we* can find it, then *they* can also. The current generation of jihadists, cartel traffickers, and La Cosa Nostra soldiers have grown up in this techno-savvy environment. There are websites that will, for a modest fee, provide a ninety-day log of incoming and outgoing calls for any "private" cell-phone number. Illegal though these services may be, the sites that provide them are accessible to anyone willing to conduct a fifteen-minute search. My covert BREACH BlackBerry was now compromised. Burnt. Toast.

Right in the middle of ALTERNATE BREACH (and OXY BLUE), I crashed the Honda Valkyrie in Connecticut. That first night, when the flurry of activity in the hospital had subsided—it appeared that I would survive—I became aware that Phil Romano (my boss's boss) and another supervisor were by my bedside. Seeing the familiar faces . . . the sense of relief was beyond words. They remained with me until well past midnight, when family arrived.

I was looking at a forced interruption of my UC activities. While in rehab at the Rusk Institute in Manhattan, there were many visits from fellow UCs and other agents. Not one to miss an opportunity, the case agent I was working with on the double-agent "dangle" brought a camera to my hospital room.

For my lawsuit?

Very funny. We're going to have the CI show these to Victor [the target's code name]. *Tell him you got worked over by the shylocks. It'll be great!*

Seriously?

Seriously.

To no avail. The sweet relationship with the foreign agent, perhaps on the verge of yielding real fruit, had withered on the vine. There's always a timeliness factor in these matters—foreign intelligence officers and criminals are time-sensitive, to say the least. Unexplained delays are *always* red flags for them. Then one day Victor was gone, just like that. Can't blame him.

In my absence from the field, Richard Bistrong fielded all of the communications in ALTERNATE BREACH, responding to the targets' emails as Pascal Latour. As to the phone calls, he answered the voice messages and missed calls himself, on grounds that his man Pascal had delegated the nuts-and-bolts work. The squad sent me a get-well card, assuring me that I would soon be back in the saddle. They meant well. However, if they were referring to a motorcycle saddle—not in this lifetime. As to the generic interpretation of their message, I was none too eager to resume my role as Ali Bongo's moneyman.

With two months to go before Health Services would clear me to return to duty, Chris and Dave were on the phone, wanting me to go to D.C. for a large UC meet, a cocktail reception with most of the subjects attending. *My arms are in casts! My right knee can't bend. I can't carry a gun or maneuver at all. What if something goes wrong?* Who would try to gun me down at a cocktail party? Nobody. But I would have to arrive, and leave, and not have my cover blown in the process. Never in history has an undercover agent gone into a meet with, almost literally, both hands tied behind his back. Not carrying a firearm wasn't really the problem; I hadn't been armed throughout BREACH. Not being able to use my arms *at all* was an issue. Barely able to open a door, I would be truly, unacceptably, vulnerable. Surveillance and cover are fine, but not enough. It was also a matter of cardinal principles: even if it was highly unlikely anyone would try anything under such circumstances, no UC in his or her right mind would do it, period. The request was absurd, and I said so, and I didn't go to D.C.

The *coup de théâtre* for ALTERNATE BREACH was going to be a large outdoor luncheon to celebrate the successful closing of all the arms sales to Gabon, with all the subjects in attendance. Also in attendance, for dessert, would be a number of SWAT teams. And when all was secure, at an appropriate distance, the media. The entire squad thought it was a great finale, an entirely appropriate conclusion consistent with their cinematic perception of the case. Not to be missed. (As was later revealed, they were already exchanging texts speculating as to the identity of the actors who would play *them* in the inevitable film.) I thought all of this was needlessly theatrical, and I arranged to be unavailable. Chris and Dave were mystified as to my lack of enthusiasm, but I had always been loath to be present at the arrest in UC ops. It had always felt inappropriate to me—rubbing salt into the wound—and I was highly unlikely to make an exception for this surreal parody of a *Mission Impossible* closing sequence. The arrestees were not the World's Top Narco-Terrorist Ring Leaders, cleverly lured to a neutral location. They could just as reliably have been called and asked to surrender themselves by appointment at the FBI's Washington field office. And between the caterers and flying in a half-dozen SWAT teams, how much did *this* shindig cost, by the way?

My enthusiasm (or lack of it) must have communicated itself effectively. Something less than two years had passed, in spring of 2011, when I was *not* called to testify at the first trial in ALTERNATE BREACH. Chris, Richard, and the others all took the stand and were excoriated by the defense attorneys. The trial lasted three months, ending in a mistrial after Judge Richard Leon dismissed key charges and the jury could not agree on a verdict on the remaining charges. Sometimes prosecutors drop a case after such a debacle. Not this time.

A few short weeks later, Chris relayed a demand from the DOJ attorneys to all associated with the op. Comb through all emails and texts on your workstation and Bureau BlackBerry associated with ALTERNATE BREACH, and forward. What proved to be a hugely time-consuming task for the tech-savvy young agents on the BREACH squad was no task at all for Pascal Latour. All of those items were on my overt (and covert) devices, already in appropriately labeled Outlook folders. They were all strictly business. I had no privacy concerns. *Just have the IT guys mirror the folders.*

A second trial commenced in September, and this time I was on call to testify. Apparently the prosecutors had decided that a new strategy was called for. Certain charges relating to money laundering had been dropped. (If called, I would testify from behind a screen: the prosecutors had already made applications with the court to conceal my identity.)

Here are the prosecutor's first words to the jury seated in federal district court in Washington, D.C., that September:

"This is a case about international bribery and the savvy business people who seek to profit from it. Normally, corrupt deals are struck in secret. If the money is funneled quietly . . . sham paperwork covers the illegal nature of the deal. The result is that most corrupt deals are never discovered by law enforcement. But this time, someone was watching, listening, and recording the bribe payers: The FBI."

Specifically, one Marc Ruskin, who was in New York City, still working OXY BLUE but also standing by to testify in Washington.

"The evidence will show that in May 2009 these defendants agreed to be part of a $15 million business deal involving the sale of weapons and other military products to a small country in Africa called Gabon. But unlike an honest business deal, the defendants didn't get this business by offering the lowest prices or the best products. Instead, they got this business, they got this deal, by agreeing to pay a bribe . . . amounting to $1.5 million to Ali Bongo, the Minister of Defense of Gabon. . . .

"So where was the $1.5 million for Ali Bongo going to come from? The defendants weren't going to take it out of their own pockets. Instead, they were going to take it from the people of Gabon and put it in the bank account of the minister. To do that, the defendants and their partners agreed to add $3 million to the price tag for the weapons and the military products they were selling. . . . The defendants and their partners would send the extra $3 million to Pascal Latour, a middleman. Pascal Latour would then funnel half of that, $1.5 million, right back to Ali Bongo for his own personal use. . . .

"And what would the people of Gabon get in return for paying this extra $3 million? Nothing. They would get ripped off. To understand how serious this is, it may help to think of it this way, ladies and gentlemen. . . . [T]he evidence will show, plain and simple, that this deal was corrupt, that these defendants knew it, and that they chose to participate in it anyway . . . We want American people and American businesses to export goods, not corruption. And to that end, there is a law called the Foreign Corrupt Practices Act, or FCPA."

This was only the second FCPA case that used an undercover agent. The first one had been in 1997, thirteen years earlier, and that had been my case as well. I agree with the prosecutors that the legislation is a good idea. We do want to export "goods, not corruption." But sometimes the best intentions . . . well, the second trial turned out as disastrously as the first one—more so, with acquittals all around following revelations concerning overly zealous investigation and prosecution. Those emails and other communications that had been subpoenaed from everyone on the team? They revealed a lot of bad behavior. I came out clean. Others didn't. This made all the papers, of course, which love corruption cases, and this episode had the additional media appeal provided by the DOJ's and FBI's apparent goof-ups.

The case was commonly referred to in the media as the "Africa Sting." *The Washington Post* went right to the heart of the issues that brought down the case in its entirety: "In text message after text message, FBI agents and their key informant joked about sex, booty calls, prostitutes, cigars, the Village People, the informant's wives and an agent's girlfriend. They even pondered who might play their roles in a movie based on their sting.

"When arrests were announced by the Justice Department, the agents and informant basked in positive press. 'It's like an atomic mushroom cloud,' the informant gloated in a text to his FBI handler.

"Since reaching court, however, there hasn't been much to brag about in the Justice Department's largest investigation of individuals accused of bribing foreign officials. In two lengthy and high-profile trials in the District's federal court, one of which ended last month, federal prosecutors failed to win a single conviction. One reason for the courtroom setbacks can be traced to the ribald texts exchanged between the informant and his FBI handlers.

"It's no secret that informants, like the one in this sting, tend to have shady pasts, traits that make them easy targets for defense attorneys. But modern communications—texts, in this case—permitted a new line of attack: Defense lawyers used the questionable messages to savage the credibility and professionalism of FBI agents, who not only seemed to share their informant's offensive sense of humor but also appeared to like him. While close relationships sometimes develop between agents and their informants, it is rare for such communications to become public. FBI agents closely guard the details of those relationships and *are generally careful about what they put into writing* (emphasis added).

"In this case, the messages shocked former prosecutors, who said the texts hurt the agents' credibility. 'It was just foolish,' said Steven Levin, a former federal prosecutor in Maryland. 'Jurors are loath to convict if they feel that both the informant and the law enforcement officers have acted improperly.'

"During the most recent trial of six men and women on charges of paying a bribe to win business with a foreign government, defense attorney Steven McCool used the texts not only to attack the character of the informant but also to accuse an agent of being a bigoted, anti-gay misogynist.

"For example, McCool asked the agent if his reference to 'da hood' in a text was meant to have 'racial overtones' and if he was expressing 'a bias against gay people' when he texted the informant about dressing up in chaps and spms [sic] while making a reference to the Village People.

"Defense attorney Paul Calli, whose client was acquitted by a judge before his case even reached the jmy [sic], said such texts showed that 'the FBI had established no appropriate boundaries' with the informant.

"The agents, who declined interview requests, testified that the off-color texts were 'operationally necessary' to build rapport with the informant and that they were not expressing biases in the messages.

"Testimony indicates the agents never thought their colorful texts, which represented a tiny fraction of the messages exchanged during the investigation, would be made public."

Let's be very clear. Much earlier in my narrative, I discussed how important it is for UC agents to insinuate themselves into their targets' often-ugly values, while taking great care that such insinuation *never gets on a tape that will be heard by a jury*. The same principle goes double for email. And, as was dramatically demonstrated in BREACH, *applies to informants as well. Just don't do it.* If it's absolutely necessary, do your "values bonding" *in person,* and when no tape is rolling.

After the mistrial, then the acquittals, the DOJ threw in the towel on ALTERNATE BREACH. As of this present writing (fall 2016), there has been just one UC operation resulting in criminal convictions under the Foreign Corrupt Practices Act. And the successful UC was not French financier Pascal Latour but the rather modest Argentine civil servant, Alejandro Perez. To tell that story in brief, I flash back to 1997, when

Craig Dotlo, my supervisor and friend in the New Rochelle office, my home base at the time, inquired about my availability to develop expertise in handling garbage, pronto. When I responded that I had long experience in managing Bureau paperwork, Craig was not amused. (It was a sore point with him, no doubt.) My destination would be the Fort Lauderdale area. This was midwinter. Sign me up, Craig.

Waste Management's incineration facility in South Florida was without a doubt the most unlikely training ground in my experience, but it had to be that way, as Craig explained. Herbert Tannenbaum, owner of Tanner Management Corp., a Long Island manufacturer of industrial-grade incinerators, had paid $50,000 in bribe money to an official in Barbados, in order to secure a $500,000 sale. A convicted co-conspirator facing eighteen months in jail had been recruited by the Bureau, and his name (I'll call him Rick) had made its way to Craig. Of course, Long Island was quite a distance from New Rochelle, and Long Island had its own FBI presence, much of it mob-related, as we have seen in TURKEY CLUB, but Craig had never been one to let a good case slip away. A little finagling and he opened the case under the auspices of the Foreign Corrupt Practices Act. Although the bribe had been paid overseas, to a foreign official, it was a crime here in the States. And a serious one at that, with significant consequences. Craig assigned old-timer Dave Clark (with whom I'd worked on RUN-DMV) to be case agent.

For this op, which we'll call INCINERATORS (I've forgotten the actual title of the case), I needed to become a foreign official with the buying power to seek a bribe from a manufacturer of industrial grade incinerators. I decided on Alejandro aka "Alex" Perez (no surprise there), now a purchasing agent for the Municipalidad de Buenos Aires. The Perez AFID was uncompromised. The papers had never disclosed it—not in RUN-DMV or any of the other ops starring Alex. In that pre-Internet environment, there was minimal likelihood of court records surfacing with any of my fictitious names. Media reports generally refer in the last paragraph, to "an undercover sting" and leave out names, both true and fictitious. The one exception in twenty years: Pascal Latour, from ALTERNATE BREACH. Those newspaper stories fingered me.

Will Godoy, my old friend from San Juan and fellow babysitter in the Papo Cancel witness-protection job, was now Legat Buenos Aires. A few phone calls in that direction resulted in a backstopped phone number and mailing address for my business card. For this one-off op, good enough. This one would be a cakewalk, I figured, featuring a week in Florida, with scheduled (by me) beach time, followed by a few meets with an unsuspecting businessman. Ah, the best-laid plans of mice and men . . .

Rick the CI, based in California, took a measured approach, planting the seeds in the course of spaced-out phone calls with Tannenbaum over the next few months. Finally, on a bright, cool afternoon in early June, at the Park Lane Hotel in Midtown Manhattan, Rick introduced me to Tannenbaum, the target. He and I had had a couple of preliminary and carefully recorded telephone conversations. As we sat in plush armchairs off the main lobby, Tannenbaum announced that he would be more than happy to negotiate the sale of incinerators for Ezeiza and Aeroparque airports, the Buenos Aires equivalents of JFK and LaGuardia. And, of course, to sweeten the pot for me. Undisturbed by Alejandro the Argentine civil servant's poor grasp of English grammar, Tannenbaum took pains to assure that I fully understood the size of the bribes I would be receiving. The two incinerating units sold for a million dollars total. Tannenbaum would inflate each invoice by $50,000, which would be directed back to me. His demeanor was nearly avuncular.

However, Tannenbaum did catch me somewhat off guard one afternoon not long thereafter, while riding in his car from his offices to his factory. I had no surveillance or backup—as usual, in the Old-Era FBI, but on this job not necessary anyway. True, riding in his car was a violation of a cardinal principle, but this guy just wasn't a thug. Wasn't armed. We were chatting about the merits of Argentine filet mignon as compared to U.S. prime rib, when he glanced over and said, "How do I know you're not an FBI agent?"

I scoffed. "Me . . . ! An FBI agent? Do you realize what you're saying? I'm the one who has to worry. Do you have any idea what the prisons are like in Argentina? If I get caught, they'll throw away the key."

That answer was totally illogical, a non sequitur, but it must have seemed irrefutable to my target, because he dropped the subject without further comment and a couple of weeks later we signed the contract for the first incinerator at a sale price of $550,000, with $50,000 of that total to be transferred to me. The second purchase would follow shortly.

Uncertain as to Tannenbaum's preferred method of transferring the illegal funds, I went fishing. The answer was an important part of the sting, of course. The dilemma, as I explained to him after signing, was how to handle my newfound wealth, because these payoffs far exceeded the petty bribes I routinely accepted back in Argentina. Not a problem, he assured me. First, he would create for my benefit a shell corporation registered in New York State. The corporate name I came up with was "Cybernet USA." (If only I—as Marc Ruskin, not Alejandro—had registered that name back at the dawn of the Internet in 1997. By now I could have sold it and retired on the profits.) As president of Cybernet, I provided alias Eduardo Dean (one of the several AFIDs I maintained in my desk in New Rochelle). Dean would never have to appear in person; all that was necessary was a valid Social Security number for the paperwork.

Tannenbaum would then introduce me to the branch president and a senior VP at a certain bank on Long Island. Which he did. In the bank's conference room, the four of us spoke confidentially. My tape was rolling. Tannenbaum explained to the banker my need for an account to be opened with discretion. Initial deposit: $50,000, to be followed soon by one of equal size. The two bank officers warned me that large cash deposits would attract unwelcome attention from regulators, then they explained how best to structure the deposits, with Tannenbaum placing the commission money into his own various corporate accounts, then arranging for a series of transfers into the Cybernet account.

Not wanting to leave *any* wiggle room at prosecution time, I pushed the envelope. I said bluntly, "You understand that no one can know of this, it is very, very important. I could go to jail in my country, if they found out I was taking bribes."

No one would find out, I could rest assured.

They opened the account then and there. In order to bring the money-laundering angle to a logical conclusion, I would need to later transfer the $50K out of the Long Island bank. Using Janus for this maneuver would have been the smart thing to do, and Craig's and my failure to do this was the beginning of trouble that I could not have foreseen in a thousand years. But this seemed pretty straightforward. When money laundering with subjects in prior cases, the financial whizzes at Janus would set up transfers from the United States to Switzerland to the

Cayman Islands, say—all in order to make it seem to the targets that the money trail was being deliberately hidden. With Tannenbaum, all I needed was a bank account somewhere, in a fictitious name. I would provide the account information to the crooked Long Island bankers, who would later transfer my bribes (paid by Tannenbaum) into this new bank. The laundering of the bribe money would now be complete. And the indictments could be prepared. Eventually, all the money would be transferred to the Bureau's coffers.

Craig was able to arrange for a contact in a local bank to open the account. In her office, I filled out the paperwork as Eduardo Dean, President of Cybernet USA. Unexpectedly, she requested Eduardo's real name, and worse yet, my real Social Security number. I understood where she was coming from—she was covering herself. If there was ever to be any blowback, she wanted to be able to point the finger at the FBI, and me in particular. I hesitated, then provided the information.

The transfers went smoothly enough. Tannenbaum deposited the money into the Long Island bank account as promised, and after the AUSAs who would prosecute the case gave us the green light, I called that crooked branch president and instructed him to transfer the money to the Eduardo Dean account. Which he did. And then I forgot about it. And then, finally—close to a year after my first meet with the target—it was time for the arrests. To avoid the Long Island traffic, my case agent Dave Clark suggested that I arrange a meeting with Tannenbaum to discuss the details of my second incinerator. *In the lobby of the New Rochelle Ramada.* Nice touch, and a first for the squad. A quick ride down the elevator from our office to the lobby, and Dave made the arrest.

Tannenbaum didn't drag it out. In August he pled to one count of conspiracy to violate the FCPA and was sentenced to one year in jail, to be followed by three years of supervised release.

Now fast-forward two years, to mid-2000 when I was a supervisor in the Safeguard Unit at FBIHQ, with an overseas posting to a U.S. Embassy within striking distance (the situation discussed in detail in a prior chapter). After fifteen years in the Bu, my first 5-Year Re-Investigation happened to be in progress. For this purpose I had completed the 127-page SF (Standard Form) -86, which the government uses for investigating officials and contractors seeking to obtain or maintain security clearances (Secret, Top Secret, etc.). Filling out one of these forms is a major pain, requiring finding all sorts of sensitive documents and details that you would never imagine having to provide. Personal, financial, all kinds of things. This form was one of the multitude of obscure administrative annoyances that divert federal agents from productive work, unknown to a (justifiably) disinterested public, until midsummer of 2015, when it was disclosed that federal Office of Personnel Management (OPM) files had been hacked in the course of two separate breaches. Details as to what exactly had been obtained by the hackers were slow to emerge, naturally enough: OPM not being eager to reveal the devastating magnitude of the breach. And then it came out. Over twenty-two *million* files, consisting primarily of SF-86s. In their entirety, including the one submitted by *FBI Director Comey*.

Any misstatement or omission when completing the SF-86 can lead, theoretically, to prosecution. More realistically, such an error will seriously jeopardize the results of the investigation. Which in the Bu means losing your job, since all special agents are required to have a Top Secret Clearance. Sitting in my office at the covert Safeguard off-site, with its picture windows facing undeveloped woodlands, Puccini playing on the CD system, I wasn't concerned. My primary professional career-related concerns at that juncture were checking for vacancies at Legat offices at various embassies and then submitting my applications. Then the phone rang. A woman from the Security Investigations Unit was on the line. She had been assigned my re-investigation and was reviewing the SF-86 along with the volume of documents she had obtained through the numerous waivers I had been required to sign, as addendums to the 86. One of the financial reports reflected a 1997 lump-sum deposit into one of my personal checking accounts. An unexplained deposit not reflected in my 86, nor in my tax returns. A deposit for . . . $50,000.

The miracle was that this sweet woman hadn't referred this little situation *directly* to the dreaded Office of Professional Responsibility (OPR). The Bu's equivalent to Internal Affairs. Had she done so, a formal investigation would have been a certainty, with my career frozen in place for a couple of years awaiting its outcome. And even when, at the end of the day, OPR found nothing, I would probably have still received a Letter of Censure (their minimum penalty), based on the theory that you must have done *something*, otherwise there wouldn't have been an investigation in the first place. And a censure is accompanied by an additional three years without career movement (other than *down*). Altogether then, this snafu could have dragged on until I was eligible for retirement, at which time I would have become a highly *uncompetitive* candidate for a first assignment at a Legal Attaché Office in a U.S. Embassy. (Although *eligible* to retire at fifty, I had no intention of doing so.)

I had lost track of how many money-laundering transactions I had been involved with over the years, but this dollar amount rang familiar. I assured my lifesaver from Security Investigations that it was all a mistake. I would get back to her forthwith, with a written explanation and documentation to back it up. Next came an emergency call to Craig Dotlo, who was still in New Rochelle. In addition to heading up C-21, he was now boss of bosses for the office. The dollar amount also rang bells for Craig. This must be the 50K payoff to Alex Perez in the Tannenbaum caper. A call from him to the branch manager at the bank in New Rochelle revealed the problem. The clerk who had created the checking account for me as Eduardo Dean, the one who was supposed to have input alias Eduardo Dean's various ID numbers, instead had input *mine*—Marc Ruskin's Social Security number. When Craig told me what had happened, I instantly remembered my misgivings before providing my true name and numbers in the first place.

Craig prepared a letter of explanation, backed by documentation from the bank, and sent it to the Security woman. The 50K was not a bribe paid to Marc Ruskin by the mob but an honest mistake by a bank officer in New Rochelle. The case of *FBI v. Marc Ruskin* was hereby circumvented. But it came within a hair's breadth of effectively destroying my FBI career.

15

Shalom

In 2010 and 2011, as I approached the mandatory retirement age of fifty-seven, I was nevertheless just about as busy as ever (though not as *intensely* busy as in the days of COMMCORR and RUN-DMV and INFRACEL and SUNBLOCK). My newest (and last) alias was Alejandro Pierre Marconi, Director General de Consultora Marconi, an Argentine national living in Buenos Aires, with an additional business office in Miami. I had access to vast sums of investment capital, monies that Argentina's wealthiest sought to place in large-scale projects. From Miami, I and my younger partner, UC agent Ricardo Dominguez, flew to San Juan every month or two. In our legend, Dominguez was a Cuban American and the only son of Marconi's former partner, and knowledgeable in commercial real estate. Together, we were seeking to build a shopping mall and/or luxury resort in the San Juan area. Of course, we understood that the requisite "commissions" must be paid to senior officials. Such bribes would be required at every stage. They were a given for every approval of zoning variances, waiver of environmental regulations, registration of contracts and deeds, multitudinous authorizations, official seals and stamps. And over the course of numerous cocktail hours and dinners in San Juan's finest restaurants, at the El San Juan, the Condado Plaza, the St. Regis Bahia Beach, and the Ritz-Carlton—anywhere, really, including the offices of these same senior officials—my partner and I made it very clear that we were willing and able to do so.

DOMINO EFFECT was a well-organized and well-funded Group I Public Corruption UC op under the direction of an ambitious and dedicated case agent, Ruben Marchand-Morales. It would last a little under a year. With an age-appropriate role, regular travel to La Isla del Encanto—had it really been twenty-five years since my first posting?—along with four-star lodging and meals, this op would be a fine note upon which to close out my FBI career. And when alias Alejandro Marconi was not in San Juan, a man who looked remarkably like him, alias Alejandro Kulikov, was on the phone and email from his office in New York (that is, my BuCubicle at 26 Federal Plaza, armed with covert cell and laptop), planning his journeys to meet with the Chinese financiers who were the subjects in a San Francisco–based Public Corruption Group II op (and impressing them with his rudimentary knowledge of Mandarin). I withhold this op's title (it was named after its primary subject) as I believe it never became public. To my knowledge the case was not destined to reach fruition, a casualty of my mandatory retirement.

And providing a fine contrast with those two high-end stings were meets at the McDonald's in the South Bronx and on West 125th Street in South Harlem, where Alejandro Huertas Veaga met Dominica to negotiate a purchase of illegal oxycodone for the OXY BLUE UC op. As laid out in the previous chapter, that sting had started off with my procuring bogus prescriptions from culpable doctors on the East Side—fair (and safe!) enough—but, to my surprise, had soon ended up with me back on the streets, buying drugs with my partner Linda. Again, "Honey" was the most important code word. But wait a minute! I'm too old for this. *I do have rocks in my head!*

And I can't forget Daniel Martinez, the international jewel thief and fence who was resuscitated five years after parting ways with the TURKEY CLUB personnel out on Long Island, with whom I had lost confidence, as we know. Daniel was now flying periodically from Miami to New York, meeting with the target in a counterintelligence Group II. (Not a False Flag sting, but just as interesting. However, I can't discuss any of those details, at least not until twenty-five or so years have passed and they are declassified.)

So, yes, a lot was going on in 2010 and 2011. I didn't feel that I was riding into the sunset on some broken-down burro. (Many agents—a lot of people in all walks of life—do feel that way, I have observed.) I was truly immersed in UC, but overshadowing all of this undercover chicanery were the pages of the calendar, which were flying by in my imagination, as in an old black-and-white film's time-transition sequence. Soon just one would remain: April 30, 2011. Some in the Bu theorize that the mandatory retirement rule reflects a justifiable belief that the special agent's profession, which necessarily entails jumping across rooftops and fast-roping from helicopters on a daily basis, is ill-suited to sexagenarians. The professional BuCynic that I had become suspected otherwise. Sure, a measure of valuable experience would be lost in the transition, but Uncle Sam can employ two brand-new agents for the price of one old agent. The bottom line rules.

Anyway, I had a plan: make myself too irreplaceable to jettison summarily on some arbitrarily designated retirement day. On April 29 I was a valued UC agent, but on April 30 I was over the hill? It was ridiculous. My five ongoing ops were too valuable to close down. They needed me. No one else could do these jobs! I therefore had applied for a one-year extension, which would require the signature of Himself: Robert Mueller, Director of the FBI. And of course before the application can hit the big man's desk it has to run the gauntlet of the entire chain of command in the New York office, including the Assistant Director, before being shipped to JEH, where it would travel from floor to floor, garnering initials, before finally arriving on the seventh floor, the executive suite. My bimonthly calls to Marie, the kindly retirement coordinator in HR at JEH—whose inbox my request currently occupied—yielded progress reports without any real intel as to what might be the final outcome. In early April— less than a month to go!—still no news. Should I be looking for a job?

While a federal pension is a wonderful thing, its size tends to be exaggerated by the media and politicians looking to cut expenditures. In just a few weeks, my income faced a 50-percent reduction while my expenses would stay at 100 percent. Then, in mid-April, Marie *called me*. Director Mueller had signed off. I had my reprieve. I had one more year on the federal dole. The various Alejandros out in the field would not all simultaneously vanish, leaving their subjects wondering and case agents wringing their hands and scurrying to reconfigure their respective ops. The luxury travel to San Juan for DOMINO EFFECT would continue.

Of all the cases, this was the one still destined to be my curtain call, the ideal cap to my career. Then BUREAUcratic mayhem struck once again. Ruben Marchand-Morales, the case agent, had been reassigned and "promoted" to a coordinator position, essentially a desk job overseeing a given office's various case categories and operational functions. There are a lot of coordinators. It gets complicated. There may be a coordinator of the coordinators.

What! Why? Soledad Colon, DOMINO EFFECT's new case agent in San Juan, had no answers, or at least none that she would share with the two UCs from the mainland. Initially, Soledad had been one of the agents assigned to support DOMINO EFFECT. After her promotion, I found her enthusiasm at the enhanced responsibility—and increased workload—was not exactly boundless. The squad supervisor, Chris Starrett, seemed to be the only one with any interest in moving forward, but his interest was not enough. Alejandro and Ricardo's four-day stays at the Condado Hilton continued for purposes of evaluating project sites and negotiations, but there was not real movement forward. No contracts were being signed. No applications being processed. The invaluable sources on the ground (that is, confidential informants) grew distant, less sure of their intel, equivocal in their statements regarding the targets (senior officials) whose compliance they had virtually guaranteed just a few months earlier. What was wrong? The answer provides us with more reasons why informants have "handlers" rather than managers or partners or directors or supervisors or bosses. They need to be carefully evaluated, developed, reassured, all while being directed, gently but firmly, toward accomplishing defined tasks. If rapport is not maintained and the informant loses confidence in the handler's ability or commitment to provide a safety net, the work product deteriorates along with the relationship. In almost all of my previous long-term ops, I had generally developed my own relationship with the informants, maintaining contact between meets to discuss strategy, sometimes simply chatting with them. (Gil Sandoval in SUNBLOCK, imprisoned at Lewisburg, is a prime example of the fruits of such an approach.) Here, in DOMINO EFFECT, Ricardo Dominguez and I did not even have the phone numbers for the informants. We were discouraged from maintaining any independent contact with them, preventing us from developing rapport. And from moving the case along. As seemed to be occurring with increasing frequency in the New-Era FBI (first in TURKEY CLUB, then ALTERNATE BREACH, now here), the case agents believed they knew better than the UCs, to the general detriment of the ops.

Over the next five or six trips to the Isla, the only progress was with our suntans. Predictably, when the case came up for mandatory review and renewal after six months, it was denied by the Undercover Operations Review Committee at JEH, and I don't blame them. On the ground in San Juan, Marconi and Dominguez disappeared without a trace, presumably seeking other venues for their large-scale investments.

The Alejandro Marconi AFID had been so meticulously backstopped it would have been a shame to put it to rest, but four months into my one-year extension—with little likelihood of yet another grace period— it seemed to me unlikely that Marconi would ever again see the light of day. But when I sent all the IDs and wallet stuffers back to Janus, I asked Val to hold onto them—just in case. An old friend, she humored me. She also put me in touch with an agent in San Antonio who was starting up a Group I targeting Mexican drug cartels. The UC would be a crooked high-stakes financier who, after gaining the confidence of the cartel bosses, would engage with them in a variety of illegal enterprises. The role called for someone with a touch of gray and credible Hispanic background. Sounded exiting. I asked for a week to give it some thought.

Paul Benoit, like myself a native of Paris, sat across from my cubicle at 26 Federal Plaza and overheard that phone call. He suggested I read a recent *New Yorker* piece on the cartels, which he happened to have in his satchel. He had come to know me fairly well over the past five years and had chosen a subtle approach—chosen wisely, and having the desired result. I read the long piece. The Mexican cartels of the 2010s were not those of the 1990s. Their appetite for killing competitors, witnesses, judges, prosecuters, *lawmen*—anyone who looked at them sideways—was unquenchable. As the reflective Marc Ruskin approached fifty-eight, maybe his accustomed response—"Well, somebody's going to have to do it, can't let an inexperienced UC take the risks"—was no longer appropriate. And it was not lost on me that once I retired, should the cartel cutthroats come looking for me, I'd be on my own, for all practical purposes. *Do I have rocks in my head?* Not anymore! I'm too old for this—for the cartels. I didn't need a week to decide. *Et bien, peut-être tu a raison,* I told Paul the following day. *I'm outta here.*

Which brings us to this poetic twist: the rabbis. New Jersey–based SA Bruce Kammerman, ex-Marine captain, SWAT team leader, fellow surveillance agent in the mid-eighties, old friend, and relatively secular Jew, had an enigma to solve. The crime was as serious as it was bizarre. The suspects and victims were all members of a singularly insular, impenetrable community: ultra-Orthodox Jews living since antiquity in a world apart, with their own social infrastructure and its own code of laws, interpreted and applied by its own judicial system, the *Beth Din*. To effectuate an Orthodox Jewish divorce, a husband has to provide his wife with a document known as a *get*: documentary proof of the dissolution of a marriage under Jewish law. If the husband refuses to give his wife the *get*, she can sue for divorce in a *beth din*, which would have the authority—moral and religious—to order the husband to issue the *get*. If the husband does not comply, he faces various penalties to pressure him into consent. Pity the poor woman whose husband still refuses to comply, under any and all circumstances. She becomes an *agunah,* a chained woman, and barred from a new marriage.

In the case confronting Bruce Kammerman, the line had been crossed: the appalling acts in question went well beyond the scope of the religious courts and their traditional enforcement mechanisms. I'll quote from the story on the case in *The New York Times* (October 10, 2013): "In Brooklyn's ultra-Orthodox Jewish neighborhoods, Mendel Epstein made a name for himself as the rabbi to see for women struggling to divorce their husbands. . . . While it's common for rabbis to take action against defiant husbands, such as barring them from synagogue life, Rabbi Epstein, 68, took matters much further, according to the authorities. . . . For hefty fees, he orchestrated the kidnapping and torture of reluctant husbands, charging their wives as much as $10,000 for a rabbinical decree permitting violence and $50,000 to hire others to carry out the deed. . . ."

All true, but Bruce's evidence against the rabbi was primarily anecdotal. The one or two wives he had interviewed were terrified by the prospect of testifying against respected elders, fearing the controversy that would follow. They would be ostracized, simple as that. Moreover, their uncorroborated testimony would have limited value in a secular court, particularly when directed at pillars of the community. An under-cover operation would be the only vehicle for a winnable case. To this end, Bruce met first with the Deputy Assistant U.S. Attorney Gil Childers, the number-two federal prosecutor for New Jersey. Childers was known for his successful prosecution of the Blind Sheik in the first World Trade Center bombing. Before Bruce could mention my candidacy for the UC job, Childers said, *No question, you're going to need Marc Ruskin*. Because experienced Jewish UCs are few in number? Who knows? I appreciated the compliment.

Bruce's idea was to set up a fictitious disputed Orthodox divorce fea-turing three UCs: the divorce-seeking wife, the uncooperative husband, and the wife's wealthy brother, who would bankroll the payoff to the target, Rabbi Epstein. A—perhaps *the*—experienced Jewish female UC had agreed in principal to play the wife. A Jewish UC based on the West Coast had been cast as her brother, alias John Miller. Would I be willing to play the uncooperative husband who had no idea what he was get-ting into? And, most importantly, could I develop a plausible scenario, one that would pass muster with a number of very intelligent subjects who were instinctively, *comprehensively* wary of the world beyond the insular Orthodox community? I would, and I could. I took a couple of weeks to do my homework prior to the strategy session Bruce conducted in the conference room at the FBI offices in Red Bank. The UC agent playing my estranged wife, Rachel, was present, along with a Janus representative, the Newark Undercover Coordinator, various squad members, and federal prosecutors. Rachel's husband John participated via conference call from California. I presented my proposed scenario, code name RABBIS GET (my name for the case, not the official one, which was not made public).

Argentina has the world's fifth-largest Jewish community, much of it Sephardic. Since Epstein and his co-conspirators were of Ashkenazi origin, they were not familiar with Sephardic customs and therefore would not be alerted to the sting by minor discrepancies. A Buenos Aires–based member of that Sephardic community, Alejandro Marconi (yes, *that* Marconi—*me*), frequently traveled to the United States, where he invested in a number of commercial real-estate projects, often with his California business associate, John Miller, Rachel's brother. At a holiday party hosted by John (Hanukkah, not Christmas!), Rachel had met Alejandro and in due course had accepted a marriage proposal. Though several years younger than Marconi, spinsterhood loomed, and the prospect of a new, observant life in South America's Jewish capital was alluring. Alas, two years later, having come to the realization that her husband was a cad, and on the verge of bankruptcy as well, Rachel returned to the States. Bitter and vindictive, Marconi refused to consent to a *get*. Refused, period.

Given that scenario, all of the Orthodox Jewish backstopping would be in Argentina. This would therefore not be just the usual driver's license, Social Security card, credit cards, and wallet-filler type of op. Though all of those routine AFID items would be required, even for myself (Alejandro Marconi would need to be a verifiable "real" person, whether he met with the subjects or not), the bulk of the backstopping would consist of the documents and trappings that are the prerequisite indicia of a routine and ordinary life in the Orthodox community. Janus justly prides itself on backstopping virtually any imaginable alias and scenario, but an Orthodox Jewish family—from marriage all the way through dissolution—no, it is unlikely that any of the Janus offices had ever been asked to even imagine such a scenario, much less pull it off. The unit had no templates, no network of contacts, in this closed society. Reverting back to my COMMCORR days of do-it-yourself backstopping, the team and I would have to work all this out on our own.

I had a leg up on the problem. When stationed in Buenos Aires as the Assistant Legal Attaché, I had become close friends with Roberto Sarfati, former director of security for the Sephardic community. Without hesitation, he agreed to be point man in Argentina. As an observant Jew, he could identify stumbling blocks before they arose, suggest solutions, and be a partner in their implementation. Sarfati would provide a certified copy of his own *Ketubah*, the Jewish marriage contract. The FBI lab at Quantico would create a new, "aged" *Ketubah* with which Rachel could authenticate her marriage when meeting Rabbi Epstein and other subjects.

It was a solid scenario—I was proud of it, frankly—but there was one problem: as a new Group I, even with much of the AFID already in place, RABBIS would take a few months to get off the ground. With *none* of the AFID in place, a year was more like it. I did not have a year left before mandatory retirement. I had less than four months to go. Undeterred, can-do Bruce promised a second extension from JEH. Boundless enthusiasm notwithstanding, he was unable to pull this rabbit out of the hat. But there was another rabbit! With authorization from JEH, Bruce and the Newark office were allowed to keep me involved as a consultant for the duration of the case. This was an excellent development: it would ease my transition to a post-Bu, no-longer-an-insider life. I had designed the scenario and would help backstop the operation (a job that would require, in the end, two years). Now, my role would continue offstage. Alejandro Marconi would be a "real" presence in the RABBIS sting, but he would never meet face-to-face with the targets.

To take my imaginary scenario and transform it into a tangible reality would require an essential trip by Bruce and the UC team to Buenos Aires. Roberto Sarfati and I set it up, and I flew down three days early as an advance man to work out final details. (A fringe benefit: the opportunity to visit with aunts and uncles, cousins, and close friends in the Argentine capital.) Thanks to Roberto, the time spent was productive, invaluable, in fact, due to the unique nature of the required backstopping. After meeting with the Chief Rabbi of the Sephardic community and visiting his temple, we attended two Orthodox weddings. Pictures of Rachel and Alejandro at the synagogue were carefully staged and taken, along with photos of the wedding reception at a well-known kosher restaurant. Other souvenir photos of better times were captured at various kosher eateries. A visit to Jewish neighborhoods and the Jewish Cultural Center that had been bombed by Hezbollah twenty years earlier (as noted in my account of my few years posted to the U.S. Embassy in Buenos Aires) rounded out everyone's education. Rachel Marconi would now be able to converse comfortably with the targets in New Jersey about where she had worshipped, socialized, and shopped a world away in Buenos Aires. Likewise for her wealthy brother John, when discussing visits to the then-happy couple and business trips arranged by Alejandro.

Back in the States after a week in Buenos Aires, equipped with the necessary props, Rachel commenced the time-consuming procedures required for obtaining a religious divorce. Prior to approaching our primary target, Rabbi Epstein, she would have to exhaust all alternative paths and aggregate the documentation generated along the way.

All of which culminated on July 18, 2013, in a *Shtar Seruv* (contempt order):

Shtar Seruv

Alejandro Marconi, with an address of 5722 South Flamingo Road, Copper City, FL, has been summoned to the Beth Din of America by Rachel Marconi regarding her request for a Jewish divorce (*Get*).

Alejandro Marconi has failed to appear in front of the Beth Din of America or an alternative Beth Din for the purpose of giving a *Get* or submitting to Beth Din adjudication of Rachel Marconi's request for a *Get*.

Alejandro Marconi is thus deemed a *mesarev/avo Iedin,* one who declines to appear in front of the Jewish courts according to Jewish law and Rachel Marconi is free to pursue any remedies permitted by secular law.

With the contempt order in hand, obtained from the *Beth Din* by a local rabbi known in the community, Rachel and John placed a call to Rabbi Martin Wolmark, the director of a local *yeshiva* and partner of Rabbi Mendel Epstein. Wolmark welcomed these new clients with sympathy and advice. He did take the precaution of asking the name of Rachel's rabbi in Lakewood (her backstopped residence). Familiar with the rabbi with whom Rachel had cultivated a relationship—she was, naturally, a member of the congregation—he took the next step and brought Rabbi Mendel Epstein into a conference call. The three of them scheduled a face-to-face meeting with Epstein for two days later, August 13, at the rabbi's home in New Jersey.

All of those intricate introductions and maneuvers were the result of more than *six months* of undercover work by Rachel—we had returned from Buenos Aires in the fall of 2012—and it was great work, the subjects had no reason to question Rachel's veracity. Just another cash client with the same old problem. In the meetings that followed, Epstein detailed to Rachel and her brother John the efficacy of his methods. The kidnapping would last only a few hours. The "tough guys" would use electric cattle prods. If a five-thousand-pound bull could be thus incentivized, a recalcitrant husband would be sure to cooperate. They always did. Best of all, there would be no traces, none of the telltale signs of traditional torture. Epstein actually chuckled. *If your husband should go to the police, who would believe such a story?* Other husbands had tried, but the authorities would not even take the complaint. Convinced, Rachel and John made a $10,000 down payment and provided the rabbis with photos of Alejandro taken in Argentina. After all, Epstein's kidnap team would have to ID their victim before the snatch. (At this stage of the sting, Bruce gave me a heads-up. *They've got the pictures of you, Marc. Keep your eyes open, just in case.* As I was living in New York City, it was a legitimate concern. I didn't want things to get out of hand. *Rachel, this is Rabbi Epstein. Good news, we came across you husband in the Diamond District, on 56th Street. He's already signed the get . . . our favorite technique worked like a charm.* No, thanks.)

As a final touch, Rachel and John played for the rabbis a recording of a call Alejandro Marconi had placed from Argentina to California—a recording that Rachel's brother John had "secretly" recorded. We had prepared the script with Bruce and rehearsed it a couple of times. Upset that a *seruv* had been issued in New Jersey, my voice nearly trembling with rage, I accused John and Rachel of having deliberately mailed a copy to my family in Argentina, in order to upset them and tarnish my reputation in the community. Not to mention the effect such a scandal would have on my local business dealings. I angrily barked that I did not recognize the authority of those Ashkenazi rabbis up north, and would not be intimidated into granting the *get*. John accused me of infidelity. He had heard rumors concerning a new girlfriend, noting that I was still married as far as Jewish law was concerned. The heated exchange continued for five minutes, long enough to create a solid impression for a future intended audience. We made sure to tone down the vitriol toward the end. We were also businessmen, after all. We didn't want to close *that* door, too.

Epstein was convinced. Who wouldn't have been? He had many photos of the couple, the *Ketubah,* the *Seruv,* the taped phone call. He was ready to move. Only one issue remained: he couldn't send his kidnap team to Buenos Aires. How could Rachel and her brother lure the husband to New Jersey? We were ready for this question, of course. John suggested a ruse. Placing business interests ahead of domestic issues, he would feign an inclination to engage in new projects with his brother-in-law, despite everything. A prime opportunity: purchasing a warehouse in a New Jersey industrial park. And John's brother-in-law was such a greedy bastard he'd surely be interested. Lured from Argentina for purposes of a property inspection, Marconi would find a reception committee, ready to initiate a persuasion session.

On the evening of October 9, 2013—a year and a half into my post-retirement—I sat in the command post of the Newark FBI office as the kidnapping attempt unfolded. I was equipped with a covert cell phone, in the event that circumstances required John to call his brother-in-law—a conversation that would be overheard by those waiting to pounce. The kidnap team, secreted in the warehouse, consisted of two rabbis and six Orthodox enforcers, wearing bandannas and ski masks, equipped with rope, surgical blades, plastic bags, and a screwdriver. Everything worked beautifully. John arrived for the bogus property inspection accompanied not by his nonexistent brother-in-law Alejandro Marconi but instead by a large contingent of SWAT operators.

The initial headline in the *Times* read: "U.S. Accuses 2 Rabbis of Kidnapping Husbands for a Fee."

Altogether, four rabbis and six others were arrested and indicted for conspiracy to commit kidnapping, attempted kidnapping, and actual kidnapping, the purpose of the crimes being to obtain money from the *agunot* (plural for *agunah*) and to threaten and coerce Jewish husbands to give their wives *gets*. The kidnapping charge itself was based on the testimony of the real husbands who had alleged that they actually had been kidnapped and tortured. The prosecutors theorized that the results of the UC op would bolster those cases. Defense attorneys replied to the accusations using the novel theory that prosecution of the defendants substantially burdened their free exercise of religion, in violation of the Religious Freedom Restoration Act. (This defense has played a pivotal role in numerous cases in recent years, albeit in very different contexts.)

What's more, the defense argued, such kidnappings were actually *mitzvah*—that is, *good deeds,* religious commandments, and that Jewish law authorized certain forms of force in furtherance of such good deeds. What *chutzpah*!

The case was tried before Federal District Judge Fredda Wolfson in Trenton. The jury took three days to deliberate.

All the subjects were acquitted on the kidnapping charges (the charges which were not based on the UC op). The prosecutors turned out to be wrong in their assumption that the *conspiracy* and *attempt* charges pertaining to intended kidnapee Alejandro Marconi would bolster the charges of actually kidnapping. The conspiracy and attempt charges held up, however. Rabbi Wolmark knew a lost cause when he smelled one and pled guilty on January 14, 2015, a month before the trial of the other rabbis, Epstein, Stimler, and Goldstein, all of whom were convicted. (David Epstein, son of Mendel Epstein was acquitted.) The "tough guys"—the enforcers—all pled guilty. Everyone would have plenty of time to perform *mitzvahs* for their fellow inmates.

And that was it. I retired on April 30, 2012—my mandatory date—they threw a party, and a week later my family was on a flight to Beijing. Six months later, I was practicing law again with offices in Lower Manhattan, only this time I saw the cases from a different perspective: I was representing defendants. My clients deserve and, I like to believe, receive the fullest expression of their legal rights, but they know the truth as well as I do: If the prosecution has good undercover work on its side, they're in real trouble.

Epilogue

When I dream, I nearly always find myself in the heart of a UC op. Planning a complex and dangerous meet with fellow agents, entering a hotel room or driving into a parking lot for a meet with a subject, checking my recording devices and weapons. I wake to the realization that there will be no more meets: this chapter is closed. Although part of me would have wanted to continue as a UC past the point where I would have had to hobble to meets with a walker, I have come to accept the transition. There are a few kinds of undercover ops that I did not get to and which I would have liked to work—but not many. My three decades were pretty full.

Today's Bu would not be quite as good a fit for me. Gone are the days of the lone wolf UC, the risk-taker out on his own, surviving by quick wits. As well, the ever-present humor and ceaseless banter, and the esprit de corps of the old Bu are becoming a thing of the past. The "paperless Bureau" that its bureaucrats have long aspired to has arrived, and with the new technology has come a generation of agent and analyst technocrats who are better suited for fighting crime facing a computer screen than a villain.

During my senior years as a BuAgent, I didn't really believe retired colleagues when they assured me that there was indeed life after the Bureau. But I have come to realize they spoke the truth, so it is with optimism and without regrets that I tip a figurative cap to my old and cherished institution, and move on.

Acknowledgments

Three professionals in the literary world are the *sine qua non* for *The Pretender*. Joe Spieler, my literary agent, believed in my idea for this book from the beginning and persevered until it became real. Mike Bryan was my literary guru, providing feedback, advice, and suggestions on matters large and small, which he dished out with humor and sagacity. Emily Angell, my editor at Thomas Dunne Books, reviewed the manuscript with a keen eye and forged a truly collaborative process. Lisa Bonvissuto, editorial assistant, brought diligence and charm to the making of this book.

For the "I've been there" advice, and the many long phone calls, big thanks to Jack Garcia (*Making Jack Falcone*) and Bob Wittman (*Priceless* and *The Devil's Diary*).

Closer to home, marketing maven Phil Ruskin, CEO at Ruskin International Communications, has provided and continues to provide indispensable assistance to this author, whose business acumen is *de minimis*. And a bow to Adina Ruskin for her invaluable assistance in getting the project launched.

Assistant Special Agent in Charge Steve Carlotta tops the list in Management; it is thanks to him that I worked as a full-time freelance undercover my last four or five years in the Bu, unencumbered by administrative responsibilities. Nor would that have been possible without the support of his boss, SAC Gerald Rose. My SSA in New York, Matt Laird, provided cover when needed, as the truly good supervisors do, and never complained that I was taking up a valuable place on his squad while contributing little to its mission.

Back at JEH, Michael Mason, Special Assistant to the Director, later Assistant Director; and Herb Cousins, Section Chief, later SAC, were reliable in their support and mentoring.

As to the FBI Special Agents, Supervisors, professionals, and others whose true names appear in the book, consider yourselves already acknowledged. The following paragraph is for those who, if they have appeared in the narrative, did so pseudonymously. Adding any information as to where or when they fit into the story would, by necessity, defeat the point of masking their identities. Thus I must limit myself to providing simply the names of those who know the roles they have played:

So, here's to you, Maureen "Moe" McDonnell, Joe Robles, Amy Solek, Jairo Lopez, George Parks, Charlie Russell, John Sinclair, Sam Santana, Ab Maldonado, Frank Flores, Marcela Barrios, Fernando Candelario, Luis Cruz, John Sokol, Don Sheehan, Dave Raiser, Roy Hoynes, Norissa, Baxter Lipscomb, Jim Rose, Jimmy Garcia, Kim Householder, Michelle Mullen, Joe Mangan, Rita Fitzpatrick, Bill May, Claudia Mannix, Danny Trompetta and Bob Kenny, Katie Harmke, Dave Stone, Prady Rivas, Amy Hirina, Brian Connolly, Rebecca, Steve Surowitz, and Lance Gambis.

Glossary of FBI Argot and Acronyms

1 Register—Sign in/out sheet for SAs (discontinued).

302—Short for FD-302, a report of investigation conducted by one or more SAs. Must be drafted within five days (much more difficult to fudge due to current technology).

515—Short for FD-515, form used to claim stats: number of arrests, drugs/assets seized, etc.

ADIC—Assistant Director in Charge, boss of one of the larger field divisions, New York, Los Angeles, Washington Field (so named to distinguish it from JEH). Pronounced "ay-dick," not by saying each letter individually. (See SAC, go figure.) The new ADIC in New York, Bill Sweeny, recently quipped at a retired SAs luncheon that according to his teenage son, the Bu finally got his title right.

AFID—Alias Fictitious Identification Documents produced by the Janus Initiative. Driver's licenses, Social Security cards, credit cards, and wallet filler (library cards, frequent flyer cards, health insurance cards, etc.). Pronounced "ay-fid."

Airtel—Communication sent between FBI offices (replaced by EC).

ALAT—Assistant Legal Attaché. SSA assigned to an FBI office in a U.S. Embassy, headed up by a Legat (see below). Generally used all upper case.

ASAC—Assistant Special Agent in Charge, traditionally the hatchet man for the Special Agent in Charge.

AUO—Administratively Uncontrollable Overtime. The ten extra hours a week required from all SAs.

Backstopping—The procedures taken to substantiate a fictitious idnentity.

Bu, BuCar, BuSteed—Synonyms for government-owned car assigned to an SA. Not to be used for personal purposes. If caught, forty-five-day suspension without pay. SAs are usually caught when they have a fender bender while shopping when off duty. Good SSAs always retroactively place the SA on duty (unless wife and kids were in car).

Bureauese—English as it appears on FBI documents: 302s, LHMs, etc.

CI—Confidential Informant. Will not testify, unless he/she agrees to become a confidential witness (CW).

CW—Confidential Witness. Same as CI, but has agreed to testify at trial.

EC—Electronic Communication. Document with strict format, used for nearly all internal communications: request for authorization to do something (trash cover, attend conference, repair car, etc.), canvass for a UCA, disseminate information, and so forth.

Field Division—A large FBI office, usually managed by an SAC. The *very* large ones, New York, L.A., Washington Field, are led by an ADIC.

FNU—First Name Unknown. As in FNU Smith. Pronounced by SAs as "Phenoo."

FOA—First Office Agent, i.e., a rookie.

FOB—Friend of the Bureau. An individual, usually working in the private sector, willing to help out, not for material gain but out of sympathy with the objectives of federal law enforcement.

Group I—Long-Term Undercover Operation (UCO), requiring FBIHQ/DOJ approval.

Group II—Short-Term Undercover Operation (UCO), usually six months to one year, approved by the ADIC/SAC of a field division.

Hello Phone—The covert phone maintained by each squad for receiving calls from informants and subjects. If the number is found in an informant's pocket by a fellow criminal, his relationship with the Bureau will not be compromised.

IT—International Terrorism.

JEH—The Hoover Building (FBIHQ), as it is referred to by those who work, or have worked, there.

LEGAT—Legal Attaché, an overseas FBI office in a U.S. Embassy, responsible for liaison with the law enforcement and intelligence services of the host country. When used all upper case, refers to the office itself, otherwise to the agent in charge (e.g., Will Godoy was Legat Buenos Aires).

LHM—Letterhead Memorandum. A letter to someone outside the FBI, summarizing information deemed suitable for dissemination. Usually sent to another government agency (OGA). Often used as a cover letter for a prosecutive report sent to the U.S. Attorney's office.

LNU—Last Name Unknown. As in John LNU. Pronounced by SAs as "Lenoo." If neither first nor last name is known, SAs do not use "Phenoo Lenoo," rather: UNSUB (see below).

OP—Office of Preference. Selected by an SA, for transfer based on seniority. One OP Transfer allowed per career. The wait for a small, highly desirable office can be twenty-plus years (as was the case for me).

One Way _____—Nickname (e.g., One Way Mary). For an agent always asking for a favor, and always too busy to lend a hand when asked.

POA—Personally Owned Automobile. As in "Why did you drive your POA, when you could have used the Bu?"

POW—Personally Owned Weapon. Firearm that an SA is authorized to carry. Up to two handguns and one long gun, from a list of approved weapons.

RA—Resident Agency. A satellite FBI office, which is part of a Field Division.

Relief Supervisor (also referred to as Relief)—An SA who fills in when the squad SSA is unavailable. First small step in road to management.

RDO—Regular Day Off. As in "I worked on Sunday, so I'm taking an RDO during the week."

SA—Special Agent, sometimes referred to as a field agent.

SAC—Special Agent in Charge. Boss of a field division (except for the big ones, run by an ADIC). Pronounced by saying each letter individually (not as "sack," which is the pronunciation used by DEA, Secret Service, etc.).

SSA—Supervisory Special Agent. In the field, manages a squad of SAs. At JEH, the bottom rung in the management ladder. I was an SSA while at the Undercover Safeguard Unit and as ALAT Buenos Aires (1998–2004).

SSRA—An SSA who is in charge of a Resident Agency while also managing a squad.

SOG—Special Operations Group.

TDY—Temporary Duty Assignment.

UC/UCA/UCE—Undercover, Undercover Agent, Undercover Employee. Used interchangeably.

UCO—Undercover Operation.

UNSUB—Unidentified Subject. Sometimes referred to as FNU LNU, tongue in cheek.